CATHOLIC SPECTACLE AND ROME'S JEWS

Catholic Spectacle and Rome's Jews

EARLY MODERN CONVERSION AND RESISTANCE

Emily Michelson

PRINCETON UNIVERSITY PRESS

PRINCETON & OXFORD

Published by Princeton University Press
41 William Street, Princeton, New Jersey 08540
99 Banbury Road, Oxford OX2 6JX

press.princeton.edu

Library of Congress Control Number 2021953502
First Paperback Printing, 2024
Paperback ISBN 978-0-691-23341-3
Cloth ISBN 978-0-691-21133-6
ISBN (e-book) 978-0-691-23329-1

British Library Cataloging-in-Publication Data is available

Editorial: Ben Tate and Josh Drake
Production Editorial: Jill Harris
Production: Danielle Amatucci
Publicity: Alyssa Sanford and Charlotte Coyne
Copyeditor: Cindy Milstein

Jacket/Cover art: Jacopo Zucchi, *Mass of Pope Gregory the Great*, 1574–1575, oil on canvas. Rome, Church of the Santissima Trinità de Pellegrini, sacristy. Photo by Tanner Nash.

This book has been composed in Miller

In memory of Kimmie
In gratitude for Bill

CONTENTS

ILLUSTRATIONS

ABBREVIATIONS

AAV   Archivio Apostolico Vaticano (formerly Archivio Segreto Vaticano)

ACDF   Archivio della Congregatione per la Dottrina della Fede

ARSI   Archivum Romanum Societatis Iesu

ASCER   Archivio Storico della Comunità Ebraica di Roma

ASF   Archivio di Stato di Firenze

ASPF   Archivio Storico de Propaganda Fide

ASR   Archivio di Stato di Roma

ASVR   Archivio Storico del Vicariato di Roma

BAV   Biblioteca Apostolica di Roma

Borg. lat.   Biblioteca Apostolica Vaticana, Fondo Borgiani latini

DBI   Dizionario Biografico degli Italiani (Treccani), https://www.treccani.it/biografico/index.html

EDIT16   Censimento nazionale delle edizioni italiane del XVI secolo, http://edit16.iccu.sbn.it/web_iccu/ihome.htm

Vat. lat.   Biblioteca Apostolica Vaticana, Fondo Vaticani latini

THROUGHOUT THIS BOOK, I use the word "sermon" to refer to all varieties of preaching forms, even when they would merit a variety of labels in Italian. Preaching genres ranged from elaborate formal sermons to simpler, more exegetical homilies. The Italian word most often used for conversionary preaching texts is *prediche* (sermons), but many are instead designated explicitly as homilies (*omelie*). The words of a convert from Judaism, preaching to former coreligionists, were typically given this latter title, as they did not follow the traditional, long-established rhetorical styles of Italian preachers. My use of the term "sermon" or "conversionary sermon" should be understood inclusively. On these distinctions, see above all Emily Michelson, *The Pulpit and the Press in Reformation Italy*, John O'Malley, *Praise and Blame in Renaissance Rome*, and Frederick McGinness, *Right Thinking and Sacred Oratory in Counter-Reformation Rome*.

The term "Roman Catholic" was not in widespread use among early modern Catholics or Jews in Italy. I use the terms "Catholic Church," "Roman Church," and occasionally "Roman Catholic Church" interchangeably.

I have translated the titles of most of the works I discuss into English, but not in cases where they are widely known by their original titles (e.g., *Bibliotheca Magna Rabbinica, Pardes Rimmonim,* or *Pugio Fidei*) or there is no English equivalent (*Eusevologio Romano*).

CATHOLIC SPECTACLE AND ROME'S JEWS

Introduction, with Pig

WE HAVE TO START with the pig. The pig reminds us that words—however dry, eloquent, or erudite—have meaty physical consequences. The sermons at the heart of this book were built from high-minded words, but at least once they coalesced around a living and energetic pig stuffed in a box.[1]

The pig was a surprising and unwelcome guest at a funeral. The funeral marked the passing of a famous and learned rabbi in Rome, Tranquillo Corcos the Elder, who died in the late 1640s. Jewish funeral processions in Rome left the cover of the ghetto, proceeding eastward, passing by the ancient church of Santa Maria in Cosmedin and near the Circus Maximus before arriving at the Jewish cemetery. Funeral processions provided one of the few occasions when Christians could observe large groups of Jews gathered together outside the ghetto for their own purposes, rather than to fulfill some ceremonial role foisted on them by others. Funerals were fraught with discomfort and the threat of violence.

This book is concerned with another kind of occasion when Christians observed a crowd of Jews in public: forced conversionary sermons, which became a defining feature of early modern Rome. Anxieties about conversion—effecting it, policing it, and proving its authenticity—saturated the early modern period. Conversionary preaching was the balm. Sermons to Jews in Rome, pressing them to convert to Catholicism, were mandated by a papal bull. They were staged weekly in public for roughly 250 years. Jewish attendance was compulsory and enforced. The content of the sermons themselves was either densely theological or sneeringly hostile—so much so that one preacher coolly informed his Jewish listeners, "I am certain that you will dislike this." But Jews were never the sole audience in

1. BAV Borg. latini (Borg. lat.) 481, fols. 172r–74r.

the room. Crowds of Christian onlookers, Roman and otherwise, also regularly attended these sermons. Their presence was expected, celebrated,
and understood from the outset to be necessary; preachers played to the
gallery. The position of Rome's "preacher to the Jews" soon became a fixed
and prestigious post. Although the legislation to establish similar sermons
extended to other parts of Italy, in Rome conversionary preaching was more
public, more consistent, and above all, utterly fundamental to early modern
Catholic self-fashioning.

Sermons and funerals differed on the surface. Sermons were imposed
from outside and resented. At heart they were intellectual, fusing theology,
scholarship, and rhetoric. Funerals, in contrast, were internal, communal,
and traditional; they fused ritual, movement, and death. This pig, however, reminds us that the two spheres were not so distant. They aggregated
violence; anger could ferment in one context and erupt in another.

The pig arrived at the rabbi's funeral courtesy of a conversionary
polemicist of exceptional zeal, Melchior Palontrotti. Perhaps it was no surprise at the time that Palontrotti did not simply seek to disrupt Corcos's
funeral but also took a coarse and satiric approach: he organized a mock
procession of local young men to counter the solemn funeral procession
of mourners. At the head of the counterprocession, corresponding to Corcos's coffin, was the box containing the live pig. At intervals, the box was
opened, the boys sang a song, and the pig's head emerged.

I don't wish to belabor the obvious here: that a pig is the primary
anti-Jewish symbol, both culturally and religiously, habitually adopted by
antagonists who wish to insult Judaism and signal their disgust with it.[2]
But neither do I wish to ignore it. Pigs and Jews had history; Palontrotti's
choice was deliberate.

Palontrotti was an expert in Hebrew language and scripture who had
devoted his life to fighting Judaism.[3] At the time of the funeral, he had

2. On January 25, 2014, three packages containing pigs' heads were posted to the
Great Synagogue of Rome, the Israeli embassy, and a museum then showing an exhibi-
tion on memories of the Holocaust. An antisemitic letter was included in one of the packages. http://roma.repubblica.it/cronaca/2014/01/25/news/teste_di_maiale_inviate_alla
_sinagoga-76891584 (January 25, 2014); http://www.ilgiornale.it/news/cronache/roma
-teste-maiale-nei-luoghi-comunit-ebraica-liberman-986053.html (January 26, 2014).

3. For Palontrotti, see Benjamin Ravid, "'Contra Judaeos' in Seventeenth-Century
Italy: Two Responses to the 'Discorso' of Simone Luzzatto by Melchiore Palontrotti and
Giulio Morosini"; Fausto Parente, "Il confronto ideologico tra l'ebraismo e la Chiesa in
Italia," 334–37; Giulio Busi, "La Breve raccolta (Venezia, 1649) del polemista antigiudaico
Melchiorre Palontrotti"; Wipertus Hugo Rudt de Collenberg, "Le baptême des Juifs à Rome
de 1614 à 1798 selon les registres de la 'Casa dei Catechumeni': Pt. 3: 1730–1798," 131.

recently capped off a decade's worth of angry treatises with a general compendium of antirabbinic arguments—the same kind that propped up forced sermons.[4] He had also played godfather to at least one convert from Judaism, giving him his own surname on February 9, 1642.[5] Palontrotti's aggressive personality comes through in the pig incident and in the fiery titles of some of his compositions, such as "A Whip against the Obstinacy and Stubbornness of the Jews."[6] In addition to his many publications *contra Judaeos*, says the manuscript describing the event, Palontrotti liked to hurl abuse (*sburlacchiava*) at synagogues. He commonly attended Jewish sermons in order to interrupt the rabbi and question his interpretation. He had a particular beef with Corcos, the chief rabbi, known as "Our Teacher" or "Our Rabbi."[7]

When the funeral procession paused, so did the counterprocession. The youths would open the casket and let the pig stick out its head as one of them shouted, "Moreno [our teacher] is in the coffin. Let's see the proof," and another, "That big head watches me; his wisdom has swelled even his bones," and yet another, "Mazel ra [the opposite of mazel tov, meaning congratulations or good fortune]! The soul of the rabbi inside a pig!"

Besides shouting, they sang a taunting song celebrating the death of Corcos. The song mocks his character and the sorrow of his followers; it describes him as cunning, lacking in faith, and full of legal and grammatical learning, but ultimately the slave of Satan.

The students cry
That the rabbi died,
Who wore tefillin
But believed like Lavan . . .

4. Melchiorre Palontrotti, *Breue raccolta d'argomenti, cauati dalla sac. Scrit. & dall'antiche tradittioni di rabbini, con le quali chiaramente si prouano i dogmi della religion christiana contra l'hebraica perfidia.*

5. ASVR Casa dei Catecumeni 178, Liber Baptizatorum 1634–75, fol. 33r.

6. Melchiorre Palontrotti, *Sferza contro l'ostinatione, et peruicacia de gl'ignoranti Ebrei.*

7. BAV Borg. lat. 481, 172r. The full passage (translated here) reads, "Melchior Pallontrotti [*sic*] of Rome was very expert in the Hebrew language and severe against the Jews. He printed [works] against their stupidities, went to synagogues and hurled abuse at them, and was often found at their sermons and interrupted them, noting their errors to the rabbi. In his time lived the principal rabbi and teacher (*morenu*), highly esteemed by all the ghetto, Rabbi Manoah. And when he died, Pallontrotti made a masquerade of the Jews who were on their way to bury Rabbi Manoah, carrying him in a coffin. But in his own [casket] he had put a live pig, with a device so that he opened the box a little bit whenever he wanted to, and the pig, called a *chazir* by the Jews, would stick its head out. The song that Pallontrotti wrote, he taught to the youths who made up his masquerade, and it is believed to be the first *giudiata* in Rome. It pretends to praise him, but it mocks him."

Our teacher is dead,
Expert in giving judgment.
We could call him Our Rabbi,
Confederate of demons.[8]

The song, we are told, was composed by Palontrotti, who taught it to his troupe. It made full use of Palontrotti's expertise as a Hebrew polemicist.[9] The song is in Italian, but almost every one of its seventy-eight lines contains at least one Hebrew word, frequently a biblical or Talmudic reference. The song concludes with a mocking stanza about the pig:

Have you read in the [Talmudic] tractate "Avoda Zara"
That pig is eaten in the world to come?
Behold our Teacher
Who, to reassure men and children,
Shows himself in the shape of a pig to everyone
Happiness to the wise! Joy to the elders!
Make a celebration, O Jews![10]

Nobody in this scenario thought words were meaningless. Words, not pigs, gave Palontrotti his livelihood. And the carefully preserved, emotionally laden story of this song shows that Palontrotti was no lone wolf. He acted with the support, tacit or explicit, of a much broader Catholic establishment.

8. Piangen' Talmidim
    ch'è morto lo Rabban
    Che portava i Tephillin
    Ma credeva come Laban . . .
    È morto lo Moreno
    Ch'era maskil nelli Dinim
    si poteva dir Rabbeno
    Confederato coi scedim
9. For further background and a full transcription, see Martina Mampieri, "When the Rabbi's Soul Entered a Pig: Melchiorre Palontrotti and His Giudiata against the Jews of Rome." Mampieri and I each independently came across the manuscript that describes this event, unbeknownst to each other.
10. Hai letto mai nello Trattato Ngavoda Zara
     Che si accola (אכל) il Chazir nel Ngolam Haba!
     Ecco il nostro Moreno
     Che per assicurar huomini e putti
     In forma di chazir si mostra a tutti
     Tutti insieme gridano
     Simcha ai chachamim, sascion a Parnassim
     Fate Chagh o Jehudim
     (n.b. The transliteration of the letter ע with "ng" reflects local Roman pronunciation.)

The manuscript that preserves the pig story was written up by Giovanni Pastrizio, an influential and well-connected professor of Hebrew; it is preserved in his collected papers. Pastrizio taught at the College of the Congregazione di Propaganda Fide, a new and robust branch of the Holy See's deliberate mission to proselytize the entire known world in the early modern period. He frames the story by describing Palontrotti's skill and erudition, recounting approvingly his history of disruptive actions. The song itself is transcribed in full, with exquisite care and meticulous attention to language. Annotations run alongside the lyrics throughout, providing both a Hebrew language original and an Italian translation for every transliterated Hebrew word, each numbered and keyed to the translation column. It is bound together with other sonnets, poems, and odes alongside material linked to Pastrizio's activities as a Hebraist, such as a poem on the Trinity, written in refutation of Judaism by a new convert on the occasion of his baptism.[11] Palontrotti's actions, carnivalesque as they seem, came straight from the world of intellectual conversionary rhetoric that animates this book.

Palontrotti's song was meant to change its listeners as well as wound them; it frames Jewishness as something to abandon in favor of Christianity. Forced conversionary sermons, too, were meant to change their hearers. They were intended to transform the lives and souls of Jewish listeners, and also their bodies, as they underwent baptism and might later birth Christian offspring. Indeed, sermons were meant to bring the death of the Jewish self and its rebirth as a Christian soul. This story, and others that will follow, encourage us to see rhetoric and violence as contiguous spheres. The pig in its box was carried directly along the thin line between speech and violence, and that line remains blurred or half erased, and sometimes eliminated entirely.

Forced preaching matters, in part because it served both as a symbol of that blurry line between speech and violence, and simultaneously, as the mask that enabled the fiction that the two were separate. Sermons to Jews were designed for this purpose. They provided the polished and public showpiece of a much broader, grimmer campaign to assert the triumph of Catholicism in Rome by subjugating and converting its Jews. As sermons earned praise and attention, they drew focus to an act of conversion by persuasion. By doing so, they enabled the more violent, coercive aspects of Rome's campaign, embodied by Palontrotti, to continue more silently at the same time, sometimes led by the very same people. Supporters of conversionary preaching could remain willfully ignorant of its darker side.

11. BAV Borg. lat. 481, 241r.

Sermons to Jews proved immensely useful to the early modern church and therefore they penetrated the society of Catholic Rome far more deeply than they penetrated Rome's ghetto. They offered many other uses and benefits for Catholic Rome besides self-congratulation. Sermons mattered most to the many people and institutions that launched and took pride in them, and so it was natural that the bulk of their impact would fall outside the ghetto. As this book will establish, sermons to Jews helped to define the New Rome of the early modern era in the eyes of locals, tourists, and visitors, including Protestants. They provided a prestigious step on the career ladder for ambitious curialists and showed off the city's intellectual heft. They became a point of pride for its Christian population. For Jews, forced preaching remained an unwelcome imposition. But out of necessity, it nonetheless fostered a tradition of creative Jewish resistance that took many forms and could even influence the direction of the sermons themselves.

Above all, sermons to Jews became a platform for debating and defending the new aspects of Catholicism that defined the early modern era. Sermons supplied an ideal opportunity to articulate and even proclaim what Catholicism now meant in the post-Reformation world, and why it was worth embracing. And no pulpit was better suited to this purpose than the conversionary one: sermons to Jews purported to address nonbelievers, who needed to learn the basics of Catholicism, but their messages also reached the many watching citizens, converts, and tourists, who were explicitly, though less openly, target audiences. Sermons to Jews rose to prominence in a tumultuous era. After the Protestant Reformation, Christian denominations in Europe competed for souls, and the Roman church sought triumphal validation for surviving the challenge. In this context, no spectacle could be more powerful than a robust public justification of Catholicism that starred its oldest antagonists. Conversionary sermons contained a paradox. They were never really intended for the conversion of Jews, at least not primarily, and Jews were never their sole audience. Their power lay in their spectacle, their widespread popularity, and the self-congratulatory fictions they allowed a population to believe about its noble missionary efforts.[12]

⁂

This book tells a story of early modern Catholicism in Rome with Judaism and Roman Jews at its center. In the early modern period, the city

12. On this point, see especially Anna Foa, "Il gioco del proselitismo: Politica delle conversioni e controllo della violenza nella Rome del Cinquecento."

of Rome re-created itself as a beacon of piety from which to proclaim a resurgent, global, triumphalist Catholicism. In the wake of the Protestant threat and Council of Trent, the Papacy and other religious institutions deliberately sought to transform the city into a model of Christian virtue. Their efforts brought not only the promotion of new devotional activities and the rebuilding of the city but also new attempts to regulate outsiders through segregation or integration. Rome's ghetto was established in 1555 amid a range of other conversionary measures.

In this grand display of devotion, Jews, the church's most ancient and challenging adversaries, were refashioned into key symbols; the great global campaign that would transform the early modern Catholic Church started at home. Rome's Jewish community was the only continuous Jewish settlement in Europe, and the oldest; Jews predated Christians in Rome. As a series of European traumas uprooted many Jewish populations, Rome's Jewish population was also growing rapidly and becoming increasingly visible. At the same time, as the beating heart and ancient seat of the Catholic Church, Rome generated most of Europe's anti-Jewish rhetoric, imagery, and conceptualizations. Thus in the *caput mundi*, the premier manufacturer of symbolic, imagined Judaism confronted Europe's most religiously symbolic population of living Jews at a fraught moment in both their histories.[13] Much of Rome's anti-Jewish policy reflected, more than anything else, these imaginings and projections. To be sure, violence and diatribe also characterized relations with Jews, real or imagined, across Europe. Often the consequences were bloodier, deadlier, and more unjust than in Italy. But theological and physical assaults are not opposites so much as sliding points on a scale, sometimes distant, yet sometimes touching. In Rome, unlike nearly everywhere else in Europe, fictive, polemicized Jews and the actual local Jewish community were in equilibrium. Living Jews and imaginary Jews had equally deep roots and equal claims to antiquity, and were equally impossible to ignore. This mixture of symbolism, realism, and performance made the case of Rome uniquely potent.

13. On imaginary Judaism and other parallel terms, see David Nirenberg, *Anti-Judaism: The Western Tradition*; Emily Michelson, "Conversionary Preaching and the Jews in Early Modern Rome"; Jeremy Cohen, *Living Letters of the Law: Ideas of the Jew in Medieval Christianity*; Jeremy Cohen, "'Synagoga Conversa': Honorius Augustodunensis, the Song of Songs, and Christianity's 'Eschatological Jew'"; Jeremy Cohen, *The Friars and the Jews: The Evolution of Medieval Anti-Judaism*; Eliane Glaser, *Judaism without Jews: Philosemitism and Christian Polemic in Early Modern England*; Eva Joanna Holmberg, *Jews in the Early Modern English Imagination: A Scattered Nation*.

This juxtaposition, unprecedented and unique, took physical form at weekly conversionary sermons. At this event, both the living Jews of Rome and imaginary Jews of Catholic theology converged in a public, spectacular way. Conversionary preaching was a staged, ritualized performance that also carried complex social implications throughout the city. It fostered street violence and pamphlet wars, drew tourists and spectators, and blurred the boundaries between real and imaginary Jews. The weekly sermons held tremendous symbolic weight for the early modern Catholic Church. From the outset they were always also a public performance, designed to address Christian spectators as well as Jews. Conversionary sermons had a broad appeal to many in Rome. They drew support, attention, and labor from Catholic institutions and innovators from across the city. Clerics, citizens, pilgrims, and tourists all flocked to the weekly spectacle, aware of its novelties and significance. Sermons to Jews remained a defining feature of Roman life throughout the early modern period. As European tourists increasingly visited ghettos, and as ethnographic interest in Jews grew, sermons to Jews gained renown as one of the features that most defined and distinguished the city of Rome. In a city known as the theater of the world, public ceremonies proclaimed Rome's most important values.[14] As a newly instituted spectacle with a broad audience, conversionary preaching offered a valuable opportunity to acknowledge interfaith tension, and transform it into an assertion of Roman piety and early modern Catholic identity.

Rome's roughly three thousand Jewish people comprised about 3 percent of its population, but their imaginary presence loomed much larger. The real Jewish people who heard the sermons were targets for proselytization and subject to the kind of deliberately offensive rhetoric they had heard from Palontrotti—or from the later preacher who made a point of telling Jewish readers how much they would dislike the book he had written from his sermons. But Jews at a sermon were also actors, playing symbolic versions of themselves for the benefit of a broad audience with other priorities than conversion. Unlike medieval public disputations between Jews and Christians, sermons took place consistently and frequently over a long period, and bespoke an increasingly international and global Catholicism. The performance of weekly sermons took its place alongside other newly created spectacles of public piety in Rome,

---

14. Pamela M. Jones, Barbara Wisch, and Simon Ditchfield, *A Companion to Early Modern Rome, 1492–1692*. See also Maria Antonietta Visceglia, *La città rituale: Roma e le sue cerimonie in età moderna*.

also intended to strengthen Catholic devotion. Conversionary sermons became the city's most powerful platform for promoting both conversion and Catholicism in a changing world. While preachers publicly offered theological critiques of Judaism as they understood it, they made their best case for choosing Catholicism over other faiths. Before a mixed audience of Jews, converts, Catholics, and other spectators, conversionary sermons celebrated the grand scope of early modern Catholicism.

This celebration thus relied on both the physical presence of Roman Jews and imagined notions of Judaism as necessary rhetorical props. It demonstrates that Jews, ideas about Jews, and rhetoric related to Jews were central to both the general evolution of early modern Catholicism and the religious landscape of early modern Rome. Conversionary preaching became a sort of vortex that absorbed the wide and contradictory variety of Catholic ideas about Jews. Early modern Catholicism cannot be understood without reference to these Jews and this spectacle. Attention to conversionary preaching rewrites the story of how the early modern Catholic Church, at the moment when it became a global religion, learned to present itself to the world.

Beneath all of these layers of meaning was a group of a few hundred people that assembled, willingly or begrudgingly, every Saturday afternoon in the Oratory of Rome's grandest new confraternity: Santissima Trinità dei Pellegrini. This book reconstructs the priorities of the preachers who ascended that pulpit, the patrons who supported them, and the Jews who resisted them. It retells some tales that are well known to scholars, but presents many others for the first time. These characters and incidents reveal the vibrancy and violence that surrounded conversionary preaching. This book brings new material to the fore as well by examining an enormous cache of nearly unknown conversionary sermons and related manuscripts begging for further study. It offers close readings of sermons, but also situates these sermons and their stories in the broader history of Rome—its spaces and people. Through these investigations, it reminds us that high-concept anti-Jewish typologies ("imaginary Judaism") never remained sealed away on an intellectual level. And it shows how living Jews, responding to these tropes, also influenced the course of early modern Catholicism.

{≈≈≈}

Conversionary preaching has left a strong cultural memory, and continues to be evoked among Roman Jews and for the benefit of visitors to Rome's

Jewish sites.[15] My approach to the topic throughout this book integrates, in innovative ways, fields of study often considered separately: Jewish studies and church history, social and theological perspectives, and urban and global histories. It seeks to balance a history of people with a history of texts to the extent that these can ever be separated. It builds on a surge of pioneering studies on both religious conversion and global Catholicism in the early modern era.[16]

This book also contributes to two long-standing historiographical challenges regarding the place of Jews in European history. The first, powerfully articulated by Debra Kaplan and Magda Teter, argues that scholars of early modern Europe continue to treat Jewish history as something isolated from mainstream historical subjects.[17] The second challenge is inherent in the ongoing scholarship on "imaginary" Jews as a permanent aspect of western European thought that has served flexible, even contradictory, political and theological purposes. As an abstract category, it bears only tenuous ties to actual Jewish communities and their history. David Nirenberg's work has provided one compelling demonstration of the deep roots of these "imaginary" or "hermeneutic" Jews. Literature on this topic, addressing many different historical periods, has mostly focused on Europe as a whole and largely theoretical concepts of Judaism, removed from its social contexts.[18] It leaves unaddressed a critical question, especially for the early modern period: How did such abstract notions relate to actual Jewish communities in Europe?

15. See, for example, the following tour guide sites: https://theromanguy.com/italy -travel-blog/hidden-gems-rome-jewish-ghetto/; https://promptguides.com/rome /attractions/jewish_ghetto.html; https://www.througheternity.com/en/blog/history/jewish -ghetto-in-rome.html.

16. For some recent examples, see Theodor Dunkelgrün and Pawel Maciejko, *Bastards and Believers: Jewish Converts and Conversion from the Bible to the Present*; Tamar Herzig, *A Convert's Tale: Art, Crime, and Jewish Apostasy in Renaissance Italy*; Robert John Clines, *A Jewish Jesuit in the Eastern Mediterranean: Early Modern Conversion, Mission, and the Construction of Identity*; Nicholas Terpstra, *Global Reformations: Transforming Early Modern Religions, Societies, and Cultures*; R. Po-chia Hsia, *A Companion to Early Modern Catholic Global Missions*; Erin Kathleen Rowe, *Black Saints in Early Modern Global Catholicism*; Karin Vélez, *The Miraculous Flying House of Loreto: Spreading Catholicism in the Early Modern World*.

17. Debra Kaplan and Magda Teter, "Out of the (Historiographic) Ghetto: European Jews and Reformation Narratives."

18. In addition to Nirenberg's *Anti-Judaism*, for different iterations of this theme, see Cohen, *Living Letters of the Law*; Jeffrey S. Shoulson, *Fictions of Conversion: Jews, Christians, and Cultures of Change in Early Modern England*; Bruno Feitler, *The Imaginary Synagogue: Anti-Jewish Literature in the Portuguese Early Modern World (16th–18th Centuries)*.

Recent histories of late medieval and early modern religion have begun to address both of these challenges. Some scholarship analyzes a deeply held Christian attitude toward Jews, as with Nirenberg's 2013 *Anti-Judaism* or Teter's 2020 *Blood Libel*. Other works rewrite broad Christian or seemingly secular narratives in a way that irrevocably integrates Jewish people, such as with Kenneth Austin's 2020 *The Jews and the Reformation* and Francesca Trivellato's 2019 *The Promise and Peril of Credit*.[19] A third approach focuses closely on the dynamics of local settings: Strasbourg and Poland for, respectively, Kaplan and Teter; Bohemia for Howard Louthan; and Rome for Marina Caffiero.[20] This book, by virtue of its close focus on one event, draws on all three approaches. It shows the involvement, and even preoccupation, of Catholic clergy and institutions with Judaism and the idea of converting Roman Jews. It also connects that interest in Judaism with wider attempts by those same institutions to evangelize the known world and make their church global. Third, it takes into account a local setting that was arguably the most compelling and high-stakes site in Europe for Jewish-Christian relations. Within the Eternal City, interreligious encounters and dynamics always bore additional symbolic weight, and especially so during the era of Roman renewal and Catholic expansion.

In layering cultural history with religious and theological approaches, this book examines the triple interaction of living Jews, living Christians, and the weighty preconceptions burdening them both. It shows, first, just how much Rome's global mission relied on interactions with Judaism, both theoretically and practically. Second, it demonstrates that imaginary and real Jews served overlapping functions in early modern Rome: conversionary rhetoric evoked imaginary Jews in the presence of real Jews. When preachers compared imaginary Jews to Catholics, Muslims, or pagans, living Jewish people in Rome suffered tangible consequences. Third, it reveals how the particular local context could also become

19. On this point, see Austin's argument that the Reformers' treatment of Jews undermined narratives of the Reformation as the herald of modernity and tolerance, and until recently remained an embarrassing topic for historians. Kenneth Austin, *The Jews and the Reformation*, xvi.

20. Debra Kaplan, *Beyond Expulsion: Jews, Christians, and Reformation Strasbourg*; Magda Teter, *Jews and Heretics in Catholic Poland: A Beleaguered Church in the Post-Reformation Era*; Magda Teter, *Sinners on Trial: Jews and Sacrilege after the Reformation*; Howard Louthan, *Converting Bohemia: Force and Persuasion in the Catholic Reformation*; Marina Caffiero, *Battesimi forzati: Storie di ebrei, cristiani e convertiti nella Roma dei papi*; Marina Caffiero, *Legami Pericolosi: Ebrei e cristiani tra eresia, libri proibiti e stregoneria*; Marina Caffiero, *Il grande mediatore: Tranquillo Vita Corcos, un rabbino nella Roma dei papi*.

universal. The patterns of that triple interaction, as set in Rome, created a powerful paradigm that could then be applied universally to a global church and its missionary targets. Ultimately, both imaginary and real Jews aided the expression of a new early modern Catholic identity.

Finally, this book also promotes recent new approaches to studying early modern Catholicism by arguing for more attention to religious minorities. A vast edifice of nineteenth- and early twentieth-century scholarship was built on institutional records of the church's many congregations; these often-prescriptive sources portrayed a monolithic, uniform, and largely successful church. In response, current scholarship emphasizes porousness and flexibility at all the borders of early modern Catholicism: geographic, theological, and personal. Recent studies stress the marginal and peripheral, domestic, and transitory as well as shifting identities, reception, appropriation, and adaptation. Some of the most fruitful results have studied interactions and reciprocal influence between Catholics and non-Catholics in distant missionary contexts.[21] This book provides a needed advancement of that approach by examining the contribution of Jews and Judaism, against which the church had so frequently defined itself. It shows that we must write the history of early modern Catholicism not only as a world religion but also as a religiously interdependent enterprise even at its core.

{⚜︎}

This book begins by re-creating the range of conversionary efforts that animated early modern Rome. The idea of "conversion" could be applied in different ways to all of Rome's religious innovation, starting with the growing desire to create committed, educated Catholics, their hearts converted from sin. But the term's more common meaning—switching religious confessions or affiliations—applied as well. In launching concerted missionary activity across the world, from Canada to Cochin, early modern Catholicism became the world's first global religion. Both internal and confessional conversion also required the physical conversion of the city of Rome into the church's exemplary capital, a new Jerusalem. At the core of these efforts lay a sweeping conversionary campaign targeting Jews.

21. For an overview of this trend, see Alexandra Bamji, Geert H. Janssen, and Mary Laven, *The Ashgate Research Companion to the Counter-Reformation*. For an exemplar, see Tara Alberts, *Conflict and Conversion: Catholicism in Southeast Asia, 1500–1700*; Matthew Coneys Wainwright and Emily Michelson, *A Companion to Religious Minorities in Early Modern Rome.*

Forced preaching to Roman Jews must therefore be seen as part of—and indeed an emblem of—the broad range of conversionary efforts that characterized the whole of early modern Rome.

For these reasons, sermons to Jews were tightly woven into both elite and popular Roman society. Chapter 2 identifies the many sorts of patrons and supporters that kept them afloat. For even one conversionary sermon to take place at all, a few weighty Catholic organizations had to contribute. Enforcing the sermons almost every week over centuries required the deep investment of many more, from confraternities to print offices to treasuries. Such institutions committed enthusiastically. Conversionary preaching looked to them like a sure success story—a self-congratulatory initiative to be proud of. It made a stellar talking point for Catholics. Preaching to Jews gained cachet and lasted. Over time, the status of conversionary preachers came to lend prestige and authority to many other initiatives in early modern Rome. Many of these other initiatives had to do with conversion, but ultimately, conversionary preaching to the Jews touched groups and people ostensibly far removed from the Saturday sermon, becoming ever more deeply woven into the religious and institutional fabric of Catholic Rome.

Conversionary preaching also drew the attention of ambitious clerics from across and outside Rome. Chapter 3 traces the varied and sometimes erratic careers of conversionary preachers, drawn in the early days from many different backgrounds. The conversionary pulpit served some of these men as a stepping-stone to greater glory. For others it was a strategic career obligation; still others found it a lifetime calling. In introducing these men and reconstructing their lives, this chapter shows that preaching to Jews immediately became a point of prestige for preachers, and remained so even as the office itself transformed from a fashion to a fixture.

Sermons to Jews always took place in the public eye, with Christians present, observing the scene. This secondary audience of Christians remained intrinsic to the entire enterprise, even though conversionary sermons ostensibly addressed only Jews. Chapter 4 details how these various onlookers—a mix of local Romans and foreign visitors—became as much a target audience as the Jews. Preachers often spoke to them directly from the pulpit. Attending a conversionary sermon formed part of the Roman devotional landscape. It joined other new acts of public piety in Rome celebrating the city's resurgence, such as the pilgrimage to the seven churches or the forty-hour devotion. It also recalled the frequent public ceremonies that enlisted Jews, such as carnival and the papal investiture. Conversionary preaching fed the voyeurism of curious tourists too, especially those whose homelands lacked large Jewish settlements. Grand tourists came to identify Rome with public sermons to Jews. Published conversionary sermons and related polemical literature extended that multilayered audience into print. In all of these ways, conversionary preaching reinforced early modern Catholic piety to a mixed and international Christian audience.

The last three chapters of the book turn more closely to the content of the sermons themselves, and the ways that preachers and audiences developed, shaped, and responded to them. Chapter 5 takes up the medieval European precedents that established "imaginary Judaism" as an enduring and powerful concept in Christian thought. Patristic conceptions of Jews reached their rhetorical peak in the public disputations of medieval Spain and Paris. Disputations determined the standard tropes and exegetical techniques for demonstrating the superiority of Christianity over Judaism. I compare this stylized rhetoric with another precedent that influenced early modern preachers: the sermons of fifteenth-century Italian mendicants. These fiery preachers addressed their preaching to Christians, but devoted ample pulpit time to practical relations between Jews and Christians in medieval towns. Their sermons resulted in palpable consequences: violence, expulsion, and economic transformation. This chapter seeks to account for continuities and differences between these two precedents, and the evolving conventions of conversionary sermons in early modern Rome.

At the same time, conversionary preaching reflected and promoted early modern Catholicism's innovations and triumphalism. Its unusual departures are best revealed in an untapped cache of over 750 manuscript sermons by Gregorio Boncompagni Corcos, the subject of chapter 6. Boncompagni Corcos, a respected conversionary preacher of the late seventeenth century, held his position for nearly forty years, and left all of his handwritten sermons in good working order, almost entirely unknown to modern scholars. In these sermons he introduced unprecedented topics discussing Catholicism's newest triumphs: recent religious orders, new saints, and the church's global reach. He made these topics into tools of Jewish conversion as well as general Catholic education. He also formulated influential arguments for the continued importance of sermons to Jews in the Roman devotional landscape, and in so doing, revealed his own personal doubts and insecurities. His preaching confirms that Judaism, the church's oldest antagonist, directly helped a resurgent early modern Catholicism to define itself while providing a context for the new "others" and new devotional priorities of the early modern period.

From the outset, Jews in Rome found ways to challenge the sermons forced on them. The final chapter reveals the evidence that Jewish people regularly and consistently resisted and refuted conversionary sermons. By the late seventeenth century, they made formal protests to objectionable content in conversionary sermons, publishing letters and treatises advocating for better treatment. Preachers, in turn, sometimes responded to Jewish protests with letters of their own. These sources also expose the many ways, small and larger, that Jewish resistance forced changes in conversionary sermons in both content and delivery. I place these interludes against the backdrop of ongoing tension and frequent, sometimes staged acts of violence between Christians and Jews in Rome. At times sermons themselves provoked further violence and ritualized mockery, blurring the distinction between theological objections to Jewish ideas and social objections to Jewish neighbors.

{⸎⸎⸎}

This book reconstructs a history of violence, trauma, and tragedy, carried out by people who firmly believed they were doing the right and moral thing. I wrote it, in part, in the knowledge that this still happens. Between the time I first began this research and its final publication, we have all moved sharply into a new political world, in which the treatment of marginalized peoples, and indeed, the shifting locations of those margins, remain current and burningly important questions. Governments fall or rise over the question of precisely how to define who is foreign and who is native, and how much so. Debates persist over whether coercion or persuasion is more just or effective, especially in cases where antagonists regard each other with suspicion, ignorance, or fear. Both my native and my adopted countries are riven by such disagreements; both unjustly continue to unsettle, expel, or enclose people in defiance of legal and human rights. The COVID-19 pandemic has only clarified how quick and deep-rooted is the general instinct to find scapegoats, however unjustified. And in both of my countries, as in many others, political and religious leaders continue to invoke Jews and Judaism, frequently disconnected from actual Jewish life or tradition, as a way of tacitly addressing or dehumanizing other audiences.

Rome's Jews provide a valuable model for considering these problems. They were simultaneously natives and foreigners, or "intimate outsiders" in Tom Cohen's useful phrase.[22] Jews had lived in Rome continuously

22. Thomas V. Cohen, "The Case of the Mysterious Coil of Rope: Street Life and Jewish Persona in Rome in the Middle of the Sixteenth Century," 221.

since before the dawn of Christianity. But the era with which this book is concerned saw a clear and deliberate shift in Rome's policy toward Jews. Where they once had been fairly well (though not entirely) tolerated, accepted, and integrated—unlike many places in Europe—they were now segregated, deliberately impoverished, and more thoroughly derided. Other minorities, less well rooted in the city, suffered from similar treatment. As Caffiero has suggested, Roman Jews, through a process of small redefinitions and legislative tweaks, found their status gradually altered; they were reimagined as heretics and so placed under the supervision of the Holy Office.[23] Although they were native Romans, they were recast as legal outsiders.

The religious polarization of early modern Europe presages the polarizations of our own era. Indeed, the stakes surely seemed even higher to early modern preachers than they do to us. For many of us, our own convictions, however strongly held, primarily concern the fate of the living, not the destiny of the dead. Preachers in the early modern world, in contrast, would have said that their mission was eternal. Any soul they failed to save faced damnation and hellfire for eternity. Their road to respectful interaction between faiths was narrow, with precipices on each side.

Then again, the stakes feel plenty high to us today as well. What does this history of early modern Rome offer to our own fraught society? In this book, I try to show how fears and concerns specific to early modern Rome were projected onto Jewish people, who suffered largely because of the preconceptions of others. It examines the particular ways that early modern Roman Jews were despised less for who they were than for what they symbolized. But it takes little imagination to see that many groups targeted today are equally victims of unjust projections, specific to the circumstances. At the risk of seeming to preach in a book that identifies preaching with violence, I want my research to make it clear how layers of misunderstanding, false labeling, and stereotyping build up gradually and take ever deeper root over centuries. Good intentions alone cannot dislodge these deeply entrenched attitudes, but an understanding of their history can help us to begin.

23. Marina Caffiero, "Gli ebrei sono eretici? L'Inquisizione romana e gli ebrei tra Cinque e Ottocento," 246–50.

CHAPTER ONE

The World of Conversion in Early Modern Rome

HE WOULD LIVE TO REGRET the conversation. Prospero di Tullio Ser-ampino, Roman Jew and proud father of five, found himself in the position of the biblical Jepthe, forced to keep a promise too hastily made and yield up a child. Prospero's chance conversation with a Dominican friar may have seemed friendly enough at first. The friar, Giovanni Domenico Nazzareno, asked Prospero how many children he had, and whether he would consider making any of them Christian. He wouldn't. But Nazzareno pushed, describing the great benefits of a Christian life, and the care and comfort that a baptized child would receive. Prospero still refused. Would it make any difference, asked the friar at last, if the pope himself conducted the baptism? A frustrated Prospero finally spat back this specific response: "If this is so, I'll give him to you, for God wants to give him to you." The documentary record emphasizes that these were the exact words he used, noting them so carefully that in the manuscript original, the handwriting becomes more precise, and in later printed versions the words are underlined or italicized.

Nazzareno, no fool, pounced. He informed Prospero that the hasty statement was binding and roped in bystanders as witnesses. Prospero objected immediately, insisting that he had not been serious. Nazzareno then pulled every string he could. He took the case to the rector of the House of Catechumens. The rector immediately consulted the conversionary preacher to the Jews, Giuseppe Ciantes. Ciantes determined that Prospero's retort constituted a legally binding promise. From there, the case circled up to the Catechumens's cardinal protector and then to the pope. Urban VIII Barberini agreed with delight to sponsor the baptism of Prospero's child personally.

In the middle of the night, and over Prospero's repeated protests, the rector of the House of Catechumens raided the Serampino house in the ghetto and emerged with two children: a thirteen-month-old girl, Gemma, and a boy, Solomon, who seemed about six. The Jews of Rome rallied around Prospero, furious, betrayed, and angry enough to turn the city upside down. The record describes them as mad dogs howling (*latrare*). The boy, Solomon, lavished with attention within the House of Catechumens, seemed to agree to convert. The rector reassessed the boy's age to be at least seven, the age of reason and free will. In response to strenuous Jewish objections, a group of officials, again including Ciantes, reviewed the case and confirmed, predictably, that both children still merited baptism. Baby Gemma would fulfill her father's promise; Solomon was converting of his own volition, having been persuaded. To the Catholics involved, the incident was a shining example of Urban VIII's benevolence. For the papal baptism, they staged an elaborate ceremony in the Dominican church of the Minerva, where Nazzareno was based. It may have been the first time a pope had ever performed such a baptism personally.[1] On March 27, 1639, the children—now called Anna Urbania and Urbanus Urbanius— wore white, silver, and gold wool. The little boy was mounted on the pope's own white horse in a triumphal procession, followed by carriages, drums, and trumpets. The crowds overflowed. The procession proceeded directly through the ghetto itself and then around much of Rome.

In some ways, this story is clearly extraordinary. Compared with other records, it stands out for the curious circumstances of the *offerta*, or offering of relatives for baptism, and its violence and drama. It is the only extended narrative in the record book of seventeenth-century baptisms; all other entries merited only two to three lines. Remedio Albano, the rector who recorded the story, proudly noted his own role in the action: "The friar came to me, Remedio Albano, Rector." To him, it demonstrated "the confusion of the cursed and obstinate Jewish rabble [*cenaglia*], and praise of the omnipotent triune god, of the glorious Virgin Mary, and . . . the holy triumphant and militant church."[2] The story, with its many officious meetings and performative legalism, also provided a valuable precedent for instances of contested baptism. The rector's narrative was printed up verbatim into a pamphlet, which was later incorporated into other collections of cases. The pamphlet appears, for example, bound inside a 1694

---

1. Domenico Rocciolo, "Fra promozione e difesa della fede: Le vicende dei catecumeni e neofiti romani in età moderna," 150. The account is ambiguous about whether Urban VIII was present or only lent his approval while Scannaroli acted for him.

2. ASVR Casa dei Catecumeni 178, Liber Baptizatorum 1634–75, fols. 17v–21v.

manuscript in the archives of the Holy Office as evidence in the baptismal case of a woman offered against her will to the House of Catechumens by her husband. In 1713, it was included in a printed collection of evidence about other ambiguous offerings of catechumens, which refers to the manuscript in the baptismal record as the original. Copies of it are also preserved elsewhere in the Inquisition archives and again in the archives of the Vicariate.[3] It has become one of the most retold stories in modern Jewish histories of Rome.[4]

But in other, possibly more important ways, this case is part of a general pattern—one slightly unusual incident in Rome's sweeping conversionary campaign. The baptism of these two children, for example, was part of a regular series of baptisms of Jews and Muslims throughout the early modern period. Just a month before he oversaw the baptism of the two children, Gianbattista Scannaroli, the suffragan bishop of Rome, had baptized two young men in the church of Santa Lucia in Selce; a month later, on Holy Saturday, he baptized two more in the basilica of Saint John Lateran.[5] Cardinals and even popes had performed extraordinary baptisms before, and would again. Dominicans and their church remained deeply involved. The celebration of conversion was already, and would remain, a priority in early modern Rome. This story, stretching from the humble priest Nazzareno to the illustrious Barberini pope, tugs on the threads that bound the entire early modern city together, revealing the wide range of institutions involved in conversionary efforts.

Nazzareno's involvement also exposes the long influence of conversionary preachers to Jews in Rome. It was the preacher Giuseppe Ciantes

3. For the 1694 manuscript, see ACDF St St CC 4 a 7, int. 2, involving one Giuditta, offered by her husband, Salvatore Se'ed. For the pamphlet as well as a discussion of these and similar cases, see Marina Caffiero, *Battesimi Forzati*, 203–56. Copies of the pamphlet are also located in ASVR Pia Casa di Catecumeni 25 (not 225 as cited elsewhere), fasc. 26; ACDF St St CC 4 a 7; ACDF St St UV 51 06.

4. E. (Emmanuel) Rodocanachi, *Le Saint-Siège et les Juifs; le ghetto à Rome*, 287; Ettore Natali, *Il ghetto di Roma. Volume primo*; Marina Caffiero, *Battesimi forzati*, 225–28, 277–78, 280–81; Alberto Zucchi, "I predicatori domenicani degli ebrei nel secolo XVII," 44–45; Wipertus Hugo Rudt de Collenberg, "Le baptême des Juifs à Rome de 1614 a 1798 selon les registres de la 'Casa dei Catecumeni': pt. 1: 1614–1676," 158. Perugini, in "L'Inquisition Romaine et les Israélites," 96, wrongly lists the date as 1659, which explains why Rodocanachi suggests that the story happened twice. These sources name the father in various ways; the manuscript original calls him Prospero Serampino. Rudt de Collenberg says it is Serapino.

5. Caffiero suggests that Gianbattista Scannarola was involved because he was a prominent jurist; from the manuscript baptismal record, it is also evident that as suffragan bishop, Scannarola had performed most of the baptisms of converts of the previous five years.

LE STOLTE
DOTTRINE
DE GLI EBREI
CON LA LORO CONFVTATIONE.

Opera

DEL PADRE MAESTRO

F. PIETRO PICHI DA TRIEVI,
Domenicano Predicatore de gli Ebrei.

Di nuouo fatta riſtampare per vtilità
de gl'Ebrei

DA F. GIO. DOMENICO NAZZARO,
dell'iſteſſo Ordine, detto il Padre ARMENO

IN ROMA, Appreſſo Manelfo Manelfi. 1640.

Con licenza de' Superiori.

FIGURE 1.1. Pietro Pichi, *Le stolte dottrine de gli ebrei con la loro confutatione.*
General Collection, Beinecke Rare Book and Manuscript Library, Yale University.

ALL'ILLVSTRISSIMO,

& Reuerendifsimo Signore,

& Padrone Offeruandifsimo

MONSIGNOR

F. GIOSEPPE CIANTI

D E' PREDICATORI

VESCOVO DI MARSICO.

◆◆◆◆◆◆

 'Honorato teftimo-
nio, ch'è piaciuto à
noftro Signore dare
al mondo de molti
meriti di V. S. Ill.ᵐᵃ
promouendola al Vefcouato di
Marfico, è ben tale che può corre-
a 2   fpon-

FIGURE 1.2. Pietro Pichi, *Le stolte dottrine de gli ebrei con la loro confutatione.*
Domenico Nazzareno's dedication to Giuseppe Ciantes. General Collection,
Beinecke Rare Book and Manuscript Library, Yale University.

who first determined that Prospero's vow could be considered binding.
Ciantes's decision allowed Nazzareno's once-private conversation to go
public, thereby engaging cardinals and popes. Moreover, Ciantes served
on the committee that concluded that neither child should be returned to
the ghetto. But the two men already shared a longer history. Nazzareno
owed Ciantes a much deeper debt. He described it a year later when he

republished an anti-Jewish tract by a previous conversionary preacher, with a new dedication to Ciantes himself (figures 1.1 and 1.2).[6] Nazzareno's letter of dedication is both congratulatory and personal. It celebrates Ciantes's "glorious efforts over the course of so many years in Rome, in the holy preaching of the true faith and the conversion of the Jews and other infidels . . . so that with the force of this light those vain shadows of their faithlessness will be largely cleared from Jewish hearts."[7]

Yet the bond between Nazzareno and Ciantes revealed how far Jewish conversion mattered in other contexts too. Nazzareno, nicknamed "the Armenian" for his origins, explicitly thanks Ciantes for individual help. He recalls his own experience as a convert to Catholicism in the House of Catechumens in Rome and the kindness Ciantes had shown him at the time. Finally, Nazzareno brings up his own plans to return to Armenia "to commit myself totally to the conversion of souls at your example." After the Council of Trent, Armenian Orthodox and other Eastern rite Christians increasingly found themselves defined as targets for Catholic missionary efforts in the church's drive for universalism.[8] In short, Nazzareno's involvement demonstrates how two conversionary preachers to Jews in Rome—the original author and the second dedicatee of this tract—fed the Roman Church's global mission.

The story of Prospero and Nazzareno is not the story of two men alone. The dispute between them drew in many major players on the Roman stage, from preachers to popes, whose interest in conversion extended far beyond Jews. Nazzareno's written dedication to Ciantes, for example, mentions the "many people zealous for the propagation of the faith" who had asked him to republish the tract. The phrase evokes the recently founded congregation of the same name that coordinated global missionary efforts. His efforts also required the involvement of the Dominican Order, the House of Catechumens, and many other cardinals. If we extend the story to include the earlier edition of Pietro Pichi's conversionary tract, we can add in the vicar of Rome, to whom it was dedicated, the Holy Office of the Inquisition, which the dedication praises, and the Master of

6. Pietro Pichi, *Le stolte dottrine de gli ebrei con la loro confutaione*. Ciantes had just left the post of preacher to the Jews and become bishop of Marsica. For the baptisms he performed as bishop, see ASVR Casa dei Catecumeni 178, Liber Baptizatorum 1634–75, fols. 35v, 37r, 41r.

7. Pichi, *Le stolte dottrine*, unpaginated, a2v–a3r.

8. Pichi, *Le stolte dottrine*. On the conversion of Eastern rite Christians, see especially Cesare Santus, "Wandering Lives: Eastern Christian Pilgrims, Alms-Collectors, and 'Refugees' in Early Modern Rome," 238–39.

the Sacred Palace, who provided an imprimatur. The complex network of institutions and people involved in conversion efforts is staggering. It reflects the extensive range of organizations that jointly animated the city and its pious activities.

Nazzareno was only one of many who linked Jewish and global conversion. Another preacher, Stefano Sirleto, had been so successful preaching to Jews thirty-five years earlier that the pope sent him to reconvert a straying bishop in Armenia.[9] Antonio Possevino, the famed Jesuit diplomat, recalled how Ignatius Loyola, founder of the Jesuit order, had held the conversion of Jews, heretics, and gentiles "close to heart" and central to the Jesuits' purpose. Ignatius set up missions in Europe and overseas for the latter two groups. His warm efforts toward Jews in Rome, "where there seemed to be hope of gathering them in," resulted in the founding of formal conversionary institutions.[10] These close connections between global and local conversion lasted into the eighteenth century. Vicento Talenti's 1753 life of Joseph Calasanz describes how the devil tried to distract Calasanz from his focus on children's education by tempting him with other missions:

> And when [the devil] wanted him to convert souls to Christ, he showed him the Indias full of idolatry, Africa and Asia full of Muslims, Europe sown with heretics, and the guardian angels of those unhappy souls begging him for help. And when the devil wanted to stay in the holy city, there were many Jews to illuminate, many sinners to convert.[11]

Talenti's devil, here, has instinctively situated Jews triply: within the city of Rome, in a pan-European setting, and globally. To these men and their milieu, preaching to Jews fit securely into the many varied conversionary efforts that characterized early modern Rome. Indeed, it fit so well that sermons to Jews could come to symbolize the whole missionizing enterprise.

---

9. BAV Urb. lat. 1072, part 2, fol. 595r., November 20, 1604. See Alberto Zucchi, "I predicatori domenicani degli ebrei in Roma"; Alberto Zucchi, "Il primo predicatore domenicano degli ebrei. Ancora sul P. Sirleto—Fr. Alessandro Franceschi." In these two articles, Zucchi first considers whether the Dominican Sirleto, known to preach to the Jews, was one of three converts, then establishes him as Stefano Sirleto, a mentally unstable and ultimately suicidal Calabrian, and finally argues that he was Cardinal Sirleto's nephew and did no dishonor to the order.

10. ARSI Opp. NN 313.

11. Vincenzo Talenti, *Vita del beato Giuseppe Calasanzio, della Madre di Dio, fondatore de' chierici poveri della Madre di Dio delle scuole pie*, 65.

Rome and Conversion

Prospero, Nazzareno, and Ciantes lived in an age of conversionary fervor. Their drama played out in its most meaningful location, in a church and especially city wherein "conversion" was both a deep concern and an ever-useful narrative principle. After centuries of threats—including the Avignon Papacy, conciliar movement, Protestant Reformation, and recent devastating Italian Wars—by the 1570s the Roman Church had emerged largely triumphant. The Papacy was firmly established in Rome, its coffers were filling, and the protracted Council of Trent had concluded. The ecclesiastical elite of early modern Rome deliberately sought to remake the city into a model of Christian virtue. Energetic religious innovation took many different forms: the growth of confraternities, founding of active religious orders, rise of new forms of public devotion, physical transformation of the city into a living model of piety, and development and expansion of overseas missions with local headquarters. The idea of "conversion," as a broad umbrella, applied in some way to nearly all of these activities. The term covered the turn to greater piety, the active embrace of Catholicism, and the transfiguration of the city itself into a theater of devotion. Karl Morrison argued that conversion is always at heart a metaphor. Even though more recent scholarship has come close to reconstructing the experience of early modern conversion, narratives retain their power: we must still attend to the various stories and models of conversion that determined how conversion was understood in early modern Rome.[12]

In the most common model of conversion, all hearts needed converting—only some from a greater distance. Early modern people commonly understood the word "conversion" to mean the heart's inner turning to piety, which often required a process of gradual inner transformation, and a lifelong process of reforming the self. Most typically, the Italian verb *convertirsi* meant adopting a monastic life. In the sixteenth and seventeenth centuries, popular books with "conversion" in their titles tended to celebrate the conversion of the sinner to God, and the return from a sinful to a devout lifestyle.[13] Equally likely, they recounted the penitential conversions of Saints Augustine, Paul, or Mary Magdalen.[14] The noun

12. Karl F. Morrison, *Understanding Conversion*, 2–27.

13. Lieke Stelling, Harald Hendrix, and Todd Richardson, *The Turn of the Soul: Representations of Religious Conversion in Early Modern Art and Literature*, 6–10.

14. See, for example, *La rappresentazione della conuersione di santa Maria Maddalena* (roughly ten editions between 1554 and 1613); *La conuersione del peccatore a Dio.*

"converts" applied most commonly in its feminine form—*convertite*—to former prostitutes who had repented or retired, entering specialized convents. True conversion thus started with an emphasis on interior piety and sometimes ended there.

Conversion was therefore an act available to and required of everybody, including those born in the church. New and old Catholics participated in the same act of turning the heart toward true devotion. In this view, a convert's baptism, while especially significant, was close kin to the activities of those born to the faith and pursuing deeper piety—being made new or being renewed. Choosing to become Catholic only validated the efforts of people who already were. Jewish women who converted first to Catholicism and then to the cloister, for example, found that their monastic vows were celebrated as a second, higher-level conversion, intensifying and confirming the first.[15]

This paradigm, inherited from medieval predecessors, taught that conversion overall was "a gradual process of testing and education induced by God from outside nature . . . indistinguishable from Christian life."[16] The understanding of conversion as a turn of the heart lay at the heart of all proselytization, whether to those becoming Catholic for the first time or those committing to a new level of piety. Activities meant to create new Catholics in the early modern period were therefore inseparable from the innovations generally classed as Catholic Reform. Both kinds of action fed the same underlying need for committed, devout, educated Catholics, who had converted their own hearts, wherever they had started from. The techniques used to bolster faith among Catholics could apply equally well to the formation of new Catholics: communal worship and action, the establishment of a pious peer group, and a new support system. All of these activities aimed to make the Roman church more appealing to more people, creating both more and better adherents.

This concept of the nature of conversion resonates, if it does not accord precisely, with the record of how religious affiliation usually changed in early modern Rome and Europe—not for purely theological reasons, but through prolonged interaction, porous cross-cultural contact, and the

---

Tragicomedia spirituale di G. Battista Leoni; Paolo Morigia, *Historia della merauigliosa conuersione, vita essemplare, e beato fine, dell'ill.ma sig.ra Lodouica Torella, contessa di Guastalla.*

15. For one such example, including a discussion on the nature of "intensification conversions," see Tamar Herzig, "The Hazards of Conversion: Nuns, Jews, and Demons in Late Renaissance Italy," 473–74.

16. Morrison, *Understanding Conversion*, 25.

deliberate choice of one culture and lifestyle over another, even if the choice was pushed along by incentives, threats, or need.[17] Even a genuine, desired conversion could still carry ambivalence, vacillation, and ongoing contact after baptism. Though converts often narrated dramatic, unwavering changes of heart, the documentary record unearths more hesitant, uneven, and convoluted stories.[18] Take the example of two Jewish siblings, Graziadio and Laura, who were baptized in Florence in the mid-seventeenth century. Each of them staged a dramatic escape from the ghetto in order to convert—Graziadio running away at fourteen, and Laura throwing herself out a window. But each of them also later fled the House of Catechumens before baptism, insisting on returning to Judaism. They each experienced many further moments of profound doubt, in both directions, before finally seeming to settle into new lives as Francesco Maria Orlandini, a Franciscan friar and highly esteemed preacher to Jews, and Suor Anna Maria Felice, a cloistered nun.

But conversionary concerns never left Orlandini. Twenty years later, he continued to trade on his track record as a recruiter to the Catholic faith, notably in a letter he addressed to the Propaganda Fide. His letter requested a transfer to a more desirable monastery, and he clearly felt that it would bolster his case to describe all the souls he had brought to baptism. Orlandini even suggested that the move might help him win over more of his family to Christianity. His whole life, he wrote, was dedicated to "building a perfect understanding of Christian truth"; this life seemed defined by missionary zeal. Yet even so, only a few years later, in 1667, Orlandini was denounced for the most scandalous apostasy: trying to recruit a neighboring nun to Judaism in secret so that they could run away (yet again) and live together as married Jews. The case drew inquisitors from three different cities in Northern Italy. Orlandini's faith (or perhaps it was pragmatism) remained forever in doubt. The process of individual conversion could take a lifetime, and did not always fall into neat or easily defined categories.[19]

17. For one discussion of this model of conversion, see Andrew Pettegree, *Reformation and the Culture of Persuasion*, 1–9, 211–17.

18. On converts telling denigrating stories to mask emotional ties to their previous religion, see Lewis R. Rambo, *Understanding Religious Conversion*, 53–54.

19. For a fuller treatment of the Blanis/Orlandini family, see Samuela Marconcini, *Per amor del cielo: farsi cristiani a Firenze tra seicento e settecento*, 140–45; Peter A. Mazur, *Conversion to Catholicism in Early Modern Italy*, 76–80, whose interpretation of Orlandini's actions I follow here. Mazur reproduced Orlandini's letter in his book (154–88); I use his translation. For a description of Orlandini's trial, see Adriano Prosperi, "L'inquisizione Romana e gli ebrei." For background on Jewish life in Renaissance Florence, see Edward L.

At the same time, another model of conversion had its uses: conversion as a radical transformation, a death and rebirth. The champions of preaching and other forms of direct mission to Jews employed this model in their rhetoric. They celebrated conversion as the creation of a new self, an act borne entirely of reason and intellectual persuasion, a dramatic, triumphant moment. This conception of conversion was common in medieval conversion narratives and remained so into the early modern period. If it was less realistic, it was nonetheless far more valuable for supporting Counter-Reformation bombast. The two children whose baptism opened this chapter did not tell their own stories, which presumably involved at least a few moments of homesickness or bewilderment. The rector Remedio Albano chose to describe their conversion as wholehearted and genuine, because it gratified his institution and own faith to put it that way.

This dual model of conversion, by turns either gradual and continuous, or severe and absolute, dates back to Saint Augustine's *Confessions*. In the lives of many converts themselves, these models were not considered opposites; converts managed to tell a story that simultaneously emphasized their deep ties to their former Jewish identity and presented an absolute transformation.[20] Modern scholarship, too, has continued to embrace both patterns and not see them as opposites. Sociologists of religion increasingly document the stages of conversion, considering it a gradual cultural shift or slow persuasion that often takes place through a set of progressive steps and is deeply contingent on historical circumstances. Moments of stark shifts or powerful transformations do occur, but the specific finite events that accompany a conversion, such as a baptism, must be framed as part of a longer and more gradual process of taking on a new culture, adopting new beliefs and practices alongside old ones, or fusing new and old cultures.[21] Indeed, some scholars argue that these necessarily fluid interactions and activities across religious borders are precisely what give those borders definition.[22]

Goldberg, *Jews and Magic in Medici Florence: The Secret World of Benedetto Blanis*; Stefanie Siegmund, *The Medici State and the Ghetto of Florence: The Construction of an Early Modern Jewish Community*.

20. Elisheva Carlebach, *Divided Souls: Converts from Judaism in Germany, 1500–1750*, 88–123.

21. Marc David Baer, "History and Religious Conversion"; 'Rambo, *Understanding Religious Conversion*, esp. 5–19; David A. Snow and Richard Machalek, "The Sociology of Conversion," 168–70.

22. Ira Katznelson and Miri Rubin, *Religious Conversion: History, Experience and Meaning*, 10–11.

Perhaps because it was so hard to capture, conversion was by definition always incomplete and therefore always suspect. Having crossed a gulf once, the second time might prove easier: "Once a convert, always convertible," as the critic James Wood put it.[23] With this in mind, many converts to Catholicism in the early modern period spent their entire postbaptismal lives constantly trying to prove their authenticity, never able to assuage in their own minds the fear that others would continue to doubt them. Gian Battista Eliano, the only early modern Jesuit of Jewish birth, found that his Jewishness followed him throughout his Mediterranean missions to the Copts. A desire to demonstrate his distance from his birth, even as his Christian missionary work forced him to grapple with it daily, made him judge the behavior of the Jews and crypto-Jews he encountered especially harshly.[24]

Christian fear of a false conversion is both specific to Jews and general to the period.[25] Converted Jews had a special significance as living proof of the truth of Christianity. If they rejected their baptism, they jeopardized Catholic claims to triumphalism and universality, and more immediately, also compromised the good standing and piety of the sponsors and institutions that had supported their conversion.[26] Recent precedent from Spain and Portugal made Jewish converts in Rome seem even more suspicious, and their case more fraught. Since Iberian Jews had been converted by force, how could their faith be trusted? But since they were not to be trusted, why make the effort to convert them? And since converts faced so much ongoing hostility from the church, what made them want to join it?[27] Proselytizers needed to ensure that converts demonstrated the real

23. James Wood, "The Radical Origins of Christianity."

24. Robert John Clines, *A Jewish Jesuit in the Eastern Mediterranean: Early Modern Conversion, Mission, and the Construction of Identity*, esp. 192–94; Carlebach, *Divided Souls*, 33–46, 115–16.

25. For an overview of early modern false identities, see Miriam Eliav-Feldon, *Renaissance Impostors and Proofs of Identity*; Natalie Zemon Davis, *Trickster Travels: A Sixteenth-Century Muslim between Worlds*; Miriam Eliav-Feldon and Tamar Herzig, *Dissimulation and Deceit in Early Modern Europe*.

26. Herzig, "The Hazards of Conversion," 488–90.

27. For an analysis of this conundrum in more detail as it relates to the Jesuit order, see Anna Foa, "'Limpieza' versus Mission: Church, Religious Orders, and Conversion in the Sixteenth Century," 304–5. On the interdependent love-hate relationship between Judaism and Christianity as it relates to conversion, see Theodor Dunkelgrün and Pawel Maciejko, *Bastards and Believers: Jewish Converts and Conversion from the Bible to the Present*, 3–8. For the instability of Jewish conversion and its effect on Protestant England, see Jeffrey S. Shoulson, *Fictions of Conversion: Jews, Christians, and Cultures of Change in Early Modern England*, 16–38.

fruits of persuasion at every turn. They knew full well that by promising economic and social perks with baptism, they might only encourage insincere conversions. And so early modern Catholics increasingly worried about sincerity and inner conviction, both in their own hearts and those of converts.[28] Anxiety about whether conversions were genuine remained a hallmark of early modern proselytization efforts and a constant companion to them.

For these purposes, a magnificent and dramatic spectacle of conversion might help allay, or at least mask, such worries. An observer could be reassured by laying eyes directly on the neophytes as they performed Christian actions in public. Surely, the observer could reason, so much effort, planning, and drama would only have been bestowed on worthy candidates. And if not, the very act of participating in such a grand ritual would surely strengthen a wavering will. Public sermons, regularly offered, easily accessible, and impressively learned and eloquent, provided the perfect stage to soothe anxieties about conversion.

The competition for souls was played for high stakes in the early modern world. The Reformation, by allowing a choice of Christian denominations in western Europe for the first time, lent new weight to all public religious actions, perhaps in Rome above all. Some of this religious fervor rode the same broad waves of reform that reconfigured early modern Catholicism throughout Europe, stemming from the Council of Trent and the example of Cardinal Carlo Borromeo for pastoral care. Rome, like other Catholic areas, bricked up the walls of convents, required bishops to take up residence in their dioceses, and adopted the new Roman liturgy and catechism.

But a great deal of religious activity was distinct to Rome or exportable as a specifically Roman devotion. Early modern popes and religious organizations undertook conscious acts of glorifying the city. They sought to rebuild Rome as the exemplary capital of a newly global religion, a New Jerusalem, a living religious spectacle, a "hothouse for nurturing all fashionable good works and displaying them to the world."[29] In so doing, they built specifically on Rome's classical past (which they sought to replace), its victories in newly Christianized parts of the world (which they considered

28. Irene Fosi, *Convertire lo straniero: forestieri e inquisizione a Roma in età moderna*, 15–20; Irene Fosi, "'Con cuore sincero e con fede non finta': conversioni a Roma in età moderna fra controllo e accoglienza."

29. Brian Pullan, "The Conversion of the Jews: The Style of Italy," 63. For Catholicism as a world religion, see Simon Ditchfield, "Decentering the Catholic Reformation: Papacy and Peoples in the Early Modern World."

a validation of their faith), and its proliferating Protestant antagonists (against whom they sought to build a model of perfect Catholicism).

The spiritual rejuvenation of Rome also required a physical renovation as Rome became the world headquarters of a global religion. Physical space was intensely contested in Rome as perhaps nowhere else in Europe.[30] The material process of rebuilding had begun a few decades after the Papacy's return to Rome in 1417. It came to include all the building activity that created Renaissance and Baroque Rome as we picture it: the construction of piazze, palazzi, fountains, churches, and straight roads, including the long line of the via Giulia stretching to the Vatican, Michelangelo's design for the Capitoline Hill, and the controversial renovations of Saint Peter's basilica.[31] Along its many newly refurbished avenues, Rome's frequent religious processions laid layer on top of layer of sacrality. Perhaps the most important role went to ancient Christian Rome as catacombs were excavated so that visitors could remember and marvel at the devotion of Christianity's earliest martyrs. Through its antiquities, the first century of Christianity in Rome was recast as an inspiration for the sixteenth.[32] Pagan antiquities played a part too. When Sixtus V indulged his taste for Egyptian obelisks and dotted the city with them, he topped them with crosses, and added statues of Saints Peter and Paul to the triumphal columns of Marcus Aurelius and Trajan.

Literary efforts complemented physical ones. Sermons at the papal court embarked on an explicit program of proclaiming the health of the Catholic Church and particular glory of Rome.[33] The Roman martyrology, drastically revised by Cardinal Cesare Baronio in the 1580s, read privately or recited liturgically across Christendom, favored early Roman martyrs; it especially emphasized the physical locations of their relics in the eternal city.[34] Guidebooks to the catacombs drew attention to the lasting and universal merit of the first Roman martyrs. Likewise, the flourishing genre of guides to modern Christian Rome cast the city as a global exemplar of piety. Camillo Fanucci's *Treatise of All the Pious Works of the Great City of Rome* reminded readers that even though heretics were incorrigibly stubborn, "nonetheless Catholics from all over will take as an example

30. See Laurie Nussdorfer, "The Politics of Space in Early Modern Rome."

31. For an overview of such projects, see Jean Delumeau, *Vie economique et sociale de Rome dans la seconde moitié du XVI siècle*; Helge Gamrath, *Roma Sancta Renovata*.

32. Simon Ditchfield, "Reading Rome as a Sacred Landscape, c. 1586–1635."

33. Frederick McGinness, *Right Thinking and Sacred Oratory in Counter-Reformation Rome*; Emily Michelson, *The Pulpit and the Press in Reformation Italy*.

34. Ditchfield, "Reading Rome as a Sacred Landscape," esp. 171–78.

Rome, and its works, which through imitation they will embrace more vigorously."[35]

Fanucci was referring specifically to Holy Years; other guidebooks reinforced the point more generally. Onofrio Panvinio began his famous guide to the Seven Churches of Rome with a sonnet dedicated to the city. His guidebook itself, in its popular vernacular edition, served to transform a physical pilgrimage unique to Rome into a mental journey of prayer available to readers far distant. Its dedication to the duchess of Gravina, Beatrice Ferella degli Orsini—already elderly, with a married granddaughter, and presumably no wish to undertake the long journey—treats the guidebook as a meditation, a fruitful addition to "continuous contemplations and prayers," a form of Roman spiritual consolation of benefit to all.[36] Where so much literature, notably Giovanni Boccaccio's *Decameron*, had mocked Rome as a den of sin and corruption, works like those of Fanucci and Panvinio offered an alternative, Counter-Reformation model. They reinforced the conceit that Rome exemplified perfect Catholic piety, as a sublime, distant archetype as well as a living city.

Such congratulatory hyperbole continued through the seventeenth century and perhaps reached its peak with Carlo Bartolomeo Piazza's *Eusevologio Romano*, an immense and magisterial survey of Rome's pious institutions, and the capstone of a series by Piazza on this theme. The *Eusevologio* tallies Rome's hospitals, national colleges, orphanages and shelters, religious colleges and seminaries, confraternities, religious companies, artistic associations, literary academies, and illustrious libraries. A dedicatory letter celebrates the city's variety and internationalism—with Rome as the mother of all. Piazza describes Rome as a "Theater of Roman beneficence to every nation in the world . . . [which] so piously generous, does not contain in itself alone all that which, to universal benefit, would gladden entire Provinces and cities."[37]

35. Camillo Fanucci, *Trattato di tutte l'opere pie dell'alma città di Roma*, 3. See, more generally, Anna Blennow and Stefano Fogelberg Rota, *Rome and the Guidebook Tradition from the Middle Ages to the 20th Century*.

36. Onofrio Panvinio, *Le Sette Chiese Romane del RPF Onofrio Panvinio*, quotation unpaginated. The sonnet is by Rinaldo Corso. On Panvinio, see Stefan Bauer, *The Invention of Papal History: Onofrio Panvinio between Renaissance and Catholic Reform*.

37. Carlo Bartolomeo Piazza, *Eusevologio Romano overo delle opere pie di Roma*, ix–x. "Eusevologio" is Piazza's own neologism, a play on words on the name of Eusebius of Caesarea (c. 260–c. 340), author of an early ecclesiastical history. The title therefore denotes a compendium of knowledge, especially ecclesiastical, and is best left in Italian. My thanks to Tim Greenwood for his help here.

The flowering of pious rhetoric and activities, perhaps inevitably, also prompted new initiatives intended to either segregate or integrate outsiders who did not fit the city's pious image—in particular sex workers, Jews, and paupers, whose numbers all increased in the sixteenth century. Nicholas Terpstra has described the practice of physically enclosing undesirables as "an early modern ethos" across Europe generally, manifest in widespread measures to purify the body of Christ through segregation, enclosure, prosecution, and expulsion.[38] Such measures were not invented in Rome, but they perfectly reflected its triumphalist priorities. Within a year of establishing the ghetto in Rome, in 1555, Pope Paul IV encouraged vagabonds to collect around Piazza del Popolo, away from the city center. In the thirty years after the Council of Trent, "an ever-increasing battery of laws" sought to expel or segregate prostitutes from Roman society.[39] As Lance Lazar and Brian Pullan have argued, these efforts differed from earlier forms of poor relief by emphasizing moral reform alongside material support. Jesuits established a trio of confraternities for those in need, all located close together in Rome. One supported repentant prostitutes, one protected girls at risk, and one hosted Jewish people considering conversion to Catholicism; it later became the House of Catechumens. Run by Jesuit-led confraternities, these organizations sought to rehabilitate (or habilitate) nonconformists into Catholic orthodoxy. None of these troubled populations was new to the city, but their abiding presence became more problematic in a Rome increasingly seeking to model perfect religion.

Activities of Catholic devotion and conversion dovetailed within Roman confraternities too, especially in newer organizations. Confraternities such as Santissima Trinità dei Pellegrini, sodalities, or other forms of religious societies provided most of the poor relief, social support, and religious devotion available to early modern Italian societies. Eager for the spiritual benefits that accrued to them, confraternities ran hospitals, buried the dead, supplied dowries, and set up aid societies for indigent groups. They also united clerical leaders and lay supporters in close collaboration. Religious orders that founded confraternities relied heavily

38. Nicholas Terpstra, *Religious Refugees in the Early Modern World: An Alternative History of the Reformation*, 74–132, esp. 91–93.

39. Lance Gabriel Lazar, *Working in the Vineyard of the Lord: Jesuit Confraternities in Early Modern Italy*; Tessa Storey, *Carnal Commerce in Counter-Reformation Rome*, 241, 67–94; Elizabeth S. Cohen, "Honor and Gender in the Streets of Early Modern Rome"; Elizabeth S. Cohen, "Seen and Known: Prostitutes in the Cityscape of Late Sixteenth-Century Rome."

on lay participants. The wealthiest could lend or donate houses; many more could join their confraternities, populate their pilgrimages and processions, and leave precious remembrances in their wills. Trinità dei Pellegrini's primary purpose was to host the pilgrims who descended on Rome in the hundreds of thousands for Holy Years. In other confraternities, members of religious orders undertook the spiritual direction of laypeople through meditations such as Ignatius Loyola's *Spiritual Exercises*, frequent confessions, and eucharistic devotion. Above all, confraternities staged elaborate processions and festivities, enacting their piety and devotion to the city at large.[40]

Displays of civic, urban piety were therefore inseparable from conversionary and renewal efforts. Public displays offered a powerful argument for choosing Catholicism over other faiths, and a reminder that both the sincerest and newest Catholics were essentially participating in the same activity. Against the carefully staged backdrop of the city, the sight of committed Catholics expressing their devotion through participation in religious spectacle provided peerless publicity for the Roman church. Word often spread through the growing number of visitors to Rome and long-term foreign sojourners. More and more such groups established bases in Rome, founding their own churches or national colleges, transforming the urban landscape and redefining Rome as a profoundly heterogeneous city. Some of these institutions, such as the Spanish Santissima Trinità dei Monti or Santa Maria in Monserrato, stayed well within denominational boundaries. Others, like the Venerable English College, provided refuge for Catholics in now-Protestant countries while tacitly playing host to their Protestant compatriots.[41] As recent scholarship has established, these institutions were never homogeneous and always porous. They connected their home regions to the rest of the city's population in intricate ways.

---

40. Pietro Stella, "Tra Roma barocca e Roma capitale: la pietà romana," 759–65; Barbara Wisch and Nerida Newbigin, *Acting on Faith: The Confraternity of the Gonfalone in Renaissance Rome*; Luigi Fiorani, "'Charità e pietate.' Confraternite e gruppi devoti nella città rinascimentale e barocca"; Matizia Maroni Lumbroso and Antonio Martini, *Le confraternite romane nelle loro chiese*, 425–27.

41. For an introduction to national churches and colleges, see Susanne Kubersky-Piredda, Alexander Koller, and Tobias Daniels, *Identità e rappresentazione: le chiese nazionali a Roma, 1450–1650*; Antal Molnár, Giovanni Pizzorusso, and Matteo Sanfilippo, *Chiese e nationes a Roma: dalla Scandinavia ai Balcani: Secoli XV–XVIII*. For the methodology of studying these institutions, see especially Irene Fosi, "'Procurar a tutt'huomo la conversione degli heretici': Roma e le conversioni nell'Impero nella prima metà del seicento"; Irene Fosi, "*Roma patria comune*? Foreigners in Early Modern Rome."

Another way to center Rome as the model capital of a world religion was to make it, at least in appearance, a clearinghouse for Catholic missions across the globe, where proselytization had to precede all other forms of devotion. Capuchins, Franciscans, and Dominicans, among other religious orders, departed Europe with the dream of saving souls. The Society of Jesus, most famously, organized missions across the globe, from Goa to Germany, Chile to China. Fourteen thousand petitions from young Jesuit men, begging to be sent to the Indies, survive only because all such letters had to be sent to Rome, where the superior general could consider them.[42] Rome became a critical node for their global missions and also a hub for Jesuit education with the founding of the Collegio Romano, later the Gregorian University.[43] Scholars are increasingly aware that most missionary connections took place outside Rome and Europe, and rightly question a fixed center-periphery dynamic. Nonetheless, it was to the city's advantage to portray itself as the nucleus of all missionary activity and seek to make that claim true. Because of missions, Rome prided itself on becoming a hub of knowledge of the wider world as well; missionaries were the vectors who filled the city with new items and information from across the globe.[44]

In this vein, the Holy See sought to consolidate the widespread missioning impulse by founding its own organization, the Congregatio de Propaganda Fide, on January 8, 1622. The date, Epiphany, honored the three Magi and thereby immediately connoted global intentions. Perhaps no other organization better embodied Rome's broad ambitions.[45] Like national colleges, the Congregation of Propaganda Fide reinforced the

42. Camilla Russell, "Imagining the 'Indies': Italian Jesuit Petitions for the Overseas Missions at the Turn of the Seventeenth Century." See also Adriano Prosperi, *Tribunali della coscienza: Inquisitori, confessori, missionari*, 600–649; Adriano Prosperi, *La vocazione: storie di gesuiti tra cinquecento e seicento*, 66.

43. Paul V. Murphy, "Jesuit Rome and Italy."

44. On decentering Rome, see especially Luke Clossey, *Salvation and Globalization in the Early Jesuit Missions* (Cambridge: Cambridge University Press, 2008), 45–67; Ditchfield, "Decentering the Catholic Reformation." On Rome's material culture, see Renata Ago, *Gusto for Things: A History of Objects in Seventeenth-Century Rome*. On Rome as a knowledge hub, see Sabina Brevaglieri, *Natural desiderio di sapere: Roma barocca fra vecchi e nuovi mondi*; Elisa Andretta and Federica Favino, "Scientific and Medical Knowledge in Early Modern Rome."

45. Giovanni Pizzorusso, "Agli antipodi di Babele: Propaganda Fide tra immagine cosmopolita e orizzonti romani (XVII–XIX secolo)"; Giovanni Pizzorusso, "I satelliti di Propaganda Fide: il Collegio Urbano e la tipografia poliglotta. Note di ricerca su due istituzioni culturali romane nel XVII secolo." Despite its pretensions, the congregation carefully focused their proselytization efforts on areas that avoided overlap with the Spanish Crown and Inquisition.

idea that Rome—the new Jerusalem—was the global capital of Christendom, now extending its reach into the four known continents: Europe, Asia, Africa, and America. The Propaganda Fide oversaw the Collegio Urbano, which brought young converts from "target" countries to Rome, trained them up, and sent them back again as missionaries. It maintained an enormous and detailed correspondence with its alumni on missions across the globe. It negotiated with nuntiates and other ecclesiastical representatives abroad. To prepare its missionaries, the Propaganda Fide also became a center for linguistic training and scholarship. Its in-house printing press was dedicated to producing doctrinal books in translations for missionaries to take with them. By the mid-seventeenth century, it could print in twenty-three languages and had become a focal point for foreign scholars in Rome. More broadly, with its grand complex of buildings in Piazza di Spagna, the Propaganda Fide became a clearinghouse for intellectual exchange about foreign countries, especially regarding eastern Europe and the Levant. As a result, its print office became an authority on Hebrew and rabbinics, with its own Hebrew professors. Global missions departing from Rome kept the conversion of Jews at their core.[46]

A Protestant of any denomination, perhaps from Scotland or Sweden, would not have escaped the fervent missionizing impulses of Roman institutions, but he would have experienced them differently than Roman Jews did. The Protestant case provides a jarring contrast with the campaign to convert Jews in the same period. Protestants from northern Europe came to Italy in growing numbers over the sixteenth and seventeenth centuries, as university students, soldiers, merchants, or tourists. Unlike foreign slaves or Roman Jews, Protestants could travel easily to and around the peninsula, if they were given a safe conduct. Many were drawn increasingly to Rome. They often visited expressly to gawk at Catholic rituals and papal splendor, hoping to confirm all they had been told about the city's famed corruption, excess, and decadence.[47] Tensions nonetheless ran high. Black rumors ran through northern Europe about the harsh and unforgiving tactics of the Inquisition, ready to persecute or proselytize Protestants when the inquisitors found them.[48] John Raymond, an Englishman

46. Giovanni Pizzorusso, "Lo 'stato temporale' della Congregazione de Propaganda Fide nel Seicento."

47. Fosi, *Convertire lo straniero*, 14–15. For nuanced examples of Protestant travel to Rome, see Rosemary Sweet, "The Changing View of Rome in the Long Eighteenth Century"; Gerrit Verhoeven, "Calvinist Pilgrimages and Popish Encounters: Religious Identity and Sacred Space on the Dutch Grand Tour (1598–1685)."

48. Fosi, *Convertire lo straniero*, 149–51.

who traveled to Rome in the 1640s, described the "horrible (in Report) Inquisition" as a danger that discouraged English travelers from the city, advising his compatriots to avoid mentioning religion: "the safest way is Dissimulation."[49] If a Protestant did convert, his first duty was to turn himself in to the Inquisition to abjure his heresies and reconcile himself to the Roman church. For many, this was a daunting deterrent.

Such a visitor—mobile, European, informed, and undeniably some kind of Christian already—required different conversionary tactics. A consensus gradually formed that medieval techniques of conversion could not apply. Instead, Protestants were best approached with "superabundant charity"—a softer, more sympathetic approach to conversion, based on gentle persuasion rather than the castigation and chastisement that had characterized so much previous missionary work, especially toward Jews.[50] From its earliest iterations in the 1560s, this effort involved prominent personalities such as Peter Canisius, the Dutch Jesuit who had earned his Catholic stripes in northern Europe. Soon afterward, Baronio, the pope's own confessor, spelled out such a policy in his *Apologeticus*, written to facilitate the final conversion of Henri IV to Catholicism. The *Apologeticus* emphasized "persuasion, reconciliation, and charity."[51] As a result, it contributed to a fundamental shift in Italy in attitudes toward Protestants. "Signori Christiani non Catholici" became a group to be flattered, not browbeaten, into Catholicism.

Attempts at formal institutions for winning over Protestants followed the path laid out in Baronio's *Apologeticus*. In 1600, Baronio's associate and fellow Oratorian, Giovenale Ancina, set up the first congregation for Protestants reconciled to Catholicism, the Congregation of Santissima Maria della Compassione. The congregation sought to support former Protestants only after their conversion. Through a mixture of regular prayer meetings, close supervision, and strategic introductions, its supervisors tried to ensure the catechism, education, socialization, patronage, and future employment of members who sought to make new lives as Catholics in Italy. As Peter Mazur points out, Ancina and his closest colleagues all

49. John Raymond, *Jo. Raymond, an Itinerary Contayning a Voyage, Made through Italy, in the Yeare 1646 and 1647*, introduction, A7b–A9a. On the Roman Inquisition's confusion regarding denominations of Protestantism in England and Scotland, see Stefano Villani, "Defining the Church of England in Italy in the Early Modern Times: British Reconciliations in the Documentation of the Inquisition of Pisa."

50. For the use of the phrase, see Mazur, *Conversion to Catholicism in Early Modern Italy*, 43–65.

51. Peter A. Mazur, "Searcher of Hearts: Cesare Baronio's History of Conversion," 214–21.

had lived and worked in religiously mixed areas. Having spent time out-side Rome, they had learned to see Protestantism as a human, not purely theological, concern. In Rome, they continued to seek out the company of recent converts.[52]

This new approach of "caresses and courtesy" could clash with the instincts and tactics of inquisitors. Jesuits in Italy, for example, fought hard to obtain and retain the privilege to absolve heresy privately in the confessional. To do so, they set themselves up in deliberate opposition to local inquisitors, capitalizing on the Holy Office's black legend and empha-sizing their own likability in comparison. Jesuits argued to the Holy See that fear of the Inquisition alone kept many Protestants from repenting, making their private alternative necessary.[53] They maintained that the gentler approach was especially necessary for well-bred university stu-dents and aristocratic travelers to Italy. In Rome, the Propaganda Fide received specific recommendations in 1625, shortly after its founding, for approaching European Protestants on new terms: they should use their most learned missionaries, polish their linguistic competence, show Prot-estants the best sights in the city, and treat them as potential future allies. The congregation and other nuncios who endorsed these recommenda-tions nonetheless had to strike a careful balance between this sympathetic approach, the harsher stance of the Holy Office, and the technical prohibi-tion on Protestants taking up residence in Italy.[54]

When a hospice for converted Protestants, the Ospizio dei Conver-tendi, finally opened in Rome in 1673, it continued to treat Protestants as potential allies and assets. Its founder, Mariano Sozzini, requested copies of the constitutions of similar houses from across Europe, including the regulations of the College of Neophytes in Rome. The Ospizio's eventual program covered catechistic as well as social rehabilitation, but also val-ued frequent prayer and promoted close contact with the spiritual orien-tation and sermons of the Oratorians. In addition, the Ospizio sought to reform the negative views of Rome that prevailed in Protestant countries. Neophytes were taken on trips to holy sites in Rome, such as catatombs and basilicas, and received as assigned reading the new guidebooks that emphasized piety and charity in Rome, such as Fanucci's *Treatise of All the*

52. Mazur, *Conversion to Catholicism in Early Modern Italy*, 45–47.

53. Jessica M. Dalton, *Between Popes, Inquisitors and Princes: How the First Jesuits Negotiated Religious Crisis in Early Modern Italy*, 62–92.

54. Fosi, *Convertire lo straniero*, 152–55; Mazur, *Conversion to Catholicism in Early Modern Italy*, 56–58. Documents regarding these recommendations can be found in ACDF TT 1 b, 122r–24v.

Pious Works of the Great City of Rome.[55] The Ospizio hosted many kinds of converts besides gentleman travelers. Many were indigent, relying on the funds from charitable organizations for new Christians. Others only converted after an extended sojourn. The vast numbers of *oltramontani* migrating to Rome required ever more support. National colleges and churches serving the Catholic faithful from Protestant countries, such as the Venerable English College and Collegium Germanicum et Hungaricum, prepared future clergy for life on the contested frontiers of Catholicism, and provided a reassuring link for their members who had adopted Catholicism and could not easily go home.[56] Converting Protestants called for an all-hands-on-deck approach to conversion much the way converting Jews did.

In most other respects, the two early modern campaigns were different, even as they shared common roots in medieval antiheretical polemics. The mission toward Jews continued to draw on medieval rhetoric and predispositions, while adding new legislation and conversionary approaches. But Protestants had no precedents. Efforts to convert them developed from the careful observation and description of individual Protestants figures in Rome, and proceeded with a policy of sweetness and persuasion. This tactic directly opposed the approach laid out in Paul IV's 1555 bull *Cum Nimis Absurdum*, which abandoned earlier popes' gentler appeals to persuasion, and explicitly redirected the conversion of the Jews into channels of humiliation and rigid discipline.[57]

Muslims in Rome also found themselves subject to conversionary fervor, but in a variety of less straightforward ways. Some Muslims had arrived in Rome in the wake of the expulsions from Spain and Portugal in the late fifteenth century, although precise numbers are difficult to quantify.[58] Many others came as captives in military victories. They worked as galley slaves in Civitavecchia, or enslaved construction or domestic workers in Rome itself, under the dominion of the pope.[59] In 1566, Pius V confirmed in a *motu propio* that if they could make their

55. Sergio Pagano, "L'Ospizio dei Convertendi di Roma tra carisma missionario e regolamentazione ecclesiastica (1671–1700)," 316, 331 passim.

56. Irene Fosi, "A proposito di nationes a Roma in età moderna: provenienza, appartenenza culturale, integrazione sociale."

57. Renata Segre, "La Controriforma: espulsioni, conversioni, isolamento," 715.

58. Egmont Lee, *Habitatores in Urbe: The Population of Renaissance Rome = la popolazione di Roma nel Rinascimento*. Thanks are due here to Francesco Lacopo for sharing his own work on this question.

59. Justine Walden, "Muslim Slaves in Early Modern Rome: The Development and Visibility of a Labouring Class."

way to Rome's civic center at the Capitoline Hill, enslaved Muslims could ask for manumission if they showed proof of baptism. Between 1516 and 1716, 641 people born Muslim were freed in this way. Most of them had come to Rome from elsewhere for this purpose.[60] Such an arrangement was rooted in the explicitly evangelical priorities of the sixteenth-century Papacy. But it presented immediate practical problems for Rome's governing bodies; an overreliance on this offer would cost them valuable slave labor in Rome and elsewhere. Like the ultimate conversion of the Jews, these priorities worked better as theories than in practice. Fear and suspicion of Muslims from varying populations far exceeded their actual numbers. The enduring strength of the Ottoman Empire, and demographic upheavals from the conquest of Constantinople, led to a rise in anti-Muslim rhetoric that dovetailed with longer-standing antipathy toward Judaism.

In the seventeenth century, this drive toward proselytization took on a scholarly aspect; it fueled an industry of Arabic language study in Rome, based at the Propaganda Fide. Future missionaries learned the language inextricably from their study of religious disputations and polemics in preparation for their missions. The goal was to reach Eastern rite Christians and Muslims abroad, not locally. Arabic instructors were generally not of Muslim origin; they were Italian students of the language or Arabic-speaking Christians (born or converted), notably Gian Battista Eliano.[61] Within Rome, baptisms of Muslims took place regularly alongside baptisms of Jews, but in smaller numbers. Muslims tended to convert as individuals, not families, and also lacked the infrastructure of sponsorship devoted to supporting Jewish converts.[62] The diarist John Evelyn recalled seeing one in 1645, with great spectacle:

---

60. Serena Di Nepi, "Saving Souls, Forgiving Bodies: A New Source and a Working Hypothesis on Slavery, Conversion and Religious Minorities in Early Modern Rome (16th–19th Centuries)." See, more generally, Ariel Salzmann, "Migrants in Chains: On the Enslavement of Muslims in Renaissance and Enlightenment Europe."

61. Aurélien Girard, "Teaching and Learning Arabic in Early Modern Rome: Shaping a Missionary Language"; John-Paul A. Ghobrial, "The Life and Hard Times of Solomon Negri: An Arabic Teacher in Early Modern Europe"; Bernard Heyberger, "Polemic Dialogues between Christians and Muslims in the Seventeenth Century"; Bernard Heyberger, "L'islam dei missionari cattolici (Medio Oriente, Seicento)"; Giovanni Pizzorusso, "La preparazione linguistica e controversistica dei missionari per l'Oriente islamico: scuole, testi, insegnanti a Roma e in Italia." For Eliano, see especially Clines, *A Jewish Jesuit in the Eastern Mediterranean*.

62. Domenico Rocciolo, "Documenti sui catecumeni e neofiti a Roma nel Seicento e Settecento," 403.

The 25th invited by a Frier Dominican whom we usualy heard preach to a number of Jewes, to be Godfather to a Converted Turk & a Jew, The Ceremonie was perform'd in the Church of S: Maria sopra la Minerva neere the Capitol, They were clad in White, then exorcis'd at their entering the church with aboundance of Ceremonies, when lead into the Quire, they were baptizd by a Bishop in Pontificalibus: The Turk lived afterwards in Rome, sold hot-water, & would bring us presents when he met us, kneeling, & kissing the hemms of our Cloaks: But the Jew was believ'd to be a Counterfeit.[63]

Evelyn dwells here on the question of genuine versus false conversion. The man he describes as a Turk has a conversion that Evelyn accepts as genuine. In Evelyn's description, he is then integrated into Roman life, gains respectable employment, and seems to play a desired role as a humble and grateful inferior. The Jewish convert, suspected of false conversion, is dismissed. He has breached the contract that his baptism suggested and disappears.

Evelyn's anxiety was widely shared. All conversionary methods, sweet or harsh, masked apprehension about the true hearts of their targets. The Reformation had brought new attention to the value of interior conversion and indeed religious choice among confessions. As Irene Fosi has demonstrated, the desire for heartfelt, interior conversion was strong enough both to encourage and then mask insincere conversions. Protestants at the ospizio, for example, were often given prearranged confessional forms to fill in, which corralled their personal narratives into formulaic ones.[64] Yet anxiety about genuine interior conversion also led, paradoxically, to a strong desire for baptisms to be public. Institutions in Rome committed ever more firmly to piety and conversion, but especially in forms that were easy to see, watch, and celebrate.

Converting Rome's Jews

The Catholic reinvention of Rome and its increased focus on confessional choice had special implications for Jews. Jews had lived in Rome from ancient times, dating their origins there to the second century BCE. In Rome, Jews had always been tolerated and protected. They enjoyed an uncommon level of privilege too, partly through the antiquity of their

63. John Evelyn, *Diary: Now First Printed in Full from the Manuscripts Belonging to Mr. John Evelyn, and as Edited by E. S. de Beer*, 376–77.

64. Fosi, "Con cuore sincero e con fede non finta"; Fosi, *Convertire lo straniero*, 67–74.

community, and partly thanks to a history of special dispensations for services to the Papacy. Popes from Gregory I to Martin V renewed the bull *Sicut Judaeis,* which offered legal protection to Jews in Rome and discouraged forcible conversions. The long Middle Ages saw an extended period of relative tolerance, stability, and civil relations between Jews and others in Rome.[65] At the same time, an ever-present undercurrent of yearning for the conversion of the Jews stirred all of Italy during the period before the Reformation. Jewish people were frequently enticed to convert— sometimes to escape judicial punishment for crimes. Local rulers found it beneficial to sponsor converts and provide ongoing support for their baptized families in a grand show of piety.[66]

But the sixteenth century witnessed enormous transformation for Rome's Jews in particular. Their community swelled as it absorbed Jews expelled from the Iberian Peninsula and Sicily in 1492; Portugal, Navarre, and Provence in 1498; and Naples and Calabria in 1510. It is possible that by 1527, only half of the Jewish people in Rome had Roman origins. This influx was unwelcome; Roman Jews offered a hundred gold ducats to Alexander VI to turn away the first Spanish contingent.[67] Within the Papal States, Paul IV's restrictive legislation and its enforcement had cascading effects, traumatizing entire communities. In Ancona, the arrest of eighty immigrants from Portugal, and the execution of twenty-five of them, deliberately made an example of the suspicious "Marrano" community and devastated eyewitnesses.[68] In Spoleto and elsewhere, banks started refusing to deal with Jews, thereby breaking up communities in the entire region; those who could, escaped entirely, while others became

65. For an overview of the Roman Jewish community, see Natali, *Il ghetto di Roma*; Attilio Milano, *Il ghetto di Roma; illustrazioni storiche*; Kenneth R. Stow, *The Jews in Rome*; Kenneth R. Stow, *Theater of Acculturation: The Roman Ghetto in the 16th Century*. For the earlier period, see Serena Di Nepi, *Surviving the Ghetto: Toward a Social History of the Jewish Community in 16th-Century Rome.* For later, see Groppi Angela, *Gli abitanti del ghetto di Roma: Descriptio hebreorum del 1733.* See also Benjamin Ravid, "Venice, Rome, and the Reversion of New Christians to Judaism: A Study in Ragione di Stato," 175. In "Converts and Conversos in Sixteenth-Century Italy: Marranos in Rome," Anna Foa reminds us that Marranos in Rome preceded 1492. See also Anna Esposito, *Un'altra Roma: minoranze nazionali e comunità ebraiche tra Medioevo e Rinascimento,* 128–29.

66. Tamar Herzig has reconstructed one significant case of this phenomenon in *A Convert's Tale* and has discussed the need for attention to fifteenth-century Jewish conversion in "The Future of Studying Jewish Conversion in Renaissance Italy."

67. Jean Delumeau, *Vie économique et sociale de Rome dans la seconde moitié du XVIe siècle,* 1:216.

68. On the conversos of Ancona as seen by a contemporary, see, most recently, Martina Mampieri, *Living under the Evil Pope: The Hebrew Chronicle of Pope Paul IV by Benjamin Nehemiah Ben Elnathan from Civitanova Marche (16th Cent.),* 85–106.

local migrants, moving from town to town in search of stability.[69] Divisions between Roman and "foreign" Jews hardened, as is evident in the names of their different synagogues, based on their places of origin.

Rome's increasingly plentiful and visible Jews became pawns in the much more widespread battle for souls. In the Middle Ages, speaking generally, conversion of the Jews was a distant ideal, growing gradually more important through the fifteenth century. But in Rome their increased numbers shifted the balance. And by the late sixteenth century, as religious denominations across Europe increasingly competed for souls, converts from Judaism became a powerful endorsement for any confession. Catholics, in particular, saw Jewish conversion as a special affirmation that could mitigate their many recent trials. In Rome, it became especially urgent. Where Roman Jews had once been protected by their economic usefulness and undeniable *romanità*, now they seemed like a failure, a threatening tear in the fabric of Catholicism, and an affront to its proud revitalization.[70] The mid-sixteenth century thus saw the first concerted, practical effort to convert Roman Jews en masse. Supporting or tolerating Judaism no longer sufficed; Jews had to be "redeemed," contained, and if possible, converted (to stability, acceptability, and Christianity).

As a result, a succession of sixteenth-century popes and cardinals intensified their long-standing attempts to convert the Jews of Rome.[71] Over the next century and a half, the campaign reflected shifting papal priorities. Theoretical concerns about conversion, strengthened by the Holy See's quest to impose a uniform belief system, increasingly found their way into the policies that administered Rome's Jewish community—for example, as justification in the papal bulls that legislated taxation. This conversionary campaign unfolded in many directions, and included both carrots and sticks. Some of these initiatives, such as distinguishing signs, Talmud burning, and conversionary preaching, had medieval precedents here revived in new form. Others, such as the House of Catechumens, the College of Neophytes, and especially the ghetto, were new to the sixteenth century. Most of the legislation required Jewish institutions to fund them fully or partially.[72]

---

69. Segre, "La Controriforma," 721–24.

70. Stow, "The Papacy and the Jews," 257–58; Lazar, *Working in the Vineyard of the Lord*, 33.

71. In "The Future of Studying Jewish Conversion in Renaissance Italy," Tamar Herzig rightly notes a strong interest in Jewish conversion in the fifteenth century and argues against seeing the Reformation as its sole cause.

72. Lazar, *Working in the Vineyard of the Lord*, 115; Alessia Lirosi, "Monacare le ebree. Il monastero romano della Ss. Annunziata ai Pantani. Una ricerca in corso," 155, 165.

A few key baptisms boosted the credibility of the entire enterprise, above all the protracted, piecemeal conversion of one branch of the Corcos family over three generations. The Corcos family prospered in Rome, having arrived from Spain after the expulsion in 1492. The first to convert was Elia Corcos, personally baptized in 1566 by Pope Pius V, who granted Elia the use of his own name, Michele Ghislieri. A generation later, in 1581, Lazzaro Corcos converted and was baptized by Pope Gregory XIII, whose natal name was Ugo Boncompagni. Lazzaro became Gregorio Boncompagni, and brought with him his wife and at least two children into the church. His extremely wealthy father, Salomone, followed a year later, taking the name Ugo Boncompagni. Salomone's conversion was encouraged and sponsored by Philip Neri, founder of the Congregation of the Oratory and a future saint. The Corcos family was ennobled and given Roman citizenship. Such grand honors and direct papal involvement were unusual—a token of respect for the prominence or at least riches that the family could offer.

These Corcos conversions made national and international news. They also sealed the Catholic future of the family, and more specifically, bound it closely to Neri and the Oratorians, who had overseen and even masterminded their religious journey. The Boncompagni Corcos built their elegant new palazzo immediately behind the church complex of the Congregation of the Oratory. The family supported the church of the Oratorians in a literal way too, providing silver lamps, damask wall tapestries, and a grand statue of Neri himself for the church's sacristy.[73] In the same manner, when Jehiel da Pesaro was baptized in Florence as Vitale Medici, in the same year as Lazzaro, his conversion launched an ongoing relationship with the church of the Santissima Annunziata. Vitale's sons went on to sponsor the rebuilding of the sacristy in the church of Santissima Annunziata in the 1630s and 1640s along with other church projects in the city. As an explicit statement of their patronage and devotion, they fitted it with an elaborate father-and-son portrait of Vitale and his son Alessandro, and a related fresco of the original Saint Vitale at the moment of his conversion.[74] Conspicuous church patronage was a welcome gesture from prominent converted families.

73. Alberto Bianco, "Cesare Baronio e la conversione dei Corcos nei documenti d'archivio della Congregazione oratoriana di Roma," 160–62.

74. On the decoration of Santissima Annunziata, see Dora Liscia Bemporad, "Arredi Sacri: Argenti per un Santuario." On Vitale's family patronage of the sacristy, see Bernice Iarocci, "The Santissima Annunziata of Florence, Medici Portraits, and the Counter Reformation in Italy," 206–26. On Vitale's sons' further patronage, see Marconcini, *Per amor del cielo*, 43–44.

Meanwhile, the Corcos conversions continued. A decade after Lazzaro's baptism, in 1592, came another triumph with the conversion of four of Ugo's fatherless nephews. Ippolito and Agostino Boncompagni, born Ruben and Salomone, tell the story of having been brought to the house of the Oratorians, where Neri gave sweets and figs to the ten-year-old Ruben, who in turn mistook him for the pope. The next day, Neri met with the boys and made them a deal: they would all pray to "the God of Abraham, Isaac, and Jacob" for illumination. If the Jewish law turned out to be right, Neri would convert to Judaism, but if the Christian law was proven superior, he hoped they would convert instead. The boys' change of heart took place during the moment when Neri said mass in the church while they waited in the library. Their baptism, celebrated by Pope Clement VIII, prompted a celebration at the house of the Oratorians, attended by cardinals and other dignitaries. Giuda, Salomone, Ruben, and Abramo became Alessandro, Agostino, Ippolito, and Clemente, respectively. Agostino would become a brother in the Congregation of the Oratory. A fifth brother followed in 1596 with his wife, becoming Francesco Maria.[75]

But even the cases that seemed most triumphant for the church also had their dark side. During all this time, the boys' mother, Gemma, had withstood the pressure to convert from Judaism, even as two other sons, her daughter, and indeed much of the rest of her family became Catholic over the course of fifteen years. When her two sons-in-law died, she snuck out of Rome with two remaining Jewish grandchildren, heading for Venice and then the Levant, but was apprehended and brought back to Rome, where she finally agreed to accept baptism long after her Catholic sons had given up any hope of her conversion. She took—or was given—the ironic name Maria Felicità Boncompagni Corcos (*felicità* means happiness).[76]

The Corcos saga reveals a range of Jewish attitudes to conversion. It gives us a fly-on-the-wall perspective on life among the Oratorian elite,

75. Gianni Incisa della Rocchetta and Nello Vian, *Il primo processo per san Filippo Neri del Codice vaticano latino 3798 e in altri esemplari dell'Archivio dell'Oratorio di Roma*, 1:92–93, testimony of Ippolito Boncompagni, August 26, 1595; Bianco, "Cesare Baronio e la conversione dei Corcos nei documenti d'archivio della Congregazione oratoriana di Roma," 162; Louis Ponnelle, Louis Bourdet, and Ralph Francis Kerr, *St. Philip Neri and the Roman Society of His Times (1515–1595)*, 523–33, 580.

76. Incisa della Rocchetta and Vian, *Il primo processo per san Filippo Neri*, 2:268–69, testimony of Agostino Boncompagni, October 19, 1600; Fiamma Satta, "Predicatori agli ebrei, catecumeni e neofiti a Roma nella prima metà del seicento," 126–27. For a recent summary of this history, see especially Marina Caffiero, *Il grande mediatore: Tranquillo Vita Corcos, un rabbino nella Roma dei papi*, 20–24.

and shows the careful construction of conversion narratives to serve personal and political interests. For that reason, it continues to stimulate scholarly interest, as it should. These events had tangible, easily identifiable benefits for Catholic policy makers. They brought wealth and glory to the church. The Corcos conversions enhanced the reputations of three popes and two future saints—Pius V, who had baptized Elia, and Neri. The testimony of the Corcos brothers forms part of the backbone of Neri's canonization trial in the early seventeenth century; the Corcos brothers appear many times in the trial records and recount the family conversions, including that of their mother. The brothers' trial testimony insistently and repeatedly credits Neri's prayers with their conversion, although Neri also helped them in material ways. And pertinent for this story, Ugo/ Salomone's direct descendant, Gregorio Boncompagni Corcos degli Scarinci, would become the most long-lasting and best-documented preacher to the Jews of Rome.

But exemplars like the Corcos family were also useful because their prominence camouflaged how many other conversions were less successful, less lucrative, or less peaceful. Ultimately, conversionary concerns overshadowed other forms of Jewish-Christian interaction, such as the Christian study of Hebrew. Gianpietro Carafa, head of the Roman Inquisition (and as Pope Paul IV, creator of the Roman ghetto), decreed the burning of the Talmud in 1553 despite widespread Christian interest in the Talmud, and despite disagreement from some of his closest associates.[77] Much of the pressure on Jews came, in Kenneth Stow's interpretation, from Paul IV's eschatological fervor, which saw the conversion of the Jews as a necessary precursor to the end of days.[78] The bonfires that resulted represent the ascendance of conversionary policy and the formation of a principle of "predisposing force" to convert the Jews.[79]

This multipronged approach papered over some intellectual contradictions. As Anna Foa has written, conversionary strategists in Italy had observed the troubling outcome of forced conversion in Spain and Portugal, and learned from it. They launched a campaign in Rome that sought to square the circle. With one hand, the Roman campaign promoted the idea of a universal church—offering religious instruction and holding out

77. Piet van Boxel, "Robert Bellarmine Reads Rashi: Rabbinic Bible Commentaries and the Burning of the Talmud," 121–22 passim.

78. Stow, "The Papacy and the Jews," 259–65.

79. Kenneth R. Stow, "The Burning of the Talmud in 1553, in the Light of Sixteenth-Century Catholic Attitudes toward the Talmud"; Stow, "The Papacy and the Jews," 261–69. See also Foa, "'Limpieza' versus Mission."

hope of genuine conversion. With the other, it offered financial and other inducements to Jews that appeased ongoing skepticism about whether converts' hearts alone could be trusted to make them true Christians.[80] A triumphalist rhetoric, layered over a rich seam of Christian Hebraic scholarship, superficially resolved these contradictions. It rewrote difficult or imperfect conversions, smoothing out details, reassigning blame, and molding the new stories into a simple theological victory for Catholicism. Grand narratives and rich spectacles helped to "reinforce the belief in the need to facilitate the conversion of the perfidious Jews by any means necessary."[81] The grander and more public they were, perhaps the truer they must be.

Jews in this context were more useful as brand-new neophytes than as Christians. After a successful conversion, they often disappeared from the record as anything more than a statistic. The opulent baptisms of Prospero's two children, too young to dissimulate and arrayed to reflect the glory of the Catholic Church, was optimally staged to reassure spectators that the church had triumphed. Once that point had been made, their later lives were seemingly less important and certainly less documented.

The first stage of the campaign directed at Jews was economic and dates from the bull *Cupientes Iudaeos* of 1542. This bull sweetened the prospect of conversion by allowing converts to keep property, giving them rights of citizenship in their place of baptism, and mandating an education in the tenets of Catholicism. It reflected Paul III's willingness to make Italy a refuge for Jews expelled from Spain and Portugal, while also making a stronger case for increased conversionary measures. Papal taxes on Jews increased throughout the sixteenth century as well. At the same time, towns throughout Italy increasingly began to rely on Christian lending houses, or *Monti di Pietà*. These were communal, Christian-owned pawnbroker banks. Where Christians were forbidden to practice usury, the essential task of small-scale lending had fallen to Jews, making them economically necessary to the smooth functioning of Christian society. Indeed, in much of Italy Jews were then prohibited from practicing most other professions besides pawnbroking. But reliance on Jewish bankers and pawnbrokers started to rankle, leading to the invention of monti di pietà in the fifteenth century. Because a Monte was communally owned, no individual Christian could be charged with usury. Christians

---

80. Foa, "'Limpieza' versus Mission."
81. On this point, see Herzig, "The Hazards of Conversion," esp. 32–34.

in need of an immediate loan no longer needed to approach Jews, hat in hand.[82]

As their dependence on Jewish bankers waned, Christians tolerated them less. This was exactly the result sought by the fiery Observant preachers who had traversed the peninsula in the fifteenth century, preaching against Italy's Jews and encouraging the establishment of alternative lending houses. Monti di Pietà appeared throughout Northern Italy over the fifteenth century. Rome's Monte di Pietà was founded during the Holy Week of 1539, after a season of Lenten preaching in its favour by Giovanni Maltei da Calvi, commissioner of the Observant Franciscans. The Monte's establishment had helped to escalate anti-Jewish violence surrounding the Good Friday passion plays of that year; as Lenten observance so frequently did in Italy, the play aggravated tensions between Christians and Jews.[83] The Roman Monte di Pietà reached financially stable footing in the same years as conversionary preaching began. It obtained its own immense, grandiose building, five minutes from the ghetto in 1604; by 1682 the Monte successfully undermined Jewish banking in Rome. When they processed from the ghetto to the building that housed conversionary sermons, Roman Jews had to walk directly past it.

Pastoral proselytization soon followed economic efforts. Only a year after *Cupientes Iudaeos*, Paul III issued *Illius qui pro dominici*, establishing the first House of Catecumens in Italy and the early modern era. The House of Catechumens, or Casa di Catecumeni, was estabished in order to shelter, feed, and instruct new Catholics in their faith. It housed primarily catechumens, who were still preparing for baptism, but also neophytes: those who had been recently baptized and were now preparing to embark on their Catholic future. Paul III's bull honored this new institution by

---

82. For an introduction to Monti di Pietà in Rome and elsewhere, see Donato Tamilia, *Il sacro monte de pietà di Roma: ricerche storiche e documenti inediti: contributo alla storia della beneficenza e alla storia economica di Roma*; Mario Tosi, *Il sacro monte di pietà di Roma e le sue amministrazioni: il banco di depositi, la depositeria generale della R. Camera Apostolica, la Zecca, la depositeria urbana, 1539–1874*; Carol Bresnahan Menning, *Charity and State in Late Renaissance Italy: The Monte di Pietà of Florence*; Federico Arcelli, *Gli statuti del 1581 del sacro monte di pietà di Roma*; Federico Arcelli, *Il sacro monte di pietà di Roma nel XVI secolo (1539–1584): Dalla costituzione del monte all'assegnazione del banco dei depositi*; Anna Esposito, "Credito, ebrei, monte di pietà a Roma tra quattro e cinquecento," 559–82; Brian Pullan, "Jewish Banks and Monti di Pietà," 53–72; Federico Arcelli, *Banking and Charity in Sixteenth-Century Italy: The Holy Monte di Pietà of Rome (1539–84)*; Barbara Wisch, "Vested Interest: Redressing Jews on Michelangelo's Sistine Ceiling," 143–72.

83. Wisch and Newbigin, *Acting on Faith*, 362, 368–70. See also the documents reprinted in Tosi, *Il sacro Monte di pietà di Roma e le sue amministrazioni*.

placing it on equal footing with some of the most respected institutions in Rome. From the outset, its activities were considered maximally important, like activities of the church itself.[84] The function of a casa was to separate from their community any Jews (and to a lesser extent, Muslims) who showed an interest in becoming Christian, immerse them in Christian education, and continue to support and teach them after baptism, preparing them to reenter the world on the Christian side.[85] Houses of Catechumens insisted on their charitable benevolence, providing the womb for the rebirth of a Christian soul. But they were immensely controlling too, supervising every aspect of their residents' lives, and serving as the "essential link" between converts and the society around them, erasing all others.[86]

The House of Catechumens began life, as has been well documented, as a Jesuit initiative: Ignatius of Loyola first established a confraternity to support catechumens in 1543, entrusting it to a secular priest, Giovanni da Torano, and twelve other priests, soon joined by lay supporters. It quickly earned powerful patrons and effective cardinal protectors.[87] The confraternity and Torani's church of San Giovanni in Mercatello were at first located at the foot of the Capitoline Hill, just outside the eventual ghetto walls. To meet the financial needs of the nascent house, popes imposed special taxes on synagogues throughout the Papal States and wherever else local princes would allow; this fell heaviest on the Jews of Rome.[88]

The Roman House of Catechumens had faced a scandal in the person of Giuseppe Torano, its first overseer, who broke violently with the Jesuits, accused them of various improprieties, and ended up imprisoned for life himself for worse accusations.[89] By the 1550s, Ignatius had become

---

84. Karl Hoffmann, *Ursprung und Anfangstätigkeit des ersten päpstlichen Missionsinstituts; ein Beitrag zur Geschichte der katholischen Juden- und Mohammedanermission im sechzehnten Jahrhundert*, 9–23. Page numbers for this title always refer to the unpublished Italian translation housed at the ASVR.

85. For the best description of the details of the founding and running of the confraternity and House of Catechumens, see Lazar, *Working in the Vineyard of the Lord*, 99–124.

86. Mazur, *Conversion to Catholicism in Early Modern Italy*, 18.

87. Lazar, *Working in the Vineyard of the Lord*, 99–124; Mazur, *Conversion to Catholicism in Early Modern Italy*, 20–21; Domenico Rocciolo, "Catecumeni e neofiti a Roma tra '500 e '800: provenienza, condizioni sociali e 'padrini' illustri"; Micaela Procaccia, "'Bona Voglia' e 'Modica Coactio': Conversioni di ebrei a Roma nel secolo XVI"; Domenico Rocciolo, "L'archivio della pia casa dei catecumeni e nofiti di Roma"; Domenico Rocciolo, "Ebrei Catecumeni alla Madonna ai Monti nel Settecento."

88. Segre, "La Controriforma," 757–58.

89. Hoffmann, *Ursprung und Anfangstätigkeit des ersten päpstlichen Missionsinstituts*, 36–39. (ASVR Italian translation.)

gradually less involved in running the House of Catechumens and its attendant activities. His withdrawal may have reflected a desire on behalf of the Papacy to integrate new Christians into the wider fabric of diocesan life. It also fits the pattern of Jesuit initiatives: found something new and necessary, set it independently on its feet, and step back.[90] The casa itself remained on solid ground. Its first head and cardinal protector was Guglielmo Sirleto, one of Rome's most learned and well-connected cardinals. Sirleto's presence brought the casa intellectual heft, a firm administrative hand, and a powerful, dedicated patron.[91]

The casa started small but expanded steadily. In its first two decades, it baptized about 140 people, of whom about 90 were male. About a dozen of this group were of Muslim, not Jewish, origin, and came from Tunisia or elsewhere in North Africa. The Roman casa primarily targeted Jews, but it also housed Muslims on an individual basis—unlike the later Venetian casa, where the proportions were roughly reversed and reflected Venice's Mediterranean links.[92] The majority of Jewish converts within the casa came from Rome or the Papal States, but the casa also accepted them from elsewhere in Italy, Europe, or other places. Of the records that note ages, males in the Roman casa were generally under twenty years old; girls who converted were generally under ten. As the casa grew, the numbers went up. Between 1614 and 1797, it saw 1,958 Jews and 1,086 Muslims baptized, with a peak of 61 Jewish baptisms in the single year 1649.[93] Records for earlier periods have not survived, nor have comprehensive records for conversions that took place elsewhere. Despite all the fanfare, surviving records show a baptism rate of 10 to 11 Jewish people a year for the seventeenth and eighteenth centuries; this suggests an overall miniscule conversion rate of 0.03 or less of the population of the ever-growing ghetto. Jews from all over the Papal States ended up in the Roman casa. About

90. Domenico Rocciolo, "Fra promozione e difesa della fede: Le vicende dei catecumeni e neofiti romani in età moderna," 147–56; Lazar, *Working in the Vineyard of the Lord*, 239–40n121. Rocciolo and Lazar disagree entirely with each other on this point.

91. For Sirleto's manner of overseeing the house, see Mazur, *Conversion to Catholicism in Early Modern Italy*, 20–25. Sirleto is notable for having almost no traditional pastoral experience. This appointment guaranteed that his primary exposure to Catholic laypeople and those outside the world of the Curia was through Christians who had been born Jewish. See Renata Segre, "Il mondo ebraico nei cardinali della Controriforma."

92. E. Natalie Rothman, *Brokering Empire: Trans-Imperial Subjects between Venice and Istanbul*, 129–30.

93. Rocciolo, "Catecumeni e neofiti a Roma tra '500 e '800," 715–17; Procaccia, "'Bona Voglia' e 'Modica Coactio,'" 153; Lazar, *Working in the Vineyard of the Lord*, 115. For the most thorough accounting, see part 1 of Rudt de Collenberg, "Le baptême des Juifs à Rome" and the subsequent volumes.

half of the total number of Jews baptized in Rome between 1500 and 1800 came from outside the city.[94]

The Casa di Catecumeni soon spun off two notable partner institutions. A convent for Jewish-born nuns—Santissima Annunziata—followed almost immediately next door to San Giovanni in Mercatello and moved to larger lodgings at San Basilio in 1562. By 1570, it housed about 70 women, neophytes and professed nuns, and in 1617, 50 nuns and 40 neophytes. Female converts who did not take vows remained in the female division of the Casa di Catecumeni. The constitutions of Santissima Annuziata forbade Catholic-born novices from joining the convent, so as to protect them from absorbing Jewish ideas. Nonetheless, to make sure that the new Christians were closely monitored and well educated, Catholics from good but impoverished families were allowed to profess so that they could be given the major leadership roles; a Jewish-born nun could not become a prioress.[95]

Converted Jewish men considering holy orders were sent, from 1577 on, to the College of Neophytes—the Collegio dei Neofiti. The college served to train conversionary preachers. It taught men "who by studying, and by becoming apt preachers could help the conversion of the Jews in Ancona, Avignon, and first in Rome, and elsewhere," as the Jesuits later put it.[96] Or in the words of Fabiano Fioghi, its first Hebrew teacher,

> Pope Gregory XIII, being so solicitous and desirous of the salvation of the soul, and of the conversion of the obstinate Jews that he continuously has them preached to by the most learned men, and [who], to exalt the holy Christian faith, has . . . founded the College for Neophytes, so that they might study and arrive at the true knowledge of holy scripture, and, by preaching to others, might bring them to the recognition of the evangelical truth.[97]

For their education, students at the Neofiti attended the Jesuit-run Roman College. The comportment required of them is described in a set of rules from 1690, written for the appointment of a new cardinal protector,

94. Rocciolo, "Catecumeni e neofiti a Roma tra '500 e '800," 723 passim.
95. Lirosi, "Monacare le ebree."
96. ARSI Opp. NN 313, fol. 18r, letter to Claudio Acquavia, after 1604.
97. Fabiano Fioghi, *Dialogo fra il cathecumino et il padre cathechizante, Composto per Fabiano Fioghi dal Monte Santo Savino, Lettore della lingua hebrea nel Collegio de Neophiti, Nel qual si risoluono molti dubij, liquali sogliono far li hebrei, contro la uerità della santa fede christiana, con efficacissime ragioni: & per li santi profeti, & per li rabini,* 2r–v.

Fulvio Astalli.[98] The college supervised the students closely; the rulebook lists the number of shirts and underclothes they must bring with them (as well as their own beds, bedding, and furniture), laundry schedule (bleaching on Saturdays, presumably with no metaphor intended), and menu (unlimited vinegar, extra spinach on the Saturday of carnival, and wine at breakfast on Christmas with an extra salad at lunch). They must be tonsured. They must observe the forty-hour devotion when it comes to their church and serve at Mass every Saturday even though it is a school day. Their morning and evening orations are written out in full. Whenever students leave the college, even in free time, they must stay in pairs, and when they encounter Jews they may neither speak to nor offend them in any way. Prefects needed to make sure that no scholar of the college ever passed by the ghetto "or any other publicly disreputable places."[99] Hebrew remained a critical part of the curriculum for these future conversionary preachers, and they could not miss daily Hebrew lessons without special permission.

The House of Catechumens quickly reached firm footing with the appropriation of a miraculous image of the Madonna and the building of a new church. Gregory XIII showed his support for the new casa by assigning it rights to the image and the revenue it generated.[100] By 1637, there was money enough to build a grand complex housing the catechumens, College of Neophytes, and convent of Santissima Annunziata, together dominating the Monti region of Rome.[101] The church, in the parish of San Salvatore ai Monti, adjoined the casa building and was embellished with coded paintings that reflected its missionary ideals—in one case, sponsored by a former preacher.[102] The three institutions were governed by the same congregation, the Congregazione dei Neofiti. From 1634 on, after some streamlining from Urban VIII, they also shared a cardinal protector. This result was more competition among the three institutions for resources and attention, but equally, a stronger and more closely bound network of conversionary organizations in seventeenth-century Rome.[103]

98. *Relationi Economiche date all'eminentiss. e reverendiss. Sig. Card. Fulvio Astalli nell'ingresso alla protettione della chiesa della Madonna Santissima de' Monti di Roma.*

99. *Relationi Economiche*, 15, 24.

100. For concise English-language details of this story, see Mazur, *Conversion to Catholicism in Early Modern Italy*, 21.

101. Mazur, *Conversion to Catholicism in Early Modern Italy*, 22–23.

102. Carolyn H. Wood and Peter Iver Kaufman, "Tacito Predicatore: The Annunciation Chapel at the Madonna Dei Monti in Rome," 634–49.

103. Lirosi, "Monacare le ebree," 165–66.

The Congregazione dei Neofiti, and specifically its College of Neo-phytes, slotted neatly into the intellectual religious profile of sixteenth- and seventeenth-century Rome. Institutes for training clergy were flour-ishing throughout the city, and so too were centers intended to provide a home base for national and ethnic groups, such as the national colleges. The College of Neophytes linked naturally to the Greek or Maronite col-leges in serving a distinctive, slightly separate Christian population. But it also connected to the city's new flagship educational structures: the Roman College—another Jesuit institution—and Urban College, run by the Congregation of Propaganda Fide.

The basic model of the Casa di Catecumeni, pioneered in Rome, spread to other cities in Northern Italy over the following decades. In all cases, their establishment and success depended on the involvement of the local ruling family, and its interest in displaying its piety by supporting con-verts. Eleanor of Austria, duchess of Mantua, built a casa, but supported Jews in need too, hoping that her generosity might inspire their conver-sion. In Modena, Duke Alfonso III d'Este abdicated, became a Capuchin, and devoted himself to the conversion of Jews.[104] Houses of Catechumens appeared over the sixteenth and seventeenth centuries in Venice, Bologna, Mantua, Ferrara, Pesaro, Reggio Emilia, Florence, Torino, Modena, and Ancona as well as possibly Perugia, Milan, and Genoa.[105] Even Livorno, known for the relative freedom and protection of its Jewish community, and the supposedly peaceful cohabitation of religions, came to found one in the last decades of the eighteenth century.[106] These other Italian houses kept up a correspondence with the Roman casa, treating it as the center and primary reference point of the whole network. They turned to Rome for help in settling the fate of a resident, and kept the cardinal protector or rector of the casa informed of relevant cases elsewhere.[107]

A House of Catechumens could provide an important anchor for its city. Venice's casa offered opportunities for noble patronage and charity, provided a labor pool of international, multilingual intermediaries, and reinforced the imperial aspects of the authority of the city. In Reggio and Modena, the houses reflected the power and sentiments of local nobles and civic organizations, in part by refusing to admit Jews from any other

---

104. Mazur, *Conversion to Catholicism in Early Modern Italy*, 25–26.

105. For a brief general introduction to Houses of Catechumens across Italy, see Mazur, *Conversion to Catholicism in Early Modern Italy*, 18–42; Marconcini, *Per amor del cielo*, 9–16; Caffiero, *Battesimi forzati*.

106. Samuela Marconcini, "La Casa dei Catecumeni di Livorno," 435–36.

107. Rocciolo, "Fra promozione e difesa della fede," 154.

region.[108] But no casa ever came close to converting its local Jewish population entirely; in some places, marginal rates of conversion fell even further after their establishment. The treatment of catechumens could be harsh and coercive.[109] Given the unsustainably high rate of failure in numerical terms, it is clear that Houses of Catechumens implicitly served other purposes more significant than mass conversion. Like sermons, their most effective function was to convert a few Jews in public, triumphal ways, reminding both Jews and onlookers of the church's authority and dominance, and contributing to the theatrical nature of the conversion spectacle.[110]

The most dramatic step of all in the broad plan for Jewish conversion was the creation of the Roman ghetto in 1555. Venice's ghetto was the first, founded in 1516. The growth of monti di pietà throughout Italy had only encouraged the idea that Jews, as moneylenders, should be constrained and defined within clear borders such as ghettos.[111] But unlike other Italian ghettos, the Roman one had more explicitly theological foundations, and sought to rupture all links between Christians and Jews. The bull *Cum Nimis Absurdum* of July 14, 1555, was one of Paul IV's first acts in office, establishing the ghetto, reviving distinguishing signs, limiting employment for Jews, and prohibiting Christian servants and wet-nurses from serving in Jewish households. It reflected Paul IV's dogmatic and intransigent approach to his office, and his drive to convert Jews for eschatological purposes. The bull drastically curtailed Jews' mobility and employment, and reduced permitted contact between Jews and Christians.[112]

The bull *Cum Nimis*, especially in its establishment of the Roman ghetto, gradually but effectively transformed both Jewish and Christian

108. Rothman, *Brokering Empire*, 125–29. For Estense regions, see Matteo Al Kalak and Ilaria Pavan, *Un'altra fede: le case dei catecumeni nei territori estensi (1583–1938)*, 27–70.

109. For two versions of a famous account of harsh treatment in the Roman casa, see Kenneth R. Stow, *Anna and Tranquillo: Catholic Anxiety and Jewish Protest in the Age of Revolutions*; Anna Del Monte, *Rubare le anime: diario di Anna Del Monte ebrea romana*.

110. Matteo Al Kalak, "Converting the Jews: Inquisition and Houses of Catechumens, from Rome to Outlying Areas," 318–19; Foa, "'Limpieza' versus Mission." For an example of a concerted attempt to convert local Jews without establishing either a House of Catechumens or a program of forced sermons, see the case of seventeenth-century Padua in Celeste McNamara, *The Bishop's Burden: Reforming the Catholic Church in Early Modern Italy*, 221–24.

111. Pullan, "Jewish Banks and Monti di Pietà."

112. For discussions of the impact of *Cum Nimis*, see Kenneth R. Stow, *Catholic Thought and Papal Jewry Policy 1555–1593*; David Berger, "Cum Nimis Absurdum and the Conversion of the Jews," 41–49; Segre, "La Controriforma," 716–17.

society as it excised Jewish people from broader Roman life; it was arguably the "most traumatic redrawing of Rome's urban space during the
early modern period."[113] The ghetto's Jews were firmly under the eye of
the Roman government at the Capitoline Hill. While the ghetto did not
effect a total segregation, its rapidly built walls suggested physical boundaries for an ever more vigilantly guarded post-Tridentine orthodoxy.[114] In
Rome, a city of spectacle and conscious example for the rest of the world,
visible boundaries mattered. The first edict prohibiting Jewish people
from entering churches, chapels, or monasteries appeared in 1566 by order
of the cardinal vicar.[115]

Conditions in the ghetto emphasized the degradation of the Jews, especially as its population soared. By the 1527 census, Jewish people represented 3.2 percent of the population of Rome, or 1,772 people in 373 families out of a city with 53,897 inhabitants. The population grew and then
held generally steady over the following two centuries, with 4,314 people
in 1656 and 4,059 in 1733.[116] The increase came from international migra-
tion, ghettoization, and immigration from elsewhere in Italy—especially
the Papal States. Jews in the Papal States had suffered a series of fluctua-
tions as successive popes gave them more or less attention over the later
sixteenth century. After Paul IV's *Cum Nimis Absurdum*, Pius IV was relatively lenient. Jews could again own some property, and keep shops and
workshops outside the ghetto.[117] And where Pius V, in the bulls *Cum nos
nuper* (1567) and *Hebraeorum gens* (1569), had prohibited Jews from own-
ing property, and expelled them from the Papal States except for Rome
and Ancona, Sixtus V's *Cristiana Pietas* reversed course. Jewish people
cautiously began to resettle the Papal States. But shortly thereafter, Clement VIII, within a month of gaining the Papacy, explicitly renewed the
harsh policies of Paul IV and Pius V over other popes. His 1593 bull *Caeca
et obdurata* again expelled Jews, this time definitively, from the papal

---

113. Nussdorfer, "The Politics of Space in Early Modern Rome." See also Kenneth R.
Stow, "The Consciousness of Closure: Roman Jewry and Its *Ghet*." For an account of the
reopening of the ghetto that supports this view, see L. Scott Lerner, "Narrating over the
Ghetto of Rome."

114. For the construction and cost of the walls, see Milano, *Il ghetto di Roma*, 188.

115. Gerd Blum, "Vasari on the Jews: Christian Canon, Conversion, and the Moses of
Michelangelo," 562–63, 570.

116. Groppi, *Gli abitanti del ghetto di Roma*; Micol Ferrara, *Dentro e fuori dal
ghetto: I luoghi della presenza ebraica a Roma tra XVI e XIX secolo*, 9; Esposito, *Un'altra
Roma*, 129–30. These should replace the calculations for 1527 that determine a figure of
3.1 percent, as cited in Peter Partner, *Renaissance Rome, 1500–1559: A Portrait of a Society*,
77.

117. Rodocanachi, *Le Saint-Siège et les Juifs; le ghetto à Rome*, 179–82.

regions, restricting them again to Rome, Ancona, and Avignon.[118] Again, many wound up in the Roman ghetto.

The ghetto itself, with its narrow footprint, lagged behind these hairpin turns of policy. Bordered on one side by the Tiber, it extended inland in a trapezoid shape for about 150 meters. Sixtus V allowed a slight extension in 1589, built by Domenico Ferrara at the expense of the Jewish community; a further small extension came only in 1825.[119] Until 1731, three adjacent city blocks formed the *ghetarello*, a small additional area where ghetto residents stored dry goods and merchandise.[120] Like the ghetto, it was walled and locked. The ghetto itself covered ony three hectares, or just under an acre. To accommodate upward of three to four thousand people, houses in the ghetto reached three or four stories, blocking out light, and forcing inhabitants into crowded and unwholesome conditions.[121]

Entrances and exits were closely monitored. The ghetto had three gates: in Piazza Giudea, Piazza di Pescaria, and toward the Quattro Capi bridge. Two more entrances were added along the edges of the Tiber during the 1589 extension.[122] These were locked at an hour or two after sunset and opened at dawn, guarded by a well-paid, non-Jewish appointee of the cardinal vicar of Rome. Yet the ghetto was not a leper colony, built and then permanently sealed (except during plagues). Despite the theological intent behind the ghetto's founding, many of its residents spent much of their day outside for work, returning at nightfall. Exiting at night was another matter, rarely permitted, and only for grand festivals.[123] And while the ghetto was not entirely closed to Christians during the day, their presence inside made everyone uneasy. When two millers led their cart through the ghetto one late afternoon in 1621—their horses unlawfully hitched, and bearing sacks full of flour during a period of famine—they were attacked by local residents, and one was killed. But the resulting trial also revealed that Jews felt collectively endangered by this incident and did their best to ensure it could not be considered a group crime.[124]

The ghetto walls that proclaimed the separation of Jews and Christians were especially eloquent on the subject of converts. The fear that a new

118. Segre, "La Controriforma," 721–38.

119. Milano, *Il ghetto di Roma*, 190–91; Ferrara, *Dentro e fuori dal ghetto*, 6–8.

120. Ferrara, *Dentro e fuori dal ghetto*, 67–72.

121. For the theological overtones of ghetto filth and Jewish management of sanitation, see Kenneth R. Stow, "Was the Ghetto Cleaner . . . ?," 169–81.

122. Ferrara, *Dentro e fuori dal ghetto*, 4–5.

123. Milano, *Il ghetto di Roma*, 195–96.

124. Simona Feci, "The Death of a Miller: A Trial Contra Hebreos in Baroque Rome," 19.

convert would stay in contact with their family prompted a wealth of legislation against fraternization. The perceived danger was spiritual: if a convert slid back into Judaism, their sin was worse than before conversion.
As a new Christian, they would now be guilty of apostasy. Repeated edicts
from the late sixteenth century onward prohibited any kind of contact
between Jews and former Jews. These grew longer and more specific as
authorities tried to identify as well as close loopholes. In the edict of 1635,
catechumens and neophytes of both genders and every social grade were
prohibited from "practicing, conversing, contracting, trafficking, negotiating, or in any other way interesting themselves" with Jewish people,
even if they used a delegate. Without a license, they were prohibited from
entering the ghetto either on feast or nonfeast days; attending synagogues,
prayer services, circumcisions, or festivals; buying meat, or receiving gifts,
food, or drink from Jewish people; hosting Jewish people in their houses
or workshops (even their own parents, siblings, or relatives of any kind);
meeting them in a tavern, or sharing food or drink; or arranging to meet
outside the city.[125] The same fear of interaction undergirded procedures in
the convent of Santissima Annunziata, which mandated both the segregation of Jewish-born nuns and installation of Catholic-born administrators.[126] This close supervision of neophytes reflects—beyond the general
standards for novices—the ever-present fear that a Jewish convert would
instinctively be drawn back to Judaism.

Legislation and anxiety coalesced around Piazza Giudea, "the ultimate
frontier of the ghetto." The piazza was a busy market space that symbolized the point of both transition and contamination between Judaism
and Catholicism. The ghetto walls and gate bisected Piazza Giudea into
two separate spaces: a Jewish half inside and a Christian half outside the
ghetto. Its double nature fostered unusual levels of concern about Jewish-
Christian contact. During times of unrest such as the *sede vacante* (Vacant
See), Roman Christians were ordered away from their half of Piazza Giudea.
New or potential Jewish converts to Catholicism were always prohibited
from entering not only Jewish houses and the Jewish ghetto but also the
Christian half of Piazza Giudea, outside the ghetto but nonetheless too
close and too tempting. Indeed, more print legislation was directed at this
space than at any other in the city.[127]

125. AAV Misc. Arm. IV.10, 17r. Edicts to this effect from 1592 to 1712 are collected on fols. 12r–32r.

126. Lirosi, "Monacare le ebree," 153.

127. Rose Marie San Juan, *Rome: A City Out of Print*, 152–60.

Naturally, all of these repeated protestations only confirm how fully meetings, parties, and relationships continued. Studies on early modern conversion have repeatedly emphasized that although formal conversionary efforts sought total and absolute transformation, the lives of converts and catechumens in Italy were inevitably more complicated, with ongoing tangled connections and affiliations.[128] Jews, Christians, and people who had been both continued to seek each other out; they continued to enjoy time in each other's houses and spaces. They might even leave each other money in their testaments, as a Jewish woman in Ferrara did in 1559 for two nuns, possibly former Jews.[129] In a parallel way, the distinguishing signs that were mandatory on Jewish clothing—and were continually renegotiated and redefined—only confirmed that Jews and Christians otherwise resembled each other and shared the same spaces.[130] But the arrival of walls and laws drew firmer boundaries, and rendered these activities more explicitly transgressive.

Enclosure therefore emphasized as well as increased separation and difference. It forced definitions on people, homogenizing each group, and making the other, over the wall, seem more exotic and foreign. The ghetto only made Roman Jews, in concentrate, seem more visible. Its walls added weight to any interaction that took place outside them. Outside the ghetto, its inhabitants, moving about the city, had ceased to be seen as ordinary residents, part of the city fabric. They became foreigners who belonged not to Rome but rather an indistinct "elsewhere." These differences extended to the mind as well as the eye. The more a population is marked as separate, the easier it becomes to imagine things about them and assume those things are true. The ghetto walls made Roman Jews more easy to reduce to a spectacle—a theater within a theater, under a constant eye.[131] Both segregation and conversion, then, fortified Catholic orthodoxy. Removing

128. Among the most recent examples, see Herzig, *A Convert's Tale*; Clines, *A Jewish Jesuit in the Eastern Mediterranean*; Nicholas Terpstra, *Global Reformations: Transforming Early Modern Religions, Societies, and Cultures*; Mazur, *Conversion to Catholicism in Early Modern Italy*; Dunkelgrün and Maciejko, *Bastards and Believers*.

129. Herzig, "The Hazards of Conversion," 475.

130. On distinguishing signs, see Flora Cassen, *Marking the Jews in Renaissance Italy: Politics, Religion, and the Power of Symbols*. On their contestation and layers of significance, see Massimo Moretti, "'Glauci Coloris': Gli Ebrei nell'iconografia sacra di età moderna"; Wisch, "Vested Interest"; Benjamin Ravid, "From Yellow to Red: On the Distinguishing Head-Covering of the Jews of Venice"; Diane Owen Hughes, "Distinguishing Signs: Ear-Rings, Jews and Franciscan Rhetoric in the Italian Renaissance City."

131. On this point, see Stow, *Theater of Acculturation*; Dana E. Katz, "'Clamber Not You up to the Casements': On Ghetto Views and Viewing"; Dana E. Katz, *The Jewish Ghetto and the Visual Imagination of Early Modern Venice*.

Jews into a ghetto served to distill and concentrate the Catholicism of the rest of the city of Rome and give it physical boundaries. Reintroducing Jews into the population as new Catholics further reinforced the city's piety.

In an era when laypeople could, at least in theory, choose among Christian confessions for the first time, the battle for hearts and minds was paramount; its chief weapons were instruction, catechism, and supervision. Within Jewish-Christian policy, conversion became the key priority, and would remain so throughout the modern period.[132] In particular, Jewish conversion, more than ever, was supposed to be based on persuasion, not coercion, to suit this new, confessional era, a "century obsessed with defining, teaching, verifying, and enforcing the rectitude of belief and the validity of interior conversion."[133] In the early years of these conversionary efforts, Jesuits and other religious orders emphasized persuasive approaches based on education and rhetoric.

Within Rome, conversions to Catholicism signaled in microcosm the desired conversion of faraway lands and refutation of Protestant successes. They also reflected long-standing millenarian beliefs that the conversion of the Jews was a necessary step in the second coming of the Messiah. The antiquity and theological importance of the Jews made their conversions a bigger coup than that of a Muslim or Protestant. The conversion of a rabbi, his son, or a family, particularly if wealthy, was especially to be celebrated.[134]

The act of conversion was fundamentally public—theatricalized and ritualized within the heavy burden Jews already bore as the primary Christian symbol of otherness.[135] Baptisms, as we have seen, were sometimes performed with great ceremony by prominent cardinals or even the pope. In those cases, baptisms often took place in the basilica of Saint John Lateran. They could also take place in Santa Maria sopra Minerva (the primary Dominican church) or even Saint Peter's. But the celebration of a baptism, whether of Jews or Muslims, belonged to the whole city. In 1649,

132. Marina Caffiero, *Forced Baptisms: Histories of Jews, Christians, and Converts in Papal Rome*, 6.

133. Lance Gabriel Lazar, "Negotiating Conversions: Catechumens and the Family in Early Modern Italy," 177.

134. Lazar, "Negotiating Conversions," 152; Lazar, *Working in the Vineyard of the Lord*, 116–17; Marina Caffiero, "I processi di canonizzazione come fonte per la storia dei rapporti tra ebrei e cristiani e delle conversioni." See also the previously cited cases of conversion in Incisa della Rocchetta and Vian, *Il primo processo per san Filippo Neri*.

135. Anna Foa, "Il gioco del proselitismo: Politica delle conversioni e controllo della violenza nella Rome del Cinquecento," 156.

for example, the peak year for conversion to Catholicism in the seventeenth century, baptisms took place in nineteen separate churches across Rome.[136]

The combination of so many different approaches, so much legislation, and so much emotional weight formed a radically concerted effort to convert Jews, and marked a different spirit from earlier efforts at proselytization.[137] Many of these measures were meant to apply all of Italy and in theory all Catholic lands, but they were most rigorous and concentrated in Rome. And whereas other local governments had a range of interests motivating their Jewish policies and a range of competing political concerns, in Rome these efforts all overlapped to point closely to conversion. Pope Pius V said as much explicitly, as reported in a letter to Cardinal Carlo Borromeo: "In fact I wish that [the Jews] had refuge in no other place but Rome, where they can be more easily converted than elsewhere."[138] By the early eighteenth century, it was possible for a conversionary preacher to erase indigenous Jewish roots in Rome and reattribute their ongoing presence solely to efforts at conversion. The preacher Antonio Teoli argued that "the Church, as a compassionate Mother, tolerates that the Jews should sojourn in the places inhabited by her faithful Christians, for the sole object and single goal of procuring their conversion."[139] In this context, conversionary efforts in the eighteenth century would take an even more violent turn, back to forced conversions and blood libels.[140]

Conversionary preaching to Jews—a sporadic medieval practice revived in the late sixteenth century—was a uniquely socially and theologically charged event. Of the many popular public events celebrating Jewish conversion, including the baptism of catechumens and execution of recidivists, sermons were perhaps the most richly symbolic.[141] More frequent, predictable, prestigious, and accessible than baptism, they became a citywide paragon. Preaching was ostensibly the technique most firmly

---

136. For this estimation, see Rocciolo, "Catecumeni e neofiti a Roma tra '500 e '800," 716. For locations of baptisms by prominent clergy, see ASVR Casa dei Catecumeni 23 N 48, neofiti battezzati da cardinali e papi, 1675 onward. For churches used for baptisms of converts in 1649, see ASVR Casa dei Catecumeni 178, Liber Baptizatorum 1634–75, fols. 48r–54v.

137. Lazar, *Working in the Vineyard of the Lord*, 105.

138. Segre, "Il mondo ebraico nei cardinali della Controriforma," 127.

139. ACDF St St BB 3 r, 13r.

140. On this eighteenth-century turn, see especially Caffiero, *Forced Baptisms*.

141. For instances of medieval papal bills permitting or prescribing preaching to Jews, see Stow, *Catholic Thought and Papal Jewry Policy*, 19–21. Stow notes three such cases, in 1245, 1278, and 1415, none of which took root. Lazar, *Working in the Vineyard of the Lord*, 115.

rooted in persuasion rather than coercion, although the congregation's forced attendance blurs the distinction. Sermons also held the greatest potential yield of converts. They promised more than they could ever deliver, but it was precisely the promise that appealed, the dream of mass conversion made visible, before the disappointingly human results had to be contemplated. This moment of pure potential, publicly visible, was a peerless symbol. Catholics who disagreed about the minutia of proselytization could still rally around the pulpit.[142] As conversionary preaching gained symbolic importance, so too did practical measures toward widespread Jewish conversion. Jews and Judaism became so central to Counter-Reformation conversion rhetoric that Rome's historic Jewish community was recast as a living image of the generic convert.

As a staged encounter, conversionary preaching differed radically from the motley, porous world of Christian-Jewish interaction. Contact and sharing space were forbidden everywhere else, and took place furtively. At sermons, they were prescribed and visible. Forced sermons provided the only venue for licit encounter between Jews and former Jews, the only place where formerly united families and friends might expect to lock eyes.[143] But the tight scripting and choreographed spectacle of the whole endeavor reminds us that sermons were a performance of Catholic ambition, which could not be disturbed in its presentation.

The idea of Jewish conversion permeated and influenced Catholic activity, institutions, and thought. When Nazzareno insisted, in his letter of dedication, that he wanted to model his Armenian mission on the work of a conversionary preacher to the Jews of Rome, he demonstrated that interest in Jewish people and Jewish history underpinned early modern global Catholicism. Conversionary preaching acted out the dream at the heart of so much worldwide effort: the possibility of success, validation, and winning new souls to the church. It was the public face of a far broader and more complex campaign directed toward both Jews and all others. Of all conversionary efforts, public sermons provide the strongest link to the general life of early modern Rome and early modern Catholicism. Where other conversionary efforts were private or occasional, this one was public and regulated. It demonstrated openly that the wider work of conversion was well underway, and suggested, crucially, that these efforts reflected conviction, not force.

142. On this point, and Roman Jews as simultaneously powerful as potential converts and Jewish others, see Foa, "Il gioco del proselitismo," esp. 155–56; Emily Michelson, "Conversionary Preaching and the Jews in Early Modern Rome."

143. Rocciolo, "Fra promozione e difesa della fede," 147–58.

From the outset, Christians of all kinds attended the sermons as a secondary audience watching the primary (Jewish) audience. Their presence remained both important and revealing throughout the early modern period. Carlo Bartolomeo Piazza, in his sweeping survey *Eusevologio Romano* from 1698, notes that conversionary hopes had always underpinned Roman tolerance of Jews. He celebrates conversionary preaching as a public devotion, writing that "the pope with many wise reasons and motives also permitted Christians at the sermons."[144] Because it was a newly instituted spectacle with a broad audience, conversionary preaching became a key staging ground for acknowledging interfaith tension, and transforming it into an assertion of Roman piety and early modern Catholic identity. And as this book will go on to demonstrate, sermons placed Judaism at the foundation of far more widespread conversionary campaigns that reached across the globe.

144. Piazza, *Eusevologio Romano*, book X, 153 fol. uiv.

CHAPTER TWO

How Sermons to Jews Worked

IT IS SATURDAY AFTERNOON, and the sides of the vast oratory are crammed with Christian spectators; the room is so tightly packed that some have to cluster near the door or cannot enter at all. Many more have lined the streets outside. The cardinals in attendance presumably have comfortable seating, but the rest of the viewers are all on their feet. In the center of the hall, a scattering of benches has been set up for 250 Roman Jews, currently progressing along the few streets that lie between the gates of ghetto and the entrance to the oratory. Once they arrive, they must give their names to a guard who stands at the door. He will check them against his list before they can take their seats. From their benches, they can study the grand, recently completed altarpiece showing the Pope Gregory Mass (figure 2.1). Although it depicts a historical scene, the painting is set in the currently unfinished Saint Peter's and is crowded with contemporary portraits. The Jewish people in the oratory can gaze directly at the recognizable face of the man responsible for bringing them there: Pope Gregory XIII, whose legislation established conversionary sermons in Rome and who also served as the painter's model for his saintly namesake. Below him, in the painting, the cardinal protector of the confraternity, Ferdinando de' Medici, regards the viewer with a stern expression, surrounded by a cluster of sumptuously dressed cardinals and confraternity members. A special carpeted area awaits the catechumens and neophytes, conveyed to the oratory from their new Christian dormitories. In theory, they have come to further their own religious education, but their presence also tells the crowd, both Christian and Jewish, that conversion is possible—that preaching can work.[1]

---

1. For crowds and benches, see Gregory Martin, *Roma Sancta*, 75–80; Emily Michelson, "Conversionary Preaching and the Jews in Early Modern Rome." For the door deputy,

The oratory is newly built and well appointed, but it has been adapted for the occasion. If there is a monstrance containing the blessed sacrament, it has been removed. The guard at the door waits with his truncheon to pounce on any Jewish misconduct. When everyone is settled, the preacher comes in. He begins with a genuflection and a personal prayer in a low voice—hands folded, eyes devoutly heavenward. These actions are familiar to the Christian onlookers from other sermons. In this case, however, the preacher prays not only for divine guidance but specifically for his words to lead the Jews to conversion. He omits the usual pre-sermon formulas and Ave Marias, spoken aloud, lest the Jews blaspheme the names of Jesus and Mary on hearing them.[2] At last, he turns to his audience. Although he is also speaking in front of both old and new Christians, it is the anticipated future Christians he addresses. "O Jews," he begins, "not only our sainted doctors preached the excellencies of Christ, but so did your ancient Rabbis as well. Today I intend to show you how true this is."[3] Under the unforgiving gazes of the painted cardinals, the rest of the crowd watches and listens as the Jews receive their instruction.

For this scene to take place even once, a wide range of Catholic organizations had to offer support. To repeat it more or less weekly for two and a half centuries required the involvement of many more, from confraternities to printing houses to treasuries. But such groups committed enthusiastically. Conversionary sermons looked to them like a sure success story, a self-congratulatory initiative. Sermons to Jews made a stellar talking

---

see especially Cuggiò, *Della giurisdittione e prerogative del vicariato di Roma: Opera del canonico Nicolò Antonio Cuggiò segretario del tribunale di Sua Eminenza*, 356–57, and further discussion in chapters 4 and 7. For the carpet, see BAV Borg. lat. 129, fol. 499r. For a reconstruction of the oratory showing its structure and opulence, see Barbara Wisch, "Promoting Piety, Coercing Conversion: The Roman Archconfraternity of the Santissima Trinità dei Pellegrini e Convalescenti and Its Oratory." I am grateful to Barbara for our valuable conversations over this shared interest. For the altarpiece, see Antonio Vannugli, "Per Jacopo Zucchi: un' 'Annunciazione' a Bagnoregio ed altre opere"; Noel O'Regan, *Institutional Patronage in Post-Tridentine Rome: Music at Santissima Trinità Dei Pellegrini, 1550–1650*, 18–20.

2. For the removal of the monstrance, see Gaetano Moroni, *Dizionario di erudizione storico-ecclesiastica da S. Pietro sino ai nostri giorni*, 23. For the truncheon, see the extended discussion in chapter 7. For a preacher's pre-sermon actions, see Serafino Razzi, *Sermoni predicabili dalla prima domenica dell'Avvento fino all'ottava Pasqua di Resurrezione*, fol. a7v–a8r. For modifications at conversionary sermons, see Giulio Bartolocci, *Bibliotheca Magna Rabbinica de scriptoribus, & scriptis Hebraicis, ordine alphabetico Hebraicè, & Latinè digestis*, 3:750.

3. Evangelista Marcellino, *Sermoni quindici sopra il salmo centonove fatti a gli Hebrei di Roma*, 36.

FIGURE 2.1. Jacopo Zucchi, *Mass of Pope Gregory the Great*, 1574–75, oil on canvas. Church of the Santissima Trinità dei Pellegrini, Rome, sacristy. Photo by Tanner Nash.

point for Catholics. Over time, the status of conversionary preachers came to lend prestige and authority to many other initiatives in early modern Rome. Many of these other initiatives had to do with conversion, but ultimately, proselytization to Jews also touched groups and people ostensibly far removed from the event. Preaching to Jews became ever more deeply woven into the religious fabric and institutional life of Catholic Rome. It gained cachet, and it lasted.

Roman Jews, in contrast, maintained only the minimal connections necessary to the weekly ritual. During the week, they had only to prepare the roster of participants and contribute to the expenses of preaching. Communication about the sermons arrived in the form of papal or episcopal edicts, or through the *fattori*—the governors of Roman Jewry. Beyond that, their primary responsibility was simply to appear at the sermons and behave as expected. Although Jewish people did react to and resist sermons, as subsequent chapters will show, the impact of conversionary preaching was far shallower in Jewish Rome than it was in Christian Rome. An examination of the history of conversionary preaching in Rome, and its web of networks and connections, shows us how deeply enmeshed and important conversionary preaching became in the eternal city, and how essential it was to the remaking of Catholicism.

Legislation and Patronage

For much of the Renaissance period, a sermon with mandatory Jewish attendance seemed like an unusually severe event. Indeed, such sermons may have violated canon law. If they did not, they certainly came close. Pope Gregory the Great had first established the principle that Jewish conversion should not be forced but instead always be voluntary. Forcing attendance at sermons, if not the act of baptism itself, skated uncomfortably close to that line. Although later popes had tried to institute regular conversionary preaching, as with Nicholas III's bull *Vineam Sorec,* they had not absolutely made attendance mandatory. Other popes, such as Martin V, had argued against sermons entirely in favor of gentler methods of conversion.[4] Any Renaissance ruler who required the Jews in his territory to

---

4. The legality of coerced conversion and its possible extension to mandatory sermon attendance is discussed by Kenneth R. Stow in the following works: *Catholic Thought and Papal Jewry Policy 1555–1593,* 20–21; *Theater of Acculturation: The Roman Ghetto in the 16th Century,* 18–19; *Anna and Tranquillo: Catholic Anxiety and Jewish Protest in the Age of Revolutions,* 168–70. See also his notes to the discussion of *Vineam Sorec* in Solomon Grayzel, *The Church and the Jews in the XIIIth century. Vol. 2, 1254–1314,* 141–45. In *Anna*

attend such a sermon, as Ercole d'Este did in Ferrara in 1496, was thus deliberately staging an exceptionally pious or zealous act. He might even appear excessive, going beyond what church authorities would mandate.[5]

But an increase in intermittent preaching to Jews over the later sixteenth century shows the engine of evangelization gathering steam in Counter-Reformation Italy. Enterprising preachers rode the wave of conversionary fervor, delivering occasional sermons to Jews on their own initiative or with personal papal support. In a letter of 1553, the belletrist Girolamo Muzio praised the efforts of the notable convert and proselytizer Alessandro Franceschi (père) for preaching a sermon that converted a Jewish boy who was deaf.[6] In 1556, Ludovico Carretto, a Florentine doctor and convert to Catholicism, published a set of documents including a conversionary sermon attributed to his six-year-old son, Giulio.[7] In 1558, Paul IV invited a noted neophyte to visit the Jews in Romagna and Le Marche. On Yom Kippur, the most solemn day in the Jewish year, the neophyte interrupted the service in the synagogue of Recanati and placed a crucifix on the ark; after the resulting fracas, two Jews were sentenced to be whipped while walking across the city in chains.[8] Marcello Ferro boasted that in 1567, he had converted two Jewish people by taking them into a church and teaching them the rudiments of Christian faith. His story appeared in the canonization trial of Filippo Neri and echoed the trial's other stories of the saint converting individual Jews through sustained

---

and Tranquillo, Stow argues that Innocent IV surely knew that forced sermon attendance was illegal, and in his notes on Grayzel, he lays out the ways that *Vineam Sorec* tacitly avoided the use of force.

5. Tamar Herzig, *A Convert's Tale: Art, Crime, and Jewish Apostasy in Renaissance Italy*, 150–51.

6. Girolamo Muzio, *Lettere catholiche del Mutio Iustinopolitano, distinte in quattro libri*, 171–72. The letter, written in Pesaro and addressed to Lattantio Fosco, auditor of the cardinal of Naples, is dated 1553. Shlomo Simonsohn, "Some Well-Known Jewish Converts during the Renaissance," 35n79; Barbara Leber, "Jewish Convert in Counter-Reformation Rome: Giovanni Paolo Eustachio," 115n23.

7. Ludovico Carretto, *Epistola de Ludovico Carretto ad Hebreos. Sermone di Giulio Innocentio suo figliolo alli Hebrei, et era quando lo fece de età de anni cinque in sei*. On Carretto, see chapter 5.

8. Renata Segre, "La Controriforma: espulsioni, conversioni, isolamento," 754. The Hebrew chronicle עמק הבכה (*'Emeq Ha-Bakha*) describes the incident and names the neophyte as Filippo, previously Joseph Moro. See Joseph ha-Kohen, *Sefer 'Emeq Ha-Bakha = The Vale of Tears: With the Chronicle of the Anonymous Corrector*, 88; Joseph ha-Kohen, *The Vale of Tears (Emek Habacha)*, 94. This association prompted many later errors, as Vittorio Colorni has noted. Segre identifies him as Filippo Hererra, né Salomone Romano. Given that Hererra died in 1546, we can assume the preacher here was Andrea de Monte né Joseph Moro. Vittore Colorni, *Salomon Romano alias Filippo Herrera convertito del Cinquecento*, 85–96.

conversation.[9] Newsletters from Rome reported new sermons to Jews on feast days from 1568.[10] By the mid-1570s, some in the circle around the Jesuit-led House of Catechumens in Rome had started to deliver regular sermons to Jews.

The papal bull that first legislated regular preaching to the Jews, *Vices Eius Nos,* capitalized on the growing trend for conversionary sermons and their greater acceptability. The bull, promulgated in 1577, was vague on detail, but showed the beginnings of Gregory XIII's long-term investment in preaching to Jews and established the direction of later sermons. *Vices Eius Nos* established the College of Neophytes. It also gave a general command to hold regular sermons for the conversion of Jews and others. Certain parts of the bull proved easier to implement than others. As specified, sermons to Jews did rely primarily on the Hebrew Bible and rabbinic texts, and took place outside the ghetto in an oratory, but except for a few early examples, they were almost never in Hebrew.[11] These patterns enabled Christian-born preachers to try their hand at conversionary sermons and kept the pulpit from becoming too niche.

After the promulgation of *Vices Eius Nos,* religious orders and confraternities rushed to participate in conversionary preaching to Jews. Two of the era's most high-ranking cardinals gave indispensable backing: Giulio Antonio Santoro, cardinal of Santa Severina, who was responsible for the Index of Forbidden Books and the Holy Office, and Guglielmo Sirleto, cardinal protector of neophytes and catechumens. Both men regularly graced conversionary sermons with their public presence, lending the sermons both validity and splendor.[12] Rome's newest and most dynamic religious

---

9. Karl Hoffmann, *Ursprung und Anfangstätigkeit des ersten päpstlichen Missionsinstituts; ein Beitrag zur Geschichte der katholischen Juden- und Mohammedanermission im sechzehnten Jahrhundert,* 83–86, 257 (Italian typescript translation); Gianni Incisa della Rocchetta and Nello Vian, *Il primo processo per san Filippo Neri del Codice vaticano latino 3798 e in altri esemplari dell'Archivio dell'Oratorio di Roma,* 88; Gerd Blum, "Vasari on the Jews: Christian Canon, Conversion, and the Moses of Michelangelo," 563.

10. Ludwig von Pastor, *History of the Popes,* 17:341–42.

11. The sermons of Andrea De Monte in BAV Neofiti 35 are an exception; notably, he also systematically organized his sermons by parashah, according to the Hebrew calendar, as specified in the bulls, but rarely practiced in print. De Monte's surname has been written as "Del Monte" or "Di Monte," but Piet van Boxel has established "De Monte" as authoritative. Piet van Boxel, *Jewish Books in Christian Hands: Theology, Exegesis and Conversion under Gregory XIII (1572–1585).* For the text of the Papal Bulls, see Francesco Gaude, Luigi Tomassetti, and Charles Cocquelines, *Bullarum, Diplomatum et Privilegiorum Sanctorum Romanorum Pontificum Taurinensis,* 188–91.

12. Both men have received extensive scholarly attention. For an overview, see their respective entries (*voci*) in the Dizionario Biografico degli Italiani (DBI). For Sirleto, see also Peter A. Mazur, *Conversion to Catholicism in Early Modern Italy,* 20–25.

orders worked especially hard to make conversionary preaching happen. The Jesuit superior general, Francesco Borgia, had long argued that this post should naturally fall to Jesuits because converting Jews and confronting heretics demanded the same high standards.[13] Indeed, some of the most revered of the first generation of Jesuits filled in as conversionary preachers in the 1570s.[14] The records of the preacher Andrea De Monte and the renowned Michel de Montaigne, who attended sermons during his sojourn in Rome, each identified one other Jesuit by name, Father Benedettino and Franciso da Toledo, respectively.[15] The converso background of many early and influential Jesuits fueled their particular and energetic efforts at conversion.[16]

In addition to the Jesuits, the Congregation of the Oratory provided much of the early inspiration and practical support. The founder of the congregation, Philip Neri, took a personal interest in conversion, as we have already seen. So too did Cesare Baronio. Indeed, Baronio's decision to reprint papal legislation in his *Annales ecclesiastici* would increase general awareness that Jews had a legacy of protection by church authorities.[17] The Congregation of the Oratory also helped with the provision of space for sermons; the confraternity of Santissima Trinità dei Pellegrini, which would host conversionary preaching for most of its history, had only recently been set up as an initiative of the congregation. Many early conversionary preachers developed under the spiritual guidance of the Congregation of the Oratory as well; even De Monte, the first official conversionary preacher, formed part of the same circle. Several other religious orders wanted in, too. Gregory Martin famously named not only the Oratorian Francesco Maria Tarugi but also the Capuchin Alfonso Lupo as

13. van Boxel, *Jewish Books in Christian Hands*, 12; Frederick McGinness, *Right Thinking and Sacred Oratory in Counter-Reformation Rome*, 38–39.

14. ARSI Opp. NN 313, 7r, 18r; ARSI Opp. NN 336, fols. 89r–90r; John Patrick Donnelly, "Antonio Possevino and Jesuits of Jewish Ancestry"; Emanuele Colombo, "The Watershed of Conversion: Antonio Possevino, New Christians, and Jews."

15. van Boxel, *Jewish Books in Christian Hands*, 23; Michel de Montaigne, *Montaigne's Travel Journal*, 956–57.

16. On Jesuits and conversos, see especially Colombo, "The Watershed of Conversion"; Robert Aleksander Maryks, *The Jesuit Order as a Synagogue of Jews: Jesuits of Jewish Ancestry and Purity-of-Blood Laws in the Early Society of Jesus*.

17. For Oratorians and conversion, see Alberto Bianco, "Cesare Baronio e la conversione dei Corcos nei documenti d'archivio della Congregazione oratoriana di Roma," 151–70; Peter A. Mazur, "Searcher of Hearts: Cesare Baronio's History of Conversion," 213–32. For the impact of the *Annales ecclesiastici* (including Odorico Rinaldi's later volumes) on Italian attitudes to Jews, see Magda Teter, *Blood Libel: On the Trail of an Antisemitic Myth*, 162–65.

early occupiers of the post.[18] Evangelista Marcellino, De Monte's longtime partner in the pulpit, was an Observant Franciscan. After him, Alessandro Franceschi, who was both a convert and Dominican, may have taken up the task in the late 1570s and 1580s, following his earlier successes as the highest-ranking Jewish-born cleric.[19]

The early Roman campaign for Jewish conversion enjoyed patronage from the most illustrious personalities and institutions in the city—both its oldest and most venerable as well as its newest and glossiest. The benefits of association were evident. The exciting new initiative seemed to signal the city's vigorous piety. Such patronage took many forms, providing labor, resources, or funding. Many churches showed an interest in Judaism and hosted sermons about Jews, often in the presence of interested high-level clerics. These included the Jesuit church of the Gesù, the Conventual church of Santi Apostoli, Chiesa Nuova (Santa Maria in Vallicella, home of the Congregation of the Oratory), and the Dominican church of Santa Maria sopra Minerva, which had a history of conversion sermons to Jews and had hosted the College of Neophytes in its early days.[20] The first Catholic-born, long-term preacher, Marcellino, arrived bearing all the cachet of his home church of Santa Maria in Aracoeli, which was nestled atop the Capitoline Hill alongside the seat of Roman government and played host to civic officials' most important liturgical ceremonies.[21] Some of the era's greatest preachers took part. Franceschino Visdomini, for example, preached a sermon in which he reconstructed what he thought Jews would say about circumcision.[22] This evidence suggests that a network of religious groups gradually built support for conversionary activities by delivering sermons on related topics to their own Catholic laity, and that the sermons elicited a degree of civic pride.

The enthusiasm of powerful individual patrons brought prestige and support to conversionary sermons. Noblewomen frequently donated property for the use of nascent confraternities, and often made paired donations

18. van Boxel, *Jewish Books in Christian Hands*, 22–24; Michelson, "Conversionary Preaching and the Jews in Early Modern Rome," 82–84.

19. Alberto Zucchi, "Il primo predicatore Domenicano degli Ebrei. Ancora sul P. Sirleto—Fr. Alessandro Franceschi." For Franceschi in general, see Mazur, *Conversion to Catholicism in Early Modern Italy*, 66–76.

20. van Boxel, *Jewish Books in Christian Hands*, 23–24.

21. Eleonora Canepari and Laurie Nussdorfer, "A Civic Identity," 33.

22. van Boxel, *Jewish Books in Christian Hands*, 23. For De Monte's note on the sermon, see BAV Neofiti 35, fol. 23v. For Visdomini, see Emily Michelson, *The Pulpit and the Press in Reformation Italy*, 54–86.

to confraternities or charities that helped prostitutes and Jews.[23] Thus in one extended family, the support of Girolama Orsini, mother of Alessandro Farnese, helped to arrange property for the confraternity of San Giuseppe for catechumens, Caterina Orsini lent out a house she owned for the use of the Monte di Pietà in its early years, and Elena Orsini provided the first space for the confraternity of Trinità dei Pellegrini to house pilgrims; it would go on to host conversionary sermons.[24] At a grander level, Queen Christina of Sweden, a long-term resident of Rome, stated in a manifesto that she considered herself the "protector of the miserable, oppressed, and downtrodden" Jews of the Roman ghetto, and intervened in a number of Jewish causes, apparently as an expression of her millenarian and messianic beliefs.[25]

Many grandees also found it useful as a public display of piety to sponsor converts. This could mean performing the baptism, serving as a role model, arranging employment in Christian society, or allowing the use of their names. Pope Julius III, born Giovanni Maria Del Monte, had given his surname to the convert Joseph Moro (Sarfati). As Andrea De Monte, Sarfati would go on to become the best-known conversionary preacher in Rome. His nephew received the surname of Pope Gregory XIII, Ugo Boncompagni, upon conversion, and the right to use the Boncompagni coat of arms.[26] Other popes and cardinals followed these examples by continuing to sponsor converts. This practice could backfire when the new Christians failed to meet a desired standard. In a city full of neophyte godsons walking around bearing the monikers of cardinals and princes—Carlo Borromeo or Ferdinando de Medici—some patrons swore off sponsoring conversions after too many namesakes got in trouble with the law, dragging a good name into disgrace.[27] Yet the honor of naming a convert remained a privilege.

23. Lance Gabriel Lazar, "Negotiating Conversions: Catechumens and the Family in Early Modern Italy," 112, 236.

24. Lazar, Negotiating Conversions: Catechumens and the Family in Early Modern Italy," 113; Matizia Maroni Lumbroso and Antonio Martini, *Le confraternite romane nelle loro chiese*, 425; Donato Tamilia, *Il sacro Monte de pietà di Roma: ricerche storiche e documenti inediti: contributo alla storia della beneficenza e alla storia economica di Roma*, 102.

25. Suzanna Åkerman, *Queen Christina of Sweden and Her Circle: The Transformation of a Seventeenth-Century Philosophical Libertine*, 178–93, esp. 193–195. My thanks to Verity Jamieson for this reference.

26. Carolyn H. Wood and Peter Iver Kaufman, "Tacito Predicatore: The Annunciation Chapel at the Madonna Dei Monti in Rome."

27. Renata Segre, "Il mondo ebraico nei cardinali della Controriforma," 127–29; Mazur, *Conversion to Catholicism in Early Modern Italy*, 31.

Written treatises helped to glorify the idea of Jewish conversion. The year 1582, when conversionary sermons first became widely popular, saw an explosion of related literature. Four close collaborators—three converts and one "cradle Catholic"—all prepared treatises that appeared in that year. De Monte's *Letter of Peace* was either composed or carefully copied in 1582, though never published.[28] Marcellino published his own sermons to the Jews in the same year. His fifteen sermons analyzed Psalm 109 (110 in Hebrew).[29] De Monte's colleague at the College of Neophytes, the Hebrew professor Marco Fabiano Fioghi, published *The Dialogue between the Catechumen and the Catechizing Father*. These treatises are closely linked. Fioghi's dialogue borrows liberally from De Monte's work and also contains a chapter dedicated to an analysis of psalm 109/110—a conversionary source far less common than other biblical passages, such as Isaiah 7 and 53.[30] Their close associate, the convert Hebraist and censor Gian Paolo Eustachio, contributed his own treatise on conversion, the *Salutary Discourses*, in 1582.[31] Together these works set the tone for a century of polemical conversionary literature. The letters of dedication that prefaced each treatise also showed off the far-reaching influence of powerful supporters. Both Fioghi and De Monte dedicated their treatises to Guglielmo Sirleto. De Monte also dedicated another work to Pope Pius V, lauding his efforts at converting Jews.[32] Marcellino's treatise thanked Santoro;

28. Fausto Parente, "Notes biographiques sur André de Monte." For De Monte's *Lettera della Pace, see* BAV Neofiti 37.

29. Evangelista Marcellino, *Sermoni quindici sopra il salmo centonove fatti a gli Hebrei di Roma*. For Marcellino, see Michelson, "Conversionary Preaching and the Jews in Early Modern Rome"; Emily Michelson, "Evangelista Marcellino: One Preacher, Two Audiences"; Miguel Gotor, *I beati del papa: Santità, inquisizione e obbedienza in età moderna*, 79–94; Angelico Piladi, *Il P. Evangelista Marcellino insigne predicatore ed ecclesiaste del secolo XVI.*

30. Fabiano Fioghi, *Dialogo fra il cathecumino et il padre cathechizante*. For Fioghi, see Fausto Parente, "Il confronto ideologico tra l'ebraismo e la Chiesa in Italia," 315–322; Renata Martano, "La missione inutile: la predicazione obbligatoria agli ebrei nella seconda meta del cinquecento"; Piet van Boxel, "Robert Bellarmine Reads Rashi: Rabbinic Bible Commentaries and the Burning of the Talmud."

31. Giovanni Paolo Eustachio, *Salutari discorsi composti da M. Giovan Paolo Eustachi Nolano. già hebbreo, hor christiano*. Eustachio became a professor of Hebrew in Rome, a censor of Hebrew books, and a specialist in Hebrew texts at the Vatican library—a position De Monte took away from him. Leber, "Jewish Convert in Counter-Reformation Rome," 82; Todd M. Endelman, *Leaving the Jewish Fold: Conversion and Radical Assimilation in Modern Jewish History*, 43–44; Franco Buzzi and Roberta Ferro, *Federico Borromeo fondatore della Biblioteca Ambrosiana: atti delle giornate di studio 25-27 novembre 2004*, 482–85.

32. This work is De Monte's unpublished *Confusion de giudei, e delle lor false opinioni*, BAV Vat. lat. 14627 (formerly Neofiti 38).

Eustachio's was dedicated to Gregory XIII. Conversionary treatises could use paratext to aim high.

These early instances of acclaim encouraged Gregory XII to promulgate a second papal bull on conversionary preaching with a firmer papal policy and more investment in the particulars. *Sancta Mater Ecclesia* (1584) confirmed the sermons as a fully established phenomenon, and in doing so, flouted canon law.[33] The bull specified in detail how sermons were to proceed and where: in every place where enough Jewish people lived to form a synagogue. Princes and rulers should support the endeavor. Sermons should take place weekly, again on Saturdays, in a space that was Christian but not consecrated. A third of the adult Jewish community should attend, both males and females over twelve. A specially trained preacher should draw his sermons from the Hebrew Bible and specifically review the same portions of texts that the listening Jews had heard that morning in synagogue. He should refute the opinions of the rabbis on those passages and replace them with interpretations related to fundamental Christian doctrines. Mindful of past concerns that mandatory sermons were too coercive, *Sancta Mater Ecclesia* included a note about rhetoric: although the sermons should keep a close focus on Jewish depravity and error, the preacher should nonetheless preach not with malice or wrath but instead with charity and restraint. As subsequent chapters will make clear, this injunction proved difficult both to define and to uphold.

Despite its immediate popularity, conversionary preaching in its early years remained subject to papal whim and experimentation, like much other sixteenth-century Jewish policy. Sixtus V's brief of October 22, 1586, *Christiana Pietas*, reduced sermons to three times a year. "In the rest of the time," the brief specified hopefully, "[the Jews] are not constrained, but can attend as they please even if not invited."[34] This ruling was consistent with Sixtus V's wider attitude toward Jews, relaxing many of the harsher policies of his predecessors, notably Paul IV. But this hiatus from weekly preaching proved relatively brief. Clement VIII's bull *Caeca et Obdurata Hebraeorum perfidia* of 1593 restored the stringencies of earlier popes, including sermons every Saturday. By the end of the century, conversionary preaching had proven its staying power. Having survived its experimental phase, it remained a regular, uninterrupted feature of early modern

33. Stow, *Theater of Acculturation*, 18, 42.

34. Moroni, *Dizionario di erudizione storico-ecclesiastica da S. Pietro sino ai nostri giorni*, 26; Arturo da Carmignano di Brenta, *San Lorenzo da Brindisi, dottore della chiesa universale (1559–1619)*, 1:281–82. For further discussions around this bull, see AAV Arm. LII 18, 47r.

Roman religious life. The conversionary pulpit was no longer open to all interested comers. In 1604, a Dominican, Stefano Sirleto, preached to the Jews and was noted in the *avvisi di Roma* (the international news-letters sent regularly from Rome) for his brilliance.[35] He was the first in an unbroken line; the official position of *predicatore degli ebrei* was then entrusted permanently to the Dominicans. Except for the occasional guest speaker, conversionary preaching remained with the Order of Preachers for as long as it continued.

The papal rulings applied outside Rome too. Preaching to Jews took place throughout the Italian peninsula, though perhaps less regularly and surely with less scrutiny. Published sermons and homilies to Jews note the city and often the church that hosted them. Girolamo Allé, Giulio Cesare Misuracchi, and Tommaso Bell'haver preached in Venice, Faustino Tasso in Naples, and Ignazio Landrini apparently in Milan.[36] Eliseus Pesenti, a Hebraist in Bergamo, apparently left a manuscript of a sermon to Jews in his Capuchin monastery.[37] Vitale Medici in Florence was among the most feted Jewish converts, touring the city's pulpits after his baptism. Paolo Sebastiano Medici incited waves of resentment around the Papal States for his violent preaching. Preaching continued with some regularity. As late as 1788, Salomon Moisé Cavaglieri requested an exemption from attending conversionary sermons in Ferrara because of his numerous commitments as a merchant.[38] But none of these places carried the burden of presenting itself as a beacon of devotion and the aspiring center of a world religion. None of them featured Jews so prominently as sites

35. Zucchi, "Il primo predicatore Domenicano degli Ebrei. Ancora sul P. Sirleto—Fr. Alessandro Franceschi." For an introduction to Roman Avvisi, see Mario Infelise, "Roman Avvisi: Information and Politics in the Seventeenth Century."

36. Girolamo Allè, *I convinti, e confusi hebrei: opera del M.R.P.M. Girolamo Alle bolognese, dell'ordine di S. Girolamo di fiesole, divisa in alcune prediche da lui predicate nell'antico, & gia patriarcal tempio di san Silvestro di venetia*; Giulio Cesare Misurachi, *Ragionamento della venuta del Messia contro la durezza & ostinatione hebraica. Fatta alla presenzo loro da me Giulio Cesare Misurachi*; Tommaso Bell'haver, *Dottrina facile et breve per redurre l'Hebreo al conoscimento del vero Messia*; Faustino Tasso, *Venti ragionamenti familiari sopra la venuta del Messia, del R.P. Faustino Tasso, minore osservante. Fatte in Napoli ad alcuni hebrei per comandamento de gl'Ill.mi e R.mi vicerè, e arcivescovo*; Ignazio Landrini, *Virginis partus eiusque filii Emmanuel diuinitatis et humanitatis scripturalis dissertatio, atque demonstratio aduersos hebraeos, & haereticos*. On many of these, see Parente, "Il confronto ideologico tra l'ebraismo e la Chiesa in Italia," 332–335.

37. Anscar Zawart, "The History of Franciscan Preaching and of Franciscan Preachers (1209–1927). A Bio-Bibliographical Study," 385.

38. ACDF St St BB 2 a, 18.

of spectacle for curious travelers. In Rome, conversionary sermons had a point to make about the city's piety.

Sources from the early years of conversionary preaching suggest that in Rome, conversionary preachers were meant to work in pairs: one, a Catholic theologian, and the other, a Jewish convert to Catholicism. De Monte and the Observant Franciscan Marcellino were the first exemplars, but there were others. As one observer boasted, "In the Oratory, every Saturday, the Jews are preached to, first by a monk, and then by a neophyte, refuting their superstitions and perfidies with the books of their same Jewish rabbis. . . . Very often many convert to the holy and apostolic Catholic faith; it is surely a very useful practice."[39] These partnerships were sometimes successful, but they were difficult to maintain. They are also difficult to reconstruct. We have an almost continuous list of Catholic-born preachers through the eighteenth century, but imperfect evidence of the neophyte preachers; they published less and did not hold an official title. Evidence of their involvement survives only in pieces. The surviving payment records for conversionary preachers list only one preacher at a time—a "cradle" Catholic.

To keep conversionary preaching afloat, the most powerful Catholic institutions in Rome had to commit together to its upkeep. Premier among these institutions was the Holy See, which promulgated papal bulls and official legislation. It retained the ultimate power to continue or suspend conversionary sermons as well as appoint preachers. Over time, the Holy Office of the Inquisition also became involved in Jewish affairs. After Gregory XIII's 1581 bull *Antiqua Judaeorum improbitas*, which enumerated the circumstances under which inquisitors could take steps against non-Christians, the Holy Office increasingly took over issues concerning Jews in Italy, particularly court cases.[40] It treated preachers to Jews as authorities in many cases involving conversion. The Vicariate of Rome had closer supervision over sermons and other matters. Its activities show better than any other institution how much commitment and organization went into maintaining conversionary sermons. The Office of the Cardinal Vicar managed local ecclesiastical affairs for the pope in his capacity as bishop of Rome. It had official responsibility for Rome's Jews, overseeing daily relations between Jews and Christians, policing

39. *Breve Ragguaglio del modo et ordini tenuti in ricevere li pellegrini ambi gli anni santi 1575 e 1600*, 63.
40. Kenneth Austin, *The Jews and the Reformation*, 116.

the ghetto, imposing and collecting fines, and similar activities. Its records survive in the Vicariate archive, as does a comprehensive manual by Niccolò Antonio Cuggiò, the priest who served as secretary to the Vicariate for the first forty years of the eighteenth century. The manual includes a detailed chapter on Jews that emphasizes the logistics of conversionary preaching.[41]

The Vicariate oversaw regular payment and security for conversionary sermons. Where necessary, it also managed disputes between preachers and Roman Jews. The post of predicatore degli ebrei became a full-time job, as one double-booked priest learned to his detriment.[42] Conversionary preachers earned fifty scudi per year for their efforts, delivered in two installments in July and December (figure 2.2).[43] This was a respectable sum, reflecting the prestige of the office, but not enough for a full professional salary; it suggests that a preacher would have had other sources of significant income as well. Fifty scudi was more than the head coachman of the Orsini family earned in the 1630s, but slightly less than its private chaplain; a popular painter could earn much more. The same amount paid the annual rent of the painter Guido Reni.[44]

The Office of the Vicariate chose the deputy too, usually a priest himself, who not only monitored behavior but also served as gatekeeper and liaison between the preacher, Vicariate, and Roman Jewish community, or università degli ebrei. The deputy was in charge of keeping the attendance roster and ensuring that Jews complied with sermon regulations. He was paid once a year as well—the smaller sum of twelve scudi; unlike a preacher, he did not have to prepare for his role (figure 2.2). But a deputy

---

41. Nicolò Antonio Cuggiò, *Della giurisdittione e prerogative del vicario di Roma*. For the distribution of governing bodies in early modern Rome, see Laurie Nussdorfer, *Civic Politics in the Rome of Urban VIII*.

42. Giovanni Crisostomo Viola di Ortonovo took on the position while also serving as parish priest of Santa Maria sopra Minerva. He resigned in less than a year. Alberto Zucchi, "Rome domenicana: note storiche: Predicatori Domenicani degli ebrei nel sec. XVIII," 119–20.

43. Cuggiò, *Della giurisdittione*, 365–67. ASVR Mandati della Segreteria del tribunale del vicariato, Registrum Mandatorum, 1706–35, lists regular payments to preachers every six months. Earlier volumes of these records are unavailable. The summary in ASVR Atti della segreteria del tribunale del cardinale vicario, tom. 5, 687r, also mentions a further tip of twenty scudi at Christmas; this is not recorded in payment lists.

44. Laurie Nussdorfer, in private correspondence; Richard E. Spear, *Painting for Profit: The Economic Lives of Seventeenth-Century Italian Painters*, 21–40. See also Renata Ago, *Gusto for Things: A History of Objects in Seventeenth-Century Rome*, xxxvii.

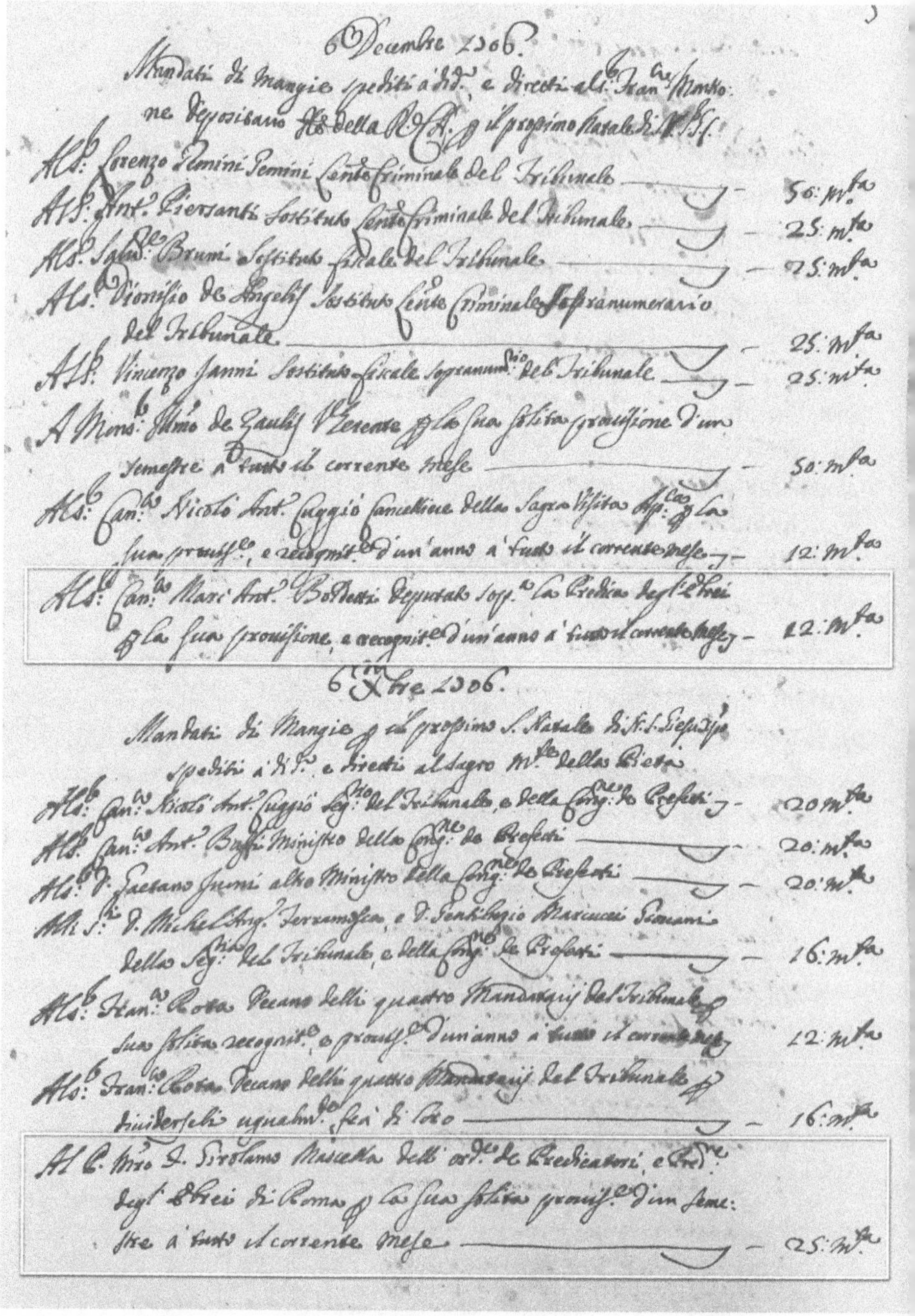

FIGURE 2.2. Eighteenth-century payments from the Vicariate to the deputy, Marcantonio Boldetti, and the preacher, Girolamo Mascella, 1706. Archivio Storico del Vicariato di Roma. Photo by Frank Lacopo.

could nonetheless be a person of rank; in the early eighteenth century the role fell to Marcantonio Boldetti, a noted Hebraist.[45]

The location of conversionary sermons in the oratory of Santissima Trinità dei Pellegrini bespeaks their prestige. The confraternity of Santissima Trinità dei Pellegrini embodied all the pious and charitable ambitions of early modern Rome. Founded in 1550 under the auspices of Neri and the Congregation of the Oratory, the confraternity's particular charge was to host the enormous waves of pilgrims that flooded Rome during Holy Years. The confraternity undertook to welcome, house, feed, preach to, catechize, and wash the feet of the faithful arriving from all over Europe and farther. The great and good of Rome rushed to take part, usually watched by gaping local onlookers. Located near the Ponte Sisto and about ten minutes away from the ghetto by foot, the confraternity grew into a huge and bustling complex. It boasted a large hall for devotional activities connected with Holy Years, a church, kitchens, dormitories, a cemetery for deceased members, and various outbuildings. For pilgrim visitors, Trinità dei Pellegrini became the public face of the city and the portal through which they encountered Rome. In addition to its work with pilgrims, Trinità dei Pellegrini took in convalescents from hospitals across the city, dowered unmarried girls, hosted the popular new forty-hour devotion, oversaw the nearby San Sisto hospice, distributed food and alms, and organized its own devotions and processions. These activities combined to make Trinità dei Pellegrini the city's largest and most successful new confraternity, and a symbol to both visitors and locals of Rome's bustling new pious energy.[46] Association with the confraternity of Trinità dei Pellegrini connected conversionary sermons with one of Rome's most prestigious religious organizations.

Trinità dei Pellegrini was chosen for conversionary sermons in part because of its general competence and suitability, but also because it had an oratory. Jewish bodies, even those supposedly on the brink of becoming Christian, presented a problem: they had been forbidden from entering

45. ASVR Mandati della Segreteria del tribunale del vicariato, Registrum Mandatorum, 1706–35, 7r, 6 Dic. 1706, notes payments to Boldetti as deputy and Girolamo Mascella as preacher; some of his writings as deputy are found in ASVR Atti della segreteria del tribunale del cardinale vicario, tom. 5. See also the entry on Boldetti in the DBI.

46. *Breve Ragguaglio*, 62–64; Fausto Garofalo, *L'ospedale della ss. Trinita' dei Pellegrini e dei Convalescenti*; Marco Borzacchini, "Il patrimonio della Trinità dei Pellegrini alla fine del cinquecento"; Carla Benocci, "Il complesso assistenziale della SS. Trinità dei Pellegrini: ricerche sullo sviluppo architettonico in relazione ad alcuni anni santi"; Luigi Fiorani, "Gli anni santi del cinque-seicento e la confraternità della SS Trinità dei Pellegrini"; O'Regan, *Institutional Patronage in Post-Tridentine Rome*; Luigi Fiorani, "Il carisma dell'ospitalità: la confraternita della Trinità dei Pellegrini nei giubilei cinque-secenteschi."

Christian churches in 1566, but for sermons they ought to be relocated to a Christian space, as *Sancta Mater Ecclesiae* had specified.[47] An oratory— consecrated, yet not a church—provided the answer. At Trinità dei Pellegrini, the oratory formed part of the overall church complex, but had its own entrance on Via delle Zoccolette. While the main facade of the church fronted a piazza, the Jews entered the oratory from the smaller back door near the Tiber. Santissima Trinità dei Pellegrini remained the location of record for conversionary sermons through the mid-eighteenth century. Piazza's *Eusevologio Romano* of 1699 still located the sermons in its oratory, and Cuggiò's eighteenth-century guide to the office of vicar of Rome confirms that "currently [the preaching] takes place in the oratory off the Santissima Trinità, as [the bull] says, and there is no other suitable space near the ghetto that is not a church."[48]

In entering the oratory, Jews found themselves in its most private devotional space: the inner sanctum of confraternal events. The oratory was the center of the confraternity's own private pious activities; this was not the cavernous hall—the ospizio—that hosted foreign pilgrims. In the oratory, the confraternity welcomed new members, prepared for processions, recited the office of the Virgin on festivals, and sang the seven psalms during Lent. This was also a primary place of instruction, with weekly half-hour gospel lessons to confreres and their families on Sundays and festivals.[49] Only at conversionary preaching did the oratory open up regularly to the public. Conversionary sermons placed Jewish people visibly at the heart of early modern religious Catholic innovation, piety, and devotion.

Occasionally a sermon was held in some other church. In 1592, Jews were forcibly packed into San Lorenzo in Damaso, the church located within the official residence of the vice chancellor of the Apostolic Chancery—a powerful lifetime appointment for a series of prominent cardinals. The event was notable enough to appear in the avvisi di Roma newsletters, The Jews were sent there to hear a Capuchin preacher—the

---

47. After 1566, Jews were most often found in churches only for conversionary motivations such as attendance at baptisms or forced sermons. For an extended review of this legislation, see Blum, "Vasari on the Jews," 562–65.

48. Cuggiò, *Della giurisdittione*, 1, 357.

49. On entering the oratory, confreres were meant to go to the altar and not rise from it until they heard the ringing of the confraternity general's bell. *Costituzioni della venerabile arciconfraternità della santissima trinità de pelegrini & convalescenti, novamente riformati e stampati*, 72; *Costituzioni della venerabile arciconfraternità della santissima trinità de pelegrini & Convalescenti, accresciuti e riformati*, 101–2.

avvisi noted that there were five hundred Jewish listeners but not even one conversion.[50] Anomalous stories like this one reinforce the links between conversionary preaching, power players in Rome, sainthood, and spectacle, and emphasized the scripted nature of Jewish participation.

Only in the mid-eighteenth century did conversionary sermons move closer to the ghetto and become more private. Outside the sacred landscape of public Catholic devotion, consideration of factors that might encourage conversions took priority for the first time. Shortly after Cuggiò's death in 1739, a letter from the era of Benedict XIV (1740–58) requested that sermons be transferred from the oratory to the church of Santa Maria del Pianto, which stood in Piazza Giudea abutting the ghetto. The letter suggested that Jews were reluctant to let their young children leave the ghetto, and sent only representatives aged twenty or over to the conversionary sermons. Conversion rates for these adults were unpromising, argued the author; a closer location might allow younger children to attend and bring the preacher better luck.[51] When Leo XII later revived conversionary sermons in 1823, after Napoleon, they were moved to the church of Saint Angelo in Pescheria, also close on the edges of the ghetto. The nearby church of San Gregorio della Divina Pietà, which currently bears a plaque commemorating conversionary sermons, never hosted them.

Prestige and Networks

As preaching to Jews became more firmly established and ever more credible within ecclesiastical circles, its preachers both gained esteem and lent it to other initiatives. As individuals, in small groups, and through institutions, conversionary preachers became valuable promoters of the broader campaign to convert Jews, and enjoyed authority in religious contexts across Rome, conversionary and otherwise.

As individuals, preachers were valuable consultants. The Holy Office often called on the expertise of conversionary preachers when it had to deal with Jews, such as in cases of contested Jewish marriage, heretical content in Jewish books and correspondence, or issues of ghetto and enclosure.[52] In many of these cases, the preachers' title provided their

---

50. BAV Urb. lat. 1060, pt. 2, 391r. See also Alberto Zucchi, "Roma domenicana: note storiche: Predicatori domenicani degli ebrei nel sec. XVIII," 126–27.

51. Zucchi, "Ragioni della predicazione agli ebrei," 258–59.

52. This is the main body for cases of contested baptism, as analyzed in Marina Caffiero, *Battesimi forzati: Storie di ebrei, cristiani e convertiti nella Roma dei papi*.

qualification. A judgment might be signed, "Luigi Pisani, Predicatore degli ebrei."[53]

For converts from Judaism, if they were learned and illustrious, delivering a sermon to Jews could launch a new career in Christianity as an exemplar of conversion. Vitale Medici, converted during a Lenten cycle in Florence, became a cause célèbre among Christians and a zealous evangelist among Jews. He was, by all standards, a catch for the church. Jehiel da Pesaro had been invited to Florence from Pesaro to be the community's doctor and rabbi, and then served for an unusually long time—three continuous years—as its governor. His conversion followed a series of conflicts within the community's leadership. In the spring following his baptism, Medici made a splash as a converted preacher, embarking on a sort of victory tour of Florentine pulpits.[54] A novel and celebrated item, he preached to confraternities on a variety of pious subjects over the next two years: diabolical temptation, the nativity of the Madonna, the last supper, the conversion of Saint Paul, and the prodigal son. He also delivered two longer, more formal sermons to Jews, with whom, predictably, his relations became increasingly hostile.[55]

The resulting publication, *Homilies to the Jews of Florence in the Church of Santa Croce*, makes these two sermons its main draw, omitting from its title any mention that the book contains mostly sermons to Christians.[56] The sermons to Jews emphasize civic pride in their delivery; the volume stresses that both sermons were given "in the magnificent city of Fiorenza" within one of its most important churches. The volume, including his two Latin orations of conversion, presents Medici as a model neophyte who could bring further conversions. Local chroniclers reinforced

53. See, for example, ACDF Doctrinalia S.O. e voti Doctrinalia 1711–13, 1; ACDF St St UV 53.

54. Medici's conversion took place in March. The Florentine date changed on March 25, not January 1; thus Marcellino's third Lenten cycle in Florence, noted as 1582 in the diaries, would have been 1583 in the Gregorian calendar, and Medici's sermons noted as May 1583 would have taken place only two months after his conversion.

55. Segre, in "Il mondo ebraico nei cardinali della Controriforma," 131n42, describes an incident where Florentine Jews attacked and gravely injured Medici as he exited the church of San Benedetto after giving the sermon on Holy Thursday.

56. Vitale Medici, *Omelie fatte alli ebrei di Firenze nella Chiesa di Santa Croce, et sermoni fatti in più compagnie della detta città*. They appear to be the only sermons published by a Jewish convert to Christianity in the sixteenth century. On Medici, see Shulamit Furstenberg-Levi, "The Book of Homilies of the Convert to Catholicism Vitale Medici: Two Models of Identity"; Shulamit Furstenberg-Levi, "The Sermons of a Rabbi Converted to Christianity: Between Synagogue and Church."

that conceit, noting that Medici's sermons had converted two listeners, and that "their goal was to lead Jews to baptism."[57]

As a new Christian bearing the name of his illustrious Florentine sponsor, and a doctor with access to a larger, wealthier clientele, Jehiel da Pesaro thrived in his new life as Vitale Medici. His family, as noted earlier, became famous patrons and donors in Florentine churches.[58] But as in Rome, it was the local Christians who gained the most. This conversion gave them reason to congratulate themselves for their piety. His case shows how conversionary activity benefited convert makers cyclically: preachers needed success stories among their listeners, converts needed to prove their new loyalties by proselytizing to the faith they had left, and successful public sermons to Jews by their former brethren reflected and ennobled the local Christian environment.

The neophyte who reproduces the rhetoric that had persuaded him was a conversionary trope in this period. Fabiano Fioghi, who taught Hebrew at the College of Neophytes in Rome, chose a dialogue form in his conversionary treatise specifically because it was the disputes he had undertaken many years earlier with a Lenten preacher, Paolo da Norcia, that had ultimately converted him: "Because I arrived at the knowledge of the truth through a disputation, thus they [his Jewish readers] will have the opportunity to know the path of salvation through this Dialogue made almost like a disputation."[59] Fioghi's treatise was published only a year before Medici's conversion. Converts also needed a sponsor and role model, and so created a sort of conversionary lineage. A conversionary preacher could endorse and guarantee the conversion of others. His approval implied the purity of the conversion, and its intellectual and theological underpinnings. Even when the preacher could not take direct credit for a conversion, his insertion into the lineage gave weight and merit to the conversion, even through the mid-eighteenth century. We saw in the previous chapter how Giovanni Domenico Nazzareno thanked the conversionary preacher Giuseppe Ciantes for his personal help. Conversionary preachers formed part of the ongoing chain of converts and

57. Settimanni, *Diario*, ASF Manoscritti 129, 199v; Agostino Lapini, *Diario Fiorentino dal 252 al 1596*, 222. Both of these authors suggest that Medici's sermons would find more success among Jews from outside Florence.

58. Stefanie Siegmund, *The Medici State and the Ghetto of Florence: The Construction of an Early Modern Jewish Community*, 279–80, 397–98; Shulamit Furstenberg-Levi, "The Boundaries between 'Jewish' and 'Catholic' Space in Counter-Reformation Florence as Seen by the Convert Vitale Medici."

59. Fioghi, *Dialogo fra il cathecumino et il padre cathechizante*, 3 v.

sponsors, and contributed to broader networks that supported conversionary institutions.

Preachers also sought to encourage broader conversionary endeavors toward Roman Jews. In these efforts, they collaborated with each other and with other converts in small groups. During his preaching career and after, De Monte worked on conversionary measures together with Fioghi and Giovanni Paolo Eustachio. De Monte and Fioghi helped to organize the Talmud burning of 1553.[60] Fioghi and Eustachio also served on a papal committee to create a collection of scriptural conversionary passages intended to appeal to both Catholics and Jews during conversionary preaching.[61] Their three conversionary treatises of 1582 all drew heavily on each other, and the three men owned copies of each other's works. Although such partnerships could contain as much competition as collaboration, they were all directed toward the shared mission of converting Roman Jews and creating favorable conditions for life as a new Christian.[62]

These small networks upheld the efforts two of the major institutions of religious conversion in Rome: the House of Catechumens and College of Neophytes. In contrast, although Jewish women attended conversionary sermons, female catechumens and neophytes seem never to have left the "Nunziatella" convent to return to sermons.[63] Because the members of the College of Neophytes were training to become preachers themselves, they spent much of their day studying Hebrew and rabbinic sources for this purpose. In the early decades of the college, De Monte served as its overseer and Fioghi as its Hebrew professor. Fioghi taught students how to use Hebrew sources in their sermons as De Monte did in his. His students would have heard De Monte preach to the Jews; for at least the first fifty years of the college's existence, neophytes living in the college returned to

60. Fausto Parente, "Les raisons et justifications de la conversion des Juifs," 27; Fausto Parente, "La Chiesa e il 'Talmud': L'atteggiamento della Chiesa e del mondo cristiano nei confronti del 'Talmud' e degli altri scritti rabbinici, con particolare riguardo all'Italia tra XV e XVI secolo," 584–85. See also Kenneth R. Stow, "The Burning of the Talmud in 1553, in the Light of Sixteenth-Century Catholic Attitudes toward the Talmud," 17–18. Filippo Herrera, mentioned above, also contributed.

61. Piet van Boxel, "Cardinal Santoro and the Expurgation of Hebrew Literature"; van Boxel, "Robert Bellarmine Reads Rashi"; van Boxel, *Jewish Books in Christian Hands*, 57–69.

62. Especially for competition among these scholars, see Leber, "Jewish Convert in Counter-Reformation Rome," 79–83. See also Gian Ludovico Masetti Zannini, "La Biblioteca di Andrea Del Monte (Josef Sarfath) e altre librerie di ebrei nel Cinquecento romano."

63. Alessia Lirosi, "Monacare le ebree. Il monastero romano della Ss. Annunziata ai Pantani. Una ricerca in corso."

Trinità dei Pellegrini to observe conversionary preachers show them how the job was done.

Preachers also played a crucial role at the casa. Newly arrived Jews had forty days to "explore their will," as the technical phrase went. If at the end of that period they had not chosen baptism, they could return home. During this initial period, the casa exerted all possible pressure on the undecided. This included regular visits from conversionary preachers, who brought all of their rhetorical skills to bear on their one-person audience. The well-known memoir of one near-convert in the eighteenth century, Anna Del Monte, describes the period she spent in the House of Catechumens resisting attempts to catechize her. Over the course of two weeks, the conversionary preacher came to exhort her on five separate occasions (as did thirty-seven other people).[64]

Over the seventeenth century, the authority of conversionary preachers spread beyond the close-knit world of Jewish converts and the institutions that supported them. Wherever Hebrew mattered, their word and influence counted. When Sapienza University in Rome recruited a chair of Hebrew language in 1696, the search committee required its candidates to be able to read and write Hebrew in both block and script alphabets as well as Latin, Arabic, and Aramaic, and also show familiarity with rabbinic and Talmudic literature, a command of Hebrew grammar, and a wide knowledge of Hebrew and Latin literature. At the interview, candidates might be asked to read and explain a page of the Bible chosen at random, parse three Hebrew verbs, or analyze Hebrew vowels. This was intellectually demanding work. A successful search needed an impeccably learned hiring committee, which in this case included Girolamo Mascella, newly appointed preacher to the Jews of Rome.[65]

The scholarly world in Rome, in full intellectual flower in the seventeenth century, had taken a distinctly conversionary turn, thereby raising the profile and opportunities for Hebrew scholars.[66] Libraries, universi-

---

64. Stow, *Anna and Tranquillo*; Mazur, *Conversion to Catholicism in Early Modern Italy*; Micaela Procaccia, "'Bona Voglia' e 'Modica Coactio': Conversioni di ebrei a Roma nel secolo XVI"; Domenico Rocciolo, "Ebrei catecumeni alla Madonna ai Monti nel Settecento"; Marina Caffiero, "'La caccia agli ebrei': Inquisizione, casa dei catecumeni e battesimi forzati nella Roma moderna."

65. For his qualifications, see BAV Borg. lat. 476, 20r. For the committee, see BAV Borg. lat. 476, 244r–v. For his appointment as preacher, see Zucchi, "Roma domenicana," 121. Mascella's largely illegible sermons are held in BAV Borg. lat. 778.

66. This was a period of enormous fruitfulness, as described vividly in Ingrid D. Rowland, *Giordano Bruno, Philosopher/Heretic*; Irene Fosi, "Usare la biblioteca: la Vaticana nella cultura europea."

ties, and many religious congregations kept a Hebraist on staff. Unlike the Christian Hebraism of the early Renaissance two centuries earlier, the Christian study of Hebrew, taking place in many kinds of scholarly institutions, was more closely linked to conversion, and took on a much stronger polemical and conversionary angle. The remit of the College of Neophytes made it a center of Hebrew language teaching, furnishing Hebraists for other institutions in Rome. Future missionaries honed their polemical and linguistic skills at the college, as did future Hebrew scholars at many Catholic institutions, such as the Vatican library, Sapienza University, or Congregation of Propaganda Fide. Training as a conversionary preacher thus improved scholars' employment prospects across Rome more generally. Those alumni who remained preachers found themselves well connected to Hebraists in other institutions.

One friendship group of three Hebraist scholars captures the world of elite Hebrew scholarship in seventeenth-century Rome and its conversionary leanings. The Cistercian Giulio Bartolocci (1613–87) remains the best known of these figures. A student of the convert and esteemed Hebrew professor Giovanni Battista Jona, Bartolocci compiled the first great bibliography of Hebrew and Jewish postrabbinic literature. At four volumes of close to a thousand pages each, Bartolocci's *Bibliotheca Magna Rabbinica* is feasibly the most important piece of Hebrew or Judaic scholarship produced in the early modern period.[67] The second, Giovanni Pastrizio (Ivan Paštrić, 1636–1708), ultimately became a professor of Hebrew as well as polemical theology and superintendent of the printing press at the Congregation of Propaganda Fide, which trained young men for global missions. Born in Croatia, Pastrizio trained at the College of Neophytes in Rome.[68] The third, Gregorio Boncompagni Corcos degli Scarinci, served as the preacher to the Jews of longest standing: thirty-nine years. He was both a Dominican and the descendant of the famous Corcos family that had converted from Judaism in the sixteenth century.

These three men shared close connections, and their friendship shows how highly Roman intellectual circles esteemed conversionary preachers. Bartolocci corresponded with Boncompagni, sending him Hebrew commentaries to review.[69] Boncompagni, in turn, relied on Bartolocci's scholarship in preparing his own works. Bartolocci's name appears throughout the margins of Boncompagni's sermon manuscripts, providing support

---

67. Bartolocci, *Bibliotheca Magna Rabbinica*. Vols. 4 and 5 (an index) were completed by Carlo Imbonati after Bartolocci's death.

68. Tomislav Mrkonjić, *Il Teologo Ivan Paštrić (Giovanni Pastrizio) (1636–1708): Vita-Opere-Concezione della Teologia-Cristologia.*

69. See BAV Borg. lat. 129, 11.

for his conversionary arguments ("See Bartolocci," sometimes with page numbers).[70] Pastrizio supplied an official but nonetheless enthusiastic imprimatur to the *Bibliotheca Magna Rabbinica* in his professorial roles at the Propaganda Fide, attesting at some length to the doctrinal orthodoxy and merit of the work. So did Boncompagni; his imprimatur as preacher to the Jews appeared repeatedly next to Pastrizio's.[71] And when Boncompagni died, his enormous corpus of papers and sermons did not stay in the Dominican convent where he lived—despite his prominence there—but instead went en masse to Pastrizio at the College of Propaganda Fide, before eventually landing in the Vatican library.

The academic and missionary activities of these three men touched scholarly institutions across Rome. As scriptor of Hebrew at the Vatican library, Bartolocci held the most illustrious post in Rome available to a Hebrew scholar, at the city's most important scholarly hub. The Vatican library had consistently kept a Hebraist on staff from the mid-sixteenth century. When the library was founded, in the fifteenth century, it collected Greek, Latin, and Hebrew manuscripts, and its Hebrew collections reflected relatively pacific Renaissance traditions of Christian Hebraism. Hebrew language and studies were an absolutely essential aspect of the great flourishing of intellectual culture in seventeenth-century Rome. But in that period, the post of scriptor of Hebrew also sometimes became a kind of bully pulpit for conversionary polemic.[72] The job of Vatican library Hebraist often went to an elite, learned convert from Judaism; in the sixteenth century, De Monte, Eustachio, and Franceschi all held the position.[73] In the seventeenth century, the scriptor and convert Giulio Morosini produced a well-known and much-requested conversionary polemic, *The Path of Faith* (figure 2.3). Its title page proudly presents his status at the Vatican library and the College of Propaganda Fide as a guarantee of the book's usefulness as a conversionary tool.[74]

70. See BAV Borg. lat. 129, 170v, 393v.

71. In the first three volumes; Boncompagni and Bartolocci both died before volume 4 was published.

72. On the Vatican library, Rome's seventeenth-century intellectual life, and the importance of Hebrew studies, see Fosi, "Usare la biblioteca," esp. 788.

73. Simonsohn, "Some Well-Known Jewish Converts during the Renaissance," 30–33; Mazur, *Conversion to Catholicism in Early Modern Italy*, 68–69.

74. Giulio Morosini, *Via della fede mostrata à gli ebrei . . . Opera non men curiosa che util principalmente per chi conversa o tratta con gli'ebrei, o predica loro.* On Morosini, see Michaela Andreatta, "The Persuasive Path: Giulio Morosini's Derekh Emunah as a Conversion Narrative"; Benjamin Ravid, " 'Contra Judaeos' in Seventeenth-Century Italy: Two Responses to the 'Discorso' of Simone Luzzatto by Melchiore Palontrotti and Giulio Morosini," 328–49; Fosi, "Usare la biblioteca," 788–89.

דרך אמונה

VIA DELLA FEDE

MOSTRATA A'GLI EBREI

DA

GIVLIO MOROSINI VENETIANO

Scrittor della Biblioteca Vaticana nella Lingua Ebraica, e Lettor
della medesima nel Collegio de Propaganda Fide.

DIVISA IN TRE PARTI.

*Nella Prima si pruoua, che non deuono osseruare la_*
Legge Mosaica, mà quella di Christo, i di cui misterij
si stabiliscono.

Nella Seconda si mostrano tutte le cerimonie, e riti loro
dal nascer sin al morire, per tutto il Calendario, e per
quel tutto che pretendono d'osseruare, e si fà veder che
son piene di superstitione, e di trasgressione.

Nella Terza si palesa, che nè meno osseruano i precetti
del Decalogo.

Opera non men curiosa, che vtile, principalmente per
chi conuersa, ò tratta con gli Ebrei, ò predica loro.

In ROMA nell'Anno M D C L X X X I I I.
Nella Stamparia della Sacra Cong. de Prop. Fide.

Con licenza de' Superiori.

FIGURE 2.3. Title page of Giulio Morosini's *Via della fede mostrata a'gli ebrei*, 1683.
General Collection, Beinecke Rare Book and Manuscript Library, Yale University.

Pastrizio's own career at the Congregation of Propaganda Fide gives an equally clear sense of the importance of Hebrew to the project of global missions. The Propaganda Fide taught Hebrew because it was necessary for Bible and theology students, including future missionaries. As professor of Hebrew, Pastrizio bought and sold Hebrew books, including many conversionary treatises, and collaborated with their authors. Pastrizio also ran the congregation's print office, where missionaries requested the necessary books for their missions.[75] The congregation's print office earned praise from contemporaries for having the equipment to deal with many diverse regions the world and supply catechisms in any language.[76]

Even though the Propaganda Fide did not directly seek the conversion of Jews, it was deeply involved in matters Jewish or Hebrew. Pastrizio spent much of his life drafting manuals on the teaching of Hebrew grammar, and his expertise as a Hebraist often proved broadly useful. When the chief rabbi of Rome published treatises seeking to win Jewish concessions from Catholic authorities, it fell to Pastrizio to check and approve his use of rabbinical sources, and his approval provided the rabbi with much-needed validation.[77] Morosini's introduction to *The Path of Faith* directly links Hebrew scholarship with global conversion. He thanks Pastrizio by name for allowing him to purchase so many Hebrew books for the Propaganda Fide and setting such a good example as a pious polyglot.[78]

The records of Pastrizio's print office also show that the Propaganda Fide regularly filled requests from scholars and alumni for Hebrew books. A 1656 graduate called Cristoforo Hans, for instance, asked specifically for Jona's Hebrew translation of the Gospels along with his translation of Robert Bellarmine's *Christian Doctrine* as well as a set of devotional books

75. For documents relating to Pastrizio's correspondence and his work at the print office, see ASPF Misc. Gen. XII; ASPF Misc. Gen. XIII; ASPF SC Stamperia I. This includes documentation relating to Morosini and Bartolocci.

76. Carlo Bartolomeo Piazza, *Eusevologio Romano overo Delle Opere Pie di Roma*, treatise 13, ch. 16, 134–37. See also Giovanni Pizzorusso, "I satelliti di Propaganda Fide: il Collegio Urbano e la Tipografia poliglotta. Note di ricerca su due istituzioni culturali romane nel XVII secolo." On the Propaganda Fide's printing equipment, see Celeste McNamara, *The Bishop's Burden: Reforming the Catholic Church in Early Modern Italy*, 231–39.

77. Pastrizio's imprimatur appears on two treatises collectd in ASVR Atti della segreteria del tribunale del cardinale vicario, tom. 5. It reads, "Le autorità Rabbiniche allegate dal detto Rabbino Tranquillo Corcos Hebreo in questa Scrittura ho confrontato con le parole Ebriache delli medesimi Autori, & ho veduto esser conformi. Di Propaganda Fide questo di' primo Marzo 1698. Giovanni Pastritio Lettore di Teologia in Propaganda mano propria." Such treatises are discussed at length in chapter 5. On the value of Pastrizio's imprimatur for that author, see Teter, *Blood Libel*, 287.

78. Morosini, *Via della Fede mostrata à gli ebrei*, 1v–2r.

and catechisms.[79] Bartolocci's *Bibliotheca Magna Rabbinica,* Morosini's *The Path of Faith,* and Jona's Hebrew Gospel appeared regularly on the office's book distribution lists. The presence of Hebrew at the Propaganda Fide exemplified the idea that the conversion of the Jews, the church's first interlocutor, provided the microcosm for the macromission: the Catholicization of the wider world.

At this most elite level of Hebrew scholarship, a man who held the post of predicatore degli ebrei would fit right in and earn high praise from his most learned contemporaries. Boncompagni proved a case in point. His friend and colleague Bartolocci dedicated a section of volume 3 of the *Bibliotheca Magna Rabbinica* to a discussion of Hebrew scholarship in Rome, including conversionary preaching. Bartolocci devoted a long column to praising Boncompagni, calling him "very expert and practiced in Jewish and Rabbinic matters," "with the greatest fruit for the souls who are being converted from Judaism." Boncompagni's knowledge of Jewish sources was so great, said Bartolocci, that his listeners could pull no objections from the Talmud to which he could not respond; as he noted, "When the lion roars, who is not afraid?" Crucially, Bartolocci reminds his readers that these sermons benefit Catholics as well as heterodox listeners. Likewise, as he turns to a discussion of conversionary polemicists, Bartolocci immediately singles out Pastrizio as the most proficient of them all in the Hebrew language. Pastrizio had in fact been Bartolocci's student. Throughout the volume, Bartolocci continues to praise both men, again stating that Pastrizio excelled in disputes against Jews in his capacity as professor of polemic. All of this praise appears in a section that highlights the prominence of Hebrew studies in Rome and in which Bartolocci lists the various monasteries and congregations that most excel.[80] The phrases in the *Bibliotheca Magna Rabbinica* also suggest real affection among three men, close personal links, and high intellectual standards.

The firm establishment of Hebrew scholarship in Roman institutions, the steady publication of tracts by, for, and about converts, and indeed the weekly ritual of the sermons themselves all had a collective effect on policy. These works shared the belief that Hebrew sources mattered. They respected the Hebrew language and assumed that Hebrew books contained valuable lessons about Christian doctrine. As later chapters will demonstrate, sermons focused primarily on theological issues, such as the nature of the Trinity and incarnation, and the litmus question of whether Jesus was in fact the Messiah. This approach differed from that of literature on Judaism prevalent elsewhere in Europe, such as in Germany and Poland. There, from the late Middle Ages onward, publications and polemics concentrated primarily on Jewish ritual and customs, generating a set of ethnographic texts known as *minhag* literature. In Italy, respect for Jewish texts did not extend to Jewish bodies, but the intellectual focus seems to have protected Jewish communities as a whole from the absolute worst of the European blood libels and other false accusations.[81] Both preachers and their Jewish audiences thus had an interest in keeping Hebrew scholarship at the center of the weekly sermons.

When Pastrizio asked Mascella to be on the search committee for that chair of Hebrew—for it was Pastrizio who organized the competition— it spoke well of the status of conversionary preachers in Rome. It meant that Mascella was considered fit to evaluate the most illustrious Hebrew scholars of the day. Another conversionary preacher, this time from France (presumably Avignon, under papal jurisdiction), also applied for the position. One of his fellow candidates was Carlo Imbonati, who would go on to complete Bartolocci's *Bibliotheca Magna Rabbinica*. A third candidate, Boldetti, would later become Mascella's deputy at conversionary sermons.[82] Scholarly circles in Rome were wider, denser, and more reliant on Hebrew than ever, rooting conversionary sermons ever more firmly at their center.

Regulating the Jewish Audience

The growing general popularity of Hebrew language study among Rome's intellectuals returned attention to conversionary sermons, where Hebrew texts were discussed publicly and skillfully. The treatment of actual Jews at conversionary sermons contrasted starkly with the esteem given to their language and scholarship elsewhere in Rome. It was imperative that Jews not only show up at conversionary sermons but also ensure that their demeanor conform to Catholic expectations. The role and behavior of Jews at conversionary sermons was thus tightly scripted through the close legislation of minute details. Sermons took place on Saturday afternoons at "twenty-two hours," which was after lunch, and they lasted about an

81. Teter, *Blood Libel*, 173–91. On ethnographic literature, see Yaakov Deutch, *Judaism in Christian Eyes: Ethnographic Descriptions of Jews and Judaism in Early Modern Europe*. For convert ethnographies in particular, see Elisheva Carlebach, *Divided Souls: Converts from Judaism in Germany, 1500–1750*, 178–99.

82. BAV Borg. lat. 746, fol. 244.

hour.[83] This timing was strategic. Because Saturday was the Sabbath, Jewish businesses would be closed, leaving their proprietors with no excuses to miss the sermons. Moreover, the Torah portion that would have been read that morning in synagogue would still be fresh in the listeners' minds when they heard it refuted in the afternoon. Finally, it was a deliberate insult to Rome's Jews to be forced to lose their one afternoon of repose to a taxing and unwelcome ordeal. The Sabbath was the high point of the week, a holy day typically spent close to home, engaged in prayer, family time, and Torah study. A command to leave the ghetto for a hostile sermon made a mockery of the biblical mandate to delight in the Sabbath and rejoice in it.

The second papal bull, *Sancta Mater Ecclesia* of 1584, as we have seen, required all Jews over the age of twelve, male or female, to attend conversionary sermons—one-third of the community, or università, at a time in rotation. In fact, this percentage was never more than an aspiration. Montaigne reported seeing sixty Jews in 1581. When Clement VIII reestablished regular preaching, he set the number at 200 men and 100 women.[84] By the end of the century the number of women required had been reduced to 50, and the overall number appears to have stayed somewhere between 250 and 300. While the original bull applied to all Jews from the age of twelve, by the end of the seventeenth century the de facto minimum age was eighteen, even though Bartolocci's contemporaneous and precise descriptions of conversionary sermons continued to insist otherwise.

How were these minimum numbers to be met? An edict preserved in the archives of the vicar's office set out in meticulous detail the procedure for the attendance roster.[85] Promulgated on September 25, 1596, when Clement VIII restored weekly sermons, it ordered that a rotation begin the following Saturday, October 5.[86] The edict required the fattori of the università to list the first and last names of all the Jews in Rome over the age of twelve, male or female, and submit the list to the Vicariate within six days. The list was to be divided into three groups. The fattori were to send the first of the three groups to the sermon on October 5, with the second group on October 12 and the third on October 19. The edict continued to spell out the pattern explicitly through November, reminding

83. ASVR Atti della segreteria del tribunale del cardinale vicario, tom. 5, 687r.
84. Montaigne, *Montaigne's Travel Journal*, 956; Attilio Milano, *Il ghetto di Roma; illustrazioni storiche*, 269.
85. ASVR Editta vicarii Urbis, Editti e Bandi 1566–1609, 14r–v.
86. The papal edict from 1593, the year sermons restarted, lays out a less detailed and presumably less successful roster. AAV Misc. Arm. VII, 346r. See also Carmignano di Brenta, *San Lorenzo da Brindisi, Dottore della Chiesa Universale (1559–1619)*, 4:108.

the fattori that the rotation must always start over from the beginning and that nobody could attend the sermon if it was not their turn. Failure to produce the list in time earned a fine of two hundred scudi—four times the annual compensation of the conversionary preacher—with other penalties reserved to the cardinal vicar at will.

In its particulars, the edict gives the impression that for the first two decades of conversionary preaching, nobody had needed or bothered to sort out how to meet the bull's requirements. And in fact, almost all surviving edicts about preaching attendance postdate this one. Clement VIII's rees-tablishment of conversionary preaching meant it was time to get serious about these sermons. They were here to stay. Regarding attendance, young, unmarried women, especially vulnerable to the stares or leers of onlookers, clearly posed a special concern.[87] A 1606 edict insisted that the attendance rules applied "to all women in turn, of every age."[88] But a later seventeenth-century deputy confirmed that in thirty-five years of experience, he had seen only married women attend sermons and no young girls.[89]

Most edicts sought to enforce attendance through fines, imposing a substantial penalty, usually twenty-five gold ducats, on the fattori of the community for every sermon that failed to meet the overall quota. Accord-ing to the edicts, individual truants also paid one scudo each for their vio-lation. Even the people whom the truants sent as their substitutes—and who therefore attended more sermons than was required of them—had to pay a small fine for violating the rules. In practice, at least according to one deputy, the actual penalty for skipping a sermon could be as low as five giulii, and even this was enforced only according to the offender's means.[90] The wearying repetition of edicts about attendance, promulgated at least a dozen times, suggests that truancy remained a perpetual problem.[91]

The various ghetto era synagogues of Rome undertook the rotation in pairs: the Castilian and Catalan, Nova and Siciliana, and Tempio and

87. Milano, *Il ghetto di Roma*, 273.

88. AAV Misc. Arm VII, 58, 327r.

89. ASVR Atti della segreteria del tribunale del cardinale vicario, tom. 55, 687r. Bartolocci's description from 1683 of conversionary preaching reelaborates the statues of *Sancta Mater Ecclesia* as if they were fully enforced. Bartolocci, *Bibliotheca Magna Rabbinica*, 3:749.

90. Compilations of the terms of these edicts are found in ASVR Editta Vicarii Urbis, Editti e Bandi 1566–1609, 13r–15r; ASVR Atti della segreteria del tribunale del cardinale vicario, tom. 55, 684r–687r.

91. Edits were issued in 1588, 1593, 1600, 1602, 1605, 1606, 1607, 1643, 1652, 1704, 1706, and 1740.

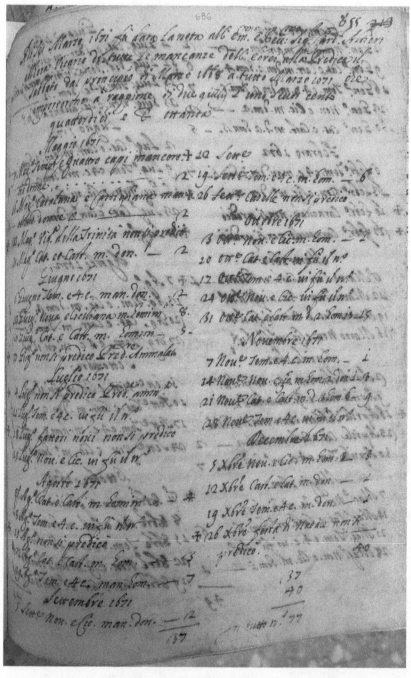

FIGURE 2.4. Tally of conversionary sermons, rosters, and absences, 1671.
Archivio Storico del Vicariato di Roma. Photo by Frank Lacopo.

Quattro Capi.[92] The office of the Vicariate kept a weekly record that included these turns, the number and gender of the absent, and cancellations (figure 2.4). Up to fifteen people missed their turn weekly, but usually no more than six or seven. The total number of absences was tallied every few months and at the end of the year in order to calculate the fines due; these could add up to hundreds of scudi.[93]

The expectation of trouble led to the frequent cancellation of sermons. Sermons were suspended regularly for Jewish festivals, Catholic festivals, and other important dates on either the Hebrew or Catholic calendar on the well-tested assumption that heightened emotions around these events would spark violence. The dates included Easter Saturday, when Jews were confined to the ghetto with their doors and windows tightly closed; Christmas or Christmas Eve when these fell on Saturdays; the day before Trinity Sunday; and the commemoration of the dead or any other time when the Oratory was taken over for special ceremonies. As a rule, Jewish people were prohibited from watching Christian festivals or processions in which they did not participate, especially if the event included a display of the Eucharist. Hence a 1629 edict requiring Jewish households that overlooked the churches of San Angelo in Pescheria and Santa Maria del Pianto, on the edges of the ghetto, to shutter their blinds and close their front doors for the entire length of the procession of the Blessed Sacrament.[94] Jewish proximity to the host was considered controversial and dangerous; shutting off physical contact only echoed and confirmed assumptions of the Jewish rejection of Christ.[95]

At other times, sermons were canceled to protect not hosts but Jews. A veneer of tension lay over the enterprise of preaching; authorities stayed alert for violence. The Jewish festivals of Hanukkah, Purim, Passover, and Shavuot along with the fast of 9 Av and autumn High Holidays all precluded a sermon on the closest Saturday. So did the installation of

92. Before the establishment of the ghetto, Rome had housed nine or ten synagogues for communities of different origin: French Sephardi, Sicilian, Castilian, Catalan, German Ashkenazi, Papal States, and various Roman. This number was by legislation diminished under the late sixteenth-century popes, as described in Milano, *Il ghetto di Roma*, 214–18, 276–77; Micol Ferrara, *Dentro e fuori dal ghetto: I luoghi della presenza ebraica a Roma tra XVI e XIX secolo*, 46–55.

93. Milano, *Il ghetto di Roma*, 277–79. Going to sermons out of turn could earn a fine of five giulii. For the calculation for 1671–72, see ASVR Atti della segreteria del tribunale del cardinale vicario, tom. 55, fol. 686r–v.

94. AAV Misc. Arm. VII, 58, 330r.

95. Dana E. Katz, "'Clamber Not You up to the Casements': On Ghetto Views and Viewing," 67–83.

new fattori or other major officers. Heavy rain could cancel a sermon, as did snow, for the safety of the Jews so as "to avoid the inconveniences and molestations done to them by Christians throwing snowballs." The preacher's deputy kept copies of the list of these exceptions.[96] Only two events could lead to an extended cancellation lasting many weeks: the Vacant See, during which Jews were subject to ritualized additional violence, and illness of a preacher. A short illness could cancel a sermon, as it did for two weeks in summer 1671, but if the preacher was gone a long time, a substitute was expected to relieve him.[97]

In the end, between festivals and exigencies, conversionary sermons were only preached on about half the Saturdays of the year or a little more; Attilio Milano calculated that only between twenty and twenty-seven sermons took place per year in the 1670s, with an average of six absences per sermon.[98] If one-third of the adult population attended each week, then any individual's own turn came up no more than nine times per year and perhaps as few as six. In fact, the number was probably even lower. As stated earlier, Rome had a fairly stable population of approximately 4,000 Jewish people (3 to 4 percent of the population of Rome) throughout the late sixteenth and seventeenth centuries, and an estimated family size of 4.3 children per family.[99] If only the parents joined the roster, roughly 425 to 450 adults were eligible each week to fill the 250 to 300 required slots. These numbers suggest that the legislation and logistics of conversionary sermons were engineered so as to provide a viable crowd for a Christian spectacle—enough to sustain the premise of weekly preaching to Jews. But they were not enough to demonstrate any real effort to reach as many Jews as possible, as often as possible.

From the outset and ever after, Jews at sermons were closely policed. In addition to bearing the usual distinguishing signs, their outer clothing was strictly monitored. They could only wear simple short cloaks to the sermon, not the luxuriously ornamented *cimarra;* if extreme cold called for both, the rougher cloak had to cover the finer one.[100] Inside

96. "L'inconvenienti e molestie che si fanno detti da Christiani con tirarli palle di neve," cited in ASVR, Atti della segreteria del tribunale del cardinale vicario, tom. 55, 687v.

97. ASVR Atti della segreteria del tribunale del cardinale vicario, tom. 55, 687v–88r, 690r; Milano, *Il ghetto di Roma*, 275–78.

98. Milano, *Il ghetto di Roma*, 275–77.

99. For the population, see Ferrara, *Dentro e fuori dal ghetto*, 9; Peter Partner, *Renaissance Rome, 1500–1559: A Portrait of a Society*, 77. For family size and fluctuation, see Stow, *Theater of Acculturation*, 137–38.

100. For 1603 legislation against the cimarra, see AAV Misc. Arm. VII, 58, 328r. For the Jewish badge in Italy, see Benjamin Ravid, "From Yellow to Red: On the Distinguishing

the oratory, conversionary preaching rested on the expectation that Jews would resist or misbehave. The Vicariate's deputy had the authority to expel Jewish listeners from the sermon and imprison the insolent in the prisons of the cardinal vicar.[101] The guard who took names at the door was frequently a neophyte who knew the crowd and could match names to faces. Jews were expected to listen in modest silence. Edicts imposed fines and punishments on Jews who disrupted the sermon.[102] The deputy patrolled the group, alert for any behavior that could be considered insolence, particularly talking, jeering, or feigning sleep. He or a *sbirro* (police officer) carried a baton or truncheon.[103] Jews objected that "policeman walk through the Oratory with sticks in their hands, as if they had to tame irrational animals with little decorum of Catholic piety, almost as if they wanted to force [the Jews] to believe using the stick." The deputy Boldetti caused special alarm within the università for being "bold enough to move on from threats to hard knocks [*fiere percossi*], especially to beating up women without any cause, or at least without warning."[104] The truncheon proved a particular sore point as it undermined the entire pretense of gentle persuasion through rhetoric.

These constraints were noteworthy to onlookers who commented on or commended them. In the earliest years of the sermons, Martin describes a deputy who works "so especially to keepe the Jewes in awe, and to rebuke them for absense or slacknesse."[105] Federico Franzini's guidebook from nearly a century later gives more detail: "So that they do not sleep, and remain humble, there is a policeman with a baton in hand, who, at the preacher's signal, touches whoever is sleeping, because upon entering the church they must give their names to one who writes it down next to the door. When the preaching is over, the policeman goes to note

---

Head-Covering of the Jews of Venice"; Diane Owen Hughes, "Distinguishing Signs: Ear-Rings, Jews and Franciscan Rhetoric in the Italian Renaissance City"; Barbara Wisch, "Vested Interest: Redressing Jews on Michelangelo's Sistine Ceiling"; Flora Cassen, *Marking the Jews in Renaissance Italy: Politics, Religion, and the Power of Symbols.*

101. Cuggiò, *Della Giurisdittione,* 356.

102. Samples are quoted in Attilio Milano, *Storia degli Ebrei in Italia,* 279. Milano also posits that monitors checked that Jews did not stuff their ears with wax or cotton to block out the sermon. I have found no independent evidence of this widely rumored practice.

103. Moroni, *Dizionario di erudizione storico-ecclesiastica da S. Pietro sino ai nostri giorni,* 25. For further discussion of the truncheon, see chapter 7.

104. ASCER 1 Ue 2, inf. 2 fascicolo 8 e 9. These objections, raised by the chief rabbi of the early eighteenth century, formed part of a larger body of Jewish resistance to the circumstances surrounding conversionary sermons (and are discussed further in chapter 7).

105. Martin, *Roma Sancta,* 77.

down the unruly, and fines them one *testone*, which is given to the poor Catechumens."[106] Piazza's 1699 depiction of conversionary sermons in his day focuses almost entirely on the kinds of Jewish "cunning" expected at sermons, such as removing their yellow hats or ribbons, and on the varieties of corporal and financial punishment meted.[107] As a further goad to obedience, Jews were required to support conversionary activities financially. They bore the expense for the construction of the benches on which they sat to hear the sermon, and the labor required to set them up and put them away every week.[108] The fines for errant behavior during sermons, truancy, or place swapping, collected and distributed periodically, were donated to charitable groups, often the House of Catechumens itself.

Forced preaching had been tried in other contexts. Tenacious nuns in Strasbourg, for example, had been forced to listen to Protestant sermons to coax them out of their convent. They resisted, but found that offers of pensions were more persuasive.[109] In Rome, instances of Jewish misbehavior only seemed to reinforce Christian assumptions of an insolently stubborn people who needed to be subdued into the true faith; it suited supervisors and onlookers to expect confirmation of that narrative. For Jews, if this was conversion by persuasion, it was so only under the most straitened circumstances. The narrow roles into which Jewish people were shoehorned at conversionary sermons created a stark disparity. The historical, embodied Jews of Rome, set up to look demeaned and disobedient, contrasted sharply with the physical grandeur of the Christian setting and the abstracted, lofty, entirely idealized study of Hebrew, the virtues and value of which could only be unveiled by Christian hands. Conversionary sermons embodied this dichotomy and put it on display to the entire city. In the pulpit, Christian scholars of Hebrew used all the hermeneutic tools and tricks they knew. They delivered an elaborate, erudite oration before an audience primed to appear unworthy of it, and before a second audience primed to see in this elaborate ritual the confirmation of their own values. This was no way to evince more than a few Jewish conversions. But from the point of view of the secondary audience, it was a successful, affirming performance. Little wonder, then, that its lead actors became authorities and luminaries far beyond the pulpit.

106. Federico Franzini, *Roma Antica e Moderna*, 240.

107. Piazza, *Eusevologio Romano*, 153.

108. ASVR Atti della segreteria del tribunale del cardinale vicario, tom. 55, 687r; Cuggiò, *Della giurisdittione*, 357; Zucchi, "Ragioni della Predicazione agli Ebrei," 260.

109. Amy Leonard, *Nails in the Wall: Catholic Nuns in Reformation Germany*, 70–71.

CHAPTER THREE

The Careers of Preachers

THE LINGUIST AND THEOLOGIAN Benedetto Biancuzzi (or Biancucci) delivered only one sermon to Jews, but he made the most of it. He had the text of the sermon printed up and then added, in his own hand, an autograph letter of dedication to Pope Paul V.[1] The letter mixed personal and universal concerns, recalling the pope's personal request that Biancuzzi preach the sermon, boasting about the novelty of its content and praying for the eventual conversion of all Jews. Up until he delivered this sermon, Biancuzzi had published only one title—a respectable literary miscellany of prominent humanist writing. He had also worked as a copyist for the better-known Hebraist Giovanni Paolo Eustachio. But in the months between delivering the sermon in October 1605 and seeing it into print in the new year, Biancuzzi was granted a post as professor of Hebrew at Sapienza University. He would be known from then on as a Hebrew scholar above all, soon publishing a prominent Hebrew grammar.[2] Was his conversionary sermon a ploy for employment—an especially public job interview? Or did it celebrate his coming appointment at Sapienza?

1. Benedetto Biancuzzi, *Lettione fatta alli Hebrei di Roma, nell'Oratorio della Santissima Trinità de' Pellegrini, & Convalescenti, li 8 di ottobre 1605 dal R. D. Benedetto Biancucci . . . Dottore Theologo, et Professore della Lingua Santa nella Sapienza Romana.* Autograph copy at BAV Stamp. Barb.V.IV.68.

2. Benedetto Biancuzzi, *Indices tres obseruationum miscellaneorum variarumque lectionum*; Benedetto Biancuzzi, *Institutiones in linguam sanctam Hebraicam.* On Biancuzzi (sometimes written "Biancucci"), see Gian Maria Mazzuchelli, *Scrittori d'Italia,* 1189–90. Mazzuchelli describes how listening Jews laughed at Biancuzzi for his exegesis. Piet van Boxel, "Robert Bellarmine Reads Rashi: Rabbinic Bible Commentaries and the Burning of the Talmud," 131; Barbara Leber, in "Jewish Convert in Counter-Reformation Rome: Giovanni Paolo Eustachio," 91, notes the association with Eustachio (wrongly named here as Domenico), as do the catalogs of the Biblioteca Ambrosiana, which holds Eustachio's two manuscripts in Biancuzzi's hand, and National Library of Israel, which has digitized copies.

Biancuzzi left no trace of any further preaching, but his single sermon clearly served a tactical purpose as his scholarly prospects rose.

Sermons to Jews proved strategically useful to others like Biancuzzi who were on their way to other careers. Yet what we might term the Biancuzzi style of preacher—the guest star—provided only one of many routes into the conversionary pulpit. Conversionary preachers came in many models. Some characterize the heady early days of conversionary preaching, when a sermon to Jews was a quick, popular way to signal ambition. Other types persisted, becoming typical of conversionary preaching's later period. In considering these men in aggregate, two things become apparent: preaching to Jews conferred status, and those designated as predicatori degli ebrei used that status to promote conversion in other contexts. This chapter asks what kind of person delivered forced sermons to Jews, and what he did with his experience. It traces the varied, sometimes-erratic careers of individual preachers inside and outside the pulpit. Such an examination shows us the close ties and continuous interplay of benefits between preachers to Jews and the Catholic institutions of Rome. It helps us to see how fully sermons and the broader network of proselytizing activities were good business. Specific, sometimes-mundane events and behaviors accumulated into the "hothouse of conversion" that was early modern Rome. Those enthusiastic for salvific activity thus found plenty of practical opportunity. Converts to Catholicism found not only employment but also approval and validation by wooing the community they had left. Cradle Catholics with the right skills and clout found a living and place to be an expert.

The many conversionary preachers of early modern Rome included ambitious clerics on the make, members of both new and old monastic orders, and converts from Judaism. Information about their lives survives in documents other than sermons. Diaries, memoirs, letters, wills, petitions, or the avvisi di Roma newsletters sometimes mention them by name. Biographies or hagiographies discuss the subject's work with Jews, occasional or frequent. Published anti-Jewish polemics often identify whether the work or author ever addressed Jews directly. Preachers to Jews used their official title in their other scholarly activities, and also can be traced in the other works they collaborated on, published, or endorsed. Finally, modern scholarly sources on conversionary preaching direct us to names we might have missed otherwise. Of these sources, the most comprehensive is a series of articles written in the 1930s by Alberto Zucchi, listing all the Dominican holders of the post.[3]

3. Alberto Zucchi, "Il predicatore degli ebrei in Roma"; Alberto Zucchi, "Il primo predi-catore domenicano degli ebrei. Ancora sul P. Sirleto—Fr. Alessandro Franceschi"; Alberto

These fragments tell us, above all, that forced preaching to Jews, especially at its outset, offered a rung on the career ladder for many ambitious clerics. For some, the conversionary pulpit became a stepping-stone to greater glory. A few found it a long-term or lifetime calling. For these men, the title of predicatore degli ebrei accompanied them beyond the pulpit. Conversionary preachers contributed to conversionary campaigns, Hebrew scholarship, anti-Jewish polemic, and the broader currents of Counter-Reformation Rome. Whether short or long, a turn in the pulpit remained a prestigious move, adding weight to a man's signature and promising a smoother entrée into powerful ecclesiastical networks.

The long history of preaching to Jews shows a reciprocal and continuous cycling of influence and prestige between individual preachers and the broader Catholic world. In its early years, that cycle was weighted toward the influential volunteers whose good reputation helped to launch and support the new, untested practice of public preaching to Jews. But even from the start, conversionary preaching already boosted careers, and the potential benefits flowed in both directions. In the seventeenth century, the balance shifted. As the post of predicatore degli ebrei found firm ground within the Dominican order, the title alone added weight and authority to other enterprises. Preachers used their respected status primarily to support Jewish conversion well outside the sermon context as well as far more broadly wherever their expertise was useful.

The precarity of conversionary preaching in its early years called for the robust support of elite and influential Catholics. Histories of the practice typically begin with Andrea De Monte, the convert from Judaism admired by Catholics and despised by Jews in equal measure.[4] While De Monte may not have directly instigated formal conversionary sermons, their early history relies on his reputation. But De Monte's story also

---

Zucchi, "Ragioni della predicazione agli ebrei"; Alberto Zucchi, "I predicatori domenicani degli ebrei nel secolo XVII"; Alberto Zucchi, "Rome domenicana: note storiche: Predicatori domenicani degli ebrei nel sec. XVIII." These articles appear in a series in *Memorie Domenicane,* and some have overlapping titles.

4. On De Monte, see Fausto Parente, "Notes Biographiques sur André de Monte"; Fausto Parente, DBI entry; Romeo De Maio, *Riforme e miti nella chiesa del cinquecento,* 349-50; Carolyn H. Wood and Peter Iver Kaufman, "Tacito Predicatore: The Annunciation Chapel at the Madonna Dei Monti in Rome"; Gian Ludovico Masetti Zannini, "La biblioteca di Andrea Del Monte (Josef Sarfath) e altre librerie di ebrei nel cinquecento romano"; Martine Boiteux, "Preaching to the Jews in Early Modern Rome: Words and Images," 301-5; Piet van Boxel, *Jewish Books in Christian Hands: Theology, Exegesis and Conversion under Gregory XIII (1572-1585),* 20-37. The anonymous letter reporting Jewish complaints against De Monte is reprinted in Fausto Parente, "Il confronto ideologico tra l'ebraismo e la Chiesa in Italia," 378-79.

demonstrates how urgently the first preachers needed to win commitment from respected, unimpeachable heavyweights in the Catholic world: writers of polemics, founders of religious orders, and seemingly infallible men who could get things done, immune to vehement Jewish resistance and backed by powerful institutions on the rise. No Jewish convert, no matter how feted or illustrious, could carry the enterprise alone and make it a success.

De Monte was a former rabbi from Fez, known as Joseph Moro or Joseph Zarfati. The dates of his birth and arrival in Rome are unknown. He converted in Rome in 1552, baptized personally by Pope Julius III Del Monte and given his surname.[5] Learned and zealous, De Monte served as a Hebraist at the Vatican library and Sapienza University, translator of Oriental texts, censor of Jewish books in Rome and Spoleto, and adviser to Cardinal Guglielmo Sirleto, his protector, on rabbinic literature. After baptism, he became the darling of the ecclesiastical elite in Rome. In 1578, he and his wife, Cristofora, another convert, were given lodging and livelihood in exchange for teaching the rudiments of Christianity to new Christians. De Monte began to preach to Jews in 1576 on his own initiative and later won an official papal appointment from Gregory XIII. He continued to preach regularly through 1581. His sermons noted dates, locations, and at times, the names of the illustrious churchmen who came to hear him preach.[6] De Monte has remained the exemplar of Jewish converts to Catholicism in early modern Italy, in part because famous foreigners in Rome such as Michel de Montaigne witnessed his preaching of 1581 and publicly praised his erudition.[7]

But Roman Jews despised De Monte, and everybody knew it. One of De Monte's Christian friends even told him as much: "The Jews have a terrible anger against you, and however much it is said that you are their servant to preach to them and teach them the holy word of God without any payment from them. . . . [T]hey don't appreciate it and would sooner hear sermons and doctrine from any other Christian than from you."[8] The author of the Hebrew chronicle *The Vale of Tears* wrote of De Monte (and

5. Parente notes in the DBI that De Monte's name does not appear in the appropriate volume of baptismal records for catechumens and no surviving records for Saint Peter's confirm his baptism.

6. Expertly discussed in van Boxel, *Jewish Books in Christian Hands*, 20–26.

7. Michel de Montaigne, *The Complete Works of Montaigne: Essays, Travel Journal*, 956–57; Gregory Martin, *Roma Sancta*, 78–82.

8. BAV Vat. lat. 6792; Parente, "Il confronto ideologico tra l'ebraismo e la Chiesa in Italia," 378–79. For a translation in French, see Charles DeJob, "Documents sur les Juifs des États pontificaux." The letter is undated and unsigned.

two others), "Lord, may their sins never be forgotten."[9] But even as De Monte continued to preach for the rest of the decade, his vehemence and nastiness as a preacher only ever earned him hatred and scorn from his primary audience. Romans remembered the Jews' animosity. As one account written a century later had it, "The Jews would not go to hear him, and fled from him as much as possible."[10] By many accounts—though we have no hard evidence—it was Jewish hostility that had first caused De Monte to seek papal support, leading in turn to the first papal bull requiring conversionary preaching in 1577.[11] De Monte was then constrained first to preach with an associate, and soon after, to give up the pulpit in 1582.[12]

Undaunted, De Monte continued as a zealous proselytizer, censor and confiscator of books, and "sotto-maestro" of the College of Neophytes.[13] He remained close to subsequent popes, Cardinal Sirleto, and Philip Neri, and worked to regulate their conversionary practices toward Jews. De Monte's zeal outlasted him. In his will, he commissioned an Annunciation chapel and altarpiece painting at the church in the House of Catechumens, known as the Santa Maria ai Monti or Madonna dei Monti. Unlike any other Annunciation scene, the verses of Isaiah 7:14–15 are displayed in clearly visibleHebrew: "Behold a virgin shall conceive and bear a son. . . . Butter and honey shall he eat." These texts had undergirded De Monte's own sermons, and he also elaborated them in his treatise *The Confusion of the Jews*. In this way, the altarpiece directly addressed Jewish converts residing in the House of Catechumens; it was designed to bolster both their new Catholic faith and the broader Counter-Reformation program of instructive painting.[14] Moreover, De Monte left behind a letter to Julius III, two polemical conversionary treatises, and a volume of

9. "אנא ה' חטאתם אל חמתה." Joseph ha-Kohen, *Sefer 'Emeq Ha-Bakha = The Vale of Tears: With the Chronicle of the Anonymous Corrector*, 19.

10. Federico Franzini, *Roma Antica e Moderna*, 240.

11. In *Il ghetto di Roma; illustrazioni storiche*, 271, Attilio Milano writes of De Monte, "Fu colui che indusse Gregorio XIII a emettere le due bolle," but names Giuseppe da Firenze as the first initator of sermons to Jews in Rome. Parente, in "Notes Biographiques sur André de Monte," 189, is more hesitant: "De Monte a été vraisemblablemane l'inspirateur de cette mesure." Leber, in "Jewish Convert in Counter-Reformation Rome," 114–15, points out that his fame does not constitute hard evidence of influence over the pope.

12. On Evangelista Marcellino as De Monte's associate, see Emily Michelson, "Evangelista Marcellino: One Preacher, Two Audiences."

13. For notes on De Monte taking bribes regarding the confiscation of books, see Karl Hoffmann, *Ursprung und Anfangstätigkeit des ersten päpstlichen Missionsinstituts; ein Beitrag zur Geschichte der katholischen Juden- und Mohammedanermission im sechzehnten Jahrhundert*, 260 (Italian typescript translation).

14. Wood and Kaufman, "Tacito Predicatore."

manuscript sermons only recently identified as his and indeed bearing his autograph.[15] These, along with his books, remained in the library of the Collegio di Neofiti before transferal to the Vatican library.[16] Though never published, the treatises, in Hebrew and Italian, had a lasting influence on converted Jews in Rome. Later converts and other Hebraists read, studied, and annotated them. In the margins of De Monte's *The Confusion of the Jews* we find doodled the words, "Francesco Maria Ferretti, Neofito," a name given to at least two converts from Judaism—one of whom is known to have spent time in the Roman casa roughly 150 years later.[17]

De Monte remained an anomaly among conversionary preachers in Rome. Among later occupiers of the post, he was the last converted Jew to win broad fame for sermons to his former brethren (though other converts did so outside Rome or for other reasons). He was also the only preacher to lose his position due to unpopularity (as documented further in chapter 6); after him, the position became increasingly well established and less vulnerable. De Monte was probably the best-documented and best-known conversionary preacher, but one of the least typical too.

A better model for a suitable conversionary preacher is De Monte's associate, Evangelista Gerbi, called Marcellino, who also published as Lorenzo Selva. Marcellino, an Observant Franciscan, was a prolific and popular preacher throughout Rome. He had won approval from three popes and had turned down two bishoprics. Starting in the 1580s, Marcellino served as the specially appointed explicator of scripture at the Observant church of Santa Maria in Aracoeli.[18] His printed output included

15. Andrea De Monte, *Oratio habita apud S.D.N. Iulium, divina providentia papam tertium*, n.d. (held at the BAV; a manuscript copy is also at BAV Vat. lat. 3561); Andrea De Monte, *Lettera della Pace* (held at BAV Neofiti 37); Andrea De Monte, *Confusione dei Giudei*, Vat. lat. 14627 [prev. Neofiti 38]). The sermons are at BAV Neofiti 35, previously attributed to Domenico Gerosolimitano, and identified in van Boxel, *Jewish Books in Christian Hands*.

16. Masetti Zannini, "La biblioteca di Andrea Del Monte," 399; Leber, "Jewish Convert in Counter-Reformation Rome," 81.

17. BAV Vat. lat. 14627 fol. 122v. For two converts named Ferretti, see Paolo Sebastiano Medici, *Conversione di Sabbato Nachamù rabbino ebreo in Ancona* (discussed further in chapter 5); ACDF Doctrinalia S.O. e voti Doctrinalia 1711–13, 1.

18. Early bibliographical sources include Cesare Campana, *Delle historie del mondo descritte dal Sig. Cesare Campana*, 570; the vita by Jacopo Peri in Evangelista Marcellino, *Prediche della passione e resurrezione di Giesu Criso nostro redentore. Fatte l'anno 1592 in Roma dal R.P.F. Vangelista Marcellino*; Federico Borromeo, *De sacris nostrorum temporum oratoribus libri quinque*; Giuseppe Dondori, *Della pietà di Pistoia*, 302–12. Modern sources include Gustavo Cantini, *I francescani d'Italia di fronte alle dottrine luterane e calviniste durante il cinquecento*. The fullest information is found in Angelico Piladi, *Il P. Evangelista Marcellino insigne predicatore ed ecclesiaste del secolo XVI*. See also Miguel

sermons, theological treatises, a popular prose romance, many books of Old Testament exegesis based on his explications, and in 1582, *On Metamorphosis, or the Transformation of the Virtuous*, a devotional novel so popular that it merited six subsequent editions and a French translation. By the 1620s, he was a candidate for sainthood. Marcellino was also the unnamed associate hired to accompany the unpopular De Monte. Where contemporary spectators noted another preacher in the pulpit with De Monte, or named "P. Marcellino and M. Andreas" together, Marcellino himself confirms their association, mentioning in writing, "My dearest Mr Andrea Monte, with whom I have been joined against the Jews for ten years now."[19] The publication of Marcellino's sermons to Jews, in the year after De Monte's removal from the pulpit, may well have marked his contribution to the debacle, making him a crucial link in the complex history of Jews, Christians, and converts in Rome.[20]

The specifically exegetical nature of Marcellino's appointment at Santa Maria in Aracoeli and his emphasis on the books of the Old Testament made him an ideal candidate to exemplify the demands of regular preaching to the Jews. Unlike De Monte, Marcellino could appear to be a devoted, even beloved preacher. Thirty years after Marcellino's death, his hagiographer described how the best Jewish families converted at his sermons, "moved by divine grace and by the loving words of the preacher."[21] His twentieth-century biographer proposed that Jewish people attended sermons simply out of love for Marcellino given that he had begun preaching to Jews before it became mandated. "The Jews went to Marcellino's preaching, not because they were constrained, but out of spontaneous desire. . . . In preaching to the Jews he was moved solely by the desire to do them good . . . and he was very endeared to them; they listened to him willingly." Whether or not this is true, Marcellino found more success than De Monte, keeping the position for at least eight years.[22] He was also a more difficult figure to demote, as an established, even revered preacher

---

Gotor, *I beati del papa: santità, inquisizione e obbedienza in età moderna*, 79–85; Michelson, "Evangelista Marcellino: One Preacher, Two Audiences"; Emily Michelson, "Dramatics in (and out of) the Pulpit in Post-Tridentine Italy."

19. "Mi dice il mio Carissimo Messer Andrea Monte, col quale già per dieci anni sono congiunto contra gli Ebrei," in Evangelista Marcellino, *Lezzioni Diciannove sopra Rut. Del RPF Vangelista Marcellino de' Minori Osservanti*, 34r.

20. Evangelista Marcellino, *Sermoni quindici sopra il salmo centonove fatti fatti a gli hebrei di Roma*.

21. Iacopo Peri, *Breve Discorso della via del P.F. Vangelista Marcellino da Pistoia . . . Raccolto da Fra Iacopo Peri*, 16–17.

22. Piladi, *Il P. Evangelista Marcellino*, 35.

and author in frequent demand for preaching Lenten sermon cycles in cities across Italy.

Marcellino's time in the pulpit seems to have wrought at least one spectacular success: the elite Florentine rabbi Jehiel da Pesaro, baptized as Vitale Medici, as discussed in chapter 1. Some contemporaries gave the credit for Jehiel's high-profile conversion to Catholicism in 1582 to Marcellino, who had just delivered that year's Lenten sermon cycle in Florence as a guest preacher. A local chronicler praised Marcellino through his new protégé. "Preaching with holy fervor, [Marcellino] brought to our holy faith, with Divine help and his own sermons, Maestro Vitale di Salomone da Pesaro, a Jew very learned in philosophy, medicine, and Jewish theology. . . . He received the water of holy baptism in Rome from the hands of his Holiness, and his sponsor was the Cardinal de Medici."[23] The chronicler suggests that when Medici himself then preached, Marcellino was his model: Medici sought to persuade other Jews "as he had been persuaded by the sermons of Padre Marcellino."[24] Marcellino's surviving sermons from Florence fit the general model of a traditional Lenten cycle rather than a conversionary model. We can easily imagine that during his sojourn as a Lenten preacher, Marcellino had mentored Medici in the more specific art, honed in Rome, of preaching conversionary sermons to Jews.[25]

But the documentary record is not entirely clear about Medici's converter. A later source attributes Medici's conversion not to Marcellino but instead to a local inquisitor, Dionisio Castacciaro (Dionigi da Costacciaro). Moreover, surviving correspondence between Dionigi da Costacciaro and the cardinal of Santa Severina corroborates this theory. The two men discussed how to spirit Jehiel out of the ghetto without provoking its other residents.[26] If this is the case, then it is important to note that some con-

---

23. Settimanni, *Diario*, ASF Manoscritti 129, 295r–v. Dionisio Pulinari, in his *Cronache dei Frati Minori della Provincia di Toscana*, 315–16, notes Marcellino's two sermon tours of Florence.

24. Settimanni, *Diario*, 299v.

25. For Marcellino's Florentine preaching, see Evangelista Marcellino, *Predica del venerdì santo fatta nel dvomo di Fiorenza, l'anno 1585 dal molto r.p.f. Vangelista Marcellino de' minori osseruanti di San Francesco*. For his time in Florence, see Gotor, *I beati del Papa*, 80–82. For Medici, see Shulamit Furstenberg-Levi, "The Boundaries between 'Jewish' and 'Catholic' Space in Counter-Reformation Florence as Seen by the Convert Vitale Medici"; Shulamit Furstenberg-Levi, "The Sermons of a Rabbi Converted to Christianity: Between Synagogue and Church"; Shulamit Furstenberg-Levi, "The Book of Homilies of the Convert to Catholicism Vitale Medici: Two Models of Identity."

26. Paolo Sebastiano Medici, *Catalogo de neofiti illustri usciti per misericordia di Dio dall'ebraismo e poi rendutisi gloriosi nel cristianesimo per esemplarità di costumi, e profondità di dottrina*, 59–60. On the correspondence, see Samuela Marconcini, *Per amor*

temporary chronicles—either in defiance of the facts or without knowing them—decided to give the credit for Jeḥiel's conversion to a preacher.
Marcellino, the charismatic and renowned visitor, made a better story,
both more benign and more pious. The notion that the protégé of such a
man went on to give sermons of his own supported the model of an ideal
preacher creating a worthy neophyte in his own image.

The conversionary pulpit hosted many other ambitious clerics eager
to capitalize on the excitement surrounding the new enterprise and to
benefit from its growing prestige. Many belonged to the first generation
of the new Society of Jesus, and would famously shape and define their
new society. Robert Bellarmine, who had polished his skills as a Hebraist while lecturing in Louvain, was ordered to preach to Jews when his
superiors recalled him to Rome—a mark of both his skill as a preacher and
the importance of this project.[27] Diego Lainez, the second superior of the
Society of Jesus and himself the descendant of a Spanish converso, supposedly contributed one of the earliest conversionary sermons in Rome
immediately after the promulgation of the papal bull *Vices Eius Nos* in
1577. Gianbattista Eliano, the only Jesuit born Jewish, may have delivered
sermons along with his other conversionary activities. These men took
their experience with them into their later apostolates. Eliano, for example, honed his preaching skills in advance of a series of famed missions
across the Mediterranean.[28]

The most notable Jesuit to preach to Jews was the scholar and diplomat Antonio Possevino, who lived in Rome in the 1570s as secretary of
the Society of Jesus. Possevino spent six months during 1577 preaching
to Jews in the Oratory of Santissima Trinità dei Pellegrini, taking over
from Bellarmine, and making him and Lainez among the first to commit
to the role following the new legislation. Possevino's sermons themselves

---

del cielo: farsi cristiani a Firenze tra Seicento e Settecento, 42–43; Furstenburg-Levi, "The
Boundaries between 'Jewish' and 'Catholic' Space." See also Lucio Biasiori and Samuela
Marconcini, "Public Secrets: Vitale Medici's Conversion and Its Impact on the Social, Religious and Urban Landscape of Late Sixteenth-Century Florence." Since "Public Secrets" is
still forthcoming, I have not been able to consult it, but it may provide more evidence on
this event.

27. van Boxel, "Robert Bellarmine Reads Rashi," 128–29; van Boxel, *Jewish Books in
Christian Hands*, 11–13.

28. Robert Aleksander Maryks, *The Jesuit Order as a Synagogue of Jews: Jesuits of
Jewish Ancestry and Purity-of-Blood Laws in the Early Society of Jesus*, 62; Hoffmann,
Ursprung und Anfangstätigkeit des ersten päpstlichen Missionsinstituts, 262–63 (Italian
typescript translation); Robert John Clines, *A Jewish Jesuit in the Eastern Mediterranean:
Early Modern Conversion, Mission, and the Construction of Identity*.

survived long enough to be noted among his papers, but are no longer extant.[29] He described his experience with Roman Jews in two other surviving manuscripts, now housed at the Jesuit archives in Rome and well known to scholars.[30] Possevino claimed fourteen conversions, including a family group. Gregory Martin confirms that Possevino was based at the Oratory as a preacher and later names him first in his list of preachers to the Jews.[31] Martin describes Possevino as a preacher who transmitted the values of Catholic Rome to his Jewish audience. "Wel therefore and charitable," says Martin, was Possevino, because "when preaching to the Jews, he desyred them to have as much care of their owne salvation, as some others had . . . which for their sakes did punish themselves to the very sheding of some droppes of bloud."[32] Martin was referring to the penitential practice of discipline with cords, widespread in Rome, when penitents would commonly pray for the souls of Jews. Possevino would go on to proselytize in Sweden later in that year, and became a prominent missionary in Scandinavia and eastern Europe.[33]

Preaching was a natural extension of broader Jesuit conversionary efforts in Rome and eventually around the world. Jesuits had founded the House of Catechumens in Rome, seen it through various birthing pains and scandals, and fought for it to receive papal and administrative support on par with the most respected institutions in the city.[34] Lance Lazar suggests that the casa's model of reflection and education in an enclosed setting grew directly out of Loyola's own conversionary experience, and later developed into a process that would be repeated throughout the Italian peninsula.[35] Preaching and broader Jesuit Jewish policy were most closely

29. The sermons are listed in the inventory of Possevino's papers now in ARSI Opp. NN 313, fol. 7. See Emanuele Colombo, "The Watershed of Conversion: Antonio Possevino, New Christians, and Jews," 39; John Patrick Donnelly, "Antonio Possevino and Jesuits of Jewish Ancestry," 5–6. Colombo refutes Donnelly's hypothesis that Possevino was probably of converso origin himself, as restated in Maryks, *The Jesuit Order as a Synagogue of Jews*, 123, 161.

30. ARSI Opp. NN 313; ARSI Opp. NN 336, fols. 89 r–90 v. The two documents contain nearly identical accounts, with Opp. NN 313 in Italian and Opp. NN 336 in Latin.

31. Martin, *Roma Sancta*, 71, 82.

32. Martin, *Roma Sancta*, 94–95.

33. John Patrick Donnelly, "Antonio Possevino: From Secretary to Papal Legate in Sweden."

34. Hoffmann, *Ursprung und Anfangstätigkeit des ersten päpstlichen Missionsinstituts*, 14 (Italian typescript translation).

35. Lance Gabriel Lazar, *Working in the Vineyard of the Lord: Jesuit Confraternities in Early Modern Italy*, 111. For details of the confraternity's foundation, see Lazar, *Working in the Vineyard of the Lord*, 99–118. Hoffmann notes the other earlier models for the casa and confraternity, including English "hospitals of converts," in *Ursprung und Anfangstätigkeit des ersten päpstlichen Missionsinstituts*, 9–14 (Italian typescript translation).

linked in Possevino, one of the leading voices to defend Jewish converts and their descendants in the debate over whether they should be permitted to join the Jesuits. In 1576, shortly before his preaching appointment, Possevino had written a detailed memorial to Everard Mercurian, the general of the Society of Jesus. The memorial argued that if the Society was to maintain its unity and commitment to Jesuit ideals, it must ignore questions of lineage and blood purity among its members. Anything less would bring schism to the order; it would stink of paganism and run contrary to Jesuit ideals.[36] During the 1570s, Possevino also drafted his magnum opus, the *Bibliotheca Selecta,* published decades later. The *Bibliotheca Selecta,* a bibliographic encyclopedia of Jesuit-approved reading, draws on Possevino's skills as a Hebraist and his experience proselytizing to Jews. Five chapters of Book 9 summarize his position on Jewish conversion, based directly on his personal experience in Rome.[37]

Possevino's experience preaching to Jews led him to take credit for the infrastructure of Roman conversion. As the Jesuits recalled it, his success at conversionary preaching, and his hopes for young converts of great presence and intelligence (in his words), encouraged him to approach two powerful cardinals, Sirleto and Giulio Antonio Santori.[38] He requested funds to establish the College of Neophytes, which would train converts as future preachers. Sirleto became the college's cardinal protector. Jesuit involvement in general and Possevino's in particular helped to place conversionary preaching on a firm footing in tangible ways.

In those early decades, when the prestige of the conversionary pulpit relied so much on individual personalities, the pulpit also rewarded individual careers in equal measure and sometimes contributed to the highest-possible tribute: sanctity. Marcellino himself was revered as a future saint at his death. Miracle stories and hagiographies collected around him, although the campaign for his canonization was brief.[39] A mission to the Jews did not hurt the cause of the future saint Lorenzo da Brindisi either. Lorenzo was a provincial general of the Capuchins in Tuscany. His mastery of the Hebrew language led Pope Clement VIII to appoint him to preach to Jews in 1592—a year in which the pope decided to renew frequent preaching. Lorenzo had previously preached to Jews in major cities

36. Maryks, *The Jesuit Order as a Synagogue of Jews,* 162–82; Thomas M. Cohen, "Racial and Ethnic Minorities in the Society of Jesus," 203–5.

37. Colombo, "The Watershed of Conversion," 37–40; van Boxel, *Jewish Books in Christian Hands,* 16–17; Donnelly, "Antonio Possevino and Jesuits of Jewish Ancestry," 6–7.

38. ARSI Opp. NN 313, 18r.

39. On Marcellino's canonization case, see Gotor, *I beati del papa,* 79–94.

in Northern Italy and was probably Marcellino's successor. In Rome, he held the post for two years before becoming an anti-Protestant missionary in Vienna and Prague. Later he would become general of the Capuchin order as well as a diplomat in the service of the pope and various dukes before his eventual canonization. Our record of his preaching practices comes from the testimony of his fellow Capuchins, particularly Francesco da Valdobbiadene, who described Lorenzo's techniques in the pulpit as a skilled Hebraist. Lorenzo made a show of mounting the pulpit with a stack of Hebrew texts, and reading scriptural passages in excellent Hebrew as well as in Latin and Italian.[40] His biographer notes that when Lorenzo asked Clement VIII for relevant books, he was given access to De Monte's personal library, which was at that time in the possession of De Monte's wife's nephew, the convert Salomone Corcos / Ugo Boncompagni.[41]

Those who testified for Lorenzo's sanctity insisted that his words were friendly and fraternal, and that his Jewish audience received him well.[42] Yet since Lorenzo was one of the few Capuchins to hold the post, we might also identify him with the friar mentioned in the Roman newsletters, or avvisi, of July 18, 1592, for whom the Jews of Rome were brought by force to hear a sermon in the church of San Lorenzo in Damaso in 1592.[43] Lorenzo had indeed preached the Lenten cycle in that same church during that same year; his biographer has established that Lorenzo's conversionary preaching in Rome lasted from Lent 1592 to spring 1594.[44] Optimistic hagiographers had to whitewash.

Preaching to Jews remained a credible sign of a future saint. Or at least, this is how it seemed to the hagiographer of Joseph Calasanz, a contemporary of Lorenzo da Brindisi and hopeful newcomer to Rome in 1592. Nearly 150 years later, when Calasanz's case for sainthood was edging toward success, the author of his vita emphasized Calasanz's attention

40. For a lengthy discussion of Lorenzo's mission to Jews, especially in Rome, see Arturo da Carmignano di Brenta, *San Lorenzo da Brindisi, Dottore della Chiesa Universale (1559–1619)*, 1:267–316, 543–47. Valdobbiadene's testimony is quoted and discussed in Andrew J. G. Drenas, "'The Standard-Bearer of the Roman Church': Lorenzo da Brindisi (1559–1619) and Capuchin Missions in the Holy Roman Empire," 24–44.

41. da Carmignano di Brenta, *San Lorenzo da Brindisi, Dottore della Chiesa Universale (1559–1619)*, 1:303; Masetti Zannini, "La biblioteca di Andrea Del Monte," 399–400. Zannini does not confirm the loan to Lorenzo.

42. Drenas, "The Standard-Bearer of the Roman Church," 43–44.

43. BAV Urb. lat. 1060, 462r. See also Zucchi, "Rome domenicana," 126–27.

44. da Carmignano di Brenta, *San Lorenzo da Brindisi, dottore della chiesa universale (1559–1619)*, 1960, 1:298–99, 543–47.

to Jews early in his Roman sojourn.[45] He tells us that Calasanz had deliberately joined the confraternity of Santissima Trinità dei Pellegrini and thrown himself into its various pious activities, which included giving sermons to Jews and bringing others to join him.[46] Calasanz's apostolate to the Jews, as recorded in this instance, was fleeting and hard to prove. What matters here is how his later hagiographer, looking back from the eighteenth century, believed that a mention of conversionary sermons would boost Calasanz's piety credentials. Whether or not Calasanz himself actually preached to Jews in his round of devotional activities, as the text suggests, this list imagines conversionary preaching comfortably alongside other Catholic acts of public devotion. It assumes not only that the conversionary pulpit was open to visitors but also that visitors entered it as an expression of their own devotion or ambition.

Even as the post of predicatore degli ebrei settled gradually into familiarity, many clerics still flocked to this pulpit, trying their hand at conversionary preaching without then taking it on as a permanent mission. Some preachers and clerics, such as Biancuzzi, Lorenzo da Brindisi, or Calasanz, seem to have considered preaching to the Jews a way to build credibility or feed a fashion. They left behind one or two sermons to Jews, or references to them, but did not otherwise devote their careers to Jewish conversion. But in two of these cases, as we have seen, such efforts with Jews formed a crucial part of the posthumous case for their canonization.

Even writers who were not primarily preachers and even those based outside Rome recognized the career-boosting potential of an occasional sermon to Jews. Girolamo Allè, a Hieronymite based in Fiesole, published nineteen mystical and devotional works that he dressed up with tantalizing titles, including: *The Unknown and Known Bride of Solomon, The Man Who Talks Little and Thinks Much,* and *The Pythagoran, Kabbalistic, Alchemical, and Judicial Chimeras Dissipated by the Wind of Truth.*[47] Among these is *The Convinced and Confused Jews* (1619), the lone surviving example of printed conversionary sermons delivered in

45. For Calasanz and the Piarist order, see Karen Liebreich, *Fallen Order: Intrigue, Heresy, and Scandal in the Rome of Galileo and Caravaggio,* which documents the order's history of child abuse. See also the entry on Calasanz (Calasanzio) in the DBI.

46. Vincenzo Talenti, *Vita del beato Giuseppe Calasanzio, della Madre di Dio, fondatore de' Chierici poveri della Madre di Dio delle scuole pie,* 76–77.

47. *La sconosciuta, e conosciuta sposa di Salomone; L'huomo che parla poco, e ragiona molto; Le chimere pitagoriche, cabalistiche, chimiche e giudiciarie dissipate dal vento della verità.* For Allè, see also Parente, "Il confronto ideologico tra l'ebraismo e la Chiesa in Italia," 326–27.

Venice.[48] In reality, the volume combines six sermons to Jews, preached over six Saturdays of Lent in the church of San Silvestro, with six sermons to Christians, preached in other churches around Venice. Yet apart from his one title on Kabbalah and a general interest in the exotic, Allè showed no lasting interest in Judaism. Writing conversionary sermons did not so much define his oeuvre as identify them as a fad.

But if it was a fad, Allè still considered it one worth spending time on. *The Convinced and Confused Jews* is a grand volume. In addition to the standard preliminaries, it includes fifteen more pieces of paratext, mostly letters and laudatory verses in praise of the author. Many of his sermon titles hint at self-promotion: "Sermon on the Glories of Christ, given in San Marco of Venice on Palm Sunday, [himself] having been chosen among other preachers preaching in Venice that year to preach to the Most Serene Republic."[49] Allè's efforts were probably inspired by a growth in conversionary treatises in the early seventeenth century and particularly by one work: Tommaso Bell'haver's (or Bellavere) *Brief and Easy Doctrine to Bring the Jew to the Knowledge of the True Messiah and Savior of the World* published in Venice in 1608.[50] Bell'haver's title page promoted his work as a useful tool for readers who might want to debate faith with Jews, and Allè may have taken up the suggestion literally. His six sermons to Jews replicate the precise order of argumentation in the first six books of Bell'haver's treatise. This may have reflected his concern to keep sermons and polemical literature at the level of doctrine too, rather than discussing Jewish custom. The strictly theological subject matter of his sermons to Jews suggests as much.[51]

The Observant Franciscan Faustino Tasso also seems to have used conversionary sermons as fuel for his aspirations. A poet, translator, publisher, and historian, Tasso published a volume of twenty conversionary sermons

48. Girolamo Allè, *I convinti, e confusi hebrei: opera del M.R.P.M. Girolamo Allè bolognese, dell'ordine di S. Girolamo di fiesole, divisa in alcune prediche da lui predicate nell'antico, & gia patriarcal tempio di San Silvestro di Venetia.*

49. "Predica della Glorie di Christo, Fatta in S. Marco di Venetia la Domenica della Palme, Essendo elletto fra gli altri Predicatori, che quell'anno predicano in Venetia per Predicare alla Serenissima Republica." Allè, *I convinti, e confusi hebrei,* 136–51.

50. Tommaso Bell'haver, *Dottrina facile et breve per redurre l'Hebreo al conoscimento del vero Messia.* See also Giovanni Battista Bellavere, *Doi breui trattati, nell'vno de' quali si raccoglieno diuerse efficaci ragioni contra gli hebrei, et nell'altro dimostrando la grauezza del peccato della lussuria si diffiniscono le sue specie.*

51. Magda Teter, *Blood Libel: On the Trail of an Antisemitic Myth,* 182, notes that Allè was protesting the Italian translation of a book on Jewish customs for women, written for Jews but accessible to Christians, with potentially detrimental effects.

to Jews in 1585—*ragionamenti* or brief homilies.[52] His printed output otherwise contains no proselytizing material. This volume could have represented Tasso's response to *Sancta Mater Ecclesia*, the recent papal bull of 1581 establishing conversionary preaching. He claimed to have delivered the sermons in Naples in the Holy Year of 1575 to only a few Jews and then repeated them in Mantua at the request of the local inquisitor to one Jewish man receptive to conversion. The sermons worked, and a baptism followed. This lone success justified the publication of Tasso's volume, but Tasso clearly used the book more ambitiously. He dedicated the homilies to Guglielmo Gonzaga, duke of Mantua and Monferrato, and boasted on the title page that they had been commissioned by the viceroy and archbishop of Naples. His letter of dedication to Gonzaga is framed with more attention to Gonazaga's support for Tasso's own Observant order and its local monastery than to efforts to convert Jews. The sermons seem to have been no more than a convenient premise in a bid for Gonzaga patronage.

In the early seventeenth century, the excitement around preaching to Jews settled down as the position came under the permanent supervision of the Dominican Order. Although a sermon to Jews remained a momentous public spectacle, the job of preaching became more specialized, permanent, and bureaucratic, and less open to ambitious one-hit wonders. Seventeenth-century sources for preachers to Jews therefore come from fewer authors, but from more consistent names and with more works from each. The establishment of a formal title, predicatore degli ebrei, only codified the high status of the position. It remained a prestigious springboard to senior ecclesiastical roles. Giuseppe Ciantes, who held the post from 1624 to 1640, was then elected bishop of Marsica; the preacher Giovanni Compagni became bishop of Sansepolcro in 1696 and Larino in 1703; his successor, Antonino Serafino Camarda, went on to become bishop of Rieti.[53] In each case, the conversionary pulpit had given its occupants a leg up.

What did these men do with their clout? How did they spend their time outside the pulpit? Investigating their overtime and after-hours activities helps us to understand the role and uses of the new position of predicatore degli ebrei in the seventeenth and early eighteenth centuries. Seventeenth-century preachers to Jews supplemented their sermons with a broader range of activities clustered around religious conversion,

---

52. Faustino Tasso, *Venti Ragionamenti familiari sopra la venuta del Messia, Del R.P. Faustino Tasso, Minore Osservante. Fatte in Napoli ad alcuni Hebrei Per comandamento de gl'Ill.mi e R.mi Vicerè, e Arcivescovo.*

53. Zucchi, "Roma domenicana," 122.

supporting and vouching for new converts. Their lives intertwined closely with those of their Jewish audiences as well as the other institutions that sought or monitored conversion. Ciantes, in his subsequent job as bishop of Marsica, personally performed the baptisms of converted Jews (and Muslims) at least three times.[54] Preachers to Jews also worked with the most important congregations and religious orders in Rome. Their activities overlapped with those of other missions and missionaries, but their special status and official title added distinction to their efforts. Whereas in the sixteenth century, would-be preachers had sought individual prestige through preaching to Jews, thus lending support to the new office, it was the stability and stature of the post itself that brought honor in the seventeenth and eighteenth centuries.

Yet for Jewish audiences, the institutionalization of the post brought new disadvantages. Not only did it signal the permanence of sermons to Jews, but it meant that a preacher had less incentive to court his listeners. With job security, popularity mattered less. The two conversionary preachers who defined the position in the early seventeenth century, Pietro Pichi and Ciantes, both twinned their sermons with overt antipathy outside the pulpit toward Roman Jews, extensively applied.

Pichi, who preached from 1624 to 1626, supplemented his position by writing and publishing four anti-Jewish polemical treatises during his years in the pulpit. Pichi taught and preached at the Dominican convent of Santa Maria sopra Minerva. He was appointed to succeed the preacher Stefano Sirleto in 1604, and held the post until 1626. He then retired to Trevi, where he died in 1637.[55] His published polemics are usually understood to reflect his oral sermons, referring directly to his experience in the pulpit: *On the Passion and Death of the Messiah, against the Jews*; *On the Birth of the God-Birthing Virgin, against the Jews*; *Letter to the Jews of Italy Which Demonstrates the Vanity of Their Penitence*; *The Foolish Doctrines of the Jews and Their Refutations*.[56] Pichi's treatises suggest an innately aggressive pulpit manner, as his *Treatise on the Passion* makes plain:

54. ASVR Casa dei Catecumeni 178, Liber Baptizatorum 1634–75, 53v, 37r, 41r.
55. Zucchi, "Il primo predicatore Domenicano degli Ebrei. Ancora sul P. Sirleto—Fr. Alessandro Franceschi"; Zucchi, "Rome domenicana," 118; Fiamma Satta, "Predicatori agli ebrei, catecumeni e neofiti a Roma nella prima metà del seicento"; Parente, "Il confronto ideologico tra l'ebraismo e la Chiesa in Italia," 328–29; François Secret, *Les kabbalistes chrétiens de la Renaissance*, 324–25; Teter, *Blood Libel*, 185–86.
56. Pietro Pichi, *Trattato della passione e morte del Messia contra gli ebrei*; Pietro Pichi, *De partu Virginis deiparae aduersùs Iudaeos libri tres*; Pietro Pichi, *Epistola a gli Ebrei d'Italia nella quale si dimostra la vanità della loro penitenza*; Pietro Pichi, *Le stolte dottrine de gli Ebrei con la loro confutatione*.

Although I have preached to you for so long, showing you your errors clearly, giving you the remedy to be able to free yourselves from them, nonetheless, although you have listened well to my words, it has not led visibly to that fruit which one might hope. . . . Thus I thought to write in this book some of those lessons that you have heard from me, and I chose those that, because you have most abhorred them, are therefore most necessary to you.[57]

Rather than seeking to establish bridges linking Judaism to Christianity, Pichi specifically emphasized all the points that he knew his audience most disliked hearing. The hostility evident in this introduction to his *Treatise on the Passion* remained consistent later. It is Pichi whose aggression led him to boast to Jewish readers in a dedication at the front of *The Foolish Doctrines*, "You will dislike this work more than a little . . . for putting you in a bad light to Christians."[58]

Pichi's violent prose was matched by Ciantes's violent actions, all the more striking because Ciantes's writings, at least what remains of them, are pacific and cerebral. Ciantes, also a Dominican, descended from a patrician Spanish family that had settled in Rome. Educated in Hebrew at the convent of Santa Maria sopra Minevera, Ciantes succeeded Pichi in the pulpit 1626, at the age of twenty-four, and held his position until his appointment as bishop of Marsica in 1640. He retired to Rome sixteen years later.[59] In retirement, he published two anti-Jewish treatises: *On the Most Holy Trinity, Clearly Proven from the Testimony of the Ancient Jews*, and immediately afterward, *On the Incarnation of the Divine Word, Clearly Defended from the Objections of the Jews with Their Own Doctrine and Greatest Theologians*. He also published the only Hebrew translation of a medieval scholastic work: the *Summa contra Gentiles* of Thomas Aquinas.[60]

These texts, by nature, did not invite violent rhetoric or direct insult. As scholars have noted, Ciantes's treatises approached the conversionary mission from a relatively irenic angle. He was primarily interested in a

57. Pichi, *Trattato della passione e morte del Messia contra gli ebrei*, 1 (A1r).

58. *Ai letttori ebrei*, in Pichi, *Le stolte dottrine de gli Ebrei con la loro confutatione*, unpaginated, f. a5r–v.

59. Satta, "Predicatori," 114–15.

60. Giuseppe Ciantes, *Della Santissima Trinità, evidentemente provata da i testimoni de gli antichi Ebrei*; Giuseppe Ciantes, *Della incarnazione del verbo divino. Evidentemente difesa dalle opposizioni degli Ebrei colle dottrine medesime de loro maggiori teologi*; Giuseppe Ciantes, *Summa diui Thomae Aquinatis ordinis Praedicatorum contra Gentiles. Quam Hebraicè eloquitur Iosephus Ciantes Romanus episcopus Marsicensis ex eodem Ordine assumptus.*

Kabbalistic interpretation of Hebrew texts, and sought above all to demonstrate close correlations between Kabbalah and Christian theology.[61] This approach may not have been more persuasive, but it sets Ciantes apart from most conversionary preachers and polemicists, including Pichi; in writing, he seems less antagonistic and more cerebral, concerned with theological and mystical points of convergence, and not with Jewish ritual or even scriptural exegesis. By focusing so closely on Kabbalistic texts over scriptural ones, Ciantes recalls the fifteenth- and early sixteenth-century Christian Kabbalists and Christian Hebraists, interested in seeking divine truths in ancient Jewish texts.[62] Based on these treatises alone, reflecting perhaps the pacifism of his old age, one might well argue that Ciantes "had a deep knowledge of and profound respect for Hebrew texts and culture, and . . . advocated for genuine cultural exchange."[63]

Yet Ciantes's intellectual loftiness masked an actively aggressive persecution of Roman Jews during his time as predicatore degli ebrei—in fact worsening any climate for cultural exchange. As discussed in chapter 1, Ciantes helped to stage and carry out the nighttime raid on the ghetto that abducted two young children after their father had only hypothetically agreed to let the pope baptize them. Ciantes then agitated to keep the children despite a whirlwind of protests and investigations. This was not the only incident. Ciantes was the unnamed preacher criticized in a letter to Urban VIII for kidnapping two other children under similar circumstances. A recent convert named Ignazio remained infatuated with a married Jewish woman, Cannosa. When Cannosa refused his advances, Ignazio reported her to the casa as a potential convert, along with her six-year-old son and younger daughter. Ciantes, along with the rector of the College of Neophytes, collected a group of converts armed with swords and truncheons; together they raided the ghetto, raised a ruckus, and abducted Cannosa. Failing to find the two children named, they took two of her other infants, still of breastfeeding age, to use as blackmail. Cannosa pleaded her case and was released. The Jews of Rome then appealed directly to the pope for intervention, beseeching Urban VIII to return Cannosa's two babies, even though one had already been baptized against all regulation.[64]

61. Yossef Schwartz, "Kabbalah and Conversion: Caramuel and Ciantes on Kabbalah as a Means for the Conversion of the Jews"; Parente, "Il confronto ideologico tra l'ebraismo e la Chiesa in Italia," 346–49; Satta, "Predicatori."

62. Schwartz, "Kabbalah and Conversion," 179–80, 182; Satta, "Predicatori," 120.

63. Boiteux, "Preaching to the Jews in Early Modern Rome: Words and Images," 311.

64. This incident is found in ACDF Res Doctrinales DB I 1618–98, 7:239r. The preacher is not named, but Ciantes held the position throughout Urban VIII's entire Papacy. My thanks to Ian Campbell for alerting me to this case.

Ciantes seems to have adopted a split persona: high-minded in print, and violent in person. His sermons—at least as understood from his later publications—provided a smoke screen for coercive conversion and were contradicted by his actions during his tenure as a preacher. Pichi's surviving works, in contrast, show a much smaller distinction between preaching and violence. The lives of both men remind us that preaching to the Jews was never entirely about persuasion, as it was proclaimed to be. Sermons formed the acceptable, intellectual surface that masked a broader, harsher campaign. In contradiction to their obligations as preachers, both of these men actually made conversion by persuasion more difficult.

Both Pichi and Ciantes, as we have seen, took time to convert their sermons into a polemic or conversionary treatise. So did nearly every other long-standing conversionary preacher. Indeed, the only full volume of conversionary sermons published in sermon format in Rome was that of Evangelista Marcellino; after him, almost no conversionary sermons from Rome made their way into print without first shifting genre.[65] A preacher might construe his treatise as a dialogue about Christian values, an extended commentary on psalms or other scripture, a letter, or a series of arguments on one topic, such as the Trinity, the Messiah, or in one case, a set of odes to Europe's most successful conversionary preacher of all time, Saint Vincent Ferrer.[66] By publishing their work as polemic, preachers added their expertise in the pulpit to a much larger body of literature. Except for legal notices, polemics were the most common form of publication in Italy relating to Jews, and they appeared steadily throughout the early modern period. Learned converted Jews composed them as a way to prove their loyalty to the church; Catholic scholars, such as the prolific Melchior Palontrotti, wrote them to capitalize on their popularity. Preachers were naturally among the most qualified polemicists and could therewith claim a broad readership for their works.

Printers and publishers found it valuable to showcase preachers' official titles at the forefront of their published work; they often added the designation of predicatore degli ebrei to the title page after the author's name. We can assume that they thought it would increase the book's value. Preachers themselves made a big point of their long experience.

---

65. The only other full volumes of conversionary sermons published in early modern Italy are those of Tasso and Allè. The only other printed sermon I have found from Rome is that of Biancuzzi.

66. Antonio Teoli, *Esercizj di cristiane virtù insegnate dal gran taumaturgo S. Vincenzo Ferreri dell'ordine de' Predicatori da praticarsi in sette Venerdì ad onore di detto santo*; Antonio Teoli, *Storia della vita e del culto di S Vincenzo Ferrerio, dell'ordine de' Predicatori.*

Pichi, dedicating his *Treatise on the Passion* to Pope Paul V, praised him for appointing conversionary preachers "of great valor" and pointed out his own decade in that pulpit.[67] Ciantes proclaimed in his work on the Trinity that "I hope in this to convince the Jews in doctrine, for which I have committed a great part of my years, in their spiritual service."[68] Gregorio Boncompagni, in his completed but unpublished treatise *News of the Principal Sects of the World,* imagined that four decades of preaching exclusively to and about Jewish people qualified him to speak about unrelated religions, proclaiming, "After having preached to the Jews of Rome ... I wanted to publish this work for the benefit of everybody, and in particular for those who want to be instructed in the true faith, from whatever sect."[69] Expertise in the pulpit gave a preacher extra authority in a crowded market and helped him to argue for the relevance of his work more broadly.

The conceit of preaching anchored and elevated the entire genre of conversionary polemic, whether or not the authors were actual preachers. Polemics relied on the crucial fiction that they could help a preacher compose his sermons, and also benefit Christian and Jewish readers. Palontrotti, with no known qualifications, could present himself as a consultant to preachers by asserting that his *Brief Collection of Arguments* was "very necessary to preachers and catechizers, [and] very useful to the Jews."[70] The Theatine missionary Giovanni Maria Vincenti contended that his treatise on the Messiah was "not only necessary to Jews, but very useful to Christians and above all to Preachers."[71] Some even promised to help a reader to play preacher if he encountered a Jewish person willing to listen. Thus Bell'haver argued that his *Easy Doctrine* "will be very useful to the preachers, and every other religious person, who, having no knowledge of the holy tongue, can rely on it in disputes and reasonings about the holy

---

67. Pichi, *Trattato della passione e morte del Messia contra gli ebrei,* 3r.

68. Ciantes, *Della Santissima Trinità,* 2r.

69. BAV Borg. lat. 47, 2r–v.

70. Melchior Palontrotti, *Breue raccolta d'argomenti, cauati dalla sac. Scrit. & dall'antiche tradittioni di rabbini, con le quali chiaramente si prouano i dogmi della religion christiana contra l'hebraica perfidia.*

71. Giovanni Maria Vicenti, *Il Messia Venuto ... non solamente necessaria a gli Hebrei, ma molto utile à Cristiani e massime à' Predicatori.* The work was placed on the Index of Prohibited Books in 1680, according to Moshe Carmeli-Weinberger's introduction to William Popper, *The Censorship of Hebrew Books.* This is confirmed in the *Index Librorum Prohibitorum usque ad annum MDCCIV. Regnante Clemente XI,* 262, which lists Vicenti's title in the index's decree of June 18, 1680.

faith with those same Jews."[72] And Giulio Morosini's *The Path of Faith* was "no less interesting than useful, principally for those who converse or deal with Jewish people, or preach to them."[73] These claims overreach. Professional preachers had a good system for composing sermons, relying mostly on model sermon books and precedents from colleagues; polemical authors, meanwhile, really sought a wider readership. But pitching a work to conversionary preachers justified a treatise, raised its game, signaled its ambition, and thereby showed the esteem given to the role.

All conversionary preachers were erudite, but some dedicated themselves especially to scholarship. The exemplar of this type of preacher was Gregorio Boncompagni Corcos degli Scarinci. As we have seen, Boncompagni was the descendant of Ugo Boncompagni, né Salomone Corcos, the wealthy Jewish patriarch whose family's celebrated conversion had brought welcome publicity to the first decades of the conversionary campaign. Gregory XIII Boncompagni extended his surname and coat of arms to the family, which then became great supporters of Philip Neri and his nascent Oratorian order, as we have seen.[74] Gregorio, raised a Catholic, studied Semitic languages from his youth onward and was appointed predicatore degli ebrei from 1649 until his death in 1688. Boncompagni is the only Dominican conversionary preacher of confirmed Jewish origin.[75]

In addition to his scholarly collaborations and friendship with Giovanni Pastrizio and Giulio Bartolocci, previously discussed, Boncompagni pursued other scholarly projects. His intellect and high status linked him to

72. "Et credo altresi, che sarà molto utile a Rever. Padri. Predicatori, & ad ogni altro persona Religiosa, etiandio, che non havesse alcuna cognitione della lingua santa, per servirsene alle ocasioni nella disputa, & nei ragionamenti della Santa Fede con gli stessi Hebrei." Bell'haver, *Dottrina facile et breve*, A6r.

73. Giulio Morosini, *Via della fede mostrata à gli ebrei . . . Opera non men curiosa che utile principalmente per chi conversa o tratta con gli'Ebrei, o predica loro*.

74. Alberto Bianco, "Cesare Baronio e la conversione dei Corcos nei documenti d'archivio della Congregazione oratoriana di Roma"; Gianni Incisa della Rocchetta and Nello Vian, *Il primo processo per san Filippo Neri del Codice vaticano latino 3798 e in altri esemplari dell'Archivio dell'Oratorio di Roma*, 126–27. Gregorio, who lived until 1688, may have been a late son to Lazzaro/Gregorio by his second wife, Lisa Buratti, who is noted in 1610, or may have been their grandson. Either way, he was born three to five decades after Lazzaro/Gregorio's conversion. See Bianco, "Cesare Baronio e la conversion dei Corcos," 159.

75. For Boncompagni, see also Boiteux, "Preaching to the Jews in Early Modern Rome: Words and Images," 312; Marina Caffiero, *Legami Pericolosi: Ebrei e cristiani tra eresia, libri proibiti e stregoneria*, 280–90. Boiteux erroneously names Boncompagni as the only convert among official conversionary preachers of the seventeenth century rather than as the descendent of converts, and in her account, mistranslates *nipote* as nephew, not grandson. Satta, in "Predicatori," speculates that the Spanish ancestors of Ciantes might have been Jewish, in which case Boncompagni was not the first.

many religious institutions across Rome, such as the Dominican college at Santa Maria sopra Minerva, where he trained. Like his Dominican predecessors, Boncompagni was later based in the basilica of Santa Maria Maggiore, where he joined the Liberian Chapter College of Penitentiaries. He was the college's chief librarian, funding its major renovation, expanding its non-Italian collection, and making it competitive with other scholarly libraries in Rome.[76] Carlo Bartolomeo Piazza, in his survey of Roman institutions, singled him out by name when he discussed the glories of Roman libraries. The library of the College of Penitentiaries, he wrote, "cedes nothing to the libraries mentioned above. It has been restored in a magnificent building, greatly amplified by the noble, copious, and well-furnished library left by P. Maestro Gregorio Scarinci Domenicano, of the Order which governs this college, a Dominican friar of great doctrine, erudition, and virtue."[77]

For Pichi, Ciantes, and most other conversionary preachers, we must deduce their pulpit rhetoric from their published work. But their greatest intellectual successor left us his actual sermons. Despite leaving no trace in print, Boncompagni left a wide bookshelf's worth of manuscripts: some notes, a treatise, and ten large volumes of conversionary sermons—a long lifetime's work.[78] These annotated sermons, along with his various other reflections and treatises, are discussed more fully in the second half of this book. Boncompagni's activities outside the pulpit suggest a more distant manner than his predecessors, more concerned with his colleagues in scholarship and evangelization than with their Jewish targets in person. For instance, Boncompagni edited De Monte's works, which were preserved in the library he oversaw at Santa Maria Maggiore.

Boncompagni also signed off on Morosini's *The Path of Faith*. Endorsing the works of new converts was common for conversionary preachers—an activity where their position was especially valuable. Well into the eighteenth century, a preacher's official title always appeared with his endorsement. As mentioned in chapter 2, the convert Francesco Maria Ferretti received an endorsement from the current *predicatore degli ebrei*,

76. Zucchi, "Rome domenicana," 120–21; PT Masetti, *Monumenta et Antiquitates veteris disciplinae ordinis praedicatorum ab anno 1216 ad 1348 praesertim in Romana provincia Praefectorumque qui eandem rexerunt Biographica Chronotaxis*, 2:152–53; Guendalina Serafinelli, "Guido Reni, Clemente Boncompagni Corcos e lo stendardo doppio di San Francesco: Rinvenimenti d'archivio."

77. Carlo Bartolomeo Piazza, *Eusevologio Romano Eusevologio Romano overo Delle Opere Pie di Roma*, part 13, cxv [volume f. P2v].

78. These are discussed at greater length in chapters 5 and 6.

Raimondo Maria Berlati, in publishing his treatise *The Truth of the Christian Faith*. Ferretti's case had been made famous by the preacher who converted him, Paolo Sebastiano Medici. Berlati approved a similar treatise by the convert and censor Giovanni Antonio Costanzi.[79] Costanzi later paid the favor forward, approving the redaction decisions of a later preacher and censor, Antonio Teoli, whom he labels as "Padre Predicatore" even in a censorship context.[80] He was perhaps repaying a debt to Teoli, who had supported Costanzi when he was newly arrived in Rome and sought to evangelize local Jewish people. Costanzi described this interaction in his treatise, noting that "this is a thing proven in an authentic attestation that I keep with me . . . by the late P. Antonio Teoli, who was then preacher to the Jews in this same city."[81]

In these endorsements, roughly a paragraph each, the preacher's job was to reassure readers that the content was orthodox as well as beneficial to Christians. Often, the preacher would approve the author's use of rabbinic sources, but he might endorse the work even if it did not include such sources. Gregorio Compagni gave an imprimatur to Giovanni Piero Pinamonte's *The Synagogue Disenchanted*, even though it was not based on Hebrew sources and made some practical arguments that preachers avoided.[82] Lorenzo Virgulti provided one of the pages of approbation for an especially unusual treatise published jointly by a bishop of Verona, Francesco Trevisani, and the Jewish woman he had converted and to whom he gave his name: Francesca Maria Trevisana.[83] This was an atypical treatise in having a woman's name on the title page, even though within the text she remained a silent interlocutor. The treatise appears to commemorate the occasion of her conversion and monachization, which represented a notable achievement for Trevisani. Trevisana's story is recounted at length at the beginning of the volume. Virgulti's

79. DBI sv "Andrea de Monte"; Morosini, *Via della fede mostrata à gli ebrei*; Francesco Maria Ferretti, *Le verità della fede cristiana*; Paolo Sebastiano Medici, *Conversione di Sabato Nachamu Rabbino ebreo in Ancona seguita l'anno 1735 descritta*; Giovanni Antonio Costanzi, *La verità della cristiana religione contro le vane lusinghe di moderni ebrei*, xi.

80. ACDF St St BB 3 r, 182r.

81. Costanzi, *La verità della cristiana religione contro le vane lusinghe di moderni ebrei*, xiii. On this interaction, see Ariel Toaff, "Giovanni Antonio Costanzi, ultimo censore di libri ebraici a Roma (1745–1756 ca.)," 208–9.

82. Giovanni Pietro Pinamonti, *La Sinagoga disingannata: overo via facile à mostrare a qualunque ebreo la falsità della sua setta*, a2r. On Pinamonti, see Teter, *Blood Libel*, 188–90.

83. Francesco Trevisani, *Conferenze pastorali istruttive sopra la verità della fede cristiana, fatte da Monsig. Francesco Trevisani con Sara figlia di Salvatore Conegliano ebreo di Ceneda, ora Suor Francesca Maria Trevisana*, unpaginated d3v.

commendation of Trevisani's *Pastoral Lectures* follows the approbations of five other clerics, including two archbishops. Of these, Virgulti's is the one able to provide reassurance that the contents satisfactorily dissolved the arguments of the rabbis and would acquaint Jews with their own errors.

As skilled Hebraists, conversionary preachers also served as or collaborated with censors of Hebrew books, who worked according to the norms of the Index of Prohibited Books, first published in 1559, and the Congregation of the Index that supported it. The church's book censorship program was not directed solely or even primarily against Jews but instead operated throughout the Catholic world.[84] The Congregation of the Index's attention to Jewish books in the Counter-Reformation primarily reflected the fear that Jewish texts would offend Catholic dogma, but also that they might tacitly support Protestant ideas.[85] Censors were often converted Jews with strong Hebrew skills. One might think censorship is an activity fundamentally opposite to conversionary preaching: hiding or expurgating Jewish texts rather than discussing them in public. But censors and preachers could see the two activities as complementary; both preaching and censorship sought to remedy the perceived dangers of rabbinic or Talmudic texts. One bowdlerized those texts; the other belittled them to Jews directly in sermons.[86] The two roles were thus closely intertwined. De Monte moved from preaching in the pulpit to censoring in the library. Ciantes, Boncompagni, and possibly Pichi moonlighted as censors during their tenure as conversionary preachers.[87] In the early eighteenth century, the conversionary preachers Virgulti and Teoli both also served as censors.

The overlap between preaching and censoring was scholarly as well as personal. Scholars of censorship have described a world of close collaboration between censors, preachers, and other Hebraists. These groups shared a goal of compiling a body of Jewish texts that would support Christianity while preserving those aspects of ancient Hebrew and Judaism that were deemed inoffensive and valuable. At its most intellectual,

84. For an introduction to book censorship in Italy, see Gigliola Fragnito, *La Bibbia al Rogo: La censura ecclesiastica e i volgarizzamenti della Scrittura (1471–1605)*; Gigliola Fragnito, *Church, Censorship and Culture in Early Modern Italy*; Giorgio Caravale, *Forbidden Prayer: Church Censorship and Devotional Literature in Renaissance Italy*.

85. Michael T. Walton and Phyllis J. Walton, "In Defense of the Church Militant: The Censorship of the Rashi Commentary in the Magna Biblia Rabbinica."

86. van Boxel, "Robert Bellarmine Reads Rashi"; van Boxel, *Jewish Books in Christian Hands*. This position contradicts somewhat the one taken in Amnon Raz-Krakotzkin, *The Censor, the Editor, and the Text: The Catholic Church and the Shaping of the Jewish Canon in the Sixteenth Century*.

87. Popper, *The Censorship of Hebrew Books*, 104; Caffiero, *Legami Pericolosi*, 293.

this collaboration could be seen as a way to preserve Jewish texts that troubled Christians instead of destroying them entirely.[88] Books were frequently corrected or expurgated as a means of keeping them in circulation. At times, censorship was performed with a light touch or more leniently in practice than stated in law; sometimes it could be performed mechanically and thoughtlessly, leading to incoherent texts. Readers and printers could also find ways to subvert censored texts.[89] But at its harshest, censorship had the effect of reinforcing the boundaries between Christians and Jews, protecting Christian minds from contamination by Jewish ideas just as the ghetto protected Christian bodies.[90] The censor Costanzi made a practice of confiscating Hebrew manuscripts from Jewish possession in Rome and Ancona, including a magnificent copy of the Zohar, and bringing them to the Biblioteca Casanatense, thus forming the basis of the library's contemporary collections.[91]

Teoli may have been the first to admit to conflict between the preaching and censorship, identifying a need for gentleness that other preachers had overlooked. A letter he addressed to the Holy Office described how his obligations as a preacher limited his scope as a censor: "I was determined (within the bounds of conscience) to produce a favorable relation [of certain books], so as not to infuriate the Jews, but to win their affection, which I consider necessary for disposing them graciously toward making my sermons bear fruit." He asked to be excused from further revisions, which "make me too hateful to the Jews, and prejudice that pious affection that I need them to have for me, so that I can, in my office as preacher, pull them graciously to awareness of our holy faith."[92]

But if censorship and preaching were so closely intertwined, why were censors much more frequently converts, while the most celebrated

---

88. van Boxel, "Robert Bellarmine Reads Rashi," 125; van Boxel, *Jewish Books in Christian Hands*, 167–71. On sixteenth-century Hebrew censorship in Italy more generally, see Gila Rosen-Prebor, "Domenico Yerushalmi: His Life, Writings and Work as a Censor"; Raz-Krakotzkin, *The Censor, the Editor, and the Text*; Amy E. Phillips, "Censorship of Hebrew Books in Sixteenth Century Italy. A Review of a Decade of English and French Language Scholarship."

89. Piet van Boxel, "Hebrew Books and Censorship in Sixteenth-Century Italy."

90. Federica Francesconi, "'This Passage Can Also Be Read Differently . . .': How Jews and Christians Censored Hebrew Texts in Early Modern Modena."

91. On Costanzi, see Biblioteca Casanatense, *Le cinquecentine ebraiche: catalogo*; Fausto Parente, "Di uno scritto antiebraico della meta del xviii secolo: la verita della cristiana religione contro le vane lusinghe de' moderni ebrei di Giovanni Antonio Costanzi (1705 ca.–1785)"; Toaff, "Giovanni Antonio Costanzi."

92. ACDF St St BB 3 r, frontispiece, 1r. Marina Caffiero has also noted the importance and novelty of Teoli's position. See Caffiero, *Legami Pericolosi*, 293–95.

preachers were almost always Catholic by birth?[93] Three possible explanations seem likely. First, censors needed mastery of a sophisticated range of Hebrew biblical, rabbinic, halachic, and liturgical literature, which learned converts would have acquired in their earlier Jewish education. Preachers, in contrast, could rely on a body of received preaching literature and conventions, and more frequently recycle a narrower set of Hebrew sources. Second, preachers required greater familiarity with Catholic theology and dogma in order to construct their own rhetorical arguments. Converts lacked this level of training, and the job of censorship did not require it. Finally, in their exceedingly public role, preachers needed more credibility and respect than the more secluded position of censor in order to embed their sermons in a wider Catholic context at a high status.

Hebrew skills also proved useful in other contexts. As previously noted, the preacher Girolamo Mascella served on the selection committee for the Hebrew language chair at Sapienza University in 1696; Boncompagni collaborated with Bartolocci and also endorsed every volume of Bartolocci's *Bibliotheca Magna Rabbinica* published during his lifetime. Virgulti, as both preacher and censor, reviewed a cache of Hebrew documents taken from the ghetto, writing up a report on their contents to the Inquisition; in other cases, he provided the Inquisition with his scholarly opinion and commentary on a list of questions about Jewish practice and its effect on Christians.[94] Luigi Pisani, a convert who preached to Jews in Rome, printed a long opinion on the legal properties of Jewish marriages. His brief formed part of a complex case of contested baptism during an engagement that much preoccupied the Holy Office. Pisani's contribution was intended to help the Inquisition decide in favor of the convert, another Francesco Maria Feretti. Pisani identified himself in these cases as a predicatore degli ebrei, although his position was less certain.[95]

Pisani's life also tells a more complicated story about conversion and preaching. As we have seen, Jewish converts to Catholicism remained

---

93. The specific sermon-related commission in van Boxel's *Jewish Books in Christian Hands* might be considered an exception to a general pattern of employing mostly converts as censors.

94. Giulio Bartolocci, *Bibliotheca magna rabbinica de scriptoribus, & scriptis Hebraicis, ordine alphabetico Hebraicè, & Latinè digestis*, vols. 1–3; BAV Borg. lat. 476, 20r, 244r–v; ACDF TT 4 b, int. 16; ACDF QQ 3 L, int. 6. For a retelling of this incident, see Caffiero, *Legami Pericolosi*, 40–42.

95. ACDF Doctrinalia S.O. e voti Doctrinalia 1711–13, 1/1, 12v; ACDF St St UV 53, 449r–50v. The convert was baptized Francesco Maria Ferretti, but is a different man from the Francesco Maria Ferretti converted by Paolo Sebastiano Medici. This convert was born Raffaele Aboab, from Pesaro; the other was Sabbato Nachamu, from Ancona.

under suspicion. In an era alert to false or expedient conversions, converts to Catholicism often felt compelled to spend their lives and careers demonstrating that their new faith was genuine. Furthermore, for learned converts in particular, a career in Hebrew language or proselytization was one of only a few career options available. A few erudite converts reached memorable heights. A great many less illustrious ones left no further trace after baptism. The documentary record of Pisani shows us a life in the middle—a rabbi and then a learned preacher who nonetheless seemed to struggle in his new situation. Pisani preached to the Jews of Rome in the late seventeenth and early eighteenth centuries. We know this in part from a treatise objecting to his sermon, written by R. Tranquillo Vita Corcos, and in part from traces he left in the records of Pastrizio. The treatise lays out Jewish objections to Pisani's aggressive rhetoric (and is discussed at greater length in chapter 7). The remaining evidence from Pastrizio's papers suggests a life of supplication.

Pisani requested one copy of Bartolocci's *Bibliotheca Magna Rabbinica* and a Hebrew translation of the gospels from Propaganda Fide "to use in the discourses that he gives by the order of our lord to the Jews on Saturday after the sermon."[96] This description casts doubt on Pisani's official status in regard to his Catholic-born colleague who delivered "the sermon," but tells us that early eighteenth-century conversionary sermons must then still have followed the practice of pairing cradle Catholics with preachers who were converts from Judaism. His use of the term *discorsi* to distinguish his preaching from the regular *prediche* (sermons) indicates two preachers of varying importance. A receipt dated eleven days later confirms that he got his books and signed for them.[97] Three weeks later, Pisani wrote to thank the congregation for helping him with his debts.[98]

Pisani entreated Pastrizio twice more privately in 1704 to lend him certain late medieval philosophical works and tractates of Talmud because he had "need of them to find out one matter for the service of God"; he promised to take good care of the books and keep them safe.[99] When writing directly to Pastrizio, he wrote sometimes in Hebrew and sometimes in a macaronic Italian, keeping the book titles and his own signature in Hebrew.

---

96. *Memoriale dell'Ebrei contro le prediche di Luigi Pisani Rabino convertito fol 496*, ASVR Atti della segreteria del tribunale del cardinale vicario, tom. 5. This treatise is discussed at length in chapter 7. For Pisani here, see ASPF SC Stamperia I, 665r.

97. ASPF SC Stamperia I, 1622–1720, 665r.

98. ASPF Misc. Gen. XIII, 89r.

99. BAV "מפני שיש לי הכרח והוא למצא ענין אחד לעבודת השם ושכרו כפול משמים." Borg. lat. 499, 86r, 87r–v.

In Hebrew he is deeply obsequious, assuring Pastrizio rewards in the world to come. Pisani's dependence on Pastrizio comes through in another record among Pastrizio's papers, describing Pisani as a former rabbi from a famous family and skilled proselytizer who had converted many rabbis himself before he suffered a downfall in 1697 for which he now required charity. The note, drafted in Pastrizio's own hand, petitions a superior on Pisani's behalf. Pastrizio's support continued; another note from 1707 shows Pisani signing in promise to repay a loan of seven scudi and fifty baiocchi, given to him as aid in time of need. Pisani, it seems, kept company with the scholarly elite, but never found firm footing.[100] Converted preachers did not always reach the heights that may have been promised to them before baptism.

By the middle decades of the seventeenth century, then, conversionary preaching became less of a marvel and more of a cog in the wider machinery of ecclesiastical bureaucracy. While dogged Christian propagandists continued to pour new treatises into the stream of anti-Jewish polemics, they seem to have been less concerned with occupying the pulpit itself. Instead, the post passed to a stable series of Dominican friars and, in some instances, converted co-preachers. Traces of novelty preachers and single sermons decline, while records of the official Dominican predicatori degli ebrei become easier to document.

Most Dominican conversionary preachers, with institutional weight behind them, felt less need to flatter their audience, evidently deciding that anti-Jewish violence in word or deed was compatible with public sermons, and would not influence the chances of winning converts. Yet this process of becoming routine does not mean that conversionary preaching became less important; on the contrary, it endured, secure in its reputation. The sixteenth-century interest in conversionary preaching did not so much dissipate in the seventeenth century as diffuse. The official title of predicatore degli ebrei brought authority and gravitas to a range of other activities, and advanced the careers of those who bore it.

100. BAV Borg. lat. 481, 219r; BAV Borg. lat. 746, 270r.

CHAPTER FOUR

Sermons to Jews
and the Public

A DIVINE VOICE told the young Joseph Calasanz to leave his native Spain, abandon his successful career as vicar general in the diocese of Urgel, and journey to Rome. Knowing that Rome had triggered the spiritual downfall of many an earnest cleric, Calasanz was reluctant at first. But he quickly found that the journey brought him success. On arrival in 1592, he adopted an intense schedule of devotional activities that he maintained for the rest of his life. These inspired him to found a series of schools as well as his own religious order to run them, ultimately leading to his canonization in 1767.[1]

The life that Calasanz built for himself in Rome, as recounted in the 1753 vita advocating his canonization, demonstrates not only the enormous range of pious and devotional activities on offer in the Eternal City but also the full kinship between Rome's conversionary efforts and its broader religious revival. When Calasanz entered the city for the first time in 1592, trying to make his way immediately to Saint Peter's basilica, he ran across the *possesso* ceremony of the newly elected Pope Clement VIII. The possesso, which wound across the city from the Vatican to the church of Saint John Lateran, was the most splendid and notable of all Roman processions, as it marked the pope's formal (legal) action, as bishop of

---

1. For this recounting, see Vincenzo Talenti, *Vita del beato Giuseppe Calasanzio, della Madre di Dio, fondatore de' Chierici poveri della Madre di Dio delle scuole pie.* For the Piarists, his religious order, see Karen Liebreich, *Fallen Order: Intrigue, Heresy, and Scandal in the Rome of Galileo and Caravaggio.*

Rome, of taking possession of his diocese.[2] But it was only one of many displays that sought simultaneously to celebrate, reinforce, and argue for Roman Catholicism; religious processions, devotions, dramas, tableaux, and intensified pilgrimages all helped to turn Rome into a setting for Counter-Reformation spectacle.

Calasanz had come to Rome precisely in order to soak up this environment and immerse himself in it. To that end, he deliberately joined the new confraternity of Santissima Trinità dei Pellegrini, which embodied the links between devotion and conversion. The confraternity, in turn, came under the umbrella guidance of the recently established Congregation of the Oratory, which as we have seen, was one of many new religious orders that made their home in Rome and sponsored some of its most dynamic religious activities. The Congregation of the Oratory, under Philip Neri's leadership, met regularly for prayer, sermons, and the spiritual direction of laypeople, and established new popular devotions that galvanized the city.[3] Over time, it also hosted some of the best sacred music in Rome in its church of Santa Maria in Vallicella (Chiesa Nuova). Neri himself took a special interest in conversion, as discussed earlier, famously meeting the young Jewish Corcos boys for the gentle conversations that led to their conversion as well as that of their brothers and mother.[4]

Calasanz's vita provides a long description of the many devotional rituals he undertook as a member of the confraternity of Santissima Trinità dei Pellegrini. These included the pilgrimage to the Seven Churches of Rome, visiting churches especially for the jubilee, catechizing heretics, caring for poor pilgrims from abroad, washing the feet of the pilgrims, seeing to their food and lodging, and preaching to the Jews in the confraternity's oratory. The vita tells us that Calasanz was an enthusiastic participant in all of these activities:

2. On the early modern possesso, see Irene Fosi, "Court and City in the Ceremony of the Possesso in the Sixteenth Century."

3. Maria Teresa Bonadonna Russo, "Il conversionismo devoto di Filippo Neri tra eredità savonaroliane e rigori inquisitoriali"; Bonadonna Russo, M. Teresa [Maria Teresa], and Niccolò Del Re, San Filippo Neri nella realtà romana del XVI secolo: atti del convegno di studio in occasione del iv centenario della morte di San Filippo Neri (1595–1995): Roma, 11–13 Maggio 1995; Luigi Fiorani, "'Charità e pietate.' Confraternite e gruppi devoti nella città rinascimentale e barocca."

4. Gianni Incisa della Rocchetta and Nello Vian, Il primo processo per san Filippo Neri del codice vaticano latino 3798 e in altri esemplari dell'Archivio dell'Oratorio di Roma; Louis Ponnelle, Louis Bordet, and Ralph Francis Kerr, St. Philip Neri and the Roman Society of His Times (1515–1595), 523–33, 580.

In addition to [all the exercises of the confraternity], was the preaching to the Jews assembled in it, and other pious works, and Giuseppe committed himself to all of them, and not only did he fulfill them by himself, but he brought the workers in his schools to do them too.[5]

Neither Calasanz nor the author of his vita seems to have seen proselytizing non-Catholics as a niche activity reserved for specialists. Nor did conversionary preaching bring them out of a Catholic orbit and into a Jewish one. To them, sermons to Jews were simply one more item in the array of public Catholic devotions that made Rome a sacred landscape.

Preaching to Jews was always a public event—a spectacle that was critically valuable to the Christian fabric of the city. From the outset, its founders expected and assumed that Christians would attend. The presence of onlookers at sermons was considered so essential that it itself became a subject of discussion within Catholic circles and even in the sermons themselves. Indeed, while sermons purported to address Jews, Jews were only the secondary audience; the Christian spectators served as the primary listeners. Conversionary preaching needed spectators because propaganda always does. Much of the event's value lay in its ritualistic, scripted nature. The tightly controlled performance suggested to onlookers that Counter-Reformation Rome truly was achieving its ideal of perfect Catholic piety—so much so that it was even succeeding in converting the Jews. The sermons also offered a model of the way Jewish-Christian relations were meant to work within that idealized vision.[6]

Drawn to a novel, prestigious experience marketed directly to them, Christian spectators duly filled the room. Sermons became a popular attraction, drawing travelers from abroad as well as locals. The spectacle of conversionary preaching in Rome was so distinctive and popular that for many visitors, it became a defining feature of the entire city, and remained one throughout the early modern period.

In order for this performance to succeed, all the actors also had to know how to play their roles. In Rome, Christians and Jews alike were well versed in the conventions of public ritual. As an act of religious theater, sermons to Jews slotted naturally into two of the city's broader ritual networks: Rome as a ceremonial city, and Jews as actors in Christian dramas. Participants and spectators applied their experience from these other networks to the Saturday sermons, affixing them firmly within the

5. Talenti, *Vita del beato Giuseppe Calasanzio*, 76–77.
6. On rituals that model an ideal society or are otherwise prescriptive, see Edward Muir, *Ritual in Early Modern Europe*, 5–6.

devotional network and ritual life of early modern Rome. The Christian framework imposed on these sermons also extended into printed sermons and sermon rhetoric. Printed sermons that claimed to address Jews were structured for a Christian readership. And preaching rhetoric deployed the word "Jew" in sermons in a way that could clearly be understood to refer to Christians, even in the presence of Jews. All of these factors demonstrate that the performance of preaching to Jews had incomparable value to Rome's "society of spectacle," which was manufactured by ecclesiastical policy and rhetoric, and imposed on all early modern Romans.

Christian and Catechumen
Attendance Discussed

As the importance of spectators grew, Christian attendance at conversionary sermons became the subject of deliberate discussion. Gregorio Boncompagni worried the subject from many angles. He considered titling a sermon "We Ask Whether Christians Should Participate in the Preaching to Jews," but ultimately abandoned the idea, leaving only the title, written out three times on a blank page.[7] He devoted another undated sermon to asking "the reason why many do not convert to the faith of Christ," and whether disputations between Catholics and infidels were useful.[8] Boncompagni ultimately preached at length on the subject directly in his sermon of July 15, 1673: "We ask whether it is permitted to preach to the Jews, dispute with Jews, and preach publicly to the Jews in the presence of Christians." His firm "yes" to this question argued that a mixed audience carried the weight of tradition and that Christians spectators would act as a check on Jewish misbehavior. But most of his reasons dwell heavily on the benefits to Christians. Boncompagni asserted explicitly what many boastful book titles only hint at: that sermons to Jews made invaluable tools for teaching necessary doctrine to Christians that they would not otherwise learn. As he put it, "Because it is good that in front of Christians the faith of Jesus Christ is confessed, praised, explained, and defended, which is not done in other sermons."[9] His sermon defends at length the pedagogical value of conversionary sermons for faithful Christians

---

7. BAV Borg. lat. 115, 378v. The title of this sermon was crossed out or overwritten the first time, written in full the second time, and showed a depletion of ink the third time.

8. BAV Borg. lat. 129, 427r–28v.

9. BAV Borg. lat. 129, 499r. The sermon and its afterlife in Giulio Bartolocci's *Bibliotheca Magna Rabbinica* are discussed at greater length in other chapters.

searching for truth and illumination. As a confessional tool, conversionary sermons were irreplaceable.[10]

Christian spectators mattered ever more, perhaps, because another critical population may have quit the show. At the outset and for at least half a century thereafter, converting Jews from the House of Catechumens and College of Neophytes continued to attend conversionary sermons. Students in the college, of course, attended as part of their training. But above all, the visible presence of both groups was a theologically necessary piece of showy propaganda. The spectacle of future and newly baptized Catholics in the pews, dressed in their especially visible black or white clothing, suggested a direct link between preaching and converting.

For the early years of conversionary preaching, the evidence that these "in-between" witnesses attended sermons is incontrovertible. After 1634, however, when the cluster of conversionary institutions moved to its permanent, grander site at Santa Maria ai Monti, the indications are less certain. The regulations for the College of Neophytes published in 1690 point to continuity: "On Saturday the host is displayed in church, and when there is a sermon, everybody should go, and to get there in time in winter, they will leave off the last half hour of school."[11] Given that the college, House of Catechumens, and church all formed part of the same connected structure, the extra half hour suggests a walk to a new neighborhood, such as from the *rione* (district) of Monti to that of Regola, which housed Trinità dei Pellegrini. But in his sermon and lists discussing Christian attendance at conversionary sermons, Boncompagni lamented the absence of these students. He noted that even though Gregory XIII had ordered neophytes from the college to attend sermons for Jews every Saturday, "Ever since they went to the Madonna dei Monti they don't come anymore, because they attend the litanies that they sing every Saturday in [that] church."[12]

In precisely this period, the confreres of Santissima Trinità dei Pellegrini received a special indulgence for attending conversionary sermons taking place on their own property. "Sermons to the Jews" appears in the lists of confraternity indulgences for the first time in 1640, shortly after the construction of the Santa Maria ai Monti complex. Confraternity members

10. BAV Borg. lat. 129, 75r–77r.

11. "Il Sabbato s'espone in Chiesa il Santissimo, e quando vi sarà il Sermone tutti v'interverranno, e per venirvi à tempo l'Inverno, lascieranno l'ultima mezz'hora di Scola." *Relationi economiche date all'eminentiss. e reverendiss. Sig. Card. Fulvio Astalli nell'ingresso alla protettione della chiesa della Madonna Santissima de' Monti di Roma*, 13.

12. BAV Borg. Lat. 129, 499r.

received an indulgence of fifty years "to those deputized *fratelli* who, wearing the sackcloth of the archconfraternity, attend the preaching to the Jews that is usually held for them in the oratory of the said confraternity."[13] Fifty years is an unusually powerful indulgence for this group. Most indulgences were only granted for seven years, five years, or a period of less than one year. Attending conversionary sermons therefore seems to have been especially meritorious. Was the presence of the confreres perhaps increasingly necessary, to fill the benches vacated by the neophytes?

As neophytes withdrew from the public sermon and Rome concurrently drew ever more foreign tourists, the nature of the preaching spectacle changed, relying more on these international visitors. Pilgrim guidebooks to Rome, a skyrocketing genre, only reinforced the notion that sermons were open to the public and worth attending.[14] Visitors to Rome had long drawn on a few standard guides, honed and revised over centuries. First among these was the *Wonders of the City of Rome*, the much-reprinted twelfth-century guide to the chief sites of ancient Rome. Pilgrims turned to the thirteenth-century *Stations of the Churches of the City of Rome* or *Indulgences of the Churches of the City of Rome*, or they combined both stations and indulgences in one volume.[15] But by the sixteenth century, old and new Roman sites appeared together in one guidebook, especially Francesco Albertini's wildly popular *Booklet of the New and Old Wonders of the City of Rome*.[16] This development enabled the rise of a new kind of pious guidebook, celebrating Rome's triumphant, rejuvenated sanctity. These reveled in celebrations of new Rome's many sacred institutions and devotions. Conversionary preaching was often a special point of pride for them; it was an event easier to find in Rome than anywhere else, and full of opportunities for self-congratulation.

Gregory Martin's *Roma Sancta* could serve as the notable English example of such guidebooks, but Italians had many more. Many of these books paid special attention to Rome's increasingly famous Jews and the campaign to convert them. *Rome Researched On-site* ignored the entire Holy Year frenzy that animated Santissima Trinità dei Pellegrini and made it famous. Instead, it defined the confraternity only as "the church and

13. ASR Trinità dei Pellegrini, 523, filza 3.

14. Martine Boiteux, "Parcours rituels romains à l'époque moderne," 52–61.

15. Maria Accame Lanzillotta and Emy Dell'Oro, *I 'Mirabilia urbis Romae'*; Christopher Kleinhenz, *Medieval Italy: An Encyclopedia*, 988 sv "Rome: Guidebooks." The titles translated above are the *Mirabilia Urbis Romae*, *Statione ecclesiarum Urbis Romae*, and *Indulgentiae ecclesiarum Urbis Romae*.

16. The title translated above is *Opusculum di Mirabilibus Novae et Veteris Urbis Romae*. Matthew Sturgis, *When in Rome: 2000 Years of Roman Sightseeing*, 118–22.

hospital of convalescents and pilgrims of Santissima Trinità, in whose oratory the Jewish people are preached to, every Saturday."[17] Other guidebooks
dwelled on the sermons at even greater length. A passage that passed
verbatim from Pompilio Totti's *Portrait of Modern Rome* to Federico
Franzini's *Ancient and Modern Rome* described the history of conversionary preaching, emphasizing its coercive elements and connections with
papal power:

> A very learned Jewish rabbi, who converted and was baptized and
> named Andrea De Monte by Pope Julius III, having compassion on his
> blind people, began to preach to them in a few Roman churches with
> great doctrine and spirit. But because the Jews would not go to hear
> him, and fled him as much as possible, he worked with Pope Greg-
> ory XIII such that under punishments as the Ordinaries determined
> the Jews were compelled for a third of them to go on Saturdays, with
> women and children from age twelve, to hear the word of God. And it
> remained that a hundred men would go, and fifty women, every Sat-
> urday after lunch, and so that they would not sleep, and would behave
> modestly, a policeman stays there with a truncheon in his hand, who,
> when the preacher alerts him, touches whoever sleeps. And because,
> when they enter this church, they go to give their names to somebody
> who stands by the door and writes it down, when the sermon ends, the
> policeman goes and notes those who are resistant, and fines them one
> *testone* each, which is applied to the poor catechumens.[18]

By the end of the century, conversionary preaching merited its own
chapter and a full discussion in a celebration of Rome, at least in the
Eusevologio Romano, that massive survey by Carlo Bartolomeo Piazza.
Piazza's discussion reviews the history of Jews in Rome from their earliest arrival, with emphasis on papal privileges toward them. In this light,
it presents Gregory XIII's legislation on preaching, described in detail,
as a continuation of papal generosity. Published in the 1690s, just at the
moment when anti-Jewish rhetoric began to veer sharply toward more
confrontation (as described in chapter 7), the *Eusevologio* stresses how
popes wanted sweetness and charity from conversionary preachers: "The
wise pope suggested that [preaching] be done with great charity and
gentleness, rather than through insult and invective, so that the light

17. "la Chiesa & Ospidale della Santissima Trinità; nel cui Oratio si predica ogni
sabbato al Popolo Ebreo." Fioravante Martinelli, *Roma ricercata nel suo sito*, 22.

18. Pompilio Totti, *Ritratto di Roma moderna*, 186–88; Federico Franzini, *Roma Antica
e Moderna*, 204.

of Catholic truth would pierce them frequently . . . he privileged those preachers destined for this sacred ministry with every favor."[19] Jewish people, in contrast, appear in his chapter as restive and resistant, in need of policing, much as in previous depictions. Piazza lists the various deceits they might employ to avoid a sermon, from switching places to pleading excuses, and dwells on the need for a deputy at the door who would recognize them. He details the punishments meted on Jewish people who transgressed. And he praises the pope for allowing Christians to attend sermons "for many wise reasons and motives," even though "the Rabbis and Heads of the Ghetto often tried to prevent this with many artifices, claims, and efforts."[20] As Rose Marie San Juan has argued, the rise of such locally produced guidebooks represented internal struggles and priorities within the city. In this case, guidebooks promoted conversionary sermons as a uniquely important event for understanding the city's values, open to visitors and worth their time.[21]

Tourist and Local Spectators at Sermons

Roman residents instinctively saw preaching to Jews as an event aimed directly at themselves too. Sermon hopping was an established aspect of Catholic devotional life in Italy, especially during the forty days of Lent, when sermons took place every day simultaneously in multiple churches. Attending a sermon with the added twist of a Jewish element was no great extra stretch for an avid sermon goer. In the Vatican archives, a manuscript diary records the daily activities of an unnamed Italian priest. When the household he served moved from Spain to Rome in the late 1570s, the diarist began to take especially careful note of the sermons he attended nearly every day of Lent. He continued the practice every year until the diary ended in 1593.[22] The priest belonged to an increasingly important entourage. During the 1580s, his employer, Ippolito Aldobrandini, was elevated to the cardinalate and later became Pope Clement VIII. Throughout the diarist's time in Rome, his patron's rising star led him increasingly to sermons in Rome's newest or grandest churches: Chiesa Nuova, San Lorenzo in Damaso, and Saint Peter's. Given his access to Rome's most

---

19. Carlo Bartolomeo Piazza, *Eusevologio Romano overo Delle Opere Pie di Roma*, 8:152–53.

20. Piazza, *Eusevologio Romano*, 153.

21. Rose Marie San Juan, *Rome: A City Out of Print*, 60.

22. Anonymous, "Diario di anonimo ecclesiastico al servizio di Ippolito Aldobrandini, 1576–93, AAV Fondo Borghese IV, 145, 145–B.

elite courts and pulpits, it is notable that the diary author also repeatedly attended the conversionary sermons forced on the Jews of Rome. As he first noted, May 6,1587, "I went to the Oratory of the Trinity to the sermon to the Jews of P. Marcellino and M. Andrea." He returned three more times that summer.[23] These dates, admittedly, represent a tiny proportion of his sermon visits over nearly two decades. By the same token, however, they indicate both the high profile of the *predica alli Giudei* and its status as equal to other public sermons.

From the earliest establishment of conversionary preaching in Rome, Christian elites supported the sermons by attending them regularly. Evangelista Marcellino's volume of printed sermons, *Sermoni quindici*, directly confirms in various ways that a Christian audience was the norm, validated by its starriest dignitaries. His book is dedicated to the cardinal of Santa Severina, Guglielmo Sirleto, who habitually attended sermons in his role as cardinal protector of the College of Neophytes. Marcellino acknowledges Sirleto's regular attendance over seven years and rhetorically excuses the cardinal from reading sermons he has already heard aloud. He also indicates the presence of many other prominent clerics, mentioning by name Gabriele Paleotti, the newly confirmed archbishop of Bologna and a close correspondent of Sirleto. The sermons' broader publicity, Marcellino explains, has led him to publish them in the vernacular version that "many, many" people have already heard.[24]

The regularity of these sermons and their rarity in other countries also attracted foreign travelers, who traveled to Rome in an ever-increasing stream from the late sixteenth century onward. Their reports make the preaching spectacle vivid to readers today. Moreover, they show how fully the idea of Roman Jews came to characterize and even define the city for foreigners, especially for travelers from countries that had long since expelled their own Jewish populations. Anthony Munday, an English writer and polemicist, spent the first four months of 1579 living in the English College in Rome. Beyond his interest in the intrigue and politics of the English College, Munday was particularly curious about the peculiarities of the city's public rituals, which he observed with religiously equivocal disdain.[25] These included preaching and discussions of Rome's Jews.

23. ASV Fondo Borghese IV, 145. Quotation on fol. 75r. Dates on fols. 75r–77v: May 27, June 3, and July 8.

24. Evangelista Marcellino, *Sermoni quindici sopra il salmo centonove fatti a gli Hebrei di Roma*, "Dedica," unpaginated fols. a2r–a4r.

25. Anthony Munday's confessional allegiance is not entirely clear. For an argument for a veiled and ambiguous Catholicism, see Donna B. Hamilton, *Anthony Munday and the*

Munday's report reflects the first years of conversionary preaching, after the 1577 bull *Vices Eius Nos* and before *Sancta Mater Ecclesiae* of 1581. As the earliest foreign description of conversionary sermons, Munday's words are notable for the prominence he gives to the act of conversion:

> From thence we go to a fair large place, in the midst whereof stand-eth a font. . . . In this font every year on Easter even they do christen Jews, such as do change to their religion. For there is a certain place appointed for sermons, whereat the Jews whether they will or no must be present, because one of their own rabbins [*sic*] preacheth to them, to convert them, as himself hath been a great while. . . . In this order they come to the sermon, and when any of them doth change his faith he taketh his yellow cap or hat off from his head, and throws it away with great violence; then will a hundred offer him a black cap or a hat, and greatly rejoice that they have so won him. All his riches he then must forsake, that goes to the pope's use.[26]

Munday's discussion of Jews starts with their potential conversion. He later adds a brief paragraph on the ghetto and its trade practices, but returns at greater length to the theme of conversion, embarking on a description of Jewish baptism double the length of his portrait of the ghetto and prominently featuring English bishops. Munday's attention to conversionary preaching confirms that sermons were public, popular spectacles. He may have exaggerated the exact numbers in the crowd, but he clearly saw a large group of onlookers who regularly surrounded the Jewish audience, hats at the ready, waiting to welcome them as Christians. Symbolizing a change of faith with a change of hat has long roots; in this case, Christian black or white hats would replace the yellow hats Jews were required to wear as a distinguishing sign.[27] In Munday's telling, the drama of the sudden conversion relies on these "hundred or so" Christian spectators. He also shows how the credit for Jewish conversion went by

Catholics, 1560–1633. See also Tracey Hill, *Anthony Munday and Civic Culture: Theatre, History, and Power in Early Modern London: 1580–1633*; Adam H. Kitzes, "The Hazards of Professional Authorship: Polemic and Fiction in Anthony Munday's English Roman Life."

26. Anthony Munday, *The English Roman Life*, 49–50.

27. Diane Owen Hughes, "Distinguishing Signs: Ear-Rings, Jews and Franciscan Rhetoric in the Italian Renaissance City"; Benjamin Ravid, "From Yellow to Red: On the Distinguishing Head-Covering of the Jews of Venice"; Flora Cassen, *Marking the Jews in Renaissance Italy: Politics, Religion, and the Power of Symbols.* For another sixteenth-century example, focusing on Marinus van Reymerswaele's *Calling of Saint Matthew* painting, see David Nirenberg, *Aesthetic Theology and Its Enemies: Judaism in Christian Painting, Poetry, and Politics,* 57.

default to sermons as a dramatic display, whether or not it was deserved. Other, more coercive prods to conversion—the ghetto, Talmud burning, efforts of individuals, and publication of conversionary polemics—play no explicit role in his retelling of events. Finally, Munday frames conversionary preaching within a broader network of Christian public ritual. Munday's depiction of conversionary preaching and Roman Jewish life forms part of his broader description of the pilgrimage to the Seven Churches of Rome—like preaching, a revived and uniquely Roman religious spectacle, overseen in large part by the Oratorians.

Other notable visitors from these earliest years confirm that conversionary sermons provided a spectacle from the first, and that Jews and sermons were becoming a tourist attraction. Michel de Montaigne, who famously visited a Jewish circumcision while in Rome in 1581, also went to see an "admirable" former rabbi combat Jewish belief from the pulpit as part of his tour of Lenten preachers across Rome. That rabbi was Andrea De Monte. Montaigne's brief lines of praise for De Monte's linguistic skill are cited in most later scholarship on conversionary preaching, but it is clear that although the sermons were newly instituted, Montaigne was doing nothing unusual in attending them. Martin, the English priest whose memoir brought public religion in Rome to life for modern readers, corroborates many of the details provided by the anonymous diarist, Munday, and Montaigne.[28] Martin describes the sermon spectacle at length, dwelling on the prominent position given to catechumens and neophytes, dressed in white and black respectively, and the illustrious, varied crowd of Christian onlookers:

> The cheefe of the Christians in this Audience is always a Cardinal, as it were by office deputed to be president of this exercise, as for other causes, so especially to keepe the Jewes in awe, and to rebuke them for absence or slacknesse, . . . with him commonly are other cardinals, sometimes eight at once, after them bishopes, referendaries, prelates of al degrees, doctors of divinitie and of the Rota, noble citizens and straungers, briefly of al countries and states, flocking hither so thinke as to no other exercise byseides, that to sitte thou must come betimes, yea if you come late there is no place for thee to stand within the doore.[29]

---

28. Michel de Montaigne, *The Complete Works of Montaigne: Essays, Travel Journals, Letters*, 956–57; Gregory Martin, *Roma Sancta*. Martin's work was not published until 1969.

29. Martin, *Roma Sancta*, 77.

For over a century after Munday, Montaigne, and Martin had left Rome, forced conversionary preaching continued to bring in foreign tourists and define the city for foreign audiences. Visitors to Rome regularly attended sermons to Jews, and by doing so, made conversionary preaching an essential feature of the city's public image abroad. Increasingly, they identified the Eternal City with its ritualized display of Jews. Some visitors, including Munday and Montaigne, attended conversionary sermons as curious outsiders, drawing perhaps as much on the nascent practices of tourism as on personal devotion. But other new arrivals to Rome, such as Calasanz and Martin, explicitly considered conversionary sermons as one item in a vast banquet of uniquely Roman devotional activities. For all of them, as for the anonymous diarist, enforced preaching to Jews was an important aspect of their own religious life in Rome. Conversionary preaching continued to draw local and international crowds.

Throughout the seventeenth century, Europeans on the grand tour made a point of visiting conversionary sermons and often considered it a highlight of their visit. Francis Skippon, who showed a strong ethnographic interest in Jewish life throughout his European travels, attended Roman conversionary sermons in the 1670s. Sandwiched between his description of the Scala Santa and Piazza Colonna, we find this account: "One Saturday we heard (about four in the afternoon) a Dominican fryar preach to the Jews, at *S. Trinità de Pellegrini;* a Jew out of every family being obliged to be present." He goes on to provide the familiar portrayals of force and vigilance at sermons, the roster system, and the required attendance numbers, focusing on financial matters: "If any are absent that are expected, they are punished with a pecuniary mulct, and the class, whose turn it is, must pay for those who are poor and unable to pay. . . . The preacher hath his stipend out of the Camera Apostolica."[30] Skippon's emphasis on the sermons' logistics and finances suggests how novel they seemed to him. His decision to describe them alongside other notable sights and separately from his visits to the ghetto indicates that he saw them less as a Jewish attraction than as a Roman one.

Maximilien Misson, whose *A New Voyage to Italy* became the standard travel guide to Italy for fifty years or more, visited Rome in the late 1680s.[31]

---

30. Francis Skippon, *An Account of a Journey Made thro' Part of the Low-Countries, Germany, Italy, and France,* 658.

31. Craig Spence, *Misson, Francis Maximilian [Formerly François Maximilien] (c. 1650–1722), Traveller and Author;* Richard Ansell, "Reading and Writing Travels: Maximilien Misson, Samuel Waring and the Afterlives of European Voyages, c.1687–1714." *A New Voyage to Italy* was translated into English and German.

Misson was a keen observer of preaching—inevitable perhaps for a Hugue-
not who had fled France to settle in England. He was not impressed with
Roman preachers: "They run about with a great deal of Noise and Heat,
but there is neither Sense nor Reason in all this."[32] He ridicules the styles
and failings of Jesuits, Capuchins, Dominicans (preachers), and Carmel-
ites in turn. These notes appear early in his narrative of Rome, introducing
volume 2 of his *New Voyage to Italy*. Misson's skepticism extended to the
treatment of Jews in Rome. In considering the baptism rituals of converts
to Catholicism, he easily dismisses miraculous claims that Jews lost their
innate stink at the ceremony:

> I know not why this sho'd be reckon'd wonderful; for those who are to
> be baptiz'd are so carefully wash'd and cleans'd, that they must needs
> become sweet, tho' they really stunk before. Besides, 'tis ridiculous to
> imagine that the Jews have a peculiar Smell. The Jews at Rome are
> poor; those who are poor are always nasty, as those who are nasty usu-
> ally stink. This is the whole Mystery.[33]

Misson's narrative about Roman Jews lists, with a critical tone, every restrictive measure imposed by Paul IV—"a terrible Enemy to 'em." This includes
mandatory sermons, which he clearly considers one of the infringements
on their liberty: "I am inform'd, that by a Decree of Gregory XIII they were
oblig'd, or at least a certain number of 'em, to hear a Christian Sermon
every Saturday in the Afternoon, but I had not yet had an opportunity to
see that Assembly."[34] From Misson, Protestant readers could learn that
Catholic preaching was worthy of attention and that Rome was bursting
with sermons. And all readers might also have learned to adopt Misson's
detached, even sympathetic view of Jewish people, considered as humans
and, in this case, victims—not only as a theological concept.

Reports and descriptions by travelers to Italy invested Jews with a
symbolic weight in the European imaginary; Jews' absence from much of
Europe made them an easy repository of fears, fascinations, and stereotypes. In other parts of Europe, where Jewish settlements were present,
the practice of Christians watching Jews was increasingly well established in
printed literature. Books on Jewish practices—*minhag* literature—typically

32. Maximilien Misson, *A New Voyage to Italy: With Curious Observations on Several Other Countries, as Germany, Switzerland, Savoy, Geneva, Flanders, and Holland.
Together with Useful Instructions for Those Who Shall Travel Thither. Done out of French*,
30. Original is *Nouvelle Voyage d'Italie*, 1691.

33. Misson, *A New Voyage to Italy*, 95.

34. Misson, *A New Voyage to Italy*, 94.

contained illustrations that generally included an image of a Christian viewer looking at Jewish subjects. These figures suggested that Judaism was knowable, not secret, and available for viewing.[35] Encountering such literature at home would presumably whet the appetite for observing Jews in person abroad.

Venice offered travelers from the north their first viewing of Jews in Italy and the novelty of seeing the oldest ghetto.[36] But Rome's Jewish community was more ancient, had more local roots, and intertwined more closely with the specifically Roman attractions of antiquity and papacy. Roman Jews took on a significant place in the English literary imagination. In England, frequent reversals of national faith in the Reformation had left the country with a sort of religious whiplash and an abiding sense that conversion was by nature unstable. In that context, as Jeffrey Shoulson has argued, the symbols of the Jew and the converso became a national fixation, as a counterweight against which to define true Christianity. The recent history of forced conversion in Spain and Portugal served as a double example to England. It "embodied simultaneously the corrupt religious practices and traditions from which English Protestantism sought to distinguish itself and the preeminent example of the costs and abuses entailed in the violent imposition of religious conformity and forced conversion."[37] Jews had been expelled from England in 1290; nonetheless (or as a result), English (and sometimes Scottish) travel accounts consistently displayed keen interest in Jews—where they lived along with how they dressed, worshipped, or looked. Their attention stemmed both from simple curiosity and a sense that the contrast between the English and the Jews held the answers to fundamental questions about identity and humanity.[38]

This special interest might be said to culminate with Thomas Nashe, whose influential 1594 satire on travel narrative, *The Unfortunate Traveller*, comes to a head with a story set among Roman Jews. At the end of his

35. Teter argues that in northern Europe, these illustrations had the effect of mitigating blood libel accusations, portraying Jews as exotic but not murderous. Magda Teter, *Blood Libel: On the Trail of an Antisemitic Myth*, 181–82.

36. Eva Joanna Holmberg, *Jews in the Early Modern English Imagination: A Scattered Nation*, 35–38.

37. Jeffrey S. Shoulson, *Fictions of Conversion: Jews, Christians, and Cultures of Change in Early Modern England*, 3, 16–29; James Shapiro, *Shakespeare and the Jews*. For the broader argument that Englishness was constructed by the absence of Jews, see Eliane Glaser, *Judaism without Jews: Philosemitism and Christian Polemic in Early Modern England*.

38. Holmberg, *Jews in the Early Modern English Imagination*, 1–6, 151–52.

long journey through Europe, the English protagonist, Jack Wilton, finds himself embroiled in sexual and murderous scandals during his Roman sojourn. The instruments of his fall are a pair of Roman Jews who deceive him and plot his death. With them, Nashe layers the stereotype of Jewish misbehavior on top of the corruption of papist Rome, untrustworthiness of Italy, and barbaric character of continental Europe.[39] Zadok and Zacharias represent the most distant moral point from England and from English rectitude and propriety. When they meet their own violent end, they figure as scapegoats, taking on the burden of Christian sin in general and Jack's in particular. Their bodies and eventual execution serve as a proxy for Jack's own fears and wrongdoings, and receive all the punishment on themselves.[40] If authors like Nashe taught English travelers to see Roman Jews as their moral opposites, the opportunity to witness their conversion must have been especially appealing. Jewish abjection at sermons, specifically when contrasted with the warm welcome given to English travelers, could feed English fascination while comfortably confirming assumptions about social hierarchy.[41]

The well-known English writer and diarist John Evelyn, who wrote extensively about his three months in Rome, seems to have brought these attitudes with him to the first conversionary sermon he attended. With these predispositions, he found Jewish grumbling, though a relatively minor infraction, to be far more offensive than the outright use of constraint and force by Christians:

> A sermon was preach'd to the Jewes at Ponte Sisto, who are constrain'd to sit, till the houre is don; but it is with so much malice in their countenances, spitting, humming, coughing & motion, that it is almost impossible they should heare a word, nor are there any converted except it be very rarely.[42]

---

39. Thomas Nashe, *The Unfortunate Traveller*, 330–70; Allyna E. Ward, "An Outlandish Travel Chronicle: Farce, History, and Fiction in Thomas Nashe's *The Unfortunate Traveller.*" See also Jennifer L. Andersen, "Anti-Puritanism, Anti-Popery, and Gallows Rhetoric in Thomas Nashe's "The Unfortunate Traveller.""

40. On bodily fears displaced onto Zadok, see Andrew Fleck, "Anatomizing the Body Politic: The Nation and the Renaissance Body in Thomas Nashe's *The Unfortunate Traveller.*"

41. On the reception of the English in Rome, see Irene Fosi, "Between Conversion and Reconquest: The Venerable English College between the Late Sixteenth and Seventeenth Centuries."

42. John Evelyn, *Diary: Now First Printed in Full from the Manuscripts Belonging to Mr. John Evelyn, and as Edited by E. S. de Beer*, 291–92. This event took place in January 1645.

Yet Evelyn continued to join in conversionary activities. His diary notes his meeting with the conversionary preacher—the unnamed Giuseppe Maria Avila—who invited him to stand as godfather to two converts. The experience, as we saw in chapter 1, did not improve Evelyn's opinion of Jewish people:

> The 25th (February) invited by a Frier Dominican whom we usualy heard preach to a number of Jewes, to be Godfather to a /Converted Turk & a Jew, The Ceremonie was perform'd in the Church of S: Maria sopra la Minerva neere the Capitol, They were clad in White, then exorcis'd at their entering the church with aboundance of Ceremonies, when lead into the Quire, they were baptizd by a Bishop in Pontificali-bus: The Turk lived afterward in Rome, sold hot-water, & would bring us presents when he met us, kneeling, & kissing the hemms of our Cloaks: But the Jew was believ'd to be a Counterfeit.[43]

Although much of Evelyn's supposedly eyewitness account came from guidebooks he consulted after his return to England, this event seems fully plausible. One Jewish and one Muslim man were indeed baptized at Santa Maria sopra Minerva on February 17, 1645, presided over by Giuseppe Ciantes, the former conversionary preacher since elevated to the bishopric of Marsica.[44] There is no record corroborating Evelyn's later doubts or his own role as godfather. But for Evelyn, the visit to a conversionary sermon had lasting consequences for his experience of the city.

The idea that Rome was a place to see Jews and watch their conversion eventually saturated European travel literature. When Nicolas Audeber visited the Roman ghetto, he noted details of living conditions and synagogue life, and composed a description of the lives of Italian Jews in general. Jews were a featured attraction on his Italian tour, and he found Rome the natural place to consider them.[45] Pierre Duval's account of his 1644 voyage to Italy describes conversionary preaching as the primary characteristic of Roman Jews, who in turn are considered a defining feature of the city. Jews and sermons appear almost immediately in his introduction to Rome: "Rome is still peopled with more than three hundred thousand souls and almost eight thousand Jews, who are obligated under pain of fines to hear, every Saturday, a sermon, usually given by a Dominican, against their sect. They also have their own quarter where they must

43. Evelyn, *Diary*, 376–77.

44. ASVR Casa dei Catecumeni 178, Liber Baptizatorum 1634–75, 37r.

45. Nicolas Audeber, *Le Voyage et observations de plusiers choses diverses qui se pevvent remarquer en Italie*.

stay at certain hours."[46] For him, sermons were worth mentioning even before the ghetto.

Richard Lassels, in *The Voyage of Italy*, felt similarly. Early on, in his book's first description of Rome, he writes,

> What shall I say of the *weekly sermon* to the Jews upon Saturday; where they are bound to be present to the number of three hundred, where the *Pope* entertains a learned *Preacher* to convince them out of their own scriptures; and those that are converted are provided for in the *Hospital* of the *Catechumens,* til they be thoroughly instructed? I have seen divers of them baptized.[47]

Lassels's guidebook became the standard of the genre, defining the grand tour as a concept, and establishing the priorities and reactions to Italy that would guide a century of future tourists.[48] It taught readers to see the conversionary pulpit as one of the city's great marvels.

Conversionary sermons were novel enough to avoid being swallowed entirely into common travel tropes. Authors of travel narratives made the sermons distinctive, through either their own experiences or the placement of their descriptions. Skippon noted especially the time of the sermon he attended and its finances, while avoiding judgment on the preachers or audience. Misson considered them a sign of oppression, but regretted his failure to watch one himself. And Evelyn and Lassels came to opposite conclusions about their value even though Evelyn had read Lassels and used his work to bolster his own. Where Evelyn remained skeptical of all conversions, Lassels accepted them at face value as effective tools of proselytization. This difference stems directly from the faith of the beholder: Lassels was a Catholic priest and dutifully toed the party line; Evelyn was not (though he was wise enough to keep this quiet when asked to stand as godfather), and thus could approach sermons with more curiosity and less stake in the outcome. But both of them, like other visitors, considered conversionary preaching a defining part of the city's unique urban fabric—even decades after its initial novelty had worn off. The sermon performance invested Jews with layers of symbolism; it cast an exotic yet specific community of Jews in the general cosmic role of "the Jews." Attending such a spectacle, the ancient church pitted against its even more ancient rival, became one of the most profoundly Roman experiences available to foreign visitors.

46. Pierre Duval, *Le Voyage et la description d'Italie . . . avec la relation du Voyage fait à Rome par Monsier le Duc e Boüillon en l'année 1644*, 219.

47. Richard Lassels, *The Voyage of Italy: Or a Compleat Journey through Italy*, 18.

48. *Oxford Dictionary of National Biography*, sv "Richard Lassels."

Conversionary Sermons within Roman Ritual Networks

Conversionary preaching, as an act of religious theater, interwove seamlessly and usefully into two of the city's broader ritual networks: Christian Rome as a ritual city, and public spectacles featuring Jews. Early modern Rome was an intensely sacralized landscape. Its public processions rested on centuries of devotional associations, from the Roman emperors to the translated Passion of Christ to renewed claims of papal sovereignty. After the Reformation, the rise of competing denominations of Christianity in western Europe encouraged the Counter-Reformation Catholic church toward triumphalist and highly visible celebrations. These celebrations focused on those aspects of worship that Protestants for the most part seemed to reject: images, senses, and bodily experiences.[49] Processions and public spectacles in Rome increasingly signaled the city's renewed Catholic piety by reinscribing it physically onto its refurbished streets and enlarged squares.[50] Alongside such long-standing ceremonies as triumphal entries, papal investitures, and solemn processions, new acts of public devotion characterized early modern Rome. Designed to celebrate and promote the city's piety, they also served political purposes. To devout Catholics, eager to see their city in a triumphant light, Rome appeared to be, as Martin reminded his readers, a "blessed Citie . . . a spectacle of fayth & good workes."[51] These devotions also prepared participants to accord roles to Jewish people in Roman ritual.

Public devotions in post-Reformation Rome hit their peak during Holy Years. Every twenty-five years, Catholic pilgrims flooded the Holy City, quadrupling its population, and traversing Rome from one end to another on the ritual visits and walks that earned them special indulgences.[52]

49. Wietse De Boer and Christine Göttler, *Religion and the Senses in Early Modern Europe*; Jill R. Fehleison, "Appealing to the Senses: The Forty Hours Celebrations in the Duchy of Chablais, 1597–98." For a counterexample to assumptions about Protestant austerity, see Bridget Heal, *A Magnificent Faith: Art and Identity in Lutheran Germany*.

50. For the term "ritual city," and an exploration of the links between ritual and politics in early modern Rome, see Maria Antonietta Visceglia, *La città rituale: Roma e le sue cerimonie in età moderna*. For Rome as a sacred landscape, see Simon Ditchfield, "Reading Rome as a Sacred Landscape, c. 1586–1635."

51. Frederick McGinness, "Preaching Ideals and Practice in Counter-Reformation Rome"; Martin, *Roma Sancta*, 8.

52. The literature on Holy Years in Rome is vast. See Tommaso Maria Alfani, *Istoria degli anni santi dal loro principio fino al presente del 1750*. See also two important twentieth-century collected volumes: Marcello Fagiolo, Maria Luisa Madonna, and Lucia Armenante, *Roma Sancta: La città delle basiliche*; Gloria Fossi, Jacques Le Goff,

At the same time, within a few generations of the Protestant Reformation, visits from northern Europe also increased, often bringing curious Protestants. These too frequently clustered around Holy Years. Catholic institutions in Rome increasingly responded with a warm welcome and showy display, in the hope that well-treated and impressed visitors would respond by embracing the faith their forebears had abandoned.[53] As a result, efforts to display Rome's sanctity and piety intensified around Holy Year activities.

Rome's most popular and characteristic public devotions, sought out by Romans and visitors alike, relied on the same constellation of protagonists and institutions that supported conversionary sermons. The most important of these for the sacralization of the Roman landscape was the pilgrimage to the Seven Churches of Rome, or *giro delle sette chiese*. This fourteen-mile route visited the seven primary basilicas of Rome, passing by the Appian Way and the catacombs of ancient martyrs. Revived by Neri in 1552 as a countermeasure to louche carnival practices, it became popular with Romans and pilgrims alike, drawing over a thousand participants at a time. The *giro delle sette chiese* effectively merged Rome's triumphantly revived piety with its ancient apostolic origins and embedded them both in Rome's unique landscape.[54] Neri and the members of his society and the oratory would eventually feed hundreds of pilgrims along the way. The ritual became an important symbol of lay piety and religious renewal.[55] But it also proved to be useful publicity for popes; Gregory XIII, Pius V, and Sixtus V all undertook the route a few times a year and on the day after carnival Sunday "as a sign of appeasement for the lapse of the people into paganism."[56]

The forty-hour devotion, or *Quarant'Ore*, which often relied on the same seven churches and many more besides, also treated the city as a network of devotional points forming a sacred landscape. To commemorate the supposed forty hours of Jesus's burial in the tomb, the consecrated

---

and Claudio M. Strinati, *La Storia dei Giubilei*, especially the essays by Irene Fosi and Genoveffa Palumbo. In addition, see Genoveffa Palumbo, *Giubileo Giubilei: pellegrini e pellegrine, riti, santi, immagini per una storia dei sacri itinerari*.

53. Irene Fosi, *Convertire lo straniero: forestieri e Inquisizione a Roma in età moderna*, 57–88; Peter A. Mazur, *Conversion to Catholicism in Early Modern Italy*, 43–65.

54. Ditchfield, "Reading Rome as a Sacred Landscape, c. 1586–1635."

55. M. Teresa [Maria Teresa] Bonadonna Russo, "La visita alle 'Sette Chiese'" attraverso i secoli," 5–19; Barbara Wisch, "The Matrix: Le Sette Chiese di Roma of 1575 and the Image of Pilgrimage." See also Boiteux, "Parcours rituels romains à l'époque moderne."

56. Richard Joseph Ingersoll, "The Ritual Use of Public Space in Renaissance Rome," 120–21.

host was "guarded" in prayer and adoration.[57] First developed in the 1520s in Milan, the practice soon spread to other liturgical feasts and other cities. In Rome, the particular promoter of the indulgence was, again, Neri, who had established the practice for the Confraternity of Santa Trinità dei Pellegrini by 1550.[58] Another confraternity, the Compagnia della Morte, carried it out every third Sunday in the church of San Lorenzo in Damaso—a church that sometimes hosted conversionary sermons and was closely tied to Trinità dei Pellegrini.[59] By the seventeenth century, papal ordinances organized the entire city into a six-month period of rotation so that the *Quarant'Ore* devotion passed from one church to another every three days, comprising ninety different churches, with no repetition. The practice had gained early support from Ignatius Loyola, who as we have seen, also helped to establish the House of Catechumens and College of Neophytes for converted Jews. In other words, the same dense network of patrons, confraternities, churches, and religious orders that already supported these other new forms of devotion would find that conversionary preaching lay naturally in their wheelhouse too.

These activities overlapped physically and emotionally as well. The church and buildings of Santissima Trinità dei Pellegrini, which hosted sermons to Jews, not only participated in these devotions but also anchored the city's Holy Year endeavors. From its construction in the late sixteenth century, its buildings were always semipublic spaces.[60] The large complex served to house, feed, and wash the feet of Holy Year pilgrims. Foot washing, rather than a solely practical measure, was in fact a highly symbolic public celebration. Local onlookers crowded in to witness the spectacle of prominent cardinals in red cassocks, their sleeves pushed up to the elbows, kneeling at the feet of typically poor and definitely dusty pilgrims hosted in the Trinità's vast central ospizio. Even Jews thronged to the foot-washing ceremony, according to one chronicler, in "infinite" numbers, and frequently even donated money while there. The chronicle notes

57. Konrad Eisenbichler, *The Boys of the Archangel Raphael: A Youth Confraternity in Florence, 1411–1785*, 163–64; Mark S. Weil, "The Devotion of the Forty Hours and Roman Baroque Illusions."

58. Weil, "The Devotion of the Forty Hours," 222; Boiteux, "Parcours rituels," 63.

59. San Lorenzo in Damaso was the titular church of San Benedetto in Arenula, the predecessor of Trinità dei Pellegrini.

60. Mariano Armellini, *Le chiese di Roma dal secolo IV al XIX*; Sandra Vasco Rocca, *SS. Trinità dei Pellegrini*, 58, 67; On the various buildings of Santissima Trinità dei Pellegrini, see Matizia Maroni Lumbroso and Antonio Martini, *Le confraternite romane nelle loro chiese*, 427–28; Barbara Wisch, "Promoting Piety, Coercing Conversion: The Roman Archconfraternity of the Santissima Trinità dei Pellegrini e Convalescenti and its Oratory."

explicitly that both male and female Jewish people attended this event. The same chronicler, describing confraternity activities for the Holy Year of 1600, notes the presence of the city's most famous cardinals, ritually washing, feeding, and serving the astonished pilgrims. When Cardinals Baronio, Visconti, and Montalto took on the foot-washing ritual, so many pilgrims and confraternities crammed in to watch that they had to be sent outside and the doors barred.[61] Popes also took part. Clement VIII came in 1600, Urban VIII in 1625, Innocent X in 1650, Clemente X in 1675, Clement XI in 1700, and Benedict XIV in 1750.

In both foot-washing and conversionary preaching, Santissima Trinità dei Pellegrini staged devotional spectacles in which various humble groups were juxtaposed with the city's most elite cardinals, all watched by a broader populace. Foot washing, like preaching, served a penitential function, not only for the humbled cardinals; pilgrims reluctant to be washed were commanded to participate "under pain of disobedience," but ultimately, "while they were being washed cried tender tears of compunction."[62] The Trinità complex became a known place for Christians to witness Catholic redemption, whether Jewish or Catholic.

These examples present a picture in which clergy, locals, and pilgrims participated in the enactment of new or newly revived religious rituals, driven by new religious orders such as the Oratorians and Jesuits, and directed by its key members. Conversionary preaching functioned as another one of these rituals. Pious Catholic sermon goers attended conversionary sermons just as they attended other sermons; they included the oratory of Trinità dei Pellegrini on their sermon circuits along with other prominent churches, particularly San Lorenzo in Damaso, Santa Maria in Aracoeli, and the brand-new Chiesa Nuova, the mother church of the Congregation of the Oratory. They attended the salvific spectacle of potential Jewish conversion just as they attended the salvific rituals of the Seven Churches of Rome, the forty-hour devotion, or Holy Year activities. The ritual practices of the eternal city primed pious Romans and visitors to understand a conversionary sermon, through its staging and setting, as familiar Catholic territory, of ready spiritual benefit to themselves, the viewers.

The Christian public that thrilled to foot washing and pilgrimage was also accustomed to seeing Jewish people play a role in other public contexts; the ceremonial role of Jews in long-standing urban rituals was widespread. Many of these ceremonies were unique or distinctive to

61. BAV Vat. lat. 6822, 278–79.
62. BAV Vat. lat. 6822, 57.

Rome. Every year on the first Saturday of carnival, for example, the chief rabbi and two governors (fattori) of the università presented themselves at the Capitoline Hill, the seat of Roman civic government, to pay symbolic and financial tribute. In front of the collected conservators of the city, other officials, and spectators, they knelt on one knee, and then recited an address of homage and fealty, begging for sympathetic treatment from the city as well as the peace and health of the pope.[63] But a better-known public ritual took place during the possesso, which had so entranced Calasanz on his arrival in the city. In the possesso, a newly elected pope processed through the city from his coronation in Saint Peter's to take possession—possesso—of his bishop's *cathedra,* the church of Saint John Lateran. The procession followed a prescribed route (the Via Sacra or Via Papalis) lined with crowds.[64] The università was responsible for readying a section of the route near the Arch of Titus, which commemorates the emperor Titus's victory over Judaea in the year 70. The responsibility, developed over the course of centuries, entailed the hanging of banners and singing of hymns of praise (*laude*).

Jews had to participate in a ritual, ceremonial encounter with the pope too. This took place not at the Arch of Titus but instead earlier in the possesso, at the moment when the pope reached the first of five preset stations for scattering coins to the crowd. This was at the start of the Via Papalis, a central artery that ran through the bustling Parione region—an area in which popes consciously sought to assert increasing dominance over the many ancient noble families whose grand palaces shaped the neighborhood.[65] At the encounter, the Jews ritually presented the pope with a richly decorated Torah scroll as an act of homage. The pope, in turn, ritually cast the scroll to the ground to represent the supersession of the Old Testament by the New Testament. Each party spoke formulaic phrases, with the former attesting to the honor of the gift, and the latter responding that although the law of Moses was holy and venerable, its Jewish interpretation was vain and condemnable. The choreographed performance of the possesso ceremony valued hierarchy, precedence, and order. But under the surface, the possesso reflected a legitimate fear of disorder. It could be

63. Attilio Milano, *Il ghetto di Roma; illustrazioni storiche,* 319–22. This practice was abolished in 1857, except for the financial payment.

64. Irene Fosi, "Court and City in the Ceremony of the Possesso in the Sixteenth Century"; Gaetano Moroni, *Dizionario di erudizione storico-ecclesiastica da S. Pietro sino ai nostri giorni,* 28–33.

65. Valeria Cafà, "The Via Papalis in Early Cinquecento Rome: A Contested Space between Roman Families and Curials," 434–37.

marked by riots in the streets, often directed at Jews.[66] The instances of violence eventually prompted authorities to move this encounter from the crowded Parione region to the open space in front of Castel Sant'Angelo in 1455.[67] The long and distressing memory of the possesso left lasting scars in Jewish communal memory, stretching well into the twentieth century.[68]

Famously, Jews also played a prominent and humiliating role in Rome's famous carnival festivities. After Pius II moved the carnival races from Monte Testaccio to the more central Porta del Popolo, the races for Jews took on a more central role. As described in sources from the fifteenth to the seventeenth centuries, Jewish men were compelled to run down what is now the Via del Corso, often naked or nearly so, goaded on by jeering spectators; sometimes elderly Jewish men were shut in barrels and rolled down the route. When Munday described the Roman carnival, he began by noticing the Jews:

> The first day of their *Carne-vale*, the Jews in Rome . . . run stark naked from *Porta populo* unto the capital . . . and all the way they gallop their great horses after them, and carry goads with sharp points of steel in them, wherewith they will prick the Jews on the naked skin, if so be they do not run faster than their horses gallop, so that you shall see some of their backs all on gore blood.

Even the winner, he observes, is pelted with oranges by "a hundred boys."[69] Nearly a century later, the traveler Francis Mortoft beheld a similar sight. He went "to see the Races which are to be run by Jewes, Barbes, and other unclean Beasts for 6 pieces of stuffe. . . . The Jewes ran this day, naked, onely they had some thing about there [*sic*] middles to hide Nature, that the Whores might not see all."[70] The effect of these races was to reinforce the permanent abasement and otherness of Jewish people, making them

66. On the possesso and violence, see Fosi, "Court and City in the Ceremony of the Possesso in the Sixteenth Century." On Jews in the Vacant See, see John M. Hunt, "Violence and Disorder in the Sede Vacante of Early Modern Rome, 1559–1655."

67. Adriano Prosperi, "Incontri rituali: il papa e gli ebrei," 2:502–3; Amnon Linder, 'The Jews Too Were Not Absent . . . Carrying Moses's Law on Their Shoulders': The Ritual Encounter of Pope and Jews from the Middle Ages to Modern Times."

68. See, for example, the discussion of papal investiture in "The Jewish Pope," a 1947 story by Yudl Marks, analyzed in Miriam Udel, "The 'Jewish Pope' in the 1940s: On Jewish Cultural and Ethnic Plasticity."

69. Munday, *The English Roman Life*, 96–97.

70. Francis Mortoft, *Francis Mortoft: His Book, Being His Travels through France and Italy, 1658–1659*, 136–37.

seem forever alien, closer to beasts than to Christians.[71] Only in 1688 were the carnival races of Jews suspended, and even then, only in exchange for a hefty annual fee.

Other public devotions could similarly co-opt Jews indirectly into ritual or prescribed roles. Hearing about "the Jews" in a devotional context could spur actions against them in a social one. The notable example for Rome is the case of Holy Year 1539, when a series of inflammatory sermons promoting the establishment of Rome's Monte di Pietà prompted anti-Jewish riots. The confraternity of the Gonfalone, whose annual Good Friday procession passed through Jewish neighborhoods on its way to the Colosseum, was so stirred up by the sermons and its own elaborate passion play that its ceremony devolved into an attack on local Jews. The plays were so incendiary that they were suspected after this incident.[72]

Forced conversionary sermons, in the same way, conscripted Jews into multiple prescriptive roles. At the moment of the sermon, the listening Jews embodied both the Jew and potential convert, both the actual community and imaginary "theological" Jew. Above all, they provided a physical, public demonstration that the work of conversion by persuasion was being done. In this way, they do not seem so different from the "People of Israel" who appeared in a devotional play staged at the church of the Gesù in the 1660s, depicting the biblical exodus from Egypt. In this play, actors represented the six hundred thousand Israelites crossing the Red Sea, which was laid out on the floor of the church with columns of smoke and fire on each side. It was a grand event, lit entirely by lamps, and drew crowds—not only confraternities in their ritual habits, but the city's most prominent cardinals and even a succession of popes.[73] But how much more powerful, then, is the play of conversionary sermons when the Jews are played by themselves?

Forced sermons to Jews slotted in naturally to a preexisting view of Rome that was both sacralized and theatricalized. Visitors who wrote about the Jews' races, including Evelyn, Munday, and Montaigne, also attended conversionary sermons; their views of Jews in one context informed the other. All of these events—possesso, carnival, and passion

71. Boiteux, "Parcours rituels"; Åsa Boholm, "Christian Construction of the Other: The Role of Jews in the Early Modern Carnival of Rome." See also Denis Mooney, "The Development of the Roman Carnival over the Eighteenth and Nineteenth Centuries."

72. Barbara Wisch, "Violent Passions: Plays, Pawnbrokers, and the Jews of Rome, 1539"; Barbara Wisch and Nerida Newbigin, *Acting on Faith: The Confraternity of the Gonfalone in Renaissance Rome.*

73. *Breve Dichiaratione e descrittione del teatro eretto in quest'anno MDxclvi ad honore e culto del santissimo sacramento nella chiesa farnesiana della compagnia di Geisu.*

play—required participants to play specific roles as participants or necessary spectators. The Jews who attended conversionary sermons had their own ceremonial role when they proceeded en masse from the ghetto to the oratory of Santissima Trinità dei Pellegrini in a reverse ritual procession. The watching, jeering Christians could see in that path echoes of the degrading carnival races. But the route could equally evoke their own many salvific processions that rendered the city a sacred topography. These actions and reactions placed conversionary sermons at the center of various sacred routes that orbited the city, such as the visits to Jubilee churches, Lenten ritual processions, the Seven Churches of Rome, the *Quarant'Ore*, pilgrimage routes, and the routes one might take to attend sermons. Religious orders, in promoting these activities, did not only give support and context to conversionary preaching but turned it firmly into one of the city's devotional hallmarks.

This interplay of pious activities suggests that Jewish-Christian interaction played a specific, necessary role in Roman public life. Catholic rituals involving Jews affirmed their position as outsiders and their necessity to the city's functioning—the status that Thomas Cohen has characterized as "intimate outsiders."[74] The long history of such events provided a continuous, if evolving, background for Jews in civic ritual, which intensified in the new post-Tridentine devotions described here. The cluster of degrading legislation of Jews in the sixteenth century reduced and exoticized many opportunities for informal interaction, previously common and unremarkable. It gave increasing prominence instead to scripted, ritualistic interventions, seeking to drive Jews and Christians further apart. Concurrently, the establishment of the Roman ghetto began a long process of impoverishing the city's Jews: at the start, new restrictions on permissible professions, heavy taxation, fines surrounding conversionary activity, and the loss of property, rental income, and social mobility; in the seventeenth century, strict legislation of permissible interest rates and the withdrawal of banking licenses.[75] The early modern papal government was keen to avoid scandal. It legislated against excessive or spontaneous attacks on Jews, but instead enabled anti-Jewish sentiment to be channeled into the calendar of devotional activities.[76] The derision of carnival,

74. Thomas V. Cohen, "The Case of the Mysterious Coil of Rope: Street Life and Jewish Persona in Rome in the Middle of the Sixteenth Century."

75. On these topics, see Milano, *Il ghetto di Roma*, 144–73; Angela Groppi, *Gli abitanti del ghetto di Roma: Descriptio hebreorum del 1733*.

76. For a potential scandal that could have been much worse, see Simona Feci, "The Death of a Miller: A Trial Contra Hebreos in Baroque Rome." For a discussion of the blood

like the subservience of the possesso, ceremonialized the particular and diminishing status of Rome's Jewish community within the city.

Thus as they sat listening to conversionary sermons, Jews carried with them an echo of their other regular public performances in a civic, city-wide context. Catholics or Protestants observing Jewish people listen to the conversionary sermons would also have been fully aware of those resonances. They would easily have grasped that their own role, too, was ritually indispensable. As Edward Muir has shown, ritual actors and viewers were mutually interdependent, with one emanating certain values, and the other confirming their efficacy and emanating values of their own.[77] Christian spectators could absorb the penitential performance of the Jewish audience while modeling the righteousness that the sermons were supposed to effect, or indeed, undertaking their own penance in response. For them, Jews provided proof by exception of their own sacrality and honor.

Rome had practice in outsourcing its indispensable sinners and then offering them as exhibits. Like Jews, sex workers found dubious fame in this spectacle city as a notable "thing to be seen" that distinguished the city. Rome's courtesans were publicly and famously visible in the city's windows and salons, noted locally and in international travel literature.[78] Jews, likewise, were a featured sight, and almost uniquely visible in Italy. In Rome, extra visibility followed both Jews and sex workers down the streets remorselessly. As Elisabeth Cohen has argued, "People, some kinds of people more than others, mark the spaces and edifices that they occupy so that, as a result, these entities are—if temporarily—looked at and known differently."[79] Uncomfortable transitional points—the walls and windows of the ghetto—made Jews seem especially vulnerable in every ghetto.[80] One Roman edict from 1629 expressly commanded all Jewish people with windows facing the church of Saint Angelo in Pescheria to

---

libel scare of 1555, see Serena Di Nepi, *Surviving the Ghetto: Toward a Social History of the Jewish Community in 16th-Century Rome*, 66–73; Martina Mampieri, *Living under the Evil Pope: The Hebrew Chronicle of Pope Paul IV by Benjamin Neḥemiah Ben Elnathan from Civitanova Marche (16th Cent.)*, 65–68.

77. Edward Muir, "The Eye of the Procession: Ritual Ways of Seeing in the Renaissance," esp. 144.

78. Elizabeth S. Cohen, "Seen and Known: Prostitutes in the Cityscape of Late Sixteenth-Century Rome." See also Tessa Storey, *Carnal Commerce in Counter-Reformation Rome.*

79. Cohen, "Seen and Known," 1.

80. Dana E. Katz, "'Clamber Not You up to the Casements': On Ghetto Views and Viewing"; Dana E. Katz, *The Jewish Ghetto and the Visual Imagination of Early Modern Venice.* Katz's emphasis on the danger of windows in Venice is also pertinent to Rome.

keep them shut up from the start of an upcoming procession until the last stragglers had past, however long that took, under pain of an enormous fine of three hundred gold scudi.[81]

The project of reclaiming public spaces for piety meant creating opportunities for pious Catholic bodies to fill the streets of Rome, and restricting the mobility of less welcome, corrupting bodies—through delimited neighborhoods, distinguishing signs or clothing, and tightly scripted rituals of subservience. Jews and prostitutes, closely associated with each other in Italy as elsewhere, endured all of these impositions. Prostitutes, too, had segregated neighborhoods and were required to run in the carnival races that functioned as shaming rituals. Where Jews in Rome had their ceremony of submission in public baptism or, for the unconverted, the possesso, prostitutes might be compelled to walk through the city in a public penitential procession, accompanied by local noblewomen, on their retirement into a specialized *convertite* convent; this happened in Ferrara in 1537.[82] As scholars have long observed, both groups were tolerated inasmuch as they absorbed the necessary evils of society—one understood as a receptacle for its sexual excesses, and the other for its financial impurities.[83]

Christian Audiences in Print

As in the pulpit, conversionary sermons in print catered primarily to a Christian readership, no matter what claims they made on their title page. Marcellino's *Fifteen Sermons,* the first volume of conversionary sermons printed in Italy, and the only one based on preaching in Rome, contains marginal notes aimed at instructing an intended audience of Christian readers new to Hebraic study. These explain the different enumeration of biblical books ("note that the text is cited here as it is in Hebrew") and carefully define various sacred texts in the sermons; Jewish listeners may or may not have known that *Midrash Tehillim* is a gloss on the Book of Psalms, but most Christian listeners and readers surely did not.[84]

81. AAV Misc. Arm. VII, 330r.

82. Diane Yvonne Ghirardo, "The Topography of Prostitution in Renaissance Ferrara." For the case of Florence, see Gillian Jack, "Sex, Salvation, and the City: The Monastery of Sant'Elisabetta delle Convertite as a Civic Institution in Florence, 1329–1627."

83. See especially Hughes, "Distinguishing Signs."

84. Marcellino, *Sermoni quindici sopra il salmo centonove fatti a gli Hebrei di Roma,* "Dedica," unpaginated fols. a2r–a4r; Milano, *Il ghetto di Roma,* 284; Lance Gabriel Lazar, *Working in the Vineyard of the Lord: Jesuit Confraternities in Early Modern Italy,* 114; Alberto Zucchi, "I Predicatori Domenicani degli Ebrei in Roma," 313–22; Carolyn H. Wood

Marcellino's manner of addressing Christians in print held true for other printed conversionary sermons and polemical literature from this period, establishing a practice that continued through the seventeenth century. As we have seen with Pietro Pichi, Giuseppe Ciantes, and others, such works always addressed multiple audiences. Like Marcellino, later authors invariably published with Christian printers and publishers, sometimes in collaboration with formerly Jewish authors. They usually wrote in the vernacular, and employed paratexts—particularly dedications—directed at a Christian readership and network of Christian patrons.[85] Benedetto Biancuzzi, the Hebrew professor at Sapienza University, delivered his lone sermon to Jews in October 1605, but the additional handwritten letter of dedication to Pope Paul V that accompanies the printed version refers to Jews as "them" and Christians as "us."[86] In many cases, the different audiences were addressed together, under the conceit that the same format and presentation might serve or appeal to them all. Tommaso Bell'haver, in Venice, suggested that his *Easy Doctrine to Bring the Jew to Knowledge of the True Messiah* would bring any Jew ("even a mediocre one") to knowledge of his own error. Yet in his letter to readers, he clarified that for Christians, "it would be a consolation and confirmation in the faith," and would be equally useful for any preacher or religious leader who knew no Hebrew, but found himself drawn into disputation or arguments of faith with Jews.[87]

Conversion made sermons sell, even if the content was predictable. "Mixed" sermon volumes, containing some sermons to Jews and others to Christians, always flaunted their conversionary aspects on the title page. In the sixteenth century, both Vitale Medici in Florence and Girolamo Allè in Venice published such sermon books.[88] Their title pages focused on the sermons to Jews over all others, even when those were the minority of the sermons in the book. Such volumes were printed in Italian (sometimes

and Peter Iver Kaufman, "Tacito Predicatore: The Annunciation Chapel at the Madonna Dei Monti in Rome," 636 passim. Quotation in Marcellino, *Sermoni quindici*, 18, 3.

85. For Hebrew books in Christian printing houses, see Amnon Raz-Krakotzkin, *The Censor, the Editor, and the Text: The Catholic Church and the Shaping of the Jewish Canon in the Sixteenth Century*. For formatting in Hebrew books, see David Stern, "The Rabbinic Bible in Its Sixteenth-Century Context."

86. Benedetto Biancuzzi, *Lettione fatta alli Hebrei di Roma, nell'Oratorio della Santissima Trinità de' Pellegrini, & Convalescenti, li 8 di ottobre 1605*. BAV Stamp. Barb.V.IV.68.

87. Tommaso Bell'haver, *Dottrina facile et breve per redurre l'Hebreo al conoscimento del vero Messia*, fols. a2r, a5r.

88. Vitale Medici, *Omelie Fatte alli Ebrei di Firenze nella Chiesa di Santa Croce, et Sermoni Fatti in Più compagnie della detta città*; Girolamo Allè, *I convinti, e confusi hebrei*.

with Latin), published by Christian publishers, and contained letters to Christian readers along with dedications to local prelates or nobles. In all of these ways, they took a Christian interest in Jewish conversion for granted.

Conversionary polemics, close cousins of sermon volumes, flooded the book market in the late sixteenth century. These, too, deliberately addressed a Catholic audience over a Jewish one. Fabiano Fioghi's treatise of 1582 sought to appeal to every possible audience; his book was intended "for the benefit and use of souls, both of the poor Jews, and of Christians, neophytes, and catechumens, who will be able to learn many secrets contained in the holy faith."[89] Giovanni Paolo Eustachio framed his conversionary treatise to Jews with a dedication to Gregory XIII, and a letter to readers describing "my Hebrew nation" and "brothers of the flesh" in the third person.[90] Bell'haver explained that he had written his *Easy and Brief Doctrine* "in order that [the Jews] will have no excuse of not having someone to show them the path of truth." Indeed, he continued, he hoped that "as the book will be relevant for Jews to reduce them to the holy faith of Christ, so too will it be a consolation to Christians and a confirmation in the same faith."[91] No treatise addressed Jews without first providing at least a knowing nod and often an outstretched hand to its Christian readers.

Even printed sermons that claimed to address Jewish people directly never made them the sole audience. Pichi's *Treatise on the Passion and Death of the Messiah*, drawn from his own sermons, came with a long and hostile letter to Jewish readers, rare among such publications. Yet it must be read against the two letters to Christians that precede it. In a dedicatory letter to Paul V, Pichi argued that "where Your Holiness has addressed himself to their benefit through works, I have striven for their salvation with my voice." An additional letter offers Christian readers extensive apologies for writing in a rough Italian for the sake of Jews who read no other vernaculars—but it promised Christian readers benefit as well: "It should not be judged useless for Christians . . . by reading it, as I hope you will do, you will not only not waste time, but you will also find taste, and spiritual consolation, seeing how clearly the Holy Scriptures demonstrate

89. Fabiano Fioghi, *Dialogo fra il cathecumino et il padre cathechizante*, , unpaginated (3V). Fioghi's dialogue was reprinted in 1611 and 1628.

90. Giovanni Paolo Eustachio, *Salutari discorsi composti da M. Giovan Paolo Eustachi Nolano. già Hebbreo, hor Christiano*, unpaginated (A2r–A4v).

91. Bell'haver, *Dottrina facile*, unpaginated letter to readers (A5r).

this most important mystery of our faith, the passion of the Saviour."[92] Pichi's successor, Ciantes, dedicated his treatise on the mysteries of the Trinity to the Master of the Sacred Palace, "since my manner of speaking pleases you," but argued that the book would similarly please "every other who is your equal in mental sharpness . . . [and] to lettered men for the truth it contains."[93]

These sermon publications do not reflect that famous environment of study and unprecedented interreligious collaboration that enabled the publication and printing of Hebrew books in Renaissance Italy. In some cases, such cooperation between Jews and Christians (often former Jews) suggested moderation and compromise, or even irenicism.[94] But publications like those of Bell'haver and Pichi fall well outside that context, and reflect no direct Jewish input on the Hebraic scholarship of their authors. Every aspect of these volumes, especially their flattery of Christians, undermined their title page protests of "for the Jews," and confirmed a standard pattern for printed and spoken sermons.

Over the later seventeenth and eighteenth centuries, Italian books which superficially aimed at converting Jews routinely advertised their wider benefits for Christian readers. Such texts draw no firm line between addressing Jews and ostentatiously scolding them while keeping an eye firmly on the Christian readership. Thus the printer who published a treatise by the Theatine preacher Giovanni Maria Vincenti confidently boasted that this work on the coming of the Messiah, "explained and proven to the Jews," was necessary "not only to Jews, but very useful to Christians, and especially to preachers, confirming . . . the truth of all the mysteries of the Christian faith."[95] Seventy years later, the same claim proved helpful on the title page of the "Jewish Catechumen instructed" by the conversionary preacher Lorenzo Virgulti; the title page presented the book as "useful also

92. Pietro Pichi, *Trattato della passione e morte del Messia contra gli ebrei*, 3r, 4r.

93. Giuseppe Ciantes, *Della Santissima Trinità, evidentemente provata da i testimoni de gli antichi Ebrei*, dedica. For further analysis, see Fiamma Satta, "Predicatori agli ebrei, catecumeni e neofiti a Roma nella prima metà del seicento."

94. Joseph Hacker and Adam Shear, *The Hebrew Book in Early Modern Italy*, 6–10; David B. Ruderman, *Early Modern Jewry: A New Cultural History*, 99–120; Piet van Boxel, "Hebrew Books and Censorship in Sixteenth-Century Italy"; Piet van Boxel, *Jewish Books in Christian Hands Theology, Exegesis and Conversion under Gregory XIII (1572–1585)*. See also Raz-Krakotzkin, *The Censor, the Editor, and the Text*.

95. Giovanni Maria Vincenti, *Il Messia venuto . . . non solamente necessaria a gli hebrei, ma molto utile à cristiani e massime à' predicatori..*

to Christians who wish to know the foundations of their faith."[96] In the long confessional era, publishers and polemicists both seemed to believe that Jewish obduracy provided an ideal foil for buttressing the faith of ordinary Catholics.

Conversionary preachers in the pulpit would thus always have had their double audience in mind and sometimes even acknowledged them aloud. To his Jewish audience, Marcellino said, "I do not doubt that this sermon of mine, for all that it is high and profound, will nonetheless be understood by my faithful, who will have taken it with that meaning and sweetness, that you have not taken."[97]

Awareness of a layered audience permeated every aspect of conversionary rhetoric. It surfaced in a preacher's occasional asides, but also wound deep into the structure of sermons themselves and especially into the word at their heart, "Jew"—a word uttered in different rhetorical contexts throughout Rome. Roman Jews at conversionary sermons heard themselves addressed with a label—"O Jews"—that could certainly apply directly to them in their particular historical context, but could equally carry an abstract meaning whenever Jewish people were absent. Christians who walked into the oratory on Saturday afternoons carried with them the preconceptions and theological concepts about Jews they had heard from other pulpits.

Although Catholic and conversionary sermons derived from different textual traditions, both kinds used the word "Jew" in similar ways. Both avoided specific references to the Roman Jewish community. Instead, the word "Jew" took on a broad, more generic meaning that never referred exclusively to the living Jewish audience, even when that audience was seated right in front of them. It is important to note that in both genres, preachers could have chosen to employ other rhetorical options instead of this more abstract usage of the word "Jew." To put it another way, Jews were always invoked in the same manner in Roman sermons whether or not they were actually present. Even in the special context of conversionary sermons, the word "Jew" was only used with a general meaning that could apply equally to an audience of Christians and Jews.

---

96. Lorenzo Virgulti, *L'ebreo catecumeno instruito ne' principali misteri della santa fede Cristiana . . . opera utile anche a i Cristiani, che desiderano di sapere i fondamenti della loro Fede.*

97. Marcellino, *Sermoni quindici*, 107.

This general call to convert is timeless. Marcellino's only concession to chronology is to acknowledge a postbiblical history in which Jews should no longer observe commandments:

> You, on the contrary, until [Christ's] coming observed [the law] very little, and after he came, you want to observe and to observe so much that, as much as possible, you do not transgress one iota . . . and now see that for fifteen hundred and eighty-two years nothing has come to you except the contrary of what you wish for.[98]

Marcellino's conversionary preaching thus considers Jews primarily as a static category. His approach to persuasion does not extend to acknowledging Jewish Roman life or personal circumstances. Even a reference to the Passover feast—a high point in the Jewish year, and one still undergoing ritual innovation in the early modern period—is treated only as an event in the past: "Just as your fathers celebrated *Pasqua* one time when they left Egypt, but then every year *made* a memorial to it, so do we make a daily and continual memorial to that which Christ did once."[99] Mentioning a current practice might have helped Marcellino's argument; he could not have been ignorant of the Jewish liturgical calendar, which was meant to determine the content of his Saturday preaching.

The manuscript record—uneven for the sixteenth century, but stronger for the seventeenth—confirms that a strictly abstract treatment of Jews was the norm in conversionary sermons, for which print and manuscript versions are similar.[100] The very invariability of conversionary sermons as an established genre suggests that they were not, as a whole, concerned with accommodating the particular circumstances of sixteenth-century Roman Jewish people or closely connected to other contemporaneous conversionary efforts.

We can also expect conversionary sermons to share characteristics with other contemporary Christian sermons, particularly those preached elsewhere in Rome during Lent and festivals. The concept of persuasion

---

98. Marcellino, *Sermoni quindici*, 49–50.

99. Marcellino, *Sermoni quindici*, 125 (emphasis added). For Passover liturgical innovations in Renaissance Italy, see Robert Bonfil, *Jewish life in Renaissance Italy*, 223.

100. Based on a survey of sixteenth- and seventeenth-century conversionary sermons in manuscript preserved at the BAV. One exception is an early conversionary sermon published by Ludovico Carretto that has little precedent or imitation—as discussed further in chapter 5. Ludovico Carretto, *Epistola de Ludovico Carretto ad Hebreos. Sermone di Giulio Innocentio suo figliolo alli Hebrei, et era quando lo fece de età de anni cinque in sei*. See Robert Bonfil, "An Infant's Missionary Sermon Addressed to the Jews of Rome in 1553"; Robert Bonfil [Reuven], "Chi era Ludovico Carretto, apostata?"

was a primary concern in all early modern sermon rhetoric.[101] Jews were an especially potent symbol in Rome's grandest pulpits, often invoked in prominent sermons.

The preacher who best embodied preaching tropes in Rome was the Conventual Franciscan Cornelio Musso (1511–74), house preacher to the illustrious Farnese family of dukes, cardinals, patrons, and one pope.[102] Musso was an apt model for Marcellino and other acclaimed preachers. His pulpit, the church of San Lorenzo in Damaso, enjoyed special prominence; the cardinal associated with it during Musso's tenure was the extraordinarily powerful Alessandro Farnese, in his capacity as vice chancellor of the Apostolic Chancery. Martin's *Roma Sancta* considers San Lorenzo in Damaso second only to Saint Peter's in its discussion of preaching. The anonymous diary author discussed earlier in this chapter visited the church almost daily during Lent in some years, and heard Alfonso Lupo preach there; Lupo had also preached to the Jews. The Lenten sermons that Musso preached in San Lorenzo in Damaso in 1539 and 1540 were polished over the course of his later career, and published in a complete set in the late 1570s, just as Marcellino was first printing his own religious works.

References to Jews saturate Musso's sermons; Jews merit more attention than any other antagonist, whether Protestants, Ottomans, or Satan himself. Musso uses them in three ways, reviewed briefly here. First, Jews are invoked regularly as part of the Lenten, specifically Franciscan, rhetoric of Jewish ingratitude, deicide, and stubbornness: "Jews, why have you violated the law against this friend? You have hated, injured, surrounded, infiltrated, oppressed, tormented, and killed him."[103] Second and more often, they served as a mirror to Christian behavior: "Do you see that even the Jews have the Bible read on Saturday in their synagogues? . . . What shame is ours, that the gospel of Christ is not read or preached every festival. . . . Go to masses . . . go to the churches, which are

101. John O'Malley, *Praise and Blame in Renaissance Rome: Rhetoric, Doctrine, and Reform in the Sacred Orators of the Papal Court, c. 1450–1521*; Frederick McGinness, *Right Thinking and Sacred Oratory in Counter-Reformation Rome*; Marc Fumaroli, *L'Âge de l'éloquence: rhétorique et 'res literaria' de la Renaissance au seuil de l'époque classique*.

102. Gustavo Cantini, "Cornelio Musso dei frati minori conventuali (1511–1574), predicatore, scrittore e teologo al Concilio di Trento"; Corrie Norman, *Humanist Taste and Franciscan Values: Cornelio Musso and Catholic Preaching in Sixteenth-Century Italy*; Emily Michelson, *The Pulpit and the Press in Reformation Italy*, 54–85; Hubert Jedin, "Der Franziskaner Cornelio Musso, Bischof von Bitonto: sein Lebensgang und seine kirchliche Wirksamkeit."

103. Cornelio Musso, *Delle Prediche Quadragesimali*, 2:434.

the houses of God!'[104] Finally and most frequently, Musso calls for their conversion: "O cruel and impious dogs, who could ever say how many times you oppressed Christ, Synagogue? . . . How much better would it be for you if you converted to Christ. He is still ready to pardon you, and to put you back in his grace." "O Jews, at the example of the Ninevites do penance at the preaching of the resuscitated Jonah, the triumphant Christ, if you do not wish to perish."[105]

In these sermons, Musso reserves exhortation only for Romans and Jews: "O Roma!" "O Giudei!" He addresses no other group directly. But unlike his Roman listeners, who really heard him, Musso's Jews did not. It was a rare exception when Jews were permitted or snuck into a prominent church such as San Lorenzo in Damaso.[106] When Musso uttered the words "O Giudei," as he did frequently, he applied them to Christian listeners.

Musso's persistent lack of specificity about Jews suggests a deliberate choice. In many ways, his rhetoric, like Marcellino's, maintained medieval conventions; Jews as Christ killers, counterexamples, and converts are traditional themes in Lenten Franciscan preaching. Nonetheless, Musso's rhetoric departs from the precedent of his own order. The fifteenth-century Observant preachers who enraptured Northern Italy often framed their harsh anti-Jewish sentiments in practical and social terms, condemning Jewish-Christian socializing and encouraging Jewish expulsion.[107] Unlike these mendicants, Musso in Rome could hardly have advocated for specific legislation regarding Jews. The Holy See set policy, and it explicitly preferred conversion to expulsion. But where he might, like Bernardino of Siena, have denounced interactions between his

104. Cornelio Musso, *Prediche sopra il Simbolo de gli Apostoli . . . Predicate in Roma la Quaresima l'Anno MDXLII nella Chiesa di S. Lorenzo in Damaso*, 436.

105. Musso, *Delle Prediche Quadragesimali*, 2:428–29, 2:386.

106. For one example, see Stephen D. Bowd, "The Conversion of Margarita: A Wedding Oration in Fifteenth-Century Brescia," 152–53. For Jews in churches in early modern Rome, see Gerd Blum, "Vasari on the Jews: Christian Canon, Conversion, and the Moses of Michelangelo." Musso's church of San Lorenzo in Damaso hosted occasional conversionary sermons, as discussed earlier.

107. Hughes, "Distinguishing Signs"; Franco Mormando, *The Preacher's Demons: Bernardino of Siena and the Social Underworld of Early Renaissance Italy*; Nirit Ben-Aryeh Debby, "Jews and Judaism in the Rhetoric of Popular Preachers: The Florentine Sermons of Giovanni Dominici (1356–1419) and Bernardino Da Siena (1380–1444)"; Roberto Rusconi, "Predicatori ed ebrei nell'arte italiana del rinascimento"; Jussi Hanska, "Mendicant Preachers as Disseminators of Anti-Jewish Literary Topoi: The Case of Luca Da Bitonto."

listeners and their Jewish neighbors, he did not. Musso's sermons contain only the broadest, most general evocations of Jews.[108]

Moreover, in Musso's Rome, living Jewish people were increasingly prominent in a Rome where imaginary Jews had always already mattered. Rome's preachers, even those who never preached directly to an audience of Jews, surely knew about the huge influx of hundreds of Jewish immigrants since 1492 and the new experimentation with Jewish segregation in Venice from 1516. Their sermons drew on intellectual exchanges between Jewish and Christian humanists, as Christian knowledge of Hebrew became standard intellectual training. Musso himself sometimes explained Hebrew words in his sermons to make an exegetical point. He explicitly linked rabbinic Jews to the newer antagonists facing the church:

> Newborn Jews absorb their paternal traditions with their milk, not those of Moses, which God wants them to read . . . but of their Talmuds, which never speak except against the Christian faith, and deprave sacred letters in their own way, no less than that which our heretics do in this miserable and calamitous era to the epistles of Saint Paul and the Gospels.[109]

Yet all Musso's sermons nonetheless avoid direct allusions to living Roman Jews. They even omit mention of Rome's new Monte di Pietà, founded in the very year Musso composed his sermons and publicly preached during the same Lenten cycle of 1539. Musso was an especially careful editor of his own sermons, intending them to last for the ages.[110] But even if he had mentioned the Monte di Pietà aloud, later removing such local color before printing his sermons, any references could only have been incidental. They would not have formed extended passages central to the text.[111] Musso's Jews are always an entirely imagined, hypothesized category, the eternal adversary or mirror of Christianity.

When Musso first preached these sermons in 1539, Roman concerns about Jews were in many ways still implicit. But during the decades of Musso's growing prestige, when he probably repeated and tinkered with them every year, as popular preachers did, papal attitudes toward Jews

---

108. For Bernardino on Jews, see Mormando, *The Preacher's Demons*, 164–218.

109. Musso, *Delle Prediche Quadragesimali*, 2:226.

110. Norman, *Humanist Taste and Franciscan Values*; John O'Malley, "Form, Content and Influence of Works about Preaching Before Trent: The Franciscan Contribution."

111. For the Monte di Pietà, see Wisch and Newbigin, *Acting on Faith*. For the difference between a spoken and printed sermon in early modern Europe, see Stefano Dall'Aglio, "Faithful to the Spoken Word: Sermons from Orality to Writing in Early Modern Italy."

had developed into legislation. By the time Musso's sermons were printed in two thick and heavily annotated volumes, conversionary procedures, both coercive and persuasive, had expanded enough to establish the conversionary pulpit that employed Marcellino, De Monte, and later Pichi, Ciantes, and Boncompagni. The reissuing of Musso's sermons throughout the rest of the century and beyond suggests their continuing relevance (even in their abstract language about Jews) to that new context.[112]

Other preachers shared Musso's rhetorical approach to Jews. Marcellino preached to Christians in a traditional manner not only from his permanent post at Santa Maria in Aracoeli but also in elite churches throughout Rome and Italy. In those sermons he, too, evoked Jews as a mirror of Christian behavior. In his commentary on the book of Ruth (a book in which Christians, incidentally, read Jewish conversion allegorically as the story of the true church), Marcellino asked whether Elimelech, Ruth's father-in-law, was justified in going to Moab, where he might fraternize with foreigners. Marcellino moved the action to Rome, berating a courtly culture too concerned with appearances and advocating greater piety for a holy city:

> And if he [Elimelech], who is partly excused ... sinned by mixing with profane peoples, what about us, who converse all day with heretics, with Jews, and with stubborn sinners? Maybe we will argue that we do this in order to retrieve them from evil? I don't think we can say that, because they are more likely to convert us, than us them. We are wretched, then, who stay in the houses of sinners all day, and in the court of Princes, doing nothing but adoring, detracting, lying, feigning, scheming, and such. ... I admit that Rome is holy, the seat of Peter, and there are tombs of martyrs and the like, but with all this there is also much ambition, and many chances to depart from God, because here there is the seeing, and the being seen, the greeting, and the being greeted, the praising, the detracting.[113]

Thus might a preacher invoke Jews to criticize his Roman listeners, and Marcellino, like Musso, often did. Marcellino's first commentary on the book of Daniel opens by describing the ancient Jews who listened to sermons as though to music, and continues:

---

112. For a full list of Musso's publications, see Norman, *Humanist Taste and Franciscan Values*, 159–62.

113. Evangelista Marcellino, *Lezzioni diciannove sopra Rut. del RPF Vangelista Marcellino de' Minori Osservanti*, 20r.

And since it seems that you trust in hearing the word of God, and go filling the churches now after this preacher, and now after that one, I judge that this hearing of yours bears no more fruit than that of the Jews, because holy preaching is no more than a musical song in your eyes . . . and you listen much and do little.[114]

Howsoever Marcellino wanted to criticize his Christian listeners, whether for frantic social climbing or indeed frantic sermon hopping, he likened them to Jews, capricious or stubborn as needed.

For both Musso and Marcellino, then, any references to living Jewish people were thickly veiled, even when the conversion of the Jews seemed paramount. Musso was deeply concerned with Jews, yet despite the example of his Franciscan predecessors, he still preached almost exclusively about the ahistorical Jews of Christian lore—even while emphasizing the need for their conversion. Marcellino's fame depended on his sermons to Roman Jews, but his rhetoric always gave priority to an abstract Judaism rendered exemplary for Christians. The sermons in this brief sample all use the same language about Jews, despite the preachers' different concerns, styles, traditions, and audiences. A generic evocation of Jews was thus the norm in all styles of Christian sermons. Whether or not any Jewish people were listening, the word "Jew" was given the same broad meaning—one that Christians could apply to themselves.

Weekly conversionary sermons focused on the option to choose Catholicism, and by doing so, helped to validate and define the borders of Catholic identity. Unlike in the possesso ceremony, the visual role of Jews in conversionary sermons was not intended only to demonstrate inferiority. Instead, the silent, listening Jews modeled the possibility of universal penitence, recalling the injunction of 1 Corinthians 12:13: "For in one Spirit were we all baptized into one body, whether Jews or Gentiles, whether bond or free; and in one Spirit we have all been made to drink."[115] As Musso had put it, "Do you see how many Jews have converted in the past few years? . . . Jews, do not linger any longer, if you want to heal from your infirmities. Christians, come to the pool of penitence, do you not see that the waters have been disturbed?"[116] For him, the sight of Jewish conversion also immediately signified Christian contrition. The opportunity to choose Catholicism thus actively applied to spectators as well. Any

114. Evangelista Marcellino, *Lettioni sopra Daneiele Profeta del RPF Vangelista Marcellino de Min. Osservanti. Fatte in Roma in Araceli*, 3.
115. Douay-Rheims translation.
116. Musso, *Delle Prediche Quadragesimali*, 1:285.

Christian attending a conversionary sermon beheld the preacher addressing Jews, but such viewers had been primed from all their other sermon
experience to hear the preacher's words—"Oh Jew, repent"—as a direct
injunction to them personally. The more they identified with the Jewish
people they beheld in front of them, the more they could also hope to
enjoy the redemption on offer. The double message from eye and ear made
sermons to Jews deeply powerful for their Christian audience.

The greatest sign of conversionary preaching's importance as a Christian
event lies in its difference from daily life. Inside the oratory, for two hours on
a Saturday afternoon, Jews, Christians, tourists, and converts sat together
beneath the same pulpit, and kept to a tightly scripted near silence. At all
other times, Jews and Christians built close ties, and converts kept in contact with their old and new communities, insisting strongly on these ties in
defiance of laws trying to keep them separate. Indeed, Rome was so famous
for its socialization between the two faiths that Boncompagni had to construct a special argument against it: "Because in Rome the Jews often keep
company in the houses of Christians, and there is no Christian who hasn't
heard discussions in matters of faith; therefore, to remove the danger that
the simple will be subverted, sermons to Jews must be public."[117]

But during a conversionary sermon—and only then—the division
between Jews and others ossified into a stylized tableau. This was, for all
participants, a moment unlike any other in their experience.[118] Unlike
other choreographed public rituals for Jews—the possesso and carnival—
sermons relied on Christian words, Christian actions, and Jewish silence.
And unlike those other rituals, sermons to Jews did not confirm Jews as
intimate outsiders, flying buttresses of the Roman church who support it
from the outside.[119] Instead, conversionary sermons cast Jewish people as
living props, hypothetical versions of themselves. In a performance that
principally addressed Christians, they were both a necessary audience and
an imaginary one. Alongside the discussions, publicity, Christian spectators, patterns of ritual, and rhetorical practices that fueled the spectacle,
the Jewish audience shaped conversionary sermons into the city's most
potent and revealing manifesto. Conversionary preaching provided Rome
with an optimal platform for staging its vision of ideal Jewish-Christian
relations, its claim as theater of the world, and its self-image as a theoretically flawless exemplar of Catholic piety.

117. BAV Borg. lat. 129, 499r.
118. Domenico Rocciolo, "Fra promozione e difesa della fede: Le vicende dei catecumeni e neofiti romani in età moderna."
119. A. N. Wilson, "Everything England Used to Be."

CHAPTER FIVE

Preaching Traditions
and Change

IT WAS THE MINISTRATIONS of the Congregation of the Oratory that in 1582 converted Salomone Corcos from Judaism to Catholicism—a spectacular victory for the Catholic Church and relevant for much of our earlier discussion. Corcos's embrace of Christianity was widely celebrated; news of it was even sent abroad.[1] The Congregation's warm treatment of Corcos, and the brothers' commitment to teaching him doctrine, was known and discussed publicly at the time. But at least one contemporary newsletter made an effort to attribute the Corcos conversion to the new spectacle of conversionary preaching instead: "Because of the continuous sermons that, by order of His Holiness, are given to the Jews in the oratory of Santissima Trinità dei Pellegrini, one of them often comes to the Christian faith, as happened to Salomone Corcos, a rich Jew with more than a hundred scudi a year."[2] Corcos was indeed one of Rome's wealthiest and most illustrious Jewish figures, and eventually brought his entire family with him into the Church—those who had not converted already. His conversion provided critical validation for the growing evangelization campaign toward Jews. But when it came to announcing the event itself, the author of this newsletter had clearly determined to give the public credit for this triumphant victory for the church to sermons, not to the Congregation of the Oratory. Regardless of the accuracy of his presentation, he felt justified in offering

---

1. Corcos's baptism is mentioned four times in the avvisi di Roma. BAV Urb. lat. 1050, 122r, 124r, 210r, 215v. See also Carolyn H. Wood and Peter Iver Kaufman, "Tacito Predicatore: The Annunciation Chapel at the Madonna Dei Monti in Rome."

2. BAV Urb. lat. 1050, 124r. See also Wood and Kaufman, "Tacito Predicatore."

this explanation for Corcos's decision. As the flagship symbol of conversion by persuasion, sermons made a compelling lede for a triumphant conversionary narrative. The high status and public nature of sermons to Jews displaced the Congregation's intimate conversations.

One hundred and fifty years later, conversionary preaching still retained enough clout that a preacher could make himself the hero of somebody else's story. The conversion of Sabbato Nachamu, as narrated by the conversionary preacher Paolo Sebastiano Medici in 1735, describes the ideal effects of a conversionary sermon. In Medici's recounting, the rabbi from Ancona felt his heart touched by God as soon as he first heard Medici explain from the pulpit that Christ was the promised Messiah of the Jews. Nachamu's next step, in this retelling, was to visit the preacher in private and present his remaining doubts. After Medici expertly resolved each one, Nachamu grew so enthusiastic to embrace the Christian faith publicly that the preacher had to beg him to restrain himself for his own safety. But the next day, again inspired by a sermon, Nachamu nonetheless stood up in front of the crowd, removed his hat, made the sign of the cross, and threw himself at the feet of a listening cardinal (whom the preacher had strategically invited in advance). Nachamu—from that moment styled in the narrative only as "the Catechumen"—proved a model convert. He was both a learned rabbi and a humble student. Like Corcos, Nachamu brought to the church added benefits: he offered his three-year-old son and his wife's unborn fetus.

Offering a relative for baptism—most often one's own child or fetus—was a formal procedure that took place before the vicegerent's court, and was understood to have the strength of a donation or vow.[3] The act was immediately binding and irrevocable. Not even the person who made the offering could revoke it if they later regretted the action. Baptismal offerings in Rome took place increasingly frequently from the sixteenth century onward, and during that time the right of offering a relative extended gradually from mother and father to any known kin and even a fiancé. Unsurprisingly, baptismal offerings caused legal and emotional havoc throughout Jewish communities.[4] Nachamu's ability to present two incontestable offspring to the church made him a tremendously valuable prize.

---

3. The vicegerent is the chief deputy of the cardinal vicar of the Diocese of Rome. A cardinal vicar has responsibility for the spiritual and administrative oversight of the diocese, on behalf of his bishop. The title of Bishop of Rome is held by the pope.

4. On offerings, see especially Marina Caffiero, *Forced Baptisms: Histories of Jews, Christians, and Converts in Papal Rome*, 73–76. The case of Anna Del Monte is notable in part because she was offered by a man claiming to be her betrothed. On her story, see

Yet as the story progresses, Medici keeps himself, not his stellar cat-echumen, at the center of the action. He describes giving Nachamu pri-vate catechism lessons in his room and arranging for him to be sent to the House of Catechumens in Rome, where Nachamu was finally bap-tized. Sabbato Nachamu became Francesco Maria Ferretti. Medici ends his retelling by including the text of Ferretti's own minisermon after bap-tism—a prayer for divine illumination. By concluding his treatise on this note, having Ferretti mimic a preacher's rhetoric, Medici suggests that the best behavior for a new convert is to imitate a conversionary preacher.[5]

Both of these stories seek to attribute conversion exclusively to preaching rather than to other factors. They insist that it was preaching—and specifi-cally, Jewish enthusiasm for the theological content of sermons—that pro-duced conversion. And indeed, few other evangelizing spectacles had ever happened in Rome with as much predictability, fanfare, or institutional backing. With the two papal bulls of *Vices Eius Nos* and *Sancta Mater Ecclesia*, preaching to Jews became, for the first time in Europe, legislated, consistent, and frequent. The sermons themselves ostensibly served (in addition to Jews) a separate population with a new and distinct religious identity: new Catholics from the Roman Jewish community. Neophytes in Rome formed an unprecedented group: not compelled into Christianity through force alone as they were in Spain, yet also more deeply rooted in their own city than were any other baptized Jews in Europe.

In theory, then, conversionary preaching in Rome provided a unique opportunity to develop a new genre of sermon, adapted to the particu-larities of its target audience. Tailoring sermon to audience was one of the strongest tenets of the preacher's art, as centuries' worth of *ars praedi-candi* (art of preaching) manuals had specified. We might therefore expect that the preacher's individual creativity and innovation as well as his skill in customization would be critical to the enterprise. If the ser-mon texts themselves really mattered to conversionary preaching, perhaps the preachers ought to say something new. Perhaps they ought to con-struct some contemporary references or find words to appeal to the entire

Kenneth R. Stow, *Anna and Tranquillo: Catholic Anxiety and Jewish Protest in the Age of Revolutions*; Anna Del Monte, *Rubare le anime: diario di Anna Del Monte ebrea romana.*

5. No copies of this pamphlet survive in Italy, but the thirty-six-hundred-word text is transcribed fully in Francesco Rovira-Bonet, *Armatura de' Forti, Ovvero, Memorie spet-tanti agl'Infedeli Ebrei che siano, o turchi*, 613–16. For its fate in Portugal, see Bruno Feitler, *The Imaginary Synagogue: Anti-Jewish Literature in the Portuguese Early Modern World (16th–18th Centuries)*, 42–44. The sole surviving copy (to my knowledge) is held at the University of Leeds.

range of listening Jews. In short, the sermons might have addressed living Jewish people, the ones who were compelled to listen and were meant to convert.

But in fact, as the sermons of Marcellino showed us, this was almost never the case. Early modern conversionary sermons were, with few exceptions, repetitive and imitative performances. They arose out of a long history of Christian-Jewish polemic, whose roots are as old as Christianity itself. If sermon rhetoric were a river, its course was well established. Its banks were solid, shored up over centuries, first by disputations and occasional conversionary sermons in the high Middle Ages, and later by mendicant friars who discussed Jews in their sermons to Christians. By the time of their reestablishment in Rome, forced sermons to Jews had little opportunity to be innovative or flexible in their content. Sermon texts almost always remained largely repetitive, even formulaic, despite the uniqueness of the occasion and audience. As a rule, determined by firm tradition, they also avoided any reference to the topics most relevant and familiar to Jewish audiences: their lives and social conditions, the range of conversionary measures available to them, recent events or papal policy, or even the tangible benefits of conversion in this world or the next.[6] Such powerful adherence to medieval norms, and the failure to develop a new preaching style that directly enticed Jews in Rome to convert, could be considered a lost opportunity for innovation and direct persuasion.

Instead, what made sermons to Jews valuable to Christians was their high theological stature—and what gave them that stature was precisely the replication and familiarity of sermon tropes centuries old. As a public spectacle, conversionary sermons served multiple functions. First, they gave a clear physical embodiment to the abstract notion of conversion through persuasion. They also suggested to the watching world that any given Jewish conversion must necessarily be genuine, based on heart and mind. As previously noted, the early modern period saw increasing concern with the authenticity or inauthenticity of conversion. And in the early modern world, true persuasion required intellectual reasoning at the highest intellectual and theological levels. A baptism that could be framed as the fruit of preaching could not also be attributed to coercion or ambition;

6. For extended analyses of particular sermons and the absence of references to contemporary Judaism, see Emily Michelson, "Evangelista Marcellino: One Preacher, Two Audiences"; Emily Michelson, "Conversionary Preaching and the Jews in Early Modern Rome." For "imaginary" Judaism, see David Nirenberg, *Anti-Judaism: The Western Tradition*.

it overcame suspicion of those factors. That is why stories about conversion emphasized the role of preaching.

Ultimately, then, converting Jewish people was not the primary function of conversionary sermons to Jews. A demonstration of preaching might convert some Jews—as a side benefit, or as with Corcos, a token showpiece of success—but the event was not tailored closely to that end. Instead, sermons to Jews conformed to prototypes of other displays aimed at strengthening the faith of Catholics. To do so, sermon content had to be predictable, recognizable, and prestigious. Sermons had to aim for stature rather than efficacy. That was the marker of their worth.

Preachers to Jews all therefore faced a common dilemma: pitching their sermons to multiple audiences while also balancing the necessary carrot of flattery and stick of rebuke in speaking to Jews. A preacher's manner of addressing Jews directly was his own decision, but presented knotty problems. How could he best flatter Jewish people into the Christian fold while still obeying the papal mandate to preach on Jewish desolation, vain hopes, and idolatrous errors? Conversely, how could he signal to Christian listeners that he was no Judeophile, without also making his supposed primary audience hate him in the process? He might choose to address this problem, as Benedetto Biancuzzi did, by limiting a sermon strictly to a careful interpretation of one book in the Hebrew Bible (in Biancuzzi's case, Daniel), rehearsing eschatological arguments about the Second Coming and refuting rabbinic interpretations. Biancuzzi, like many preachers, also found the ancient preachers' mandate of *captatio benevolentia* (capturing the goodwill of the listeners) largely irrelevant to this pulpit. He laced his sermon with tirades against his audience: "You who are living today, and claim to study scripture and the rabbis, and claim to be (though you are not really) so anxious for this coming."[7] He accused "modern rabbis"—an impersonal, all-purpose category—of malignity in refusing to embrace anti-Jewish polemics and he concluded his sermon on an apocalyptic note: the true Israel of faithful believers would be brought to the celestial Jerusalem at the end of times. In Biancuzzi's reckoning, the carrot generally lost to the stick.

For as long as conversionary sermons lasted, their mix of components varied primarily in its proportions, not its content, approach, or novelty. Each preacher would have to concoct his own blend of insults, promises, and scriptural exegesis, trying to appeal to multiple audiences often at direct cross-purposes with each other. These two conditions—the prestige

---

7. Benedetto Biancuzzi, *Lettione fatta alli Hebrei di Roma*, 4.

of conversionary preaching and the contradictory rhetorical challenge it posed—faced every man who ascended the pulpit.

By asking whether conversionary sermons constituted a lost opportunity in rhetoric, we can recognize that what mattered most in their success was not a directly resulting baptism but rather adherence to a formula that met Christian expectations. By identifying the historical components of that formula, we understand how sermons performed by offering the idea of persuasion by rhetoric as a conceit. By examining the content of these sermons, we can appreciate how they could claim such high status: they permitted preachers to show off their expertise and skills as learned Hebraists, enabling the fiction that Jewish people only ever converted for the most erudite theological arguments. Furthermore, by analyzing the language with which preachers addressed Jews (one of the areas where preachers could innovate the most), we see the distance that could lie between the intellectual conceit of persuasion and the actual experience of it. Preachers spoke to and about Jews in ways that were more or less insulting, and always treated them as hypothetical, hermeneutic, or imaginary. This chapter will consider these issues chronologically from the medieval precedents for conversionary sermons through the early modern period.

Rhetorical Precedents

Two powerful categories of medieval sermon rhetoric determined the general formula for early modern conversionary preaching. Both of these categories contributed to the complex interplay between Christians and Jews in sermon rhetoric, and helped to determine how a preacher might speak publicly about Jews. First, literature arising out of the context of medieval polemics was primarily textual, rational, and exegetical. Largely dominated by Dominicans, it was ostensibly aimed directly at Jews for their conversion. Yet the implicit Christian audience had always been understood to be both more important and more worthy. Converted Jewish preachers in the thirteenth and fourteenth centuries "appear to have been driven by a desire to please Christians and harm Jews."[8] Second, the anti-Jewish preaching of medieval mendicants, which flourished somewhat later, did not claim to address Jews directly but did discuss them extensively. This preaching was dominated in Italy by Franciscans, but was

---

8. Paola Tartakoff, *Between Christian and Jew: Conversion and Inquisition in the Crown of Aragon, 1250–1391*, 89–90.

strongly influenced by the preaching of the Spanish Dominican Vincent Ferrer. It was largely scathing, bitter, and incendiary.

The theological differences between Christians and Jews became an increasingly public matter throughout the late Middle Ages. Public disputations included the Maimonidean controversies of the early thirteenth century, Paris Talmud burning of 1240, Barcelona disputation of 1263, and especially the early fifteenth-century disputation at Tortosa that lasted for nearly two years, and that saw mass conversions alongside constraints and attacks on Jewish people. As heresy, orthodoxy, and conversion gained importance throughout southern Europe, these debates sought to demonstrate that Jewish texts could prove the superiority of Christianity.[9] The disputations in particular bolstered a growing tradition of conversionary or polemical *adversus Judaeos* literature composed by mendicants and converts, most notably the Dominicans Raymond Peñaforte and Ramon Martì, and the convert Paul Christiani.[10] More broadly, they helped to make disputation a defining feature of intellectual and public life in the medieval period.[11]

Medieval disputations, and the treatises and sermons arising from them, determined the basic forms of conversionary rhetoric. The Hebrew Bible along with the rabbinic texts of the Mishnah, Talmud, and Midrash could all be reinterpreted as supporting Christian doctrine. Within this vast corpus of texts, certain passages became touchstones for Christian polemics, such as Isaiah 7:14, which appears to predict a virgin birth, or much later, the commentaries of R. David Kimḥi (the RaDaK).[12] These were deployed repeatedly to support a standard set of arguments: that the Messiah has already come, that Jesus is the Messiah, that Jesus was born of a virgin, that God is triune, and that the Mosaic law has been superseded.[13] Proselytizers sought to demonstrate mastery of Jewish texts to prove their own interpretations true and the Jewish readings false.

9. Robert Chazan, *Fashioning Jewish Identity in Medieval Western Christendom*, 7–10 passim.

10. The field of Jewish-Christian relations in the twelfth and thirteenth centuries is vast. The scholarship cited in the course of this discussion is not intended to be comprehensive.

11. Shlomo Simonsohn, *The Apostolic See and the Jews*, 316–22; Alex J. Novikoff, *The Medieval Culture of Disputation: Pedagogy, Practice, and Performance.*

12. "Therefore the Lord himself shall give you a sign; Behold, a virgin shall conceive, and bear a son, and shall call his name Immanuel." King James Version.

13. Fausto Parente, "Il confronto ideologico tra l'ebraismo e la Chiesa in Italia"; Fausto Parente, "La Chiesa e il 'Talmud': L'atteggiamento della Chiesa e del mondo cristiano nei confronti del 'Talmud' e degli altri scritti rabbinici, con particolare riguardo all'Italia tra XV e XVI secolo"; Robin J. E. Vose, *Dominicans, Muslims and Jews in the Medieval Crown of Aragon*, 139–44; Chazan, *Fashioning Jewish Identity in Medieval Western Christendom*, 19–20.

The thirteenth century also saw a new form of attack on the Talmud. The earliest Christian argumentation against Jews had been exegetical, arguing for the superiority of one biblical interpretation over another. But growing Christian interest in and study of the Talmud fostered a new approach that would continue to permeate and sometimes dominate anti-Jewish polemic. This approach posited that biblical Judaism was the true Judaism and that rabbinic Judaism was a later perversion. According to this interpretation, the rabbis of the Talmud were fully aware that the Old Testament and early Midrashic literature confirmed the truth of Christianity. But they used the Talmud to conceal this knowledge from their faithful, filling it with deceitful and tortuous reasoning along with far-fetched interpretations of scripture. Christian polemicists who took this line came to see modern Judaism as a corruption of biblical Judaism. The polemical dichotomies and tropes they established would last for centuries: clever rabbis deceiving the innocent faithful (even as the faithful were also considered theologically blind and stubborn); "true" versus "false" Judaism, a distinction determined by Christians; and the superiority of ancient Judaism over any form of contemporary Judaism.[14] As one eighteenth-century tract had it, "[Jews] are followers of their false masters, [who are] inventors of a deceitful, capricious law full of superstitions, errors, and obscenities."[15] Both the Old Testament and the Talmud contained true passages in this view, but these needed to be identified and interpreted correctly, and distinguished from the many parts of Hebrew literature that polemicists considered false and damaging to the church.[16]

All of these notions about the merits and flaws in Jewish texts found verbal expression in medieval disputations, and these led directly to some of the first conversionary sermons. Conversionary preaching evolved out of disputations, particularly in the case of Christiani, who argued against Rabbi Moses ben Nachman (Nachmanides) at the Barcelona disputation and then continued preaching to Jews thereafter. Christiani's position relied on selecting out the "good" passages from the Bible, Mishna, and Talmud, and rejecting the passages that he thought insulted or damaged the church. His approach influenced the major polemical writers of the period, such as Peñaforte and especially Martì, whose comprehensive

---

14. On the Christian concept of the synagogue as blind, see Schlauch, "The Allegory of Church and Synagogue." For an extended example of its iconography, see Katz, *The Jew in the Art of the Italian Renaissance*, 69–98.

15. Francesco Maria Ferretti, *Le Verità della fede cristiana*, 313.

16. See especially Parente, "Il confronto ideologico tra l'ebraismo e la Chiesa in Italia"; Parente, "La Chiesa e il 'Talmud.'"

treatise *Pugio Fidei* ensured that this reasoning would influence all Jewish-Christian argumentation for centuries.[17]

The entire act of staging a disputation, as scholars have long noted, seemed to suggest a kind of parity between Christians and Jews, validating their fundamental similarities. By offering detailed counterreadings of Jewish textual traditions, the Christian proselytizers confirmed the parallel importance within both faiths of exegesis, close reading, and textual interpretation. Both groups, however unnaturally, exchanged religious ideas and both "had to function in the same cultural world of contested religious truths."[18] At disputations, Jews were given the right to respond, at least artificially; indeed, the response of Nachmanides in Barcelona is one of the most famous texts of medieval Jewish history.[19]

Nonetheless, the disputations were above all a performance, not a debate, and their theatrical nature (like the resulting sermons) also made them inflexible.[20] Since their object was to use ancient texts to prove eternal truths, they could not, by definition, address local or specific circumstances. Their arguments were meant to be based on reason and be universally applicable. They were indeed universally applied; the same texts, interpretations, and polemics that fueled medieval disputations formed the basis of sixteenth- and seventeenth-century conversion rhetoric (and beyond). As a result, the Jews addressed in such literature were never the real Jewish communities of a specific time and place. Instead they were the "imaginary" Jews, the ancient theological antagonists of Christianity—a category broad, fluid, and universal enough to be able to absorb the broad, fluid, and universal arguments leveled against it. In this way, the genre that developed from disputations to address Jews directly could still only use the most abstract terms. And in this way, disputations became a genre designed not only by but also for Christian audiences.

Other medieval preaching traditions allowed more vibrant, specific discussions of Jews to flourish, but possibly for the worse. The mendicant preaching revival of the later Middle Ages, led by Observant Franciscans,

17. For the best summaries of these developments, see Simonsohn, *The Apostolic See and the Jews*, 288–342; Parente, "Il confronto ideologico tra l'ebraismo e la Chiesa in Italia"; Parente, "La Chiesa e il 'Talmud.'"

18. Quoted in Jonathan M. Elukin, *Living Together, Living Apart: Rethinking Jewish-Christian Relations in the Middle Ages*, 67.

19. David Berger, "Mission to the Jews and Jewish-Christian Contacts in the Polemical Literature of the High Middle Ages"; Robert Chazan, *Barcelona and Beyond: The Disputation of 1263 and Its Aftermath.*

20. Tartakoff, *Between Christian and Jew*, 88–91; Vose, *Dominicans, Muslims and Jews in the Medieval Crown of Aragon*, 127–28, 135.

offered a different model for the public discussion of Jews. The preaching of these friars may have owed a small debt to the Barcelona disputations and the preaching of Christiani.[21] But their preaching style, content, and social context were entirely different. In an age of financial crisis, plague, and upheaval, mendicant friars preached in a way that turned Jewish people into pointed targets of social unrest, especially in fifteenth-century Italy.[22] Celebrated preachers, particularly Bernardino of Siena, Bernardino of Feltre, and Giovanni of Capistrano, engaged in the rabble-rousing excoriation of Jews. They framed their discussions in practical and social terms.[23] Bernardino of Siena explicitly forbade social interactions such as medical care, financial loans, or even borrowing utensils. Especially during the Passion cycle, Bernardino's preaching mixed together prohibitions, excoriation, and groundless antisemitic myths.[24]

These friars were often motivated by the perceived threat of Jewish violence (or proselytization) against Christians and their desire to eliminate usury. In many Italian cities, their sermons led directly to anti-Jewish violence and legislation in local communities, especially in cases where preachers revived ancient ritual murder accusations.[25] They encouraged the imposition of distinguishing signs, restrictions on freedom of movement and commerce, and in many places, expulsion.[26] Preachers also successfully promoted the foundation of Monti di Pietà, Christian lending societies deliberately aimed at uprooting Jewish bankers. For good or ill (usually ill), these mendicants treated Jewish people not as an imagined theological example but instead as a real physical presence, living in cities

21. Harvey J. Hames, *The Art of Conversion: Christianity and Kabbalah in the Thirteenth Century*, 113–14.

22. Chazan, *Fashioning Jewish Identity*, 7–10, argues for a specific sense of threat in late medieval Italy.

23. Nirit Ben-Aryeh Debby, "Jews and Judaism in the Rhetoric of Popular Preachers: The Florentine Sermons of Giovanni Dominici (1356–1419) and Bernardino da Siena (1380–1444)."

24. Franco Mormando, *The Preacher's Demons: Bernardino of Siena and the Social Underworld of Early Renaissance Italy*, 164–218.

25. R. Po-Chia Hsia, *The Myth of Ritual Murder: Jews and Magic in Reformation Germany*. For Italy, see, most recently, Jussi Hanska, "Mendicant Preachers as Disseminators of Anti-Jewish Literary Topoi: The Case of Luca Da Bitonto."

26. For an introduction to this well-studied subject, see Roberto Rusconi, "Predicatori ed ebrei nell'arte italiana del rinascimento"; Debby, "Jews and Judaism in the Rhetoric of Popular Preachers," passim; Diane Owen Hughes, "Distinguishing Signs: Ear-Rings, Jews and Franciscan Rhetoric in the Italian Renaissance City." For a brief discussion of how this pattern could vary across Italy, see Stefanie Siegmund, *The Medici State and the Ghetto of Florence: The Construction of an Early Modern Jewish Community*, 94–95.

alongside the Christian audiences for these sermons.[27] Their sermons set a precedent for how to preach about Jews in front of Christians—a model for the early modern conversionary sermon that drew a Christian audience as part of its mission.

The medieval mendicant model owed much of its styling to the sermons of Ferrer, a Spanish Dominican preacher of the late fourteenth and early fifteenth centuries who also remained a model for conversionary preachers into the early modern period. Ferrer spent much of his life traveling across Spain to preach to Jews and supposedly converted them in enormous numbers.[28] He directly inspired later Roman preachers of the seventeenth and eighteenth centuries. Gregorio Boncompagni Corcos dedicated one volume of his sermons to "Saint Vincent Ferrer who converted twenty-nine thousand Jews" and lamented his own inadequacy in comparison.[29] And in 1735, the conversionary preacher Antonio Teoli produced a glowing, magisterial biography of Ferrer, eight hundred pages long, complete with a large and detailed foldout engraving of the saint surrounded by clusters of cherubs. According to Teoli, Ferrer had calmed an anti-Jewish riot with his authoritative and prudent preaching, and had engineered the conversion of thirteen thousand Valencian Jews in one day. According to Teoli's account, Ferrer would set aside spaces for Jews at each sermon, with a military guard to protect them. He held private discourses with rabbis, who conceded his superior knowledge of Talmud. Whole families or synagogues regularly converted during his sermons, so that the total number of Jewish souls conquered reached over two hundred thousand.[30]

Some of Rome's most driven agents of conversion found another compelling model in the Dominican friar Girolamo Savonarola, the famed apocalyptic preacher of Florence in the 1490s. During his brief but potent interval as spiritual leader of Florence, Savonarola sought the expulsion or conversion of Jews, especially by encouraging the foundation of Florence's

27. Mormando, *The Preacher's Demons*, 164–69, analyses distinctions in Bernardino of Siena's sermons between ancient and contemporary Jews, and argues that Jews were not a special target for Bernardino, although his sermons caused demonstrable harm.

28. Vose, *Dominicans, Muslims and Jews in the Medieval Crown of Aragon*; Laura Ackerman Smoller, *The Saint and the Chopped-Up Baby: The Cult of Vincent Ferrer in Medieval and Early Modern Europe*; Philip Daileader, *Saint Vincent Ferrer, His World and Life: Religion and Society in Late Medieval Europe*.

29. BAV Borg. lat. 114, 1r. For more on this dedication, see p. 232.

30. Antonio Teoli, *Storia della vita e del culto di S Vincenzo Ferrerio, dell'ordine de' Predicatori. Composta dal P Lettore Fr Antonino Teoli della congregazione di S sabina del medesimo Ordine, e Predicatore agli Ebrei di Roma*, 47–49, 397–404.

Monte di Pietà.[31] This was an explicitly anti-Jewish move, and part of his vision of Florence as a pure and holy New Jerusalem purged of infidels. To support the Monte di Pietà, Savonarola organized a grand Palm Sunday procession in 1496, starring the city's children, all dressed in white. The event collected sufficient funds to launch the bank. Savonarola's sermon on that Palm Sunday cast Florence as a biblical city, the fulfillment of a prophecy by the biblical prophet Zacharias; his closing words urged Florentines to accept Christ as their especial king.[32] Savonarola inspired an enduring movement of followers—the *piagnoni*—and his influence and religious zeal reached across much of Italy, lasting for generations. Savonarola's legacy particularly shaped the spiritual formation of Philip Neri, born and raised in Florence, and thus influenced Neri's impact on Rome, from the musical and liturgical styles of the Oratorian Chiesa Nuova to the preoccupation with Jewish conversion.[33] Ferrer, Savonarola, and the generations of mendicant preachers around them left lasting traces in their societies, not least the notion that true Christian devotion was incompatible with having Jewish neighbors.

Disputations (and the sermons they engendered) were more theological and strictly exegetical, while mendicant sermons about Jews could be more dramatic and threateningly precise. Both of these medieval traditions—disputations and mendicant preaching—contained elements that closely shaped the contours of early modern conversionary sermons, despite their apparently contradictory rhetorical modes. Yet other determining factors arose in the early modern period: the rise of Christian Hebraism, developments in Italian preaching, and the legislation of papal bulls.

The rise of Christian Hebraism in the fifteenth and sixteenth centuries, especially in Italy, added a new layer to old rhetorical patterns. As Christians learned Hebrew mystical traditions, they began to use Kabbalah to reinforce the notion that an earlier, truer Jewish wisdom had been corrupted by the willfulness and deceit of later rabbis. Kabbalistic strains of

31. On this episode, see Siegmund, *The Medici State and the Ghetto of Florence*, 51, 94–95; Barbara Wisch, "Vested Interest: Redressing Jews on Michelangelo's Sistine Ceiling," 151–52; F. R. Salter, "The Jews in Fifteenth-Century Florence and Savonarola's Establishment of a Mons Pietatis."

32. For a translation of the sermon and many rich descriptions of the event by contemporaries, see Girolamo Savonarola, *Selected Writings of Girolamo Savonarola: Religion and Politics, 1490–1498*, 222–43.

33. On Savonarola's influence, see Louis Ponnelle, Louis Bordet, and Ralph Francis Kerr, *St. Philip Neri and the Roman Society of His Times (1515–1595)*, 55. On musical transmission from Savonarola to Neri, see Anne Piéjus, "Il savonarolismo di san Filippo Neri attraverso poesie e canti"; Patrick Macey, "The Lauda and the Cult of Savonarola," 479.

Christian Hebraism found solid ground in Italy, with a well-known community of Christian Kabbalists in the later fifteenth century—notably Egidio da Viterbo and Giovanni Pico della Mirandola.[34] These interests fueled much of the Hebrew scholarly activity that animated congregations and libraries across early modern Rome, including the printed treatises of the preacher Giuseppe Ciantes and the surviving correspondence of the Hebraist Giovanni Pastrizio.[35] As Magda Teter has argued, the strength of Christian Hebraism in Italy is one part of a specifically Italian model of literature related to Judaism. Unlike the sociological or ethnographic literature that characterized writing about Jews elsewhere in Europe, the Italian approach focused on theology rather than practice, direct knowledge of Jewish people from social mixing, and awareness of the history of Jewish-Christian relations. The result was better knowledge of Jews and Judaism, and greater skepticism of the worst accusations against them. From the sixteenth century onward, accusations of blood libels in Italy, though they did recur, resulted in acquittals or the dismissal of charges.[36]

Preachers to Jews were also indebted to Italian sermon literature in general—a broad genre that itself evolved enormously in the Reformation era and afterward. Italian preaching to Christians usually tended toward either feats of rhetorical acrobatics or straightforward exegetical homilies that stayed close to scripture. But both styles allowed current events to find their way in. The celebrated preacher Franceschino Visdomini, for instance, gave a sermon on the death of Mary I of England, and another on the opening of the third session of the Council of Trent, both republished as examples of notable preaching.[37] Big news such as an important death or a military victory often merited its own sermon; so did religious campaigns, such as the one to establish Rome's Monte di Pietà in 1539. Visdomini preached a few conversionary sermons to Jews too, according to the records of Andrea De Monte.[38] In theory, therefore, the famous

34. For Christian Hebraism in general, see Allison P. Coudert and Jeffrey S. Shoulson, *Hebraica Veritas? Christian Hebraists and the Study of Judaism in Early Modern Europe*; Joanna Weinberg, "A Sixteenth-Century Hebraic Approach to the New Testament," 231–50; Stephen G. Burnett, *Philosemitism and Christian Hebraism in the Reformation Era (1500–1620)*; Stephen G. Burnett, *Christian Hebraism in the Reformation Era (1500–1660): Authors, Books, and the Transmission of Jewish Learning.*

35. Irene Fosi, "Usare la biblioteca: la Vaticana nella cultura europea."

36. Magda Teter, *Blood Libel: On the Trail of an Antisemitic Myth*, 182–91.

37. Republished in Thomaso Porcacchi, *Delle Prediche di Diversi Illustri Theologi, et Catholici predicatori della Parola di Dio*. For Visdomini's sermon on Mary I, see Emily Michelson, "An Italian Explains the English Reformation (with God's Help)."

38. Piet van Boxel, *Jewish Books in Christian Hands: Theology, Exegesis and Conversion under Gregory XIII (1572–1585)*, 23–24. These are noted in BAV Neofiti 35.

sermons of famous local preachers might have encouraged preachers to Jews, in a new era of proselytizing fervor, to tackle the modern world from the pulpit.

But papal bulls added ever more specific constraints to conversionary sermon content. The 1415 bull *Etsi Doctoris* had given early instructions for conversionary preaching in light of the Tortosa disputations. Amid a host of other legislation regarding Jews, the bull ordered the Jews of Spain to attend Ferrer-style conversionary sermons three times a year. These sermons should, first, explain that the Messiah had already come; second, elaborate the errors and heresies contained in the Talmud; and third, remind the Jews of their perpetual servitude and captivity.[39] At the establishment of Roman conversionary sermons, the bull *Sancta Mater Ecclesia* laid out a longer list of topics. Sermons to Jews should emphasize the advent and incarnation of Christ: his birth, life, miracles, passion, death, burial, descent into hell, resurrection, ascension, and the later confirmation of his gospel through the miracles and preaching of saints and apostles. They should point out the desolation and dispersion of the Jews, the frustration of their vain hopes, and the duplicity of their rabbis in promoting false interpretations of scripture. These were highbrow arguments intended for eternity; they did not descend to the current-day enticements of, for example, tax breaks after baptism or the relative luxuries on offer in the House of Catechumens.

Discussions of deceitful rabbis generally implicated the Talmud; the direction of early modern conversionary sermons owed a great deal to the keen Christian interest in reading rabbinic literature and other Hebrew books. In particular, a high-level committee of two converts from Judaism and five cradle Catholics developed a careful strategy to convert the Jews. They sought to collect convincing, erudite evidence of correct Christian readings of scriptural passages that Jews had misinterpreted, and compiled their findings into a manual for conversionary preachers. This manual contained primarily extracts from major Jewish biblical commentaries as well as Jewish theological works on topics relevant to sermons and other material. The close involvement of Robert Bellarmine and Cardinal Giulio Antonio Santoro in the compilation, alongside a flock of Hebraists, theologians, and editors, demonstrates the importance of this work at the highest levels of the church, as Piet van Boxel has argued.[40] The

---

39. Simonsohn, *The Apostolic See and the Jews*, 321–22; Daileader, *Saint Vincent Ferrer, His World and Life*, 119–20.

40. Piet van Boxel, "Hebrew Books and Censorship in Sixteenth-Century Italy."

high status and scholarly dedication of the committee members further accentuate the attention and significance given to regulating conversionary sermons.

Such powerful precedents and long lists of instructions limited the stylistic range for preachers, who largely kept within the narrowest boundaries developed for them over centuries. The models they had to follow set strict set limits on their own flexibility as composers of sermons to Jews. Individual preachers might vary in their relative focus on exegesis, doctrine, or refutation, but the weight of tradition and legislation left them little room for further creativity or evolution. The history of medieval Jewish-Christian polemic had established that the goal of a conversionary sermon was to prove the superiority of Christian theology over Jewish theology in the physical presence of both groups. In the end, this was not quite the same as giving Jews convincing reasons to become Christian.

Rhetoric, 1550–1650

Conversionary preaching in early modern Rome represents a substantially new preaching ritual, but one in which sermon texts had little room to develop, as we have seen. Indeed, their formula for success lay precisely in having a formula. The early case of Ludovico Carretto shows just how fixed some of the tropes of conversionary preaching already were by the early modern era, even before legislation in the 1570s made them a regular weekly event. Carretto, brother of the Jewish chronicler Joseph ha-Kohen, was a doctor who converted to Christianity late in life after a dispute with his family. His account of this event survives in the unusual form of a trio of letters from Ludovico, published in 1556: one to the wife who refused to follow him; another to his still-Jewish children and the community he left; and the third to his infant son, Giulio Innocentio, raised a Catholic.[41]

Crowning these efforts is a fourth text: a sermon delivered in Rome by Giulio Innocentio himself. This sermon is so deeply implausible that any attempted credibility is beyond the point. The boy's putative sermon

---

41. Ludovico Carretto, *Epistola de Ludovico Carretto ad Hebreos. Sermon di Giulio Innocentio suo figliolo alli Hebrei, et era quando lo fece de età de anni cinque in sei*. See Robert [Reuven] Bonfil, "Chi era Ludovico Carretto, apostata?," 51–58; Robert Bonfil, "An Infant's Missionary Sermon Addressed to the Jews of Rome in 1553." Bonfil has identified Carretto as Todros ha-Kohen, a doctor and brother of Joseph ha-Kohen, the noted Jewish chronicler who wrote *Emek HaBacha*. He has traced references to Carretto in Joseph ha-Kohen's letters. Carretto appears briefly in Giulio Bartolocci, *Bibliotheca Magna Rabbinica de scriptoribus, & scriptis Hebraicis, ordine alphabetico Hebraicè, & Latinè digestis*, 4:420, 4:564.

has five parts, full of Latin scriptural references. It promised that "if you pay attention today, from ignorant you will become wise, from blind, seeing, from deaf, hearing, from servitude, free."[42] Yet at the time of writing, Giulio Innocentio was no older than five or six. His father had left him in the care of the nascent casa while seeking work in Paris. Giulio Innocentio's sermon is entirely unoriginal, derived from medieval disputations—an impersonal work of showmanship. The point of the sermon is not that it might actually represent the original work of a small child but rather that it amplified already-standard formulaic performances of conversion. It draws strength from the related trope of the genius boy preacher, although typically even the brightest young boys only repeated sermons and did not compose them. Above all, Giulio Innocentio's sermon served to anchor Carretto's conversion, frame it as a success despite the intransigent relatives, and remind readers of a conversion's inherent potential.[43]

Like many conversion narratives, Carretto's individual and intimate story was repackaged for a broader audience, and it found one. The pamphlet appeared twice in Paris in a Latin translation from Hebrew, and then once in Italian in the 1550s.[44] The Latin version—as a long discourse with the letter to Giulio Innocentio appended—survived in print into the seventeenth century, appended to the 1614 Latin edition of Johannes Buxtorf's influential *Jüden-Schül, Synagoga Iudaica*.[45] In the Italian version, Carretto's pamphlet sets up a contrast between sermons and other conversionary tools, such as personal narratives. His letters recount the dream that prompted his conversion and life since then; like many conversion narratives, it relies on tropes, but the details are personal to him.[46] But throughout, Giulio Innocentio's sermon continues to bear a disproportionate weight. It is the longest item in the collection and is emphasized in

42. Carretto, *Epistola de Ludovico Carretto ad Hebreos*. The text is also transcribed in Bonfil, "An Infant's Missionary Sermon Addressed to the Jews of Rome in 1553," 161–71.

43. For a corroborating interpretation of the power of newly baptized young children, see Tamar Herzig, *A Convert's Tale: Art, Crime, and Jewish Apostasy in Renaissance Italy*, 95.

44. For the Latin translation, see Weinberg, "A Sixteenth-Century Hebraic Approach to the New Testament," 240–41. Carretto's conversion was noted at the time in one or two English sources.

45. Johannes Buxtorf, *Synagoga Iudaica hoc est, Schola Iudaeorum in qua nativitas, institutio, religio, vita, mors, sepulturaq[ue]; ipsorum è libris eorundem a M. Johanne Buxdorfio . . . graphice descripta est*. For Buxtorf, see Stephen G. Burnett, *From Christian Hebraism to Jewish Studies: Johannes Buxtorf (1564-1629) and Hebrew Learning in the Seventeenth Century*.

46. Peter A. Mazur and Abigail Shinn, "Introduction: Conversion Narratives in the Early Modern World."

its overall title. The boy's implausible youth, below the age of reason, is invoked repeatedly to reinforce the cachet of his supposed words. Conversionary sermons would not be formally established in Rome for another two decades, but already they were treated as prestigious and triumphant.

The Carretto incident produced the first printed conversionary sermon in Rome. Giulio Innocentio's sermon aptly foretold both the impersonal abstractions of the conversionary sermon genre and the prestige accorded to it. In Rome, the conversionary sermon would maintain that stature for centuries. But in most other ways, the genre moved swiftly away from Carretto's presentation, with its personal letters, strong emotions, and family stories. Later conversion accounts like Carretto's, for instance, did not continue to be published in or with conversionary sermons. Instead, they appeared typically in abjurations, baptism speeches, or polemical treatises.[47] Nor did subsequent conversionary sermons include personal letters, as Carretto's package did. Typically, the only letters found in published sermons were dedications and notes to readers. Even preachers who were themselves converts tended to avoid intimate narratives in their sermons. Instead, sermons generally stuck to theological proofs, stayed separate from other tools of persuasion, and left personal stories to other genres.

For balancing different ways of addressing a Jewish audience and showing how different rhetorical conventions could converge in the conversionary pulpit, we should turn to the lone volume of published conversionary sermons left by Evangelista Marcellino. His *Fifteen Sermons* was the most complete example of such preaching ever printed.[48] As an Observant Franciscan and lifetime preacher, Marcellino would have been trained in the preaching traditions of his order. He used those traditions in his main pulpit at the Franciscan mother church of Santa Maria in Aracoeli and the prominent churches around Italy where he also preached. Marcellino was the only conversionary preacher who held simultaneous long-term positions preaching separately to Jews and Christians in different contexts. He therefore had many occasions to draw on highly developed Franciscan rhetoric, both the precedents of his Franciscan forebears and his contemporaries in Rome. Indeed, the star preacher of the late sixteenth century, the Conventual Franciscan Francesco Panigarola, held

---

47. Irene Fosi, "Percorsi di salvezza. Preparare le strade, accogliere, convertire nella Roma barocca"; Stephen D. Bowd, "The Conversion of Margarita: A Wedding Oration in Fifteenth-Century Brescia."

48. Evangelista Marcellino, *Sermoni quindici sopra il salmo centonove fatti a gli Hebrei di Roma.*

a residency in Aracoeli in the early 1580s during Marcellino's period of conversionary preaching.[49]

Marcellino devoted all fifteen sermons to commenting on one psalm even though the psalm itself only contains seven verses. In Psalm 109/110, "Dixit Dominus Domino meo sede a dextris meis / The Lord said unto my Lord, Sit thou at my right hand, until I make thine enemies thy footstool," God promises victory to his chosen people and crushing defeat to their enemies. Marcellino offers his audience a new way to read the psalm: "There is no doubt that the Chaldean translation you follow gives a totally different sense from what we believe, which is the truth."[50] His sermons combine exhortations to convert with criticisms for stubbornness, adherence to ritual observance, and willful blindness to the truth. They cover some of the prescribed topics for conversionary sermons, such as the nativity and sacrifice of Christ, the significance of the Trinity, the virginity of Mary, and the necessary misery of Jews. But Marcellino always approaches these theological questions through the dispassionate lens of Hebrew grammar.[51] One sermon, for example, takes as its main subject the flexibility of Hebrew vowels and the multiple interpretations that can therefore result; another takes issue with the verb voices in the Hebrew in order to promote a Christian interpretation of the verse over a rabbinic one. Throughout, Marcellino argues for the superiority of Christian translations and interpretations over Jewish textual traditions, exploiting the weaknesses of Hebrew grammar and the ambiguities of translation.

Marcellino's *Fifteen Sermons* set a precedent for speaking directly to Christians while treating physically present Jews as an abstract category. His expertise in close grammatical readings of Jewish sources serves the broader contention that the psalm, like all Jewish texts, actually demonstrates Christian dogma. His arguments reflect years of study, and they would have been confusing to the less learned of his Jewish listeners. Marcellino refers to Jews primarily in general terms. He might address his listeners directly, if vaguely, as "O Giudei" or even "carissimi Hebrei," but his sermons do not mention the particular circumstances of Roman Jews as cohabitants of the same city as himself, nor the constellation of

49. On the rivalry between Marcellino and Panigarola, see Emily Michelson, "Dramatics in (and out of) the Pulpit in Post-Tridentine Italy."

50. "Non è dubbio . . . che la translatione Caldaica che voi seguitate fa un senso totalmente diverso da quello che noi crediamo; & che è la verità." Marcellino, *Sermoni quindici*, 13.

51. For common themes in medieval polemic, see Jeremy Cohen, *The Friars and the Jews: The Evolution of Medieval Anti-Judaism*. For their iteration in Marcellino's preaching, see Michelson, "Evangelista Marcellino: One Preacher, Two Audiences."

conversionary efforts aimed at them. Even though he often evokes "the modern rabbis," the Jews he describes are transhistorical, their sins eternal and their character unchanging, forever subject to the labels used by scriptural prophets: "O Jews, for how long will you display that mendacious style, for which God reprimands you so often through Jeremiah, chapter 8? For how long will you be so heavyhearted that nothing delights you except vanity and lies, as David says in Psalm 4?"[52]

These sermons offered a winning formula for making preaching seem intellectual and prestigious. They combined deep theological knowledge with expert mastery of the Hebrew language, offering the fantasy that Jews would convert for nothing less. As we have seen, surviving accounts of Marcellino's preaching by would-be hagiographers portrayed him as a huge success—both beloved and effective among Jews.[53] Certainly, compared to other preachers, Marcellino's rhetoric was consistently honest and straightforward, but also relatively cerebral, theological, and mild on the rant scale. But standards were low for defining "loving words." As frequently as Marcellino opened his sermons with the words "dearest Jews," we cannot know how such endearments sounded alongside his many criticisms: "We can consider how you are more stubborn than your ancestors were. . . . Leave off such stubbornness, you miserable ones"; "How long will you be so heavyhearted that you waste your time on nothing but vanity and lies?"; and "Don't you concede that Moses calls you idiotic, a people without counsel or prudence, because you neither know, nor understand, nor see?" Such insults drew in part on the rhetorical tradition of Marcellino's Observant forebears. Bernardino of Siena, later sanctified, was renowned for ribbing his listeners. Perhaps to Catholic ears, these comments could seem affectionate and teasing, hating the sin more than the sinner. Yet to an audience that had lived through Talmud burning and ghettoization, they might have sounded less well-meaning.

Thus Marcellino's strengths in textual analysis sit somewhat awkwardly with their intended purpose of gentle persuasion. As instruments of conversion, the sermons seem at best blunt and only partially effectual in leading to actual conversions. Unrelenting rebukes and insults are rarely effective in this regard; indeed, De Monte was removed from the pulpit precisely because his harsh scorn for the Jews worked at cross-purposes.[54]

52. Marcellino, *Sermoni quindici*, 22.

53. Iacopo Peri, *Breve Discorso della via del P.F. Vangelista Marcellino da Pistoia . . . Raccolto da Fra Iacopo Peri.*

54. Renata Martano, "La missione inutile: la predicazione obbligatoria agli ebrei nella seconda metà del cinquecento," 108–9.

But more broadly, none of the practical advantages of conversion appear in them; one might have expected tempting descriptions of the Christian life or even afterlife, but Marcellino offers only the vinegar and never the honey. In these sermons, converts are to be convinced only by accepting the hermeneutical superiority of Christian over Jewish interpretations of text

Marcellino and De Monte, colleagues in the pulpit in the late 1570s, were neither identical nor quite opposites in their styles. Where Marcellino could draw on a lifetime of Franciscan tropes, De Monte, who was born in Fez and converted in Rome in the 1550s, was far less deeply rooted in monastic traditions and mendicant rhetoric. As with many converts, his animosity was more personal than historical or theological.[55] De Monte's surviving works show that he went further than Marcellino in berating Jews, making scorn for his former brethren his focus. Whereas Marcellino's sermons hew closely to exegetical arguments, seeking to prove Catholic doctrine through close readings and grammatical analysis, the works of converts introduced new tones as well as new argumentation. De Monte's major treatise, the *Confusion of the Jews and Their False Opinions*, famously contains a level of animosity toward Jewish people that exceeds Marcellino's. He routinely called his readers "petty Jews" and describes their depravity: "the God of the Jews today, who mourns so and is despondent because of their evilness"; "all in all, they [the Jews] were idolatrous, lustful, and homicidal."[56] As we know, De Monte's contempt for his former brethren cost him the position, while Marcellino's preaching later helped his candidacy for sainthood.

De Monte's *Confusion of the Jews* was never published, but a large fair copy ready for publication is now housed in the Vatican library.[57] Like many subsequent conversionary treatises, it set out to prove the truth of various Christian doctrines, and also the falseness of Jewish ritual and doctrine. De Monte's thirty-three chapters—a number presumably chosen to reflect the years of Christ's life—begin with an overview of biblical Jewish history, offer various arguments for the inevitability of Christianity, and then review specific Jewish beliefs or rituals with an eye to discrediting them. Roughly half the chapters examine the nature of the Messiah and his divinity. The treatise sets out to prove using Talmudic

---

55. Barbara Leber, "Jewish Convert in Counter-Reformation Rome: Giovanni Paolo Eustachio," 187–89, notes the wide variation in levels of hostility that converts, including the three discussed here, displayed toward Jews.

56. Andrea De Monte, *Confusione de giudei, e delle lor false opinioni, in* BAV Vat. lat. 14627 (formerly Neofiti 38), fol. 49r, fol. 54r.

57. BAV Vat. lat. 14627 (formerly Neofiti 38).

practices that the Messiah has already come, and reviews Christian beliefs that the Messiah's incarnation, birth from a virgin, suffering, resurrection, and salvific powers were all both necessary and predicted. De Monte draws parallels between Old and New Testament texts, and relies on (or refutes) Midrashic and other rabbinic texts. Despite his book's physical and intellectual weight, he suggests, implausibly, that it is explicitly meant to educate a wide range of audiences: Christians, catechumens, Jews, and even preachers, "who are not learned in Jewish matters, but will be fully informed by this work, and then there will be great confusion and ignominy among the stubborn Jews." As with his other treatise, *On the Truth of the Coming of the Messiah to the Jews (Letter of Peace)*, De Monte hoped for a wide Jewish readership. De Monte had sent copies of his *Letter of Peace* to various synagogues, and boasted that the *Confusion*, too, could be read publicly even "in the workshops of any artisan."[58]

All the subsequent authors who left lone sermons or single-sermon volumes to Jews followed similar patterns. Like their predecessors, they generally did not address the practical benefits of conversion nor seek to adapt their arguments to the circumstances of early modern Roman Jews. Instead, they examined texts on the virginity of Mary, the nature of the Messiah, and supersession. In all cases, they blamed ancient rabbis for misinterpretation of scripture. The books showed off their authors' scholarly skills and theological arguments—virtuoso variations on an unvarying theme.[59] It was precisely their ability to conform to expectations that made them successful. Yet meeting those expectations made it impossible for them to treat the listening Jews in anything but an abstract, imaginary way.

The authors of such sermons and treatises emphasized their worthiness as converters with thorough mastery of the relevant theological arguments. Again, their main purpose was to demonstrate coverage of pre-established points of doctrine rather than to offer innovative reasons to convert. Fabiano Fioghi, like De Monte, asserted at length that the life of Jesus proved his messianic status, and added many detailed chapters

58. Andrea De Monte, *Della verità della venuta del Messia alli Hebrei (Lettera di Pace)*, in BAV Neofiti 37. Both quotations at BAV Vat. lat. 14627 (formerly Neofiti 38), fol. 4. For copies of the *Letter of Peace* sent to synagogues, see Bartolocci, *Bibliotheca Magna Rabbinica*, 3:819a; Parente's entry on De Monte in the DBI. On these manuscripts, see Gustavo Sacerdote, *I codici ebraici della Pia Casa dei Neofiti in Roma*, 27–29, notes.

59. Biancuzzi, *Lettione fatta alli Hebrei di Roma, nell'Oratorio della Santissima Trinità de' Pellegrini, & Convalescenti, li 8 di ottobre 1605*; Faustino Tasso, *Venti Ragionamenti familiari sopra la venuta del Messia, Del R.P. Faustino Tasso, Minore Osservante. Fatte in Napoli ad alcuni Hebrei per comandamento de gl'Ill.mi e R.mi Viceré, e Arcivescovo.*

refuting supposed Jewish doubts one by one. Fioghi added further detailed refutations of specific Jewish rituals, notably regarding diet and animal slaughter, marital relations, circumcision, and festivals. Giovanni Paolo Eustachio's well-regarded *Salutary Discourses,* published the same year, mostly summarized all the polemical treatises that preceded it, including that of Fioghi.[60] In most cases, the language of the treatises was erudite, reasonably polite, and formulaic, especially among authors such as Fioghi and Eustachio, who were converts, eager to promote their new faith and prove their own orthodoxy. Writing a conversionary treatise— sometimes with a personal narrative—became a standard practice among learned neophytes. And converts remained permanently under suspicion and could rarely risk a departure from the standard polemical arguments. These books promoted conversion by example and publicity as well as by conformity and erudition.

The popularity of conversionary themes gave them further purchase well outside specialized polemical literature. The most widely published sermon author of the period, the Spanish Dominican Luis de Granada, devoted the final pages of his magisterial *Simbolo della Fede* (Apostles' Creed) to a series of dialogues between a catechumen and his teacher. Translated from the Spanish, the fourth part of his treatise took up chapters related to Judaism. An heir to the mendicant tradition, Luis's language is more explicitly insulting. He includes discussions of the theological blindness and misery of contemporary Jews, and the trickery of Jewish rabbis in concealing Christian truth while vilifying the true church.[61] His theological chapters focus on the falsity of the Talmud and supersession of Jewish rituals. Luis de Granada was among the most published preachers in Europe. In its Italian translation, his *Simbolo della Fede* remained in print into the middle of the eighteenth century in over twenty separate editions. His titles were published in nine languages, in cities across Europe, from Scotland to Lithuania.[62] Granada's work serves as a reminder that conversionary themes sold well outside specialized literature, and shows how readers inevitably absorbed authors' views about Jews along with theological arguments.

The very traits that made these volumes successful—their recondite erudition, self-congratulatory tone, and anti-Jewish insults—equally made them unfit tools for an active, direct conversion campaign. An author's accusations of willful Jewish blindness, stubbornness, trickery, or slander

60. For the content of Eustachio's discourses as standard in content and nonvilifying in tone, see Leber, "Jewish Convert in Counter-Reformation Rome," 145–93.

61. Luis de Granata, *Il Simbolo della Fede,* part 4, 129–36, 218–44.

62. See www.ustc.ac.uk.

would not easily make Jewish readers sympathetic to him or his church. His detailed criticisms of textual passages and theological discussions of supersession were unlikely to win over Jewish women or children, who were expected to be literate, but not educated to disputation level.[63] Yet the conversion of women, children, or families was highly prized. Women converted less often than men in both the sixteenth and seventeenth centuries, but were particularly desirable for the potential of baptizing their children. The conversion of entire families, such as the Corcos family, as we have seen, was a widely celebrated event.[64] Despite the boasting in printed sermons and polemics, these works were instruments of limited use in reaching some of the era's most valuable converts.

Preachers were aware of the gap between the language they were trained to use and the language that might successfully achieve a conversion by persuasion. De Monte himself was convinced that conversion was impossible; over a century later, another cleric complained, "No matter how much we have tried, the Jews still will not convert."[65] Marcellino recognized how hard it was to persuade through sermons alone; in his commentary on the book of Ruth, he asked, "O how strong is the cult of either the Holy, or the superstitious religion, which we take with our mother's milk, O how difficult it is for us to leave our native practices, with which we grow up, and why do we think it is so difficult to convert the Jews?"[66] Conversionary preachers sometimes conceived of their work as a sort of Sisyphean task, that they were increasingly compelled to repeat, but that even in the context of reinvigorated conversionary efforts, would never be completed.

These patterns continued well beyond Marcellino's era, as seen in the work of the two Dominican preachers who would hold the post for most of the next fifty years. The work of Giuseppe Ciantes and Pietro Pichi survives in the polemical anti-Jewish treatises each of them published.[67] As the

63. On the education of Jewish children, male and female, in Rome, see Kenneth R. Stow, *Theater of Acculturation: The Roman Ghetto in the 16th Century*, 79–80, 178–79.

64. On the benefits of studying the conversion of women specifically, see Tamar Herzig, "The Future of Studying Jewish Conversion in Renaissance Italy." On the Corcos conversion, see Alberto Bianco, "Cesare Baronio e la conversione dei Corcos nei documenti d'archivio della Congregazione oratoriana di Roma."

65. Martano, "La missione inutile," 109; Brian Pullan, "The Conversion of the Jews: The Style of Italy"; Kenneth R. Stow, *Catholic Thought and Papal Jewry Policy 1555–1593*, 201.

66. Evangelista Marcellino, *Lezzioni Diciannove sopra Rut. del RPF Vangelista Marcellino de' Minori Osservanti*, 29r–v.

67. Fiamma Satta, "Predicatori agli ebrei, catecumeni e neofiti a Roma nella prima metà del seicento"; Marina Caffiero, *Legami pericolosi: Ebrei e cristiani tra eresia, libri proibiti e stregoneria*, 291–93; Martine Boiteux, "Preaching to the Jews in Early Modern Rome: Words and Images," 311–12. Most helpful is Alberto Zucchi, "Rome domenicana:

first preachers to hold long tenures in the post, they remained influential long after they ceased preaching. Their publications show notable differences in their character and intellectual interests, but both highlight the opportunity to mix intellectual rigor with personal insult. Indeed, Pichi seemed to relish the combination, even though Gregory XIII had directly instructed preachers to be moderate and not malicious. When Pichi gleefully anticipated the resentment of Jewish readers, telling them he was sure they would dislike his work "more than a little," he was deliberately insulting both their character and theology, "and I am sure that you will complain about me for having published to the world your stupid doctrines, putting you in a bad light to Christians."[68]

Pichi's explicitly malicious tone is evident in his three surviving polemical works: A *Letter to the Jews*, *The Foolish Doctrines of the Jews and Their Refutation*, and *On the Passion and Death of the Messiah, against the Jews*.[69] The titles alone indicate a level of anti-Jewish animosity lacking in many other sermons, such as those of Marcellino, though reminiscent of De Monte's works.[70] His direct addresses to Jews bear this out. Pichi's *Letter to the Jews*, published on the occasion of Yom Kippur, the Jewish day of repentance, does not flatter:

> I have observed for the space of fifteen years, when (even up to now) I have been preaching to you continuously, that all of your observances and ceremonies in your laws are work of no worth; they are vain things thrown to the wind. . . . Be sure that while you persevere in this your obstinance, you will never be fulfilled, and your prayers, orations, fasts, and observances are tossed and lost, because God does not accept them, does not contemplate them, but hates and abhors them.[71]

These words are addressed deliberately to those Jewish people who had not heard him preach in person. "To make you know the vanity of

---

note storiche: Predicatori Domenicani degli Ebrei nel sec. XVIII," 118–20. For an introduction to these preachers, see also chapter 3.

68. Pietro Pichi, *Le stolte dottrine de gli Ebrei con la loro confutatione*, unpaginated, f. a5r–v.

69. Pietro Pichi, *Trattato della passione e morte del Messia contra gli ebrei;* Pietro Pichi, *Epistola a gli Ebrei d'Italia nella quale si dimostra la vanità della loro penitenza;* Pietro Pichi, *Le stolte dottrine de gli Ebrei con la loro confutatione. Opera del P. maestro F. Pietro Pichi da Trieui domenicano.*

70. For a comparison of Pichi and Ciantes, see Satta, "Predicatori"; Parente, "Il confronto ideologico tra l'ebraismo e la Chiesa in Italia."

71. Pichi, *Epistola a gli ebrei d'Italia nella quale si dimostra la vanità della loro penitenza*, unpaginated, Ar1–Ar3.

your repentance . . . , I wanted to write you this letter, particularly to those who are spread throughout Italy because you are rarely, or never, preached to."[72] Similarly, his letter to Jewish readers in his treatise on the Passion berates them for having listened to his sermons for so many years with so little fruit. A few have converted, he admits, but not enough. Pichi's disdain and contempt for his Jewish audience in these letters exceed the level established by Marcellino and others, and remain consistent across all of his surviving works. His insults might suggest a less abstract, more personal treatment of Jews, but certainly not with the aim of gently coaxing them toward baptism.

Pichi's editorial choices demonstrate how a preacher's individual voice and attitude could pierce through a long and rigid tradition. His works focus especially on proving Jewish error, rather than emphasizing Christian truths through Jewish texts or comparing Christian with Jewish exegesis.[73]

Pichi approached even conventional topics more vehemently than other authors. When he wrote about the Messiah, he dwelled on the violence of the Passion. This was a deliberate choice to stress the suffering of Christ along with the insults and castigation of the Jews, where other conversionary literature on the Messiah typically avoided the Passion altogether. Given the same topic, the convert-preacher Giulio Cesare Misuracchi limited his discussion of the Messiah to broad conceptual typologies and general exhortations to convert. Tommaso Bell'haver composed fifty-one chapters on the Messiah, but devoted only one of them to the Passion and suffering. Both of their works were published within a decade of Pichi's treatise. Pichi's treatment, in contrast, examines at length the scriptural proofs "that the Messiah must suffer punishment, flagellation, and death in order to redeem the world," to assert that Christ fulfilled these prophesies.[74] Pichi certainly knew how to employ milder arguments, and did so when discussing biblical prophecy and the divinity of the Messiah, but with the Passion he intentionally chose a more antagonistic approach than necessary.[75]

72. Pichi, *Epistola a gli ebrei d'Italia nella quale si dimostra la vanità della loro penitenza*, Ar2–Ar3.

73. Parente, "Il confronto ideologico tra l'ebraismo e la Chiesa in Italia," 329–30.

74. Pichi, *Trattato della passione e morte del Messia contra gli ebrei*, 7.

75. Giulio Cesare Misuracchi, *Ragionamento della venuta del Messia contro la durezza & ostinatione hebraica contro la durezza & ostinatione hebraica*; Tommaso Bell'haver, *Dottrina facile et breve per redurre l'Hebreo al conoscimento del vero Messia*. On Misuracchi's treatise, see Parente, "Il confronto ideologico tra l'ebraismo e la Chiesa in Italia," 331.

Pichi's *Foolish Doctrines* is more extreme than his other treatises, departing further from the papal bull that regulated his preaching. It emphasizes marginal (or wholly invented) beliefs in early modern Jewish thought, making them seem mainstream by elaborately refuting them. In one case, Pichi presents the notion of the transmigration of souls into animals as a common Jewish theory, borne from a misreading of key verses. Taking a verse from Psalm 13, "I will sing unto the Lord, because he hath dealt bountifully [*gamal*] with me," he makes a point of explaining that *gamal* must not be considered a reference to the psalmist's success in avoiding transformation into a camel [also *gamal* in Hebrew]. Instead, he insists on its more common meaning of redemption, in accordance with most rabbinic interpretations.[76] This point did not need making. It is true that the transmigration of souls, or metempsychosis, became a common folk belief in the later sixteenth and early seventeenth centuries, following the publication of a Hebrew work on the subject in 1552 and the growth in popularity of Lurianic Kabbalah.[77] Indeed, *Foolish Doctrines* coincided with the peak of the career of Chayim Vital, who would write a major work on reincarnation himself.[78] But none of this discussion was relevant to most of his listeners, who would have read the verse straightforwardly anyway.[79] He seems to have gone out of his way to contort and vilify Jewish belief. This tactic would have won him few converts among Rome's rabbinic elite—the missionary's prize. Instead, it foretold the seventeenth-century tactic of scrutinizing Jewish rituals over exegesis or even theology.[80]

Yet along with his invectives, Pichi published in a way that ensured that Christians were equally aware of his rhetoric. His dedication to Cardinal Francesco Sacrati, at the start of the *Letter to the Jews*, positioned his own labors alongside the cardinal's efforts to strengthen the faith. Scriptural annotations in Latin for a Christian readership accompanied the text of the letter itself. His *Treatise on the Passion*, as we have seen, contained a letter to Paul V and another to Christian readers, preceding the letter to Jewish readers. The letter to Christians points out the usefulness

76. Pietro Pichi, *Le Stolte Dottrine de gli Ebrei con la loro confutatione*, 64–67 (D7r–E2r).

77. Gershom Scholem, *Major Trends in Jewish Mysticism*, 281–84; Gershom Scholem, *Kabbalah*, 341–44.

78. *Sefer HaGilgulim*, written before Vital's death in 1620 and published circa 1684.

79. See, for example, the widely read medieval commentary of Avraham Ibn Ezra, who reads this verse as a call to place one's faith in divine mercy.

80. Satta, "Predicatori," 116–17; Boiteux, "Preaching to the Jews in Early Modern Rome," 311.

for Christians of understanding these mysteries; for their benefit, Pichi explains, he has provided Latin citations in the margins. And the *Foolish Doctrines*, alongside the usual prefaces, includes two odes in Italian praising Pichi's conversionary efforts. Pichi also dedicated the first edition of the *Foolish Doctrines* to the cardinal vicar of Rome, Giovanni Garsia Mellini, praising him for overseeing sermons to Jews: "He shows utmost vigilance in the conversion of the Jews through the ardent zeal that he has for their salvation, so that he ensures that the holy Christian faith is preached to them continuously."[81]

Pichi, more than Marcellino or any other conversionary preacher, remained an authority for later preachers, who read and cited him as they composed their own sermons. As we have seen, the priest Giovanni Domenico Nazzareno republished Pichi's *Foolish Doctrines* in 1640 as a tribute to Pichi's successor, Ciantes. Pichi's name also appears in an anonymous document (possibly authored by Gregorio Boncompagni), which appears to contain notes for a conversionary sermon; it explores in depth Pichi's explications of different sins attributed to Jews and refers to his "Italian treatise on the Passion." The eighteenth-century preacher and censor Antonio Teoli often cited Pichi in order to justify his own stances on Hebrew books, referring to him as "the celebrated preacher to the Jews, Master Pichi."[82] Boncompagni consulted Pichi's works regularly as he wrote his own sermons. His manuscripts frequently name Pichi in the margins, especially in his interpretations of Isaiah and discussions of the Messiah. Boncompagni clearly had access to both Pichi's actual sermons in manuscript and his later printed works. He notes whether he is reading a printed treatise, sheaf of papers, or sermon manuscript: "See Pichi on the Passion," "Pichi 114/163/263," and "Pichi, page 270." Boncompagni even distinguished between different sermons on the same topic: "Pichi sermon on the Beneficio of 1611 and 1616 at the start."[83] Pichi's arguments provided enough meat for another century of sermons to Jews. Whether or not later preachers mimicked his scathing tone, Pichi's works gave them licence to resort to it, or served as a benchmark for comparison.

Ciantes, although he left his conversionary post in 1640 to become bishop of Marsica, seems to have remained engaged with attempts to convert Jews throughout his life. As discussed in chapters 1 and 3, he oversaw at least two cases of coerced baptism of young children. And at least twice

---

81. Pichi, *Le Stolte Dottrine*, unpaginated.
82. ACDF St St BB 3 r, 96r.
83. BAV Borg. lat. 746, fols. 181r–v passim; ACDF St St BB 3 r, 52v–53r, 96r, 98r, 99v.

during his episcopacy, he returned to his former church of Santa Maria Sopra Minerva to preside over the baptism of Jewish people; we find his name in the baptismal records of the House of Catechumens.[84] In retirement, he returned to Rome and published two conversionary treatises as well as his Hebrew translation of Aquinas's *Summa Theologica.*

As we have come to expect, Ciantes's three published works are pitched to elite Christian readers. Ciantes dedicated his translation of Aquinas to Alexander VII and his two treatises to Giacinto Libelli, Master of the Sacred Palace. He placed his works in a Catholic conversionary context, arguing that it was Libelli's job to prepare and administer the "healthy food for the sick stomach" that Ciantes's words had first made palatable. And he suggested that the treatise would appeal most to somebody with Libelli's level of intelligence.[85] From these statements, it might seem that Ciantes sought his legacy less as a convert maker to Roman Jews than as a theorist among the Catholic intelligentsia.

Ciantes's scholarship offers elaborate examples of his specialist knowledge as a Christian scholar of Jewish mysticism. This was a well-developed field in Italy, after a century of enthusiastic Christian Hebraism and interest in Kabbalistic texts.[86] His two treatises combine rabbinical commentaries with readings of mystical Jewish texts, reinterpreted in favor of Christianity.[87] Ciantes's deep familiarity with Jewish mystical literature is evident from the range of his references. One treatise interprets the Kabbalistic concept of *sephirot*, or divine emanations, in a way compatible with Catholic ideas of incarnation. The other reiterates a theory of three lights that in a Christian reading, can be made to correspond with the Trinity.[88] Both treatises draw primarily from the *Pardes Rimmonim*

84. ASVR Casa dei Catecumeni 178, Liber Baptizatorum 1634–75, 35v, 41r.

85. Giuseppe Ciantes, *Della Santissima Trinità, evidentemente provata da i testimoni de gli antichi Ebrei,* unpaginated, 2r.

86. François Secret, *Les kabbalistes chrétiens de la Renaissance;* Leber, "Jewish Convert in Counter-Reformation Rome." Despite a long tradition of Christian Kabbalistic thought that appropriated but lay generally outside Jewish intellectual traditions, Ciantes focuses almost exclusively on Jewish mystical texts; he only cites Christian interpreters from the late sixteenth century onward. On Christian Kabbalah in general, see Joseph Dan, *The Christian Kabbalah: Jewish Mystical Books and Their Christian Interpreters: A Symposium;* Coudert and Shoulson, *Hebraica Veritas?* On Ciantes's thought, see Parente, "Il confronto ideologico tra l'ebraismo e la Chiesa in Italia," 346–49.

87. Yossef Schwartz, "Kabbalah and Conversion: Caramuel and Ciantes on Kabbalah as a Means for the Conversion of the Jews"; Satta, "Predicatori." The works in question are Ciantes, *Della Santissima Trinità; Giuseppe Ciantes, Della incarnazione del Verbo Divino. Evidentemente difesa dalle opposizioni degli Ebrei colle dottrine medesime de loro maggiori teologi.*

88. Satta, "Predicatori," 120, argues that Ciantes extrapolates this concept from Christian sources, particularly the Gospel of John, and reconciles it with Kabbalistic thought, rather than the reverse.

treatise of Rabbi Moshe Cordovero, a sixteenth-century Kabbalist, and on thirteenth-century works attributed to Rabbi Hai Gaon.[89] Ciantes's translation of Aquinas is intended as a further tool whereby Jews could rectify those mistakes in their doctrine that stem from misinterpretations of Kabbalah. All of these exercises seem designed to make Catholic doctrine more palatable to Jews, and Jewish doctrine less distant from Christianity.[90]

It is easy to conclude that such expertise would have impressed learned Christian Hebraists while presumably flying over the heads of many potential Jewish listeners or readers. Rome was not a hub of Jewish intellectual exchange to the same extent as Venice or Ferrara at the time. But Ciantes's pursuit of mystical topics shows how difficult and sometimes simplistic such a dichotomy can be. Ciantes may indeed have chosen his erudite arguments in a genuine, well-considered attempt to persuade them. He did write that he hoped "to convince the Jews (in whose spiritual service I occupied a great many years) of these doctrines, and to show them that they are as obligated as we are to believe in the Unity and Trinity of God."[91] I say this because his career coincided with a surge in both Jewish and Christian interest in Jewish mysticism, which converged in Italy, a critical center of Jewish thought after the expulsion from Spain. Ciantes's focus on the work of Cordovero closely echoed the interests of Italian Jewish Kabbalists, who made Cordovero's approach the "most authoritative brand of Kabbalah," at least briefly.[92] The mystical and messianic fervor of the Sabbatean movement that captured Italian (and worldwide) Jewry two decades later was already building.[93]

In that context, a profound Jewish interest in Ciantes's cerebral approach is entirely plausible. In choosing to engage with the most exciting recent developments in Jewish thought, then, Ciantes might well have

89. On Ciantes's specific sources for his ideas, see Raphael Ebgi, "Vincenzo Cicogna: A Forgotten Christian Kabbalist," 402–3. On the thirteenth-century Jewish origins of this concept, see Gershom Scholem, *Origins of the Kabbalah*, 349–54. On Jewish awareness of Christian trinitarian thought during the development of the core texts of the Kabbalah, see especially Yehuda Liebes, *Studies in the Zohar*, 139–45. On Ciantes's legacy for introducing the thought of Cordovero to Christian scholars, see Daniel Stolzenberg, "Egyptian Oedipus: Antiquarianism, Oriental Studies and Occult Philosophy in the Work of Athanasius Kircher," 205–10.

90. Schwartz, "Kabbalah and Conversion," 179–80, 189. Schwartz suggests that Ciantes fundamentally disdained Kabbalah as an inferior system of interpretation. On this translation, see D. J. Fitzgerald, "A Seventeenth Century Hebrew Translation of Saint Thomas," 71–78.

91. Ciantes, *Della Santissima Trinità*, unpaginated.

92. Moshe Idel, "Major Currents in Italian Kabbalah between 1560 and 1660," 349–50.

93. See, in general, Matt Goldish, "Mystical Messianism." Specifically, see Gershom Scholem, *Sabbatai Ṣevi: The Mystical Messiah, 1626–1676*.

addressed the priorities of at least some of his Jewish listeners directly and urgently. But the chasm between his erudite words and well-documented violent actions suggests otherwise. His ability to find points of intellectual harmony never translated to greater respect for Jewish people themselves. Nor did it allow him to consider his interlocutors as individuals living in a specific, shared time and context.

The works of Pichi and Ciantes joined a robust corpus of anti-Jewish polemics; the genre had continued strong into the seventeenth century. Many of the authors were cradle Catholics. By the time Melchior Palontrotti disrupted the funeral of Tranquillo Corcos, for example, he had already an extensive body of pamphlet literature against Jews. His prolific pen produced half a dozen commentaries on psalms arguing polemical points of doctrine, and a collection of treatieses. But where scholars once maintained that conversionary interest waned after the sixteenth century, and that the task of writing polemics shifted from converts to Christians, today's greater access to early modern sources and databases seems to disprove this hypothesis.[94] The convert Misuracchi's *Reasoning about the Coming of the Messiah, against Jewish Rigidity and Obstinacy, Done by Me in Their Presence* saw at least seven editions in the first half of the century.[95] Three other converts published works with Misuracchi's identical title in the same years.[96] Similar works appeared from the converts Antonio Caraffa, Torquato della Rosa, and Francesco Negri.[97]

94. Martano, "La missione inutile," extrapolates from the demise of the convert-preacher to the demise of the convert-author in the seventeenth century. Leber, "Jewish Convert in Counter-Reformation Rome," 110–11, describes the waning of enthusiasm for conversionary matters after the sixteenth century.

95. Misuracchi, *Ragionamento della venuta del Messia contro la durezza & ostinatione hebraica contro la durezza & ostinatione hebraica*. Other editions included publication in Genoa, 1624; Siena, 1624; Modena, 1626; Modena and Milan, 1627; Milan c. 1642.

96. *Francesco Negri, Ragionamento della venuta del messia. Contra la durezza, & ostinatione hebraica. Fatto alla presenza loro da me Francesco Negri ebreo fatto christiano, & rabino di Sacra Scrittura*; Alessanro Orsino, *Ragionamento della venuta del messia, contra la durezza, & ostinatione hebraica. Fatto alla presenza loro da me Alessandro Orsino ebreo fatto christiano & rabino di Sacra Scrittura*; Giacomo Natta, *Ragionamento della venuta del messia, contra la durezza, & ostinatione hebraica fatto alla presenza loro, da me Giacomo Natta hebreo fatto christiano, & rabino di Sacra Scrittura*.

97. Antonio Caraffa, *Trionfo della santa croce, sermone spirituale, sopra l'annuntiatione della beatissima Vergine. Data in luce per Antonio Caraffa romano, già rabino hebreo fatto christiano*; Torquato della Rosa, *Salutario discorso, contra l'hostinatione de gl'Hebrei, nel qual si tratta, e ragiona sopra tre articoli. . . . Composto da me Torquato della Rosa, già rabbino hebreo, & hora per gratia di Dio, fatto christiano*; Francesco Negri, *Breue, & vtilissimo discorso contra la perfida ostinatione delli Hebrei . . . Fatica di Francesco Negri già rabino hebreo, & hora per gratia dello Spirito Santo christiano*.

Giulio Morosini's fifteen-hundred-page *The Path of Faith*, published in 1684, eclipsed them all, becoming the work of record for Catholic arguments against Judaism. Publishing a conversionary treatise seems to have remained a particular rite of passage into the seventeenth century for learned converts, with examples from Francesco Maria Ferretti, Giovanni Antonio Costanzi, and Francesco Trevisani and his convert Francesca Trevisana.[98] These contain some variation—the seventeenth-century examples include more conversion stories, for instance, and Costanzi's includes a set of Jewish objections to conversion and then proceeds to respond to them. But they all proceed according to ever more well-established norms, proving their erudition and Catholic bona fides.

The first and second generations of conversionary preachers, then, redeveloped the themes they had inherited from medieval *adversus Judaeos* literature into new spoken and written genres for the early modern period. Notably, both converts and cradle Catholics participated in this effort, both as preachers and polemicists. Converts could often take a more personal as well as derisive tone; they provided a model for others to follow while also demonstrating a clean break from their past and irrefutable allegiance to their new faith. Cradle Catholics could show off the scholarly skills they had acquired, assume a loftier tone toward Jewish readers, and perhaps speak with greater authority to Christian ones. The range of arguments provided, however, remained largely faithful to the many strict limits that popes and precedents had imposed on conversionary rhetoric, and did not address the immediate experiences of Roman Jews. Sermon literature was invariably geared toward a Christian audience, who expected to hear their own faith both celebrated and reinforced at the highest intellectual levels.

Surprises, 1649–88

By the time that Boncompagni took up the post of preacher to the Jews in 1649, he might have imagined there was little left for him to do. Medieval *adversus Judaeos* arguments were well established and still widely read; indeed, the first printed edition of Martí's *Pugio Fidei* (Dagger of Faith), which would appear in 1651, was probably already in preparation when

---

98. Ferretti, *Le verità della fede cristiana*; Giovanni Antonio Costanzi, *La verità della cristiana religione contro le vane lusinghe di moderni ebrei*; Francesco Trevisani, *Conferenze pastorali istruttive sopra la verità della fede cristiana, fatte da Monsig. Francesco Trevisani con Sara figlia di Salvatore Conegliano Ebreo di Ceneda, ora Suor Francesca Maria Trevisana.*

Boncompagni started preaching two years earlier.[99] The compositions of Boncompagni's own predecessors in the pulpit—particularly Marcellino, Pichi, and Ciantes—were readily available in print, alongside many other works. And for much of his career, Boncompagni did conform to expectations. He produced sermons on the weekly Torah portion, frequently referring to it with the words "you heard this morning." His arguments echoed the reasoning laid out by previous polemicists. Many sermons maintained that "the Jews [today] are not now like those ancient ones that were the people of God, and that we Christians are more favored by God."[100] Others took up the perennial themes of the Trinity, the divinity of Jesus, and the Passion, or offered Christological readings of the Hebrew Bible. Yet others elaborated a hypothetical disputation with Jews and offered rebuttals to their supposed assertions. Some contended that Jewish rituals and practices had been superseded.[101] In thirty-nine years of weekly sermons, Boncompagni had ample time to elaborate on all the standard topics.

In a survey of conversionary preachers, Boncompagni stands out not simply for his longevity but also for his tone—a pulpit manner that seems consistently more measured, neutral, and doctrinal than Pichi's harangues or Ciantes's Kabbalistic departures in printed works. In his manuscripts, Boncompagni stays closer to the papal mandate for sermon content, and maintains a more textual and impersonal style of argument. A sermon on the suffering of the Messiah discusses Christ's necessary torment, but is structured by systematic refutations of rabbinic interpretations, without rebuking or insulting the audience extensively. "This is the doctrine your rabbis teach you when you come to sermons. . . . Now listen because I want to confound you with what this rabbi says, [elsewhere] in the same book."[102] His sermons usually follow the weekly Torah portion or cluster around traditional conversionary topics. Those that do discuss Jewish ritual are tied to the Hebrew calendar, and lean more toward observation and description without prurience: "In these days, O Jewish brethren, you are celebrating Sukkot in memory of the exodus from Egypt, which the Lord did for you with great favors and graces . . . in memory of which you make these booths as the law commands you."[103] Questions of tone mattered to him; he left notes for a sermon titled "Whether It Is Better to

---

99. Raymond Martin, *Pugio fidei Raymundi Martini ordinis Praedicatorum aduersus Mauros, et Iudaeos.*

100. BAV Borg. lat. 115, 332r.

101. For examples, see BAV Borg. lat. 505, 506, 555.

102. BAV Borg. lat. 506, 238r.

103. BAV Borg. lat. 505, 484v.

Preach to the Jews with Sweetness or Harshness."[104] These notes are brief and inconclusive; they recount how the biblical figures Pinchas [Phineas] and Elijah engaged in violence. But the vast majority of his sermons, at least compared to Pichi's direct insults in print, are pacific.

This evidence is only partial. We cannot directly equate Boncompagni's manuscript record of his sermons, delivered orally and written to meet regular weekly deadlines, with Pichi's and Ciantes's printed treatises, which they published separately from their time in the pulpit, the fruit of longer reflection. We already know from the case of Ciantes that a single conversionary preacher's attitude could vary dramatically by context; his pacific, Kabbalistic treatises did not reflect his zealous pulpit activity. What he and Pichi eventually published did not reflect the whole of their approach to Jewish conversion and cannot be equated with Boncompagni's extensive legacy. But by considering all of these works together, we see clearly how printed publications alone seldom tell a complete story. When we have the actual record of oral sermons, written down close to their moment of delivery, we are able to see evidence of flexibility that we might not otherwise guess at. That flexibility is tacitly interwoven with the stricter power of papal legislation and narrow templates of various polemical genres. We are reminded that when a preacher chose to print, the results might serve as a sample of or contrast to his weekly sermons, but not as a full representation of his thought. Indeed, the next chapter will show that the primary work Boncompagni himself intended to publish was more bombastic and more broadly pitched than his weekly sermons, where his approach remained cerebral and detached.

Yet for all Boncompagni's careful reserve, Rome's Jews still remained stubbornly unconverted, despite developing deep familiarity with the range of arguments presented to them. What exactly, Boncompagni seems to have thought, was the point? Why continue, if after a century, the weekly effort of writing sermons was still mostly ineffective? This overarching question plagued Boncompagni personally, and he tried to work out some answers through his sermon writing. The format, value, and persistence of conversionary preaching itself became a repeated subject of his sermons, and his reflections took on a broader life well outside the pulpit. The unfinished and undated sermon on whether to preach with sweetness or harshness was one of a few on similar themes. This sermon, probably drafted toward the end of Boncompagni's career, was not developed. It contains only an eight-line stub of an answer, citing three cases of Jewish violence: Moses after the golden calf, Pinchas and the Midianite woman, and Elijah and the prophets of Baal. Whether these were examples to be followed or refuted is unclear, but the question was clearly on his mind as he attempted to justify his own lengthy career.

His most important sermon on this topic is unusually frank. Boncompagni spoke openly and in detail about a question that pressed him: "We ask if it is permitted to preach to the Jews, dispute with a Jew, and preach publicly to the Jews in the presence of Christians. And we resolve the doubts of the Jews."[105] Raising this question directly implicated the whole purpose of his life's work. Nor was this the only time Boncompagni wondered about his job's import and effects. The last page of another volume of sermon manuscripts offers a list of seventeen "reasons to preach to the Jews" (figure 5.1). This list combines standard doctrinal arguments about Jewish errors that must be corrected with broader hypothetical suggestions about why Jews had not yet converted. On the one hand, Boncompagni offers some old standards such as, "It is not true what they believe: that their current Judaism is like the ancient one. Christian doctrine is older than the faithlessness and malice of the Jews; Judaism today consists in nothing but contradicting the gospel." Jewish people don't like crucifixes, he admits, or the invocation of saints, or the Eucharist. But he also suggests that Jews have remained Jewish because they believe they are the true people of God, and because "they say it is too difficult to change religion, and that they love the one they were born and raised in."[106]

With the arguments in this list, Boncompagni admits that Jews might be put off by the multiplication of Christian sects and find it difficult to identify the true faith. He explains away such concerns by contending that it is part of the human condition for people to have different opinions and understand things in their own way. Yet he seems to lack awareness of the apparent contradiction in this assertion about sect differences. He even notes that Judaism contains its own divisions, but names the first-century Pharisees, Sadducees, Essenes, and later Karaites.[107] Here again is an opportunity lost: while seeking to demonstrate broad awareness of human commonalities, he resorts to ancient and outdated distinctions within Judaism.

These sermon stubs and bullet-pointed lists show Boncompagni arguing for the ongoing value of sermons to Jews, both as a conversionary

105. BAV Borg. lat. 129, 75r.
106. BAV Borg. lat. 115, 470r–v.
107. BAV Borg. lat. 115, 470r.

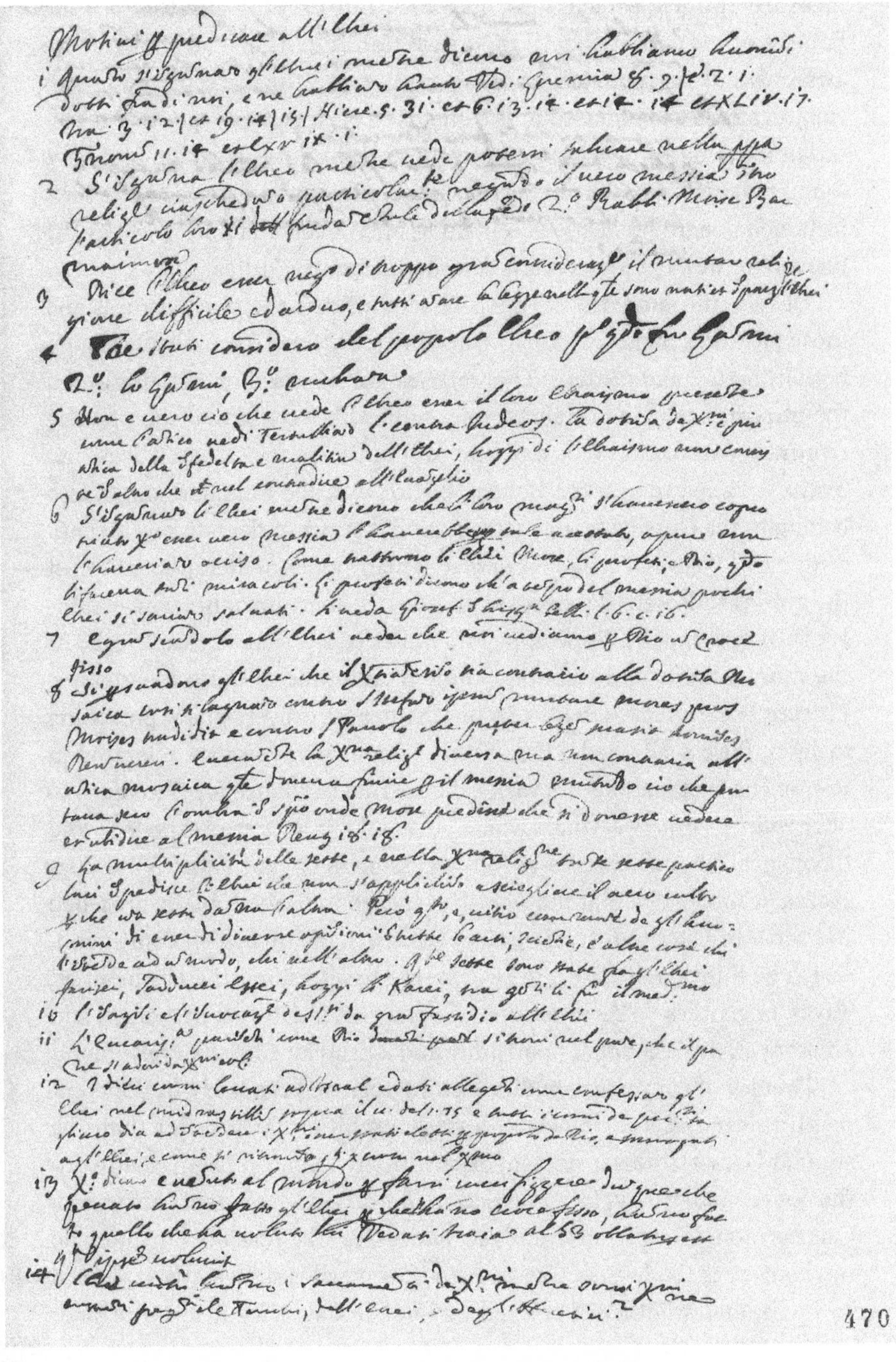

470

FIGURE 5.1. Reasons to preach to the Jews. Borg. lat. 115, 470r.
© 2021 Biblioteca Apostolica Vaticana.

measure and a spectacle for Christians. But they also underscore the failures of the conversionary rhetorical tradition. If he had shown more awareness of his audience, bringing as examples the five separate Jewish congregations then housed in the ghetto or even perhaps the Jewish sectarian movements of seventeenth-century central Europe, he might have found that his words fell on more hospitable Jewish ears. Instead, the Jews in Boncompagni's reflections remain as abstracted and ahistorical as the unevolving Jews in Marcellino's sermons a century earlier.

Despite the similarity between Boncompagni's rhetorical choices and those of earlier preachers, Boncompagni's reflections themselves are new, both in nature and content. They suggest an increased uncertainty about the importance of conversionary sermons and a sense that the practice required justification in a way that had not been true when it was first instituted a century earlier. Boncompagni's lists and rationales might also belong to the classifying and categorizing instinct of the late seventeenth century.[108] Lists and catalogs populated many kinds of literature, not least the guides to Rome that brought visitors to Boncompagni's conversionary sermons. Indeed, Boncompagni's bullet points find a possible echo in the most weighty and elaborate guide of all of these: Carlo Bartolomeo Piazza's *Eusevologio Romano*. In his chapter on conversionary preaching to Jews, Piazza supplied a list of nine reasons why Jews are tolerated in Rome. His explanations are variously pastoral (a chance for Christians to offer charity), practical (there would be scandal if Jews were expelled), and theological (they are witnesses to the Passion of Christ). At no point does Piazza acknowledge that the Jewish presence in Rome actually preceded the birth of Christianity. He ends with the hope of Jewish conversion, which he thinks more likely to be achieved by Christians than by heretics, Turks, or gentiles.[109] As in sermons, Piazza's listed Jews are imaginary and ahistorical, a missionary opportunity and a prop for Christian reflection.

Themes of conversion and preaching recurred regularly in Boncompagni's sermons, and showed a level of ambition far broader than the standard exhortations one might expect to Jews. Boncompagni clearly saw the conversion of Jews as a microcosm of every other form of conversion. One sermon, likely from the 1670s, addresses "the reason why many do not convert to the faith of Christ, even if its merit is sufficiently explained to them, and whether it is good or not for Catholics to dispute with

108. Paula Findlen, *Possessing Nature: Museums, Collecting, and Scientific Culture in Early Modern Italy*.

109. Carlo Bartolomeo Piazza, *Eusevologio Romano overo Delle Opere Pie di Roma*, 8:149–50.

infidels."[110] Another, dated 1673, addresses the conversion of the gentiles through the preaching of the apostles."[111] At other times, Boncompagni wrote sermons on the conversion of the gentiles generally, or that sought to explain why other (clearly mistaken) religions had survived for so long, such as, "In Which We Resolve the Doubts on Why All the Nations in the World Do Not See the True Messiah in Christ."[112] Boncompagni's magnum opus, a polemical treatise prepared for publication, sought to win over not just Jewish people but also "the principal sects of the world: philosophers, astrologers, Machiavellians, idolaters, Jews, Muslims, heretics, and Christians."[113] His expertise, he apparently felt, was in defending Catholicism, not in persuading Jews.

The rhetoric and content of sermons to Jews changed relatively little over the early modern period. While some preachers were more exegetical, others more intent on ritual, and yet others more mystical, they all kept within the strict rhetorical limits that had developed over centuries. Above all, conversionary preaching almost never addressed the concerns of the early modern Roman Jewish people who were listening. It did not acknowledge Rome's Jews directly, even though Rome housed the least easily ignored group of Jews in Europe. The ancient role Jews played in sermons, defined by Augustine, was that of necessary witnesses testifying to the truth of Christianity. This role protected them from extermination. But by the same token, it also discredited any evolution or variation within Judaism.[114] The Jews discussed in conversionary sermons were a wholly hypothetical and theological category, not a living religious or social community.

This arrangement suited the Jews of Rome too. If they had to sit through a long and hostile conversionary sermon, better it should focus on dry theological matters and not refer directly to themselves. A sermon that revisited the nature of the Trinity and the "correct" interpretation of Isaiah 7:14 was far safer than a sermon that criticized current Jewish practice. The less a Christian audience connected the imaginary Jews in the sermon with the real Jewish people on the benches, the safer the walk home from the oratory would be. The Jews of Rome knew about the history of attacks

110. BAV Borg. lat. 129, 427r–v. Some of Boncompagni's volumes have precise dates for each sermon, and others do not.

111. BAV Borg. lat. 129, 121r–v.

112. BAV Borg. lat. 114, fol. 255; BAV Borg. lat. 505, 126r–33r.

113. BAV Borg. lat. 47, 1r–3v.

114. See especially Paula Fredriksen, *Augustine and the Jews: A Christian Defense of Jews and Judaism.*

and expulsions that had followed incendiary mendicant sermons about Jews, and remembered the repeated attempts in their own day to legislate and contain Christian violence against them. They also knew about the blood libel—the myth of Jews murdering Christian children. The most infamous and deadly instance, the 1475 case of Simon of Trent, was Italian. Simon's cause had gained recent support from Gregory XIII, Sixtus V, and Cesare Baronio.[115] For good reason, then, as the final chapter will show, Jews objected when conversionary preachers departed from theological topics, and began to disparage Jewish ritual as their mendicant predecessors or northern European counterparts had done, even reviving the blood libel. In response to preaching they considered inappropriate, Jews countered more strongly and publicly than ever before, producing the first printed protests against conversionary sermons. Theological, Kabbalistic, or grammatically focused sermons, on the other hand, elicited less protest because they caused less harm to their Jewish listeners.

The more formulaic and predictable the rhetoric of these sermons, the more valuable they were to Christians too. In their familiarity and repetition, they fulfilled their primary intended purpose—not so much to convert Jews as to enact the concept of conversion through persuasion. The more sermons fulfilled the expectations of watchers by rehearsing familiar arguments, the more they suggested that the conversionary campaign was a success, and that its means and motives were pure. The rhetoric of sermons and printed polemics to Jews addressed primarily Christians. Boncompagni's many musings on the function of these sermons offer the final proof that even Christians understood that preaching to the Jews was a fiction, and the idea of its effectiveness toward Jews was primarily a smoke screen.

But sermons also served another function, even beyond their dubious ability to convert Jews and proven ability to fortify Christians. Conversionary rhetoric was not useful to Jews but instead highly useful for selling conversion as a theological and intellectual conviction. It became, as Boncompagni's sermon on Christian spectators shows, a valuable platform for working out difficult problems. At a time when the early modern church and city were expanding so broadly, and were beset by so many unprecedented challenges, such platforms were increasingly necessary but difficult to find. Indeed, few other opportunities surfaced for speculating on the

---

115. On Simon of Trent, see Teter, *Blood Libel*, 99–106, 110–27; Stephen D. Bowd and J. Donald Cullington, *"On Everyone's Lips": Humanists, Jews, and the Tale of Simon of Trent*; R. Po-Chia Hsia, *Trent 1475: Stories of a Ritual Murder Trial*.

nature of Catholicism, justifying and defending it, and considering why it continued to matter in a rapidly changing world. Despite their medieval heritage, conversionary sermons would come to provide one of the most effective opportunities for promoting a Catholicism that was distinctively early modern. This would require a preacher to abandon the rhetorical traditions built up over centuries of disputing with Jews. The surprise in Boncompagni's sermons is the number of times he found it necessary to depart drastically from his brief, and use his pulpit to discuss contemporary topics and unprecedented current events.

CHAPTER SIX

Saints, Turks, and Heretics

GREGORIO BONCOMPAGNI CORCOS AND
EARLY MODERN CATHOLICISM

THE FIRST SAINT born in the Western Hemisphere was Rose of Lima, beatified in April 1668 and canonized in 1671. The figure of Rose of Lima personified the expanding reach of the Roman church, suggesting that the conversion of the entire globe was within its grasp. Judaism played no obvious part in Rose of Lima's quick rise to sanctity. After her death in 1617, her case sped through the rigorous canonization process, propelled by Dominican campaigning, European royal patronage, extraordinary popular devotion, and her own passionate, deeply appealing, mystical asceticism.[1] As Gregorio Boncompagni Corcos degli Scarinci put it, the odor of Rose's peerless sanctity had reached from one pole to the other, "from the antipodes to this our hemisphere," proclaimed everywhere by the vicar of Christ (in Rome) and made visible in medals of precious metals.[2] The only holdouts against her holy example were the Jews. Within two months of Rose's beatification, Boncompagni had turned her story into a lesson for the Jews of Rome. In his sermon on June 16, 1668, he chastised them for "staying distant from the scent of her sanctity" because of their fears and thorny doubts. In Boncompagni's view, a tutorial on Catholic saint worship was deeply warranted, and Rose of Lima provided the best possible syllabus.

---

1. Frank Graziano, *Wounds of Love: The Mystical Marriage of Saint Rose of Lima*, 89–109.

2. BAV Borg. lat. 790, 81r.

Over the course of nearly half a century of preaching to Jews, Gregorio Boncompagni (as he called himself) often ignored the narrow instructions for his profession. He used his platform as predicatore degli ebrei to introduce topics that strayed far from the original papal guidelines, landing firmly in contemporary society. Thanks to him, in the later seventeenth century, preaching to Jews became instead a platform for explaining, defending, and promoting a new, global Catholicism—both to Jews and a variety of Christian audiences. His sermon on Rose of Lima provided a general discussion of how sanctity worked in Roman Catholicism, relevant to any listener new to Catholic theology, whether Roman Jew, Protestant spectator, or unschooled Catholic. Boncompagni also offered sermons on the new enemies of an increasingly global Catholicism, the new saints of the seventeenth century, and the introspective tendencies of the baroque world. In doing so, he showed how there was no better platform for celebrating the new Catholicism of the early modern period than in a pulpit ostensibly aimed at Jewish listeners.

Boncompagni and His Sermons

Boncompagni embodies the establishment intellectual Catholicism of seventeenth-century Rome, joining and actively supporting its scholarly revival and stupendous growth. He shone within the Dominican Order as a student of Semitic languages, which he studied from childhood. Even during his lifetime, Boncompagni won high praise for his devout scholarship and preaching. As discussed in previous chapters, he enjoyed connections with elite Dominican institutions in Rome and developed a close friendship with some of the city's top Christian scholars of Hebrew, who praised him for his fearless, dramatic, and successful sermons.

As readers now know, for his entire adult life Boncompagni also served as preacher to the Jews of Rome. His tenure as the official predicatore degli ebrei in Rome endured for thirty-nine years, from 1649 to 1688, the most stable period in the three-hundred-year history of conversionary preaching to Jews in Rome. Boncompagni was ideally situated to bring glory to his profession, with roots that were simultaneously notable for their Judaism and impeccably Catholic. He was the scion of the Corcos family whose conversion over the mid-sixteenth century had been so widely celebrated, and had included some of the most eminent individual Jewish converts of early modern Italy. As wealthy Catholics, the ennobled family had direct access to social and ecclesiastical power. The Boncompagni-Corcos palazzo sat just steps from the home of the Congregation of the Oratory, which had arranged the family's conversion, and which the wealthy family continued to support.[3]

Although his ancestry surely helped to determine his career, Boncompagni was not himself a convert. He was raised in a wholly Catholic environment and acquired his direct knowledge of Judaism through his studies. But he studied hard. At the library he oversaw in the College of Penitentiaries at the basilica of Santa Maria Maggiore, Boncompagni edited and conserved a rare copy of one of the primary texts of Jewish conversion in Rome: Andrea De Monte's *Letter of Peace*. De Monte's wife was Boncompagni's great-great-aunt.[4] A few decades after Boncompagni's death, the polemicist-convert Paolo Sebastiano Medici praised the fervent faith and preaching of Boncompagni, along with his brother Francesco Maria and the entire Corcos clan:

> For the space of about forty years, he preached every Saturday to the Jews in Rome. Moved and persuaded by his goodness and doctrine, many of the Jews left their perfidy and embraced the faith of Christ. . . . Great was the piety and devotion that these fervent Christians demonstrated toward the worship of God.[5]

Through his education, professional activities, and scholarly network, Boncompagni represented the mainstream orthodox line in his conversionary rhetoric and doctrinal preaching.

Boncompagni possessed two contradictory qualities necessary for anyone holding a long, repetitive job over many decades: an organized mind and an inner creative streak. Given his long tenure in the pulpit, he was

3. Gianni Incisa della Rocchetta and Nello Vian, *Il primo processo per san Filippo Neri del Codice vaticano latino 3798 e in altri esemplari dell'Archivio dell'Oratorio di Roma*, 2:268–69, testimony of Agostino Boncompagni, October 19, 1600; Fiamma Satta, "Predicatori agli ebrei, catecumeni e neofiti a Roma nella prima metà del seicento," 126–27; Alberto Bianco, "Cesare Baronio e la conversione dei Corcos nei documenti d'archivio della Congregazione oratoriana di Roma"; Carolyn H. Wood and Peter Iver Kaufman, "Tacito Predicatore: The Annunciation Chapel at the Madonna Dei Monti in Rome."

4. PT Masetti, *Monumenta et Antiquitates veteris disciplinae ordinis praedicatorum ab anno 1216 ad 1348 praesertim in Romana provincia Praefectorumque qui eandem rexerunt Biographica Chronotaxis*, 2:152–53; Alberto Zucchi, 'Rome domenicana: note storiche: Predicatori Domenicani degli Ebrei nel sec. XVIII," 120–21; Guendalina Serafinelli, "Guido Reni, Clemente Boncompagni Corcos e lo stendardo doppio di San Francesco: Rinvenimenti d'archivio." See also Martine Boiteux, "Preaching to the Jews in Early Modern Rome: Words and Images"; Marina Caffiero, *Legami Pericolosi: Ebrei e cristiani tra eresia, libri proibiti e stregoneria*, 282–83.

5. Paolo Sebastiano Medici, *Catalogo de neofiti illustri usciti per misericordia di Dio dall'ebraismo e poi rendutisi gloriosi nel cristianesimo per esemplarità di costumi, e profondità di dottrina*, 57–58.

obliged to develop new themes for old subjects, as the same biblical stories and festivals returned year after year in the Jewish calendar. Hypothetically, if a preacher gave one new sermon every week for 39 years, he would accumulate over two thousand sermons. Realistically, the number should be much lower, taking into account the ebb and flow of the Jewish calendar, the frequent cancellation of sermons, and the tradition common to Italian preaching of reusing sermon material.[6] Yet 350 years later, more than a thousand of Boncompagni's sermons still exist; rather than recycling a previous year's sermon, he seems to have written new ones regularly. The results are collected into about ten large manuscript volumes of conversionary sermons, most of them running to a few hundred pages—a lifetime's worth of weekly sermons and assorted other writings.

These sermons and some related literature made their way into the papers of Boncompagni's colleague Giovanni Pastrizio at the Propaganda Fide, and from there into the Vatican library.[7] In some volumes, the sermons are written in a variety of hands, from elegant sloping calligraphy to Boncompagni's own dark, unruly scrawl. In any given compilation, the width of the margins varies from sermon to sermon, and so does the quantity of annotation, summary material, and paratext in the margins. So too does the use of Hebrew. Some sermons provide biblical source texts in careful Hebrew print under each title, in the margins, or at the end of each sermon. Some have the Hebrew verses integrated into the text. And many, especially in Boncompagni's own hand, skip the Hebrew alphabet entirely, and transliterate the relative verses and titles into Italian letters reflecting the *giudeo-romanesco* pronunciation of Roman Jews. He was always careful to underline quotations and separate them from the body of the sermon.

The politics of the outside world rarely intruded, save for notes about the weather if it affected the sermon, and truly exceptional cases. In one striking example, a note at the bottom of one page calls attention to the peak crisis moment of Sabbatean messianism: "In this year there disappeared a false Messiah called Sabbatai Tzvi, who the Jews said had ... done many, many miracles, and then he was discovered to be false and

6. For Italian sermon material, see especially Emily Michelson, *The Pulpit and the Press in Reformation Italy*; Frederick McGinness, *Right Thinking and Sacred Oratory in Counter-Reformation Rome*; Stefano Dall'Aglio, "Faithful to the Spoken Word: Sermons from Orality to Writing in Early Modern Italy."

7. For full volumes of Boncompagni's sermons, see BAV Borg. lat. 113, 114, 115, 122, 123, 124, 129, 505, 506, 555. Other volumes that I know to comprise or contain works by Boncompagni include BAV Borg. lat. 19, 47, 192, 790.

turned Turk."[8] Another notes the beatification of Pius V in 1672 and describes some of the efforts behind the scenes.[9]

Most of his sermon volumes open with Boncompagni's signature and a declaration of the contents, but even when these are absent, we can surmise that Boncompagni mostly compiled them himself. We know this first from the order of the sermons. Almost every volume proceeds in the same logical order. Sermons on the same topic from different years are always grouped together, so that three or four sermons for a given weekly Torah portion, delivered in different years, appear one after the other. Typically, a volume of Boncompagni's sermons begins with the first week of the Jewish year and proceeds through to the end. These sermons are followed by sermons on explicitly Christian topics, and then by a series on Jewish festivals and sometimes rituals. While the papal legislation had mandated that conversionary sermons follow the order of Jewish Torah portions, printed sermons never do. This rule was followed only in manuscript, reflecting the oral delivery of sermons and not their later repackaging for print.

Boncompagni's works, even in manuscript, kept readers in mind. Many volumes are hand paginated. In most instances, numerals in the top right-hand corners do not prove authorship, but in this case, they do. He sometimes provided performance notes for himself or others, or made reference to his own page numbers, such as, "All this [matter] can be found in this book, page 127."[10] Many volumes contain brief opening addresses, tables of contents, and catchwords, most commonly used for reading aloud. The bound volumes are too large to tuck under the arm on the way to a sermon, but they are likely to have been copied and bound for private circulation later, presumably at Boncompgani's Santa Maria Maggiore, Pastrizio's Propaganda Fide, or the College of Neophytes. The introduction to one two-volume collection admits as much. Boncompagni offers a demurral, though it should fool nobody: "I have bound these sermons together not because they will be seen by anybody, which my works do not merit, but only because they remain useful to me to use again." That

8. BAV Borg. lat. 115, 243r, after a sermon given on May 8, 1666. See also the printed pamphlet discussing, though not naming, Sabbatai Tsvi at the back of BAV Borg. lat. 129, fol. 502. For an overview on Sabbatai Tsvi, see Kenneth Austin, *The Jews and the Reformation*, 181–84. For more detail, see Gershom Scholem, *Sabbatai Ṣevi: The Mystical Messiah, 1626–1676*. For the Sabbatean impact in Italy, see Stefano Villani, "Between Information and Proselytism: Seventeenth-Century Italian Texts on Sabbatai Zevi, Their Various Editions and Their Circulation, in Print and Manuscript."

9. BAV Borg. lat. 115, 260r.

10. BAV Borg. lat. 123, fol. 8v.

disclaimer appears in a preface labeled "to readers" and includes explanations of editorial decisions that only readers would need to know.[11] These notes remind us again that sermons to Jews were understood simultaneously as a performance and a source of genuine pedagogical value for Christian readers.

When Boncompagni began preaching, conversionary sermons had been taking place regularly in Rome for almost seventy-five years. It is tempting to think that perhaps the introduction of new topics was inevitable in order to keep the sermons fresh. But sermons had developed within the strict rhetorical and theological conventions established hundreds of years earlier, after which Pope Gregory XIII had been specific in legislating their content for a Roman context. Indeed, as the descendant of converts, Boncompagni probably had less leeway to experiment or show flexibility in his sermons than someone else with a wholly Catholic pedigree might have had.

And yet, experiment he did. Boncompagni's sermons, almost entirely unknown until now, reveal extraordinary surprises about conversion, early modern Catholicism, and the mind of a conversionary preacher. Most of the sermons, to be fair, follow the traditional themes. But over his long career, Boncompagni also amassed a remarkable amount of new material in the form of unprecedented topics for sermons to Jews. These fall into three general categories: religions other than Catholicism and Judaism, particularly Protestant groups and Islam; recent saints and the current events that enveloped their lives; and reflections on conversionary preaching as a practice and his own role in it. Given the force of tradition and the constraints surrounding conversionary preaching, it is astonishing both that Boncompagni even hazarded these new topics and that his attempts survived for our benefit.

New Antagonists

Boncompagni invoked Protestants rarely, yet with careful strategy. Take the case of one sermon on the topic of "heretical sects." It appears, undated, in a collection of sermons delivered between 1645 and the early 1660s. The sermon discusses the inferiority of Judaism, the mutability of the law, and the identity of the Messiah. It also demonstrates how a Catholic preacher

11. BAV Borg. lat. 506. The preface also discusses the act of transliteration and apologizes for the sermons' lack of editing. My thanks here to Anne Coldiron for sharing with me her expertise on bound manuscripts for reading.

might raise the specter of Protestantism as both a conversionary tactic and useful lesson for Jews.

At first, Protestants appear mostly as a pretext, allowing the preacher to pose hypothetical questions. Boncompagni imagines Jewish people asking why there are so many different Christian sects and so much uncertainty about which is the true law of God. This setup allows him to acknowledge that all Christians might seem the same to Jews, and to present a definition of Catholicism that deliberately disparages Protestant sects, especially the Protestant term "Reformed":

> I hear the Jew saying, "I am not so sure, because each person confirms that 'the law that I follow was given by God,' but the Christians are not so certain that their law is the law of God . . . and for this uncertainty Christians are separated into heretical opinions, since some are from the Arian sect, others of Luther, others of Donatus, others of Bucer, and others of Oecolampadius, and so forth. The preacher preaches to us [Jews] continuously that we should make ourselves Christian. What kind of Christians are we dealing with? He [the preacher] will say 'with Catholics,' but everybody claims to be Catholic; the Christian sects are infinite, and all of those whom the Catholics call heretics call themselves 'Reformed Christians.'"[12]

Boncompagni's denunciation of Protestantism here is deliberately simplistic, but its form had deep roots in Catholic polemic. By lumping sixteenth-century reformers in with fourth-century heretics—Arius and Donatus alongside John Calvin and Martin Luther—Catholic preachers could imply that they were all the same: a repetitive, familiar old enemy, easily vanquished. And in brashly listing so many names, preachers emphasized division among their adversaries. Italian preachers had made much of this argument during the first decades of the Reformation, contrasting the constancy of the Roman Church with the endless discord and splintering of the rebels.[13] Boncompagni bends this line of argumentation toward Jewish groups and finds ways to align them with his view of Protestant sects. Both, for example, misread scripture: one by misinterpreting the Messiah, and the other by misinterpreting the authority of the church.

12. BAV Borg. lat. 123, 8r.

13. For this kind of technique, see Michelson, *The Pulpit and the Press in Reformation Italy*, 54–86.

It seems slightly risky for Boncompagni to suggest that anybody might think all Christian sects might be indistinguishable or ask why potential Jewish neophytes should choose his form of Christianity over all the others. So naturally, the sermon goes on both to define Catholicism and defend it. Boncompagni defines Catholicism as the only form of Christianity that is obedient to the pope and defends it by stressing the need for authority in the church. This was a clever tactic. In Rome especially, the promise of authority made a strong selling point in a sermon. The resurgent, relatively stable seventeenth-century papacy contrasted favorably with the history of violent divisions among northern Protestant confessions.

Portraying Catholicism in its best local light was a common rhetorical tactic. In other regions of Europe, whether Catholic or contested, Catholic preachers chose to highlight different arguments that best reflected regional exigencies. In early modern Ireland, their rhetoric was often as political and sectarian as it was doctrinal; in Hungary, the controversialist Péter Pázmány linked the rise of Lutheranism to the Turkish offensive, seeking to discredit both religions.[14] Preachers in Bohemia emphasized the relationship of clergy and laity, class relations, and the construction of national identity.[15] At other times, Catholics concentrated on refuting Protestantism by criticizing its newfangled ideas. In Rome, within sight of the imposing dome of Saint Peter's basilica, Boncompagni defines Protestants differently. He portrays them primarily as Christians who are disobedient to Peter as vicar of Christ and have thereby strayed into wrong doctrine. Their "reformation" has reformed the wrong practices: "Those heretics who are called 'reformed Christians'—in what are they reformed? In negating sacraments? In removing obedience to the legitimate successor of Peter? In removing celibacy? Monastic life? . . . I would like Christianity to be reformed into more exact obedience."[16] In response to these depictions of wayward Protestants, he cites various passages in the Hebrew Bible calling for a single authoritative leader or proving the need for one. Any possible Jewish doubts about the nature of Christian authority are defused with references to the primacy of the Papacy. By laying out what makes Catholics right and Protestants wrong but still Christian,

14. Tadhg Ó hAnnracháin, *Catholic Europe, 1592–1648: Centre and Peripheries*, 55–56, 130–31.

15. Howard Louthan, *Converting Bohemia: Force and Persuasion in the Catholic Reformation*, 226–33.

16. BAV Borg. lat. 123, 9r.

Boncompagni turns his sermon into a general introductory lesson for Jews and other uninitiated listeners. Instead of a sermon suggesting that Jews should convert, or finding fault with the Jewish theological tradition, his preaching has become a platform for a broader curriculum on early modern Catholicism.

This particular sermon had another lasting influence: it formed the basis for Boncompagni's final word on Protestantism in his undiscovered magnum opus. Among his papers is a volume clearly intended as his capstone achievement: *News of the Principal Sects of the World, That Is, of Philosophers, Astrologers, Machiavellians, Idolaters, Jews, Muslims, Heretics, and Christians.*[17] Never published, the manuscript was nonetheless fully prepared for press, with a table of contents and letter to readers. We know that it was meant to be the great summation of his life's work by the volume's size (five hundred folios), its organization (ninety-six chapters, many echoing the topics in his sermons), and above all, by the blank space left in the introductory letter, which says, "After having preached to the Jews of Rome for the space of _____ years, I wanted to bring this work to light for the benefit of everyone, and in particular of those who would like to be instructed in the true faith."[18] Boncompagni's treatise is set up as a dialogue between a catechumen and his catechizing father. Much of it is pitched broadly: the need for religion along with characteristics of the divine and human nature, sin, the afterlife, and redemption. Other parts refute specific sects, and the final section promotes Catholic-specific doctrines and argues for the divine authority of the Roman church.

Within all of this flurry of activity, Boncompagni devoted only one chapter explicitly to Protestants, although many other chapters address implicitly anti-Protestant doctrinal questions such as papal succession. This chapter is clearly drawn from the sermon on heretical sects discussed above; it revisits much of the same material and expands on it. The treatise retreads the topics of the sermon: how to distinguish among Christian sects, the primacy of Peter, the need for authority, and the chaos that results from its absence. In this way, it also tells us how an idea might evolve between speech and print in early modern Rome. In his sermon to Jews about Lutherans, Boncompagni had spoken specifically about

17. Gregorio Boncompagni, *Notitia delle sette principali del mondo, cioe' di filosofi, astrologi, machiavellisti, idolatri, ebrei, maomettani, heretici, e de Cristiani;* BAV Borg. lat. 47.

18. "Dopo haver predicato all'ebrei di Roma per lo spatio di [blank] anni mi sono voluto dar in luce quest'opera a beneficio di tutti et in particolare di quelle che vorranno esser ammaestrati nella vera fede." BAV Borg. lat 47, 2v.

Judaism and Jews as they relate to his disagreements with Protestantism, as we have seen. But in the treatise, he mostly leaves out Judaism entirely, except to note that the scriptures were first written in Hebrew and should not be approached without knowledge of ancient languages. Instead, for the broader readership, he adds more fire and fury:

> [Against] the second point [supposed claim of Protestants], which is that [their] church has always been there, but unknown and invisible. If all men were geese, maybe this would be understandable. But even if they maintained that the brain of a goose still had the slightest bit of human understanding, they still could not [make this argument]; the proposition is so impertinent.[19]

Boncompagni here frames Protestantism as an idea based on faulty theological logic; he suggests that no person who thought rationally would find reason to opt for it. He also restates his position that Protestants are contrary and cannot agree (presumably he thought them stupider than geese). He carries this attitude into his next point: Protestant disagreements over scripture. Without a central authority, he insists that they cannot help falling into discord, even when the meaning is supposedly obvious:

> About points written in the clearest terms, such as "this is my body." The spirit of men has fabricated two hundred opinions, all different. What will happen then in much thornier [textual] difficulties? Everybody claims to have the true sense, so to whom should we look? Don't you know this is actually a means to foment a thousand divisions? If there were no judge in authority to end these differences . . . what would happen?[20]

With this claim, Boncompagni attempts to mount an argument that would endorse Catholicism while refuting both Protestantism and Judaism simultaneously. In that context, any subpoints that discredited only one antagonist while exonerating the other, or could rebound against Catholicism, would be useless. This conundrum eliminated one of the primary Catholic claims against Protestantism—that it lacked antiquity and continuity—because the same could be said of Catholicism when compared to Judaism. It also ruled out one of the primary Catholic claims against Judaism—that Jews failed to recognize Christ as the Messiah—because it did not apply to Protestants, who definitely did. Of the various

---

19. BAV Borg. lat. 47, 329v.
20. BAV Borg. lat. 47, 332r–v.

polemical arguments that the Roman church arrayed against heretics, only one packed the necessary double punch. This was the argument that Catholicism, with its central authority, produced order over disharmony and chaos.[21] Boncompagni deliberately chose to cite the verse "this is my body"—the most contentious verse in the New Testament and famously the subject of virulent disagreements at the Marburg Colloquy—so as to contrast it with a "judge in authority to end these differences." By basing his defense of his church on the principle of order and authority, Boncompagni allowed his definition of Catholicism and its worth to be shaped inherently by both Judaism and Protestantism, both in the narrower, more specific context of conversionary sermons to Jews and the broader outlook of his treatise.

Why did Boncompagni decide in the first place that discussion of Protestants, Muslims, and other contemporary topics belonged in his preaching to Jews? And why, then, was he so simplistic and vague about what Protestantism was? First, I would suggest, because he believed that Jewish people were more likely to convert if he convinced them that Catholicism was superior not only to Judaism but also to all forms of Christianity. But second, because he knew well that many Protestants would also have attended these sermons, as we have seen—more than ever, perhaps, in the later seventeenth century. His sermon on Protestants suggests an awareness of their presence; here was a chance to promote Catholic belief to them too. The conversion of elite Protestants, when it happened, was highly prized in Rome.[22] It was wise for a preacher to opt to treat them delicately from the pulpit. If Boncompagni did not dwell on Protestant errors in detail, he doubled his chance of winning souls.

Boncompagni's treatment of Protestants, in both his sermons and treatise, shows us how in early modern Rome, conversionary efforts could triangulate. An argument against Protestantism was useful for defining what made a Christian sect valid or invalid. An argument against Judaism was useful for endorsing Catholicism on a wider scale; it enabled a broader, comparative discussion of religious denominations. Arguments against both together, such as a general defence of papal primacy, might turn the heart of more than one kind of skeptic at once.

What happens when an imagined Islam joins this mix? In fact, Islam or what Boncompagni called "the Turkish threat" was a far more urgent

---

21. Michelson, *The Pulpit and the Press in Reformation Italy*, 76–78.

22. Irene Fosi, "Percorsi di salvezza. Preparare le strade, accogliere, convertire nella Roma barocca."

concern than Protestantism in Boncompagni's manuscripts. Imagined Muslims appear far more frequently than imagined Protestants in Boncompagni's sermons and treatise—either as an immediate menace or a useful rhetorical device. Islam merits a full series of sermons given in September and October 1674 as well as a string of chapters in his capstone *News of the Principal Sects of the World.* One of these sermons takes the form of an (unfinished) dialogue between Jews, Christians, and Muslims that survives in manuscript.[23] Boncompagni frequently invokes Muslims as part of a triad of non-Catholics, alongside Jews and heretics, and seems deeply concerned about them.

On the one hand, Boncompagni's approach to Islam, like his understanding of Judaism, was largely not his own invention. It drew on longstanding Catholic tropes of anti-Islamic rhetoric and polemic.[24] Boncompagni's work described the scandalous life of Muḥammad and his cunning; it portrayed the survival of Islam as a rebuke to Christianity; and above all, it promoted the notion that Islam converts by the sword alone.[25] Like generations of Catholic polemicists, Boncompagni failed to recognize his antagonists fully. He labels them as an undifferentiated group of *Turchi* or sometimes *Macomettani*, and treats them as an enduring, largely constant antagonist.[26] Muslims sometimes appear in his work as warrior enemies, typically in his discussions of the Battle of Lepanto. But more often he considers them a thorn in the side of Catholic religious conviction. These were common, even weary, and ill-informed stereotypes, dating back at least as far as Aquinas's *Summa contra Gentiles*, which, we can assume, a Dominican such as Boncompagni would have known better than most proselytizers. Other themes, such as the survival of Islam as a rebuke to Christianity, appeared later in the history of Christian anti-Islamic writing. Of the many possible Catholic approaches to Islam, Boncompagni in fact chose only a limited few. His works avoid the discussions of eschatology, Satanism, or crusade that other polemicists employed.[27] Instead,

23. BAV Borg. lat. 506, 370r–79v.

24. For a brief introduction to this theme, see Norman Daniel, *Islam and the West: The Making of an Image*; Nancy Bishaha, *Creating East and West: Renaissance Humanists and the Ottoman Turks.*

25. For a summary of the long history of Christians in Europe defining Islam by violence, see Noel Malcolm, *Useful Enemies: Islam and the Ottoman Empire in Western Political Thought, 1450–1750*, 35–36.

26. Margaret Meserve argues for European miscomprehensions of Ottoman Turks in particular, although in a more differentiated and complex way than appears in Boncompagni's works. Margaret Meserve, *Empires of Islam in Renaissance Historical Thought*, 4–13.

27. Bishaha, *Creating East and West*, 135–73; Daniel, *Islam and the West*, 271–75.

he recycled only a few Christian tropes against Islam and showed little engagement with Muslim texts.

In his treatise, Boncompagni follows the same route. Compared to his sermons on the same topic, his treatise is less nuanced and more negative, and concentrates on the history of early Islam. The treatise concedes little merit to Islam. Its first three chapters treat the early history of the prophet Muḥammad, his lack of true prophecy, and his slyness. Boncompagni devotes special attention to circumcision as a practice unique to Islam and Judaism. He also takes up what he considers particularly Muslim fallacies regarding polygamy and paradise, and defends the Catholic belief in celibacy against heretics, Turks, and Jews.[28] Some of this material draws on topics he had previously developed in sermons, particularly the base origins of the prophet and evils of polygamy. The rest assess the quality of Muslim law and custom—its imperfections, vanity, ignorance, and errors—with a visible level of credulity:

> [Muḥammad], finally, knew that through the study of sciences, and especially philosophy, one comes easily to the knowledge of truth. And knowing, however, that it was impossible that his followers would not have their eyes opened after they had studied for a while and would see the [__ness] and vanity of his sect, in order to keep them permanently buried in the [__s] of ignorance, I find it an astonishing deceit that although it was entirely useless, he forbade them to study logic, especially philosophy.[29]

Boncompagni's arguments sometimes race far ahead of his evidence or reasoning. This passage is one example. Shortly afterward, he is obliged to justify the fact that many of the Christian apostles were just as poor and ignorant as the supposedly unquestioning followers of Islam. Just like the Muslims he criticizes, the apostles did not gain their own knowledge of truth from the extended study of logic and philosophy. Boncompagni undertakes some rapid backpedaling, maintaining that the apostles' spiritual gifts were miraculous; they "were rendered learned, and in receiving the Holy Spirit they were given, with the gift of languages, everything necessary to convert the world."[30] In this way, he sometimes runs into trouble as he follows his argument to a logical conclusion. In his treatise, his discussion of Islam on the whole is couched in much more polemical

---

28. BAV Borg. lat. 47, 154r–221v.
29. BAV Borg. lat. 47, 177r.
30. BAV Borg. lat. 47, 165r.

language than in his sermons and grants Muslims little merit. His reliance on long-standing tropes and his failure to move beyond them reflect not only his own belief, but also the arguments that he thought would play best in the broader scope of the treatise; they underscore his intent to publish.

In his sermons, on the other hand, Boncompagni's discussions of Islam focus on its survival, strength, and undeniable power, whether religiously or politically, with a tone of more grudging respect. He also asks tougher questions, more related to the specific conversionary demands of his profession, and undertakes more extended reasoning. He is especially concerned with trying to understand why Islam has endured despite its obvious (to him) falseness and therefore looks for ways to undermine its legitimacy. *News of the Principal Sects of the World*, in contrast, provides less analysis and instead attempts to discredit the validity of Islam through salacious stories about the prophet Muḥammad, although these could equally be deployed in sermons for religious arguments. In his sermons, Boncompagni portrays Islam as simultaneously cruel and debauched. It allows little freedom of thought; it retains its followers through force, and by allowing them many wives and a paradise "where all the pleasures of the senses can be enjoyed."[31] He concludes that Islam has only survived, in part, as a rebuke to Christians, who are divided where Muslims are unified, but conversely, as a base, natural human phenomenon as well. Muslims do, he concedes, perform some good works such as shunning idolatry, but he asserts that since they act without faith or grace, they do not earn eternal life.

Boncompagni's method in these sermons is to justify the longevity and political power of Islam, proving its worth as an antagonist, but reassuring his audience that its clout on earth is deceptive. He pitches Islam as a tyrannical system that brooks no dissent and punishes all transgressions. Boncompagni holds that an attraction to Muḥammad's riches explains the popularity of Islam, in contrast to Catholicism, which is founded in poverty and rare, God-given miracles. Nonetheless, even with these caricatures, these sermons grapple with real issues: the survival of Islam; its theological appeal; the question of God's rewards; the moral behavior of religious adherents.

Yet in these concerns about how religions seek to dominate each other, Boncompagni's discussion of Islam in subtle ways also comes to reflect the specific context of the conversion of Jews, despite his reliance on widely used stereotypes. He reworks these old ideas to give them specific meaning in a conversionary context. In one case, he invokes the idea of Islam

31. BAV Borg. lat. 129, 445r.

so that he can treat Protestants and Catholics as united in their Christianity, a useful tactic before a Jewish audience. In one of his "Turkish" sermons, he tries to convince his Jewish listeners that because Christians now outnumber Muslims, Christians must be the true chosen people. But the numbers of Catholics alone do not suffice for this claim. Muslims outnumber them. In order to make the reasoning work, he must count Protestants as Christians and stress their commonalities:

> Others are Christians who worship Christ as God and baptize, but don't believe everything that Catholics believe. They reject the pope or other articles; these are schismatics or heretics. Now it's true that Turks outnumber Catholics, but that they are more [numerous] than Christians who worship Christ and are baptized? This [also does not count] the innumerable Christians in Turkish countries, while in Christian countries there are no Turks, or [they] are only there in passing.[32]

Such an argument would have been unthinkable a century earlier, when the Catholic preachers commonly described Protestant sects as the devil's newest scheme.[33] But in Boncompagni's time, the threat of imminent Reformation in Italy had faded. In the context of ongoing fears about Islam, Protestants seemed like a lesser danger. They could be recruited to stand in as Christians and boost their numbers, as a familiar enemy and manageable threat. Indeed as a concept, Protestants had become a useful asset, allowing a preacher to hone his argument about Catholic superiority by playing off his church against other forms of Christianity.

Boncompagni uses a discussion of preaching to keep focus on the conversionary setting and reveals how important Catholics considered sermons to be:

> Turks at the beginning began at its [Islam's] origins with the fury of the sword, and preserve it always with the force of arms, which cannot be said about the Christian religion, which had its origins in the preaching of the holy apostles, poor fishermen. And now most Christians enjoy liberty of prudence, which means that each one [belongs to] the sect he wants. And even if they differ in particular dogmas, they come together in baptism and the adoration of Christ, and so therefore their great number of Christians is miraculous, and the number of Turks is natural."[34]

---

32. BAV Borg. lat. 129, 446r.

33. On preachers' conceptions of Protestants, see Michelson, *The Pulpit and the Press in Reformation Italy.*

34. BAV Borg. lat. 129, 446v.

Again, he emphasizes what Protestants and Catholics have in common. They have choice and liberty, share certain sacraments, and worship Christ. Muslims, to him, survive only through force and the sword. In this sermon, Jews provide the hypothetical interlocutor. Their presence enables Boncompagni yet again to present his definition of true Christianity in contrast with other denominations. It is even possible that an argument that depended on the theological alliance of Protestants and Catholics could *only* have been floated in a sermon to Jews, not to Christians.

But at the same time, it is ironic and even poignant to make this particular argument—preaching as a peaceful contrast with the sword—during a forced sermon to Jews, where the persuasive element was a thin veneer over a high-pressure coercive campaign. Yet Boncompagni embraces this distinction. His discussion of preaching shows how important it was to Catholics. In fact, Boncompagni defines preaching as the primary activity that distinguishes Christians, whether Catholic or Protestant, from Muslims:

> Changing religions [to Islam] owed more to the sword than to the sermon, then. The miracle is that anybody in the world converted to Christ for the preaching of the holy apostles, and not that the populations subject to Muḥammad through the sword continue to follow his sect. Something done through force is worth nothing. God is no tyrant; he can, without the sword, fortify the heart to free the soul. Therefore I admire the number of Christians and not of Turks, because the Turks are numerous through force, and Christians through love.[35]

Although this passage seems to consider only Islam explicitly, it also has broader impact: it serves as a backhanded justification of conversionary preaching to Jews. Boncompagni here sets up a false dichotomy in which preaching is the opposite of violence. He assumes that if a religion contains preaching, it is necessarily a nonviolent religion. Conversely, a "sword" religion converts exclusively through force and violence, and never by persuasion. If this is so, then any conversions to Christianity must necessarily be credited to its sermons, not to force or coercion. And it follows further that the institution and continuation of conversionary sermons—and thereby the ongoing existence of conversionary preachers such as himself—are the essence of what makes Catholicism a religion of love and not of the sword.

35. BAV Borg. lat. 129, 447r.

Even Boncompagni, however, must admit that Catholic conversionary tactics rely on extensive pressure, which some might call force. He
acknowledges this contradiction in his argument by putting it in the
mouths of rhetorical Jews:

> But I hear the Jew saying that Christians are also Christians by force
> because two things maintain Christians: the Holy Office and the mantle
> of Saint Peter. I respond that the Holy Office punishes and chastises the
> sacrilegious, but does not force anyone to become Christian, rather to
> remain Christian. A very just thing. If this tribunal did not exist, there
> would be too much of a shortage in governing the church of Christ.[36]

In other words, Boncompagni admits that the Roman Church includes
coercive institutions such as the Inquisition, but insists that the Inquisition's use of force doesn't count because it is intended for Christians,
not potential converts. By the seventeenth century, of course, the Roman
Inquisition also had official oversight of Roman Jewry and dealt with
many cases regarding conversion, but Boncompagni ignores this incon-
venient truth. (The mantle of Saint Peter, he reasons, is no worse than
the biblical order of Levites and the Jewish maintenance of rabbis.) A
thoughtful respondent might also ask about the status of the Congregation of Propaganda Fide, founded for the purpose of converting foreigners.
A note in the margins addresses this very query: "The Congregation of
Propaganda Fide doesn't have weapons to make people Christian by force,
but good missionaries."[37]

With arguments such as these, Boncompagni maintains tropes and
dichotomies built up over centuries, willfully misrepresenting Islam in
order to promote Christianity and simplifying Protestantism in order to
promote papal Catholicism.[38] Protestants and Muslims, as rhetorical
devices, are perhaps even more extravagantly imaginary than the Jews,
and far less immediate. This is nothing new, except that Boncompagni
seems almost to admit that his argumentation relies on impressive mental
gymnastics. In order to explain away contradictions, he ends up bringing
the early modern world and its new Catholic institutions into his sermons:
the Inquisition and Propaganda Fide. Backed into a corner, he is forced
to innovate, even as he layers these innovations over hoary stereotypes. By
then reworking some of this material into a treatise against all heresies,

---

36. BAV Borg. lat. 129, 447r.
37. BAV Borg. lat. 129, 447r.
38. But see his sermon on the sect of philosophers in BAV Borg. lat. 122, 227v–28v.

he also displays the hubris of a conversionary preacher: he suggests that a lifetime of preaching exclusively to Jews makes him an authority on all sorts of other sects, well outside his purview and experience.

Jews here serve as a rhetorical foil as they do in so many of Boncompagni's sermons, allowing him to pile up his claims and address possible objections: "But you will say . . ."; "But I hear the Jew say . . ."; and "You will add . . ." This common rhetorical device shows how religious boundaries can shift on a theoretical plane: the borders of confession are sharpened by one privileged group against stereotypes of the demeaned other and continue to shift as different imaginary antagonists step up to the ring. The antagonists are as necessary as the preacher himself. Perhaps Boncompagni was aware of this dependence—or at least he exemplified it—when he chose to construct one of his sermons for the last week of the Jewish liturgical year as an explicit interreligious dialogue. The dialogue features a rhetorical Jew, rhetorical Muslim, and rhetorical Christian. It unfolds in predictable fashion; the novelty is Boncompagni's belief that this format was worth offering in lieu of a sermon.

Then again, Muslims, Jews, and Protestants were never only rhetorical devices. These imagined interreligious conversations did not grow in a test tube or privileged Catholic vacuum. Living Jewish people regularly attended every one of these sermons, as did Catholic spectators, and often Protestants too. Muslims or people born Muslim were also present in Rome in a variety of visible ways.[39] As this book shows, sermons engendered genuine resistance and dialogue among proselytizing Catholics, visiting Protestants, and Roman Jews, altering the experience of all participants. It is the necessary presence of multiple religious confessions, real and imagined, that makes preaching to Jews one of the most powerful and rhetorically significant platforms in the early modern world.

New Saints

Canonized saints were not an approved topic for sermons to Jews, except in the theological defense of Mary's immaculate conception and virgin birth; they were too recent. Saints Peter, Augustine, or Jerome might

---

39. On Muslims in Rome, see Marina Caffiero, "Non solo schiavi. La presenza dei musulmani a Roma in età moderna: il lavoro di un gruppo di ricerca"; Serena Di Nepi, "Saving Souls, Forgiving Bodies: A New Source and a Working Hypothesis on Slavery, Conversion and Religious Minorities in Early Modern Rome (16th–19th Centuries)"; Justine Walden, "Muslim Slaves in Early Modern Rome: The Development and Visibility of a Labouring Class."

reasonably make an appearance, but in Boncompagni's sermons, they did not. He avoided discussion of apostles, early church fathers, and medieval saints—even Saint Dominic, patron of his order. On the rare occasions when he did compose sermons about saints, they were shockingly modern characters, almost in living memory, and all recently canonized or beatified. This was a marked departure from tradition and the tenets of *Sancta Mater Ecclesia*. Boncompagni preached to the Jews about four contemporary saints: Francis Xavier (1506–52), one of the original Jesuits and renowned apostle to the Far East; François de Sales (1557–1622), bishop of Geneva in exile, known for his work in the religiously contested or largely Calvinist territories of France/Savoy; Rose of Lima (1586–1617), the first saint born in the Americas and the first non-European saint of the early modern period; and Michele Ghislieri (1504–72), former head of the Inquisition and, as Pope Pius V, pope during the Battle of Lepanto against Ottoman forces. Conversionary preaching had never reflected the contemporary world with such immediacy as in Boncompagni's works.

The manuscript record suggests that these sermons meant a great deal to Boncompagni. He preached on Rose of Lima in June 1668, almost immediately after her beatification in April. Unusually, two separate copies of his sermon on Rose of Lima survive: one in an anthology of selected sermons, and the other in a set of notes for another sermon.[40] Francis Xavier got a sermon on his feast day, December 3, for the fiftieth anniversary of his 1622 canonization.[41] François de Sales, like Rose of Lima, was beatified and then canonized during Boncompagni's preaching career in, respectively, 1661 and 1665. Boncompagni's detailed sermon on him is undated, but it appears in a collection from the 1650s and 1660s, and could well celebrate his new status.[42]

But it was the Dominican Pius V whose sermons required all Boncompagni's efforts. The first attempt at a sermon, undated, must have been delivered almost immediately after Pius's beatification on May 1, 1672. It compares Pius V to various biblical figures in a fairly repetitive list.[43] A more substantial sermon followed on May 28, 1672, called "On the Sermon of Pius V to the Jews."[44] This sermon reviews the pope's biography and accomplishments in detail. It also contains a full justification for Boncompagni's decision to preach on the pope, culminating in the marginal

40. BAV Borg. lat 122, 152r–v, notes 153r–v; BAV Borg. lat. 790.
41. BAV Borg. lat. 115, 71r–v.
42. BAV Borg. lat. 122, 150v–52r.
43. BAV Borg. lat. 115, 315r–v. Pius V would be canonized in 1712.
44. BAV Borg. lat. 115, 312r–15r.

summary, "The sermon on Pius V to the Jews is not vain but useful, not incredible but credible, not detestable but of great value and religion." Despite Boncompagni's vehemence, this second sermon was never given, as the marginal note further explains, because it was raining.[45] A third sermon explains at the outset why Boncompagni had felt compelled to defend his choice of this subject; it was after hearing the first sermon that the listening rabbis had swarmed him, crying that the subject was "horrible, incredible, and vain," redolent of idolatry.[46] On this third attempt, Boncompagni reworked the themes from his biographical, rained-out second sermon, dwelling on details of the Battle of Lepanto. Finally, on June 25, 1672, Boncompagni delivered a fourth sermon, combining a history of Lepanto, praise for its Italian captain Marcantonio Colonna, and praise for Pius V, recasting the whole in biblical terms.[47]

In short, Boncompagni composed four separate sermons on the deceased pope and battled hostile elements, human and climatic, to deliver at least two of them. The struggle caused him to explain and defend his unusual actions, structuring entire sermons around self-justification and giving us rare insight into a preacher's mind.

These characters and sermons arrive after a moment of crisis in the saint-making process. Boncompagni's sermons on saints mark a critical point in the history and early modern revival of saint making, which in turn reflect a new set of values for the early modern church. A Reformation era hiatus in official canonizations lasted from 1523 to 1588, ending with the launch of the Sacred Congregation of Rites and Ceremonies to oversee canonizations. In the 1620s and 1630s, Urban VIII imposed stricter rules and greater uniformity. These included a fifty-year mandatory waiting period between death and canonization, and the formalization of beatification as a necessary step to sainthood. Another hiatus followed between 1629 and 1658. The first saint beatified under the new system was François de Sales, in 1662 (the after-death waiting period was waived). Boncompagni must have known this when he preached on de Sales.[48]

45. BAV Borg. lat. 115, 312r.

46. BAV Borg. lat. 115, 487r–90v.

47. BAV Borg. lat. 129, 491r–94v.

48. Peter Burke, "How to Become a Counter-Reformation Saint," esp. 131–32. For an earlier iteration of this argument, see Pierre Delooz, "Pour une étude sociologique de la sainteté canonisée dans l'eglise catholique," also translated in Stephen Wilson, *Saints and Their Cults: Studies in Religious Sociology, Folklore, and History*, 189–216. See also Simon Ditchfield, "How Not to Be a Counter-Reformation Saint: The Attempted Canonization of Pope Gregory X, 1622–45," 379–81. On sanctity and saint making in the Counter-Reformation period, see Clare Copeland, "Sanctity."

Boncompagni's chosen saints represented the Catholic values of the seventeenth century, as described by Peter Burke and others, who have argued that saints are cultural indicators reflecting the values of the era in which they are canonized. None were laypeople. Two were pastors, one a mystic, and one a missionary. None were especially concerned with Judaism during their earthly lives. Boncompagni could have given many sermons on individual saints with more obvious links to Jews. He could have chosen the apostle Paul or his own Dominican forebear Vincent Ferrer, whose canonization depended on stories of mass conversion from Judaism, or Bernardino of Siena, who preached extensively against Jews in Italy.[49] He did not. Instead, he chose universal figures, widely revered. With this choice of saints—one from the Americas, one foreign missionary, one who fought the Ottoman fleet, and one who worked against Protestantism—Boncompagni used his conversionary platform to mount a much broader defense of early modern Catholicism.

Massaging the stories of these saints to fit into both locally Jewish and broadly Catholic frameworks required some careful rhetorical manipulation. Promoting a saint was always a political and selective process, with some events from the saint's life shoved into the spotlight to make a point, and more problematic moments obscured or recast with new interpretations.[50] Nor did the saints' official vitae and iconography contain the whole of their official propaganda; saints' sermons attracted multiple audiences, and so different elements mattered at different times.[51] When Boncompagni discussed these saints, he drew from rich traditions of writing and preaching about saints' lives, including the tradition of strategic selection of detail. His sermons on Pius V could draw on a growing international body of sources.[52] Boncompagni seems heavily indebted to the hagiography by Girolamo Catena, much promoted by Pius's protégé, Pope Sixtus V, and eschews the grandiloquent and flowery styles of other saint sermons

49. Laura Ackerman Smoller, *The Saint and the Chopped-Up Baby: The Cult of Vincent Ferrer in Medieval and Early Modern Europe*; Nirit Ben-Aryeh Debby, "Jews and Judaism in the Rhetoric of Popular Preachers: The Florentine Sermons of Giovanni Dominici (1356–1419) and Bernardino Da Siena (1380–1444)"; Franco Mormando, *The Preacher's Demons: Bernardino of Siena and the Social Underworld of Early Renaissance Italy*.

50. For one stellar example, see Smoller, *The Saint and the Chopped-Up Baby*, 121–59.

51. Erin Kathleen Rowe, "The Spanish Minerva: Imagining Teresa of Avila as Patron Saint in Seventeenth-Century Spain."

52. Miguel Gotor, "Le vite di San Pio V dal 1572 al 1712 tra censura, agiografia e storia"; Roberto Rusconi, *Santo Padre: la santità del papa da San Pietro a Giovanni Paolo II*; Miles Pattenden, "Antonio de Fuenmayor's Life of Pius V: A Pope in Early Modern Spanish Historiography."

from seventeenth-century Italy.[53] Sermons for Rose of Lima emphasized the factors that most defined her in many hagiographies, such as the odor of her sanctity. But Boncompagni mostly leaves out other aspects of her life, such as her ongoing extreme acts of bodily mortification, highlighting instead the constancy and firmness of her love for God.[54]

Boncompagni occasionally repeats salacious or dramatic stories, typically included in saints' lives, that present the saint as a model of sanctity for others. He recounts how de Sales was tricked into being left alone with a famous courtesan as a challenge, but spat in her face and fled when she made an advance, maintaining his chastity and rectitude with her as well as with other noble yet sinful women. He describes Francis Xavier barefoot, in iron chains, begging for food and eating others' leftovers.[55] Rose of Lima is portrayed as stoic: "from the youngest age she never cried or let out the least little sigh." He depicts her patience when the cartilage of a fistulous ear was cut away and the wound cauterized, and when physicians had to cut a piece of flesh out of her nostril.[56] This is all a very seventeenth-century way of portraying saints: heroic virtue, heroic suffering, and attention to sensual details.

But most of the time, Boncompagni dwells on those parts of the saints' lives that brought them into contact with other religions or could serve as an exemplar for new Christians. Fittingly, he uses the saints to discuss conversion. He describes how de Sales was recruited by the Conte de Medici (possibly Alessandro Ottaviano de Medici) and the duke of Savoy to work in the contested region of Chablais, and even aspired to convert James I of England. He uses Francis Xavier's life to introduce the general concept of an apostolate:

> We Christians call apostles those who have been sent to the peoples to preach the faith of Our Lord Jesus Christ throughout the world, and because Saint Francis Xavier was sent by apostolic faith as nuncio to the new world to convert souls to Christ . . . and for the pilgrimages he made . . . and the great number of people he baptized, and the miracles he did, for so much he merits this name of apostle to the Indies . . . and

---

53. Pamela M. Jones, "The Pope as Saint: Pius V in the Eyes of Sixtus V," 49–55. For a different style of seventeenth-century Italian saint sermon, see Quinto Marini, "Francesco Fulvio Frugoni oratore tra devozione e potere."

54. For the general argument that Rose of Lima is best understood as a construction of arguments, with different meanings in different contexts, that obscure her actual personhood, see Graziano, *Wounds of Love.*

55. BAV Borg. lat. 122, 150v; BAV Borg. lat. 115, 71r.

56. BAV Borg. lat. 790, 85v.

not only was he a noble but he was apostolic nuncio, legate of Pope Paul III and emissary of the king of Portugal. He converted many hundreds of thousands of men to Christ in the Indies including many great princes and kings.[57]

This passage does not specifically refer to the conversion of Jews. Jews serve here, as they so often do, as a premise, standing in for everybody who might not know what an apostle is. At other times, Boncompagni drew—or invented—more direct connections between his saints and Jewish conversion:

> Today the Christian church celebrates the feast of Saint Francis Xavier, who for being an apostle to the Indies, for having converted so many Indians to the faith of Jesus Christ, and for the desire that I have for his intercession in the conversion of Jews, I would like to speak about his apostolate, as this seems to me the greatest prerogative of this glorious saint, and therefore appropriate for Jews more than for Christians.[58]

> Frances de Sales was so powerful and capable in converting souls; may he wish that from heaven he gives force to me to convert these Jews."[59]

The preacher's invocations here tread a careful line; these figures are meant to be an inspiration for Jews, but they are also, to his mind, too far above his degraded audience and cannot provide a direct template for imitation. Instead, Boncompagni frames the saints in his sermons so that they serve a quadruple rhetorical function with regard to Jews: first, as distant models of virtue for Jews to admire; second, as a more immediate model for the preacher Boncompagni himself to imitate as a convert maker; third, as intercessors who could assist in Boncompagni's holy task; and fourth, as holy figures who have, in front of a public audience of Jews and non-Jews alike, tipped the scales decisively on the side of church and preacher. In this way, he draws his chosen saints into his own proselytizing mission.

At the same time, Boncompagni's sermons on saints also reveal a broader agenda with certain recurring themes. In addition to conversion, he particularly emphasizes miracles, the authority of the church, and sanctity. These are some of the most contested doctrines of the Reformation era—points of key difference not only with Judaism but with Protestant

---

57. BAV Borg. lat. 115, 171r. The Medici reference is in Borg. lat. 122, 151r, and says, "il Conte de Medici che fu Leone 11." Ottaviano later became Pope Leo XI.

58. BAV Borg. lat. 115, 17r.

59. BAV Borg. lat. 122, 151v.

denominations. They would become the defining features of early modern Catholicism.

Boncompagni used saintly miracles to impress his audience and demonstrate the authority of the church. In his sermons on Pius V, these activities are closely linked. In Boncompagni's account of the Battle of Lepanto, Pius V shows the miraculous gift of prophecy in predicting victory. Pius also reveals a supernatural ability to change the course of the wind of Lepanto, making it reverse direction and blow cannon smoke backward over the Turkish armies.[60] Boncompagni shows a taste for statistics as well. More than once, he runs the figures comparing Ottoman and Christian galleys, galleasses, and soldiers to suggest a miraculous victory. Above all, he relies on the huge numbers of witnesses—140—and testimonials from Pius V's canonization trial, as if piling up the statistics would alone be enough to convince the Jews.

This obsession with quantities is borne out in his other saint sermons, especially his discussion of de Sales's canonization trial. Numbers equal proof: "There certainly are reasons to believe the illustrious facts of [de Sales] because they have been proven by more and more trials, . . . by five or six bishops with magistral letters, . . . with supreme papal authority."[61] So does status. Boncompagni stresses the high rank of the examiners and witnesses. He names the organizations and companies that oversaw de Sales's trials, and verified his miracles along with the involvement of kings and queens, including the queen of England as well as the duke and duchess of Savoy, eight other princes, ten dukes, seven duchesses, twenty other nobles, sixty-eight cities, twenty-nine parliaments, twenty-one abbots, forty different religious houses, and sixty-nine monasteries. The authority of so many witnesses and the piling on of numbers are of course meant to affirm the authority of the Roman church. In his insistence, following a century of Protestants criticizing the very construction of sanctity, Boncompagni fits firmly in the early modern revival of hagiography as a polemical response to the Reformation. His efforts in the pulpit coincided with the birth of the Bollandist Society, dedicated to creating a comprehensive, scholarly collection of all the lives of the saints (the *Acta Sanctorum*).[62] In his urge to amass statistics, Boncompagni also

60. BAV Borg. lat. 129, 387v–88r.

61. BAV Borg. lat. 122, 150v–51r.

62. See Euan Cameron, *Enchanted Europe: Superstition, Reason, and Religion, 1250–1750*, 196–210; Carlos M. N. Eire, *Reformations: The Early Modern World, 1450–1650*, 402–3. The Bollandist publication of the *Acta Sanctorum* began in 1643 and completed its original goal of covering the liturgical year in 1940.

embodied the specifically early modern Catholic quest to reconcile church authority with unprovable beliefs, and fill the growing crevices of doubt with more and more insistence as well as ecclesiastical intervention.[63]

For all of his orthodoxy, Boncompagni knew that he was nonetheless courting controversy by preaching about saints to Jews and confronted the problem head-on:

> Someone will say to me that this sermon to the Jews is in vain because they don't believe. I say that if these [sermons] are in vain, then all the sermons of Christians to Jews are vain. "No," you will say, "it is necessary to preach to them with efficacious reason and argumentation." I respond that the mysteries of the faith are above any reason and cannot be proven with reason.[64]

Boncompagni builds this kind of justification into every one of his saint sermons, as if he knew they courted controversy but still believed in their cause. He considers the same point in his sermon on Rose of Lima: "For what purpose is the sermon on Beata Rosa to the Jews? [Because] whoever negates the root negates the trunk, branches, and the whole tree—the Jews negate Christ, and so they negate all the saints of Christ."[65] He goes on, in the first instance, to describe how Rose of Lima helps him personally in his own argumentation by providing a model of humility and simplicity as well as, again, powerful intercession. Boncompagni truly seems to believe that sermons about saints such as Rose offered useful lessons and would convince Jews to embrace Catholicism: "We have no better validation of the true faithful than the proof that the saints come from Christians, and that saints are those who lived at a heroic scale, and that God worked miracles and grace through them."[66] Another saint's life—in this case, Pius V—offers an ideal and convincing topic for a sermon to Jews. Boncompagni describes Pius's saintly life, emphasizing his studies, his campaigns against heresy, and especially his success in converting many heretics and Jews.

Indeed, Boncompagni bends over backward to link Pius V to Rome's Jews. He reviews some of the pope's Jewish policy, mentioning his expulsion of Jews from the Papal States. And he singles out in detail the famous

---

63. On the increasing struggles of the early modern Catholic Church to "make belief the product of authorization rather than experience," see Ethan H. Shagan, *The Birth of Modern Belief: Faith and Judgment from the Middle Ages to the Enlightenment*, 146–65.

64. BAV Borg. lat. 122, 151v.

65. BAV Borg. lat. 790, 82v–83r.

66. BAV Borg. lat. 115, 312r.

baptism of his own ancestor: "He baptized Elia Corcos, principle among the Jews, with three children, with his own hands, in Saint Peter's, gave him the papal surname . . . palaces and many riches, and a king's burial to the one [family member] who died during his lifetime."[67] Apparently Corcos had brought three hundred Jews with him into Christianity. This is statistically impossible, but as we know, Corcos's conversion did herald the baptism of the rest of his family over the following decades.[68] Boncompagni omits any mention of his own Corcos heritage, but he does provide here the only known instance of a conversionary sermon mentioning a contemporary conversion.

Yet Boncompagni's argument for saintly sermons goes well beyond Jews, serving a much broader purpose. In arguing in favor of saints, Boncompagni again suggests a wholly new approach to conversionary preaching: that the purpose of preaching was not to contest Jews on their own ground of Hebrew scripture and rabbinic literature but rather to offer a broad curriculum on how to think and believe like Catholics. He acts on this proposal, turning his sermon on Rose of Lima and one on Pius V into an extended introduction to Catholic concepts of sanctity. These sermons examine the question of whether sanctity is idolatry, address concerns that human witnesses might be flawed, and explain the distinctions between *dulia*—the level of veneration due to saints—and other forms of veneration. These discussions of sanctity depart radically from expectations for sermons to Jews or the laws regulating them.

Sanctity made an ideal launching pad for this new style of sermon because it was also the most distinctive feature of early modern Catholicism and its strongest asset. Sanctity displayed the ideals of Catholic character and behavior in a personal form. It could persuade through individual stories of superhuman heroic virtue and suffering. Sanctity had the weight of authority behind it—seen in Boncompagni's inventories of testimonies and witnesses—as well as the ineffable inspiration of miracles. The belief that true, miraculous holiness could suffuse certain people and objects distinguished Catholicism from Protestant sects; saints were the hallmark of early modern Catholic identity. And sanctity allowed for some self-congratulation about the church's growing reach. For Boncompagni, it was precisely the global nature of Francis Xavier's successes in India and

67. BAV Borg. lat. 115, 312v.

68. Gaetano Moroni, *Dizionario di erudizione storico-ecclesiastica da S. Pietro sino ai nostri giorni*, 26; Marina Caffiero, *Il grande mediatore: Tranquillo Vita Corcos, un rabbino nella Roma dei papi*, 20–21. The surname Boncompagni came from a later pope and later conversions within this family.

the Far East, and the far-reaching fragrance Rose of Lima's sanctity that highlighted Jewish obstinacy:

> The Jew responds, "I have not seen these things [miracles], but I say, "You didn't see the miracles of Moses either." These, the whole world sees, and sees them because Christ and the apostles preach them . . . these are things that Christians recount; if they were not true, they would not recount them, what interest would they have in them?[69]

In such passages, it is precisely the miracles outside Europe that provide the greatest rebuke to Judaism. In Boncompagni's eyes, the growing acceptance of Catholicism—its active, deliberate acceptance across the globe—makes the Jewish refusal to convert seem more willful and misled than ever.

Boncompagni and His Doubts

Perhaps the most compelling revelation among Boncompagni's manuscripts is not the sermon texts themselves but rather the personality revealed by reading his sermons together with the asides, comments, and annotations in their margins. These divulge something of the inner life of a preacher and proselytizer, and the constraints within which he lived. Recent and important studies of early modern conversion focus, rightly, on the experience of the converted and the narratives they created.[70] Instead, Boncompagni gives us an exceptional opportunity to see further into the experience of the converter or convert maker. His asides are not wholly spontaneous—as he writes, he keeps one eye on a public audience—but they are nevertheless valuable. Such notes might even give us one platform for introducing the idea of a "converter narrative." A converter narrative is an especially useful concept for the medieval and early modern period, an age saturated with concerns about conversion. The growing Catholic world, above all, was particularly resonant with narratives by converts themselves, whether contested, mistrusted, or hailed in triumph.

In a converter narrative, we are likely to find similar or parallel patterns to those that scholars have identified for conversion narratives and models of conversion. Conversion narratives in the early modern world were often tightly scripted, molded to reflect external constraints and

69. BAV Borg. lat. 115, 71v.

70. Peter A. Mazur and Abigail Shinn, "Introduction: Conversion Narratives in the Early Modern World"; Elisheva Carlebach, *Divided Souls: Converts from Judaism in Germany, 1500–1750*, 88–123.

conventions. Models of conversion narrative are never universal; readers must always account for local conventions.[71] Within such narratives, individual motives are sometimes discernable, but frequently only by reading against the grain.[72] Finally, no narrative of conversion should seek to separate religious from practical motives or see them as opposites. Practical and spiritual reasons for converting could easily overlap.[73]

These patterns largely hold true for Boncompagni as a converter. His written harvest was always going to conform, for the most part, to the norms of legislation for conversionary sermons, and more generally, to the constraints of the church and institutions that formed him. His personal concerns about conversion are largely determined by the unique local circumstances of the Roman conversionary campaign—from the regular presence of Christian spectators to the novel choice of Francis Xavier as a sermon subject.

Yet the question of what conversion was, why it mattered, and when it counted concerned Boncompagni personally throughout his writing life. As discussed previously, this question led him to consider the act of conversion frequently in his own sermons, compose an extended meditation on why conversionary preaching should continue, and later summarize his conclusions into lists for broader distribution. Within an inflexible system, these compositions show his concern to justify the status quo. At the same time, Boncompagni also considered his own role in that system. His position as conversionary preacher was simultaneously both convenient—as the descendant of converts, possibly predetermined—and full of personal conviction and commitment to his mission.

We find this conviction, above all, in the notes to or about himself that survive in his manuscripts. A typical frontispiece of one manuscript prepared for publication reads, "*Stracciafoglio* [notebook of papers] by f. Gregorio, very ignorant preacher to the Jews."[74] This seems like standard modest frontispiece rhetoric, but its sincerity is borne out by other comments elsewhere in his papers. Boncompagni's level of humility and dedication to his work seems to go beyond the obsequious self-abasement of early modern authors in general. At the same time, Boncompagni's introspective asides

71. Ira Katznelson and Miri Rubin, *Religious Conversion: History, Experience and Meaning*, 10–11.

72. Irene Fosi, *Convertire lo straniero: forestieri e Inquisizione a Roma in età moderna*, 67–73.

73. "Conversions of 'convenience' and conversions of 'conviction' were not altogether dissimilar." Todd M. Endelman, *Leaving the Jewish Fold: Conversion and Radical Assimilation in Modern Jewish History*, 15.

74. BAV Borg. lat. 129, 1r.

and consideration of his own person accord with the Catholic turn toward more systematic meditative practices and consideration of the self.[75] Just as he wished for the help of de Sales and Rose of Lima in his profession, he believed he, too, should operate at a superhuman level:

> I wish that it would happen to me what happened to Saint Patrick, that saint who baptized seven crowned kings, who converted Scotland, England, and Ireland, who revived seventy dead, refuting in one day the obstinacy of those to whom he preached. He traversed the world in his pastorate, and pulled a young girl out from the fires of hell, and converted all those countries, and made a great many of those who heard him into saints [?] [thanks to] the fear of that fire.[76]

These criticisms lasted his whole life, but they also reveal a level of reflection that readers rarely find in early modern preaching literature. As he entered old age, he thought back over the career that had shaped his life, writing on the spare end of a page listing biblical verses for a sermon (figure 6.1):

> This sermon was the first done by me, Gregorio. It is worth nothing; it was pure practice. The Jews negated it with total ease [although] they only knew the basics of the gospel, which is negated by the Jews. I didn't [revoke] it lest my ignorance show. It was on the 24th of June 1649. Nobody should take up preaching to Jews who is not a good theologian, and does not know the canons of the old testament, and does not know how to read without reading Rabbot, Gemara, [Isaiah], Yolcut. It is necessary to have R. Abravanel on the prophets and confute him. Today, when I have preached to the Jews forty years already, it being 1689, I say, that if I had to begin preaching again, I would not wish to do any other office than to preach to Jews, not to Christians, only to Jews, to preach in the order put by holy scripture with commentaries.[77]

With this confession, Boncompagni suggests that a lifetime of doubt was assuaged, and even then only partially, by a late realization of his own

75. For a detailed exploration, see Moshe Sluhovsky, *Becoming a New Self: Practices of Belief in Early Modern Catholicism*.

76. BAV Borg. lat. 506, 244v.

77. BAV Borg. lat. 505, 184r. The first group of texts listed here refers to, probably, the volumes of Midrash that gloss the Pentateuch along with the five Megillot (scrolls) of Song of Songs, Esther, Ruth, Lamentations, and Ecclesiastes, known collectively as Midrash Rabbah or Midrash Rabbot; the Bablylonian Talmud; the Jerusalem Talmud; and the biblical commentary known as the Yalkut Shimoni.

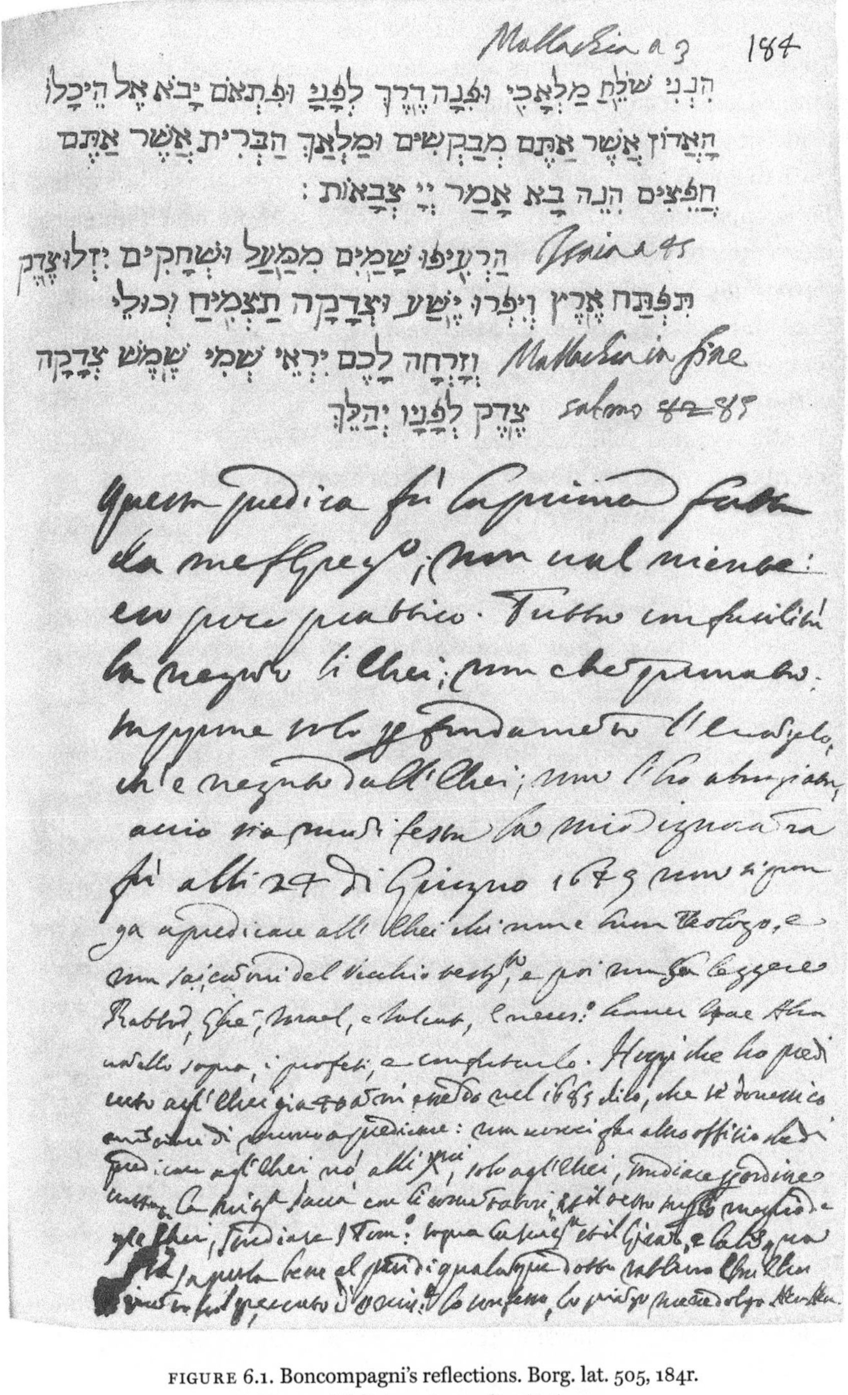
Mallachia a 3 184

הִנְנִי שֹׁלֵחַ מַלְאָכִי וּפִנָּה דֶרֶךְ לְפָנָי וּפִתְאֹם יָבֹא אֶל הֵיכָלוֹ הָאָדוֹן אֲשֶׁר אַתֶּם מְבַקְשִׁים וּמַלְאַךְ הַבְּרִית אֲשֶׁר אַתֶּם חֲפֵצִים הִנֵּה בָא אָמַר יְיָ צְבָאוֹת׃

Isaia a 45 הַרְעִיפוּ שָׁמַיִם מִמַּעַל וּשְׁחָקִים יִזְּלוּ צֶדֶק תִּפְתַּח אֶרֶץ וְיִפְרוּ יֶשַׁע וּצְדָקָה תַצְמִיחַ וְכוּלֵי

Mallachia in fine וְזָרְחָה לָכֶם יִרְאֵי שְׁמִי שֶׁמֶשׁ צְדָקָה

salmo ~~84~~ 85 צֶדֶק לְפָנָיו יְהַלֵּךְ

FIGURE 6.1. Boncompagni's reflections. Borg. lat. 505, 184r.
© 2021 Biblioteca Apostolica Vaticana.

expertise and skill. Throughout his life, he placed high expectations on conversionary preaching and considered himself deficient in comparison. To tell his collected volumes apart, he sometimes named them for different Dominican proselytizing saints of the era and judged himself in contrast to them. One volume is named for Luis Beltrán, known for his work in South America. Beltrán was canonized in 1671, the same year that Boncompagni seems to have begun compiling the volume, although the pages apparently lasted longer than he expected. The cover page reads "*Stracciafoglio* [collection of papers] by the miserable sinner Fra Gregorio Boncompagni degli Scarinci. May everyone pray for his sinning soul so that God may forgive the errors committed in the sermons given by him to the Jews of Rome from 1649 until 1671. 1672. 1673. 1674. 1675. 1676. 1678."[78] A similar volume is named for Vincent Ferrer. In that instance, his inscription, which counts as some of his last written words—reads:

> This book is a *stracciafoglio* titled "Saint Vincent Ferrer Who Converted Twenty-Nine Thousand Jews." And I . . . who up to now have preached to them I believe forty years, I doubt that I have ever converted even one, because even if many were baptized in my time, I don't believe that any one of them converted because of my sermons, because of my very great ignorance, my negligence, and for my enormous malice, because I preached with words, and not with good and holy words. *Misere mei.*[79]

By his own standards, then, Boncompagni seems to have considered himself a disappointment. Although he made strenuous efforts to pitch his preaching to multiple audiences, argued repeatedly on behalf of those audiences, and insisted that preaching to Jews explicitly strengthened the faith of Christian spectators, none of these factors was a marker of success. Neither did he seek lasting fame through frequent publication. He compared himself only with extraordinary saints and pinned his hopes on the ultimately unknowable hearts of his Jewish listeners. By those measures, he was doomed to fail.

Boncompagni remained, all of his life, an exemplary and largely conventional preacher. Most of his sermons hewed closely to tradition, refuting Jewish interpretations of scripture with dogged Catholic rebuttals. In this and many other ways, he resembled his Dominican predecessors in the pulpit. And they, too, generally offered some variation in their sermon topics and styles. It is possible that the unusually large range of topics in

78. BAV Borg. lat. 115, 1r.
79. BAV Borg. lat. 114, 1r.

his sermons reflects only the difference between his own works that survive in manuscript and the work of other preachers that were printed. But even so, the variety of unexpected themes in Boncompagni's sermon far exceeds the norms for conversionary sermons. The breadth of his reach, insistence on discussing recent events (such as canonizations), repeated attention to certain topics, and visible insecurity all suggest a sense of personal urgency. Other preachers with less of a surviving paper trail may have felt this too, but in Boncompagni it is unmistakable. He sought avidly both to defend his own position as preacher and to champion his own Catholic confession.

Boncompagni's little-known manuscript sermons demonstrate how fully Jews and Judaism, both real and imaginary, played a central role in the construction of early modern Catholicism. Jews served, above all, as interlocutors; the sermons are built around their supposed objections and concerns: "The Jew says . . . and I respond." As we have seen, this rhetorical style relies on hypothetical, imaginary Jews—a foil that allowed Boncompagni to talk about whatever he wished. Judaism, of course, had always served this purpose in the formation of Catholic theology. And the Catholic Church had extensive experience more generally in promoting its own brand of Christianity against its enemies, and defining itself against various alternative beliefs and institutions by branding them heretical.[80] Boncompagni's sermons show how much these outsiders were in fact inside, under the skin, shaping the content and style of early modern expressions of Catholic identity.

But Boncompagni's sermons were also populated by real Jewish people. Jewish objection to a sermon on Pius V led Boncompagni to dig in his heels and create more detailed, more dogmatic sermons on the beatified pope, and lay out his justification for doing so. Whether real or imagined, the voices of the other enabled Boncompagni, a superlative mainstream ambassador for Catholic orthodoxy, to articulate and explicitly develop Catholic positions. The encounter—again, both real and imagined—between Boncompagni and his audience affected his composition of these sermons, their delivery, and his choices about the Catholicism he wanted to portray and indeed sell. Their presence applied explicitly, and perhaps most powerfully, to new and contested elements of Catholicism: its world reach and new saints. In these sermons, not only are the

---

80. For this process more generally, see Peter Biller, "Christians and Heretics"; John H. Arnold, *Inquisition and Power: Catharism and the Confessing Subject in Medieval Languedoc*.

newest elements of Catholicism considered relevant to its thinking about Jews, but Jews become indispensable to the church's ways of thinking about and defining itself.[81]

Boncompagni's approach to "imaginary others" makes most sense if we see preaching to Jews as a broadly ambitious enterprise, aiming far beyond its supposedly limited audience, even while it eschewed real intellectual engagement with other faiths. Boncompagni's career accompanied a seventeenth-century revival in public, theatrical religious disputations held in other religiously fraught parts of the globe.[82] It may equally reflect the returning popularity of medieval polemic and pseudoconversionary polemical dialogue, especially among Catholic mendicants and missionaries.[83] Boncompagni's sermons are best understood primarily as an opportunity for performing and justifying Catholicism on a public stage, celebrating its triumphalism before a variety of audiences in a post-Reformation, early modern world. His writings make it clear just how much that celebration was closely, definitively shaped both by Judaism and other religions outside Catholicism.

81. For a parallel example of Catholic clergy who assumed continuity between converting local Jews and engaging with other religions on a global stage, see Celeste McNamara, *The Bishop's Burden: Reforming the Catholic Church in Early Modern Italy*, 213–15.

82. David Robinson, "Religious Disputations as Theatre: Staging Religious Difference in France after the Wars of Religion," 32–37; Gary K. Waite, *Jews and Muslims in Seventeenth-Century Discourse: From Religious Enemies to Allies and Friends*.

83. Daniel, *Islam and the West*, 286–88; Bernard Heyberger, "Polemic Dialogues between Christians and Muslims in the Seventeenth Century." For another example, see Filippo Guadagnoli, *Apologia pro christiana religione*.

CHAPTER SEVEN

Jewish Responses

HE STANDS WITH HIS HAT in his hand, expression wary, eyes watch-
ful. Even in an unflattering sketch, there is no mistaking the gravity of his
expression. He seems, with his slightly open mouth and proffered hat, to
be asking for something. And indeed he was. This is Rabbi Tranquillo Vita
(Ḥezekiah Chaim Manoaḥ) Corcos (1660–1730), the greatest defender of
Roman Jewry in its history, as captured in 1723 by the great caricaturist
Pier Leone Ghezzi (figure 7.1).[1] Corcos's widespread advocacy on behalf
of Roman Jews is well known; indeed, he had such standing that Jews
across Italy sought him out to advocate for them. A searing denunciation
of the infamous polemical preacher Paolo Sebastiano Medici gave Corcos
a first foray into a lifetime of careful diplomacy with Catholic institutions
in Rome. Other concerns followed. Corcos's many erudite, meticulously
argued letters and treatises to the Holy Office or Vicariate of Rome took
on topics grave or practical—rent rates in the ghetto, the sale of meat,
blood libels, and the Jewish badge—lending new stature and focus to
Jewish interaction with Catholic authorities. Corcos's treatise against Paolo
Sebastiano Medici also begat further written objections to other conversionary preachers and practices surrounding conversionary sermons.[2] On the
surface, such protests may appear to be private confrontations between

---

1. BAV Ott. lat. 3114, 19r. On Ghezzi, see Edward J. Olszewski, "The New World of
Pier Leone Ghezzi"; Maria Cristina Dorati da Empoli, *Pier Leone Ghezzi: un protagonista del Settecento romano*, 195. See also Attilio Milano, *Il ghetto di Roma; illustrazioni
storiche*, fig. 83. For Corcos's appearance, with an argument that Ghezzi's sketch represents the emergence of some antisemitic visual tropes, see Asher Salah, "Rabbinical
Dress in Italy.".

2. Marina Caffiero, *Legami Pericolosi: Ebrei e cristiani tra eresia, libri proibiti e
stregoneria*; Marina Caffiero, "Il rabbino, il convertito e la superstizione ebraica. La

FIGURE 7.1. Rabbi Tranquillo Corcos. Ott. lat. 3114, 19r.
© 2021 Biblioteca Apostolica Vaticana.

two parties: a conversionary preacher and an objecting rabbi. But in practice, these two figures represent the public faces of larger networks: the Roman Jewish community that Corcos represented and the many Catholic institutions that supported conversionary preachers.

This chapter looks beyond Catholic and institutional sources to examine the Jewish response to conversionary preaching. By the late seventeenth century, Jews made formal protests to objectionable content in sermons, publishing letters and treatises advocating for better treatment, primarily through Corcos. Preachers, in turn, sometimes responded to Jewish protests with letters of their own. But these treatises against conversionary preaching also built on a long-standing, continuous, and hitherto-unknown tradition of popular resistance. Roman Jews waged a multipronged battle against the Saturday sermons, with weapons apposite to all sectors of their society. They sought to signal their opposition to conversionary preaching and change whatever elements of it they could. Their tactics included general antagonism and passive resistance, lobbies against aspects of preaching legislation, and systematic refutations of sermons, many unknown until now. These efforts met with some success and had lasting influence. Yet such resistance to sermons was fraught with danger. Sermons took place against a backdrop of anti-Jewish tension that could easily and predictably ripen into violence. I place these interludes against the backdrop of ongoing strain and frequent, sometimes staged acts of violence between Christians and Jews in Rome. The sight of Jewish people grouped in public for a conversionary sermon seemed to recall other tense atmospheres, such as Vacant Sees and funerals. At times, sermons themselves provoked further violence and ritualized mockery, blurring the distinction between theological objections to Judaism and social objections to Jews as neighbors. Even in Italy, which was more abstract and cerebral in its anti-Judaism than other parts of Europe, words and deeds did not prove far apart.

---

polemica a distanza fra Tranquillo Vita Corcos e Paolo Sebastiano Medici"; Kenneth R. Stow, "The Jewish Dog and 'Shehitah,'" esp. 189–92. On Corcos's negotiations regarding the Jewish badge, see Massimo Moretti, "'Glauci Coloris': Gli Ebrei nell'iconografia sacra di età moderna," 30–32; Marina Caffiero, *Il grande mediatore: Tranquillo Vita Corcos, un rabbino nella Roma dei papi*.

Corcos's Written Objections to Conversionary Preachers

Corcos wrote three treatises objecting to specific conversionary preachers and their practices. Two of these preachers were converts from Judaism—softer targets perhaps, and more deeply resented—but all three caused offense in their sermons. The earliest treatise was the one that confronted Medici. Medici, who was born in Livorno in 1671, converted from Judaism at sixteen. As a Catholic, he went on to become a conversionary preacher throughout Tuscany. He was known for his vitriol, even during his young adulthood. The Jews of Borgo San Sepolcro first objected to his harsh language, and in 1697, Corcos took up the cause with an erudite thirty-page printed pamphlet addressed to the Holy Office of the Inquisition.[3] A note among Pastrizio's papers suggests that Medici converted because he failed to become a rabbi and was later excluded from the Dominican Order for his "unpleasant qualities" before embarking on speaking nonsense in his sermons.[4]

Corcos's treatise against Medici sets out for the first time the enduring themes he would employ in all of his future objections to conversionary preachers. It seeks to placate and flatter Christian authority figures while insisting on better behavior from their representatives. Corcos's chief argument in this case, as in the later ones, concerns the language of the sermon. In his treatise against Medici, he objects that Medici has departed from his brief—the norms and rules that regulated the content of conversionary sermons. Shared communal standards allow for long-standing peaceful relations as well as respect between Jews and Catholics, and, he says, even enable Jews to agree to attend conversionary sermons: "We don't refuse to go to sermons in these times."[5] Corcos maintains that Medici, in contrast, has abandoned these norms: where conversionary sermons are meant to stick to theology and exegesis, Medici has begun to preach instead about Jewish rituals and character. According to Corcos, Medici has deliberately

---

3. Tranquillo Vita Corcos, *Memoriale dell'Ebrei contro le prediche di P. Sebastiano Medici Ebreo convertito*, bound in ASVR Atti della segreteria del tribunale del cardinale vicario, tom. 5. For Medici, see Fausto Parente, "Il confronto ideologico tra l'ebraismo e la chiesa in Italia," 365–69; the entry on Medici in the DBI; Caffiero, "Il rabbino, il convertito e la superstizione ebraica"; Elliott S. Horowitz, "The Eve of the Circumcision: A Chapter in the History of Jewish Nightlife."

4. BAV Borg. lat. 192, 418r.

5. "Onde nessuno di noi repugna ne i tempi proprij l'intervenire alle Prediche nelle loro Chiese." Corcos, *Memoriale dell'Ebrei contro le prediche di P. Sebastiano Medici Ebreo convertito*, 445r, A-r.

misinterpreted Jewish law and practice in the most insulting way possible in order, asserts Corcos, "to make us incompatible" with Catholics.[6] Decades after Medici's death, Roman Jews would still recall his "insufferable pride," and his willingness to inveigh against and discredit them in his sermons and discourses.[7]

Corcos's response targets divisions within Christendom, and emphasizes similarities between Christians and Jews. It argues that Medici should not judge a whole population by the mistakes or extremes of one person, "just as you should not call Christians generally impious just because Luther and Calvin were."[8] Corcos tries to repair the damage Medici has wrought by dwelling on ritual similarities between Jews and Catholics, such as confession and the Ten Commandments, and suggesting that the only major division between the two groups is the question of whether or not the Messiah has already come.

This approach cuts to the heart of the problem of forced preaching: whether conversion requires sympathy between preacher and audience. Corcos contends that Medici's violent rhetoric is counterproductive. Where he was meant to persuade Jews toward Catholicism, he instead breeds hatred and resentment. "He shows himself little devoted to the conversion of the Jews, making use of a style continually rejected by the Holy Office," asserts Corcos. "If you want to smooth the way toward persuading the listener of your claim, it is necessary to make the listener feel kindly toward you, so that he may approve your mode of speaking, rather than to aggravate our people with punctures and improprieties. . . . This is instead an embitterment of our souls that renders us further away [*alieni*] from the Christian people." Insults do not work; they do not dispose the audience to agree with the preacher.[9]

To Corcos, violent speech generates violent action. He accuses Medici's preaching of causing violence against Jews in Bologna, Florence, and elsewhere, "where this said preacher not only in the pulpit but also in private

---

6. Corcos, *Memoriale dell'Ebrei contro le prediche di P. Sebastiano Medici Ebreo convertito*, A3r.

7. ASCER Inventario Fondo università degli ebrei, 3 inf. 1, 91r.

8. "Ne per esser stati empij Lutero e Calvino, si devono dire generalmente empij li Christiani. Corcos, *Memoriale dell'Ebrei contro le prediche di P. Sebastiano Medici Ebreo convertito*, A3v/6.

9. Corcos, *Memoriale dell'Ebrei contro le prediche di P. Sebastiano Medici Ebreo convertito*, P.A-v. On the term *natione*, which I have translated here as "people" and which refers to distinct ethnoreligious groups in early modern Italy, see especially Molnár, Antal, Giovanni Pizzorusso, and Matteo Sanfilippo, *Chiese e Nationes a Roma: dalla Scandinavia ai Balcani: Secoli XV–XVIII*.

discourse goes about lacerating the Jews, and is deaf to any admonition and rebuke," even from high-ranking Catholic clerics in those places.[10] This, too, is an argument that would recur in his other treatises and shows Corcos taking responsibility for Jews outside Rome.

Claims against Medici were especially acute in 1697 because Medici was about to publish a book on Jewish rites—a rare Italian foray into this prurient genre. Corcos appealed to the inquisitor to prevent its publication. The consequences were mixed.[11] On the one hand, Medici ceased preaching, and did not publish the book on rites until after Corcos died, but on the other hand, he did not stay silent. He went on to become a professor of scripture and a prolific author of anti-Jewish polemic. Medici's works included a detailed catalog of illustrious neophytes, with which he intended to demonstrate how learned and wise were the Jews who had chosen Christianity. This, and the eventual guide to rites and rituals, went on to provide popular fodder for anti-Jewish sentiment both in Italy and elsewhere in Europe for centuries. This is a case where Corcos lost the war but proved, critically, that battles could be won; the publication of Medici's *Rites and Customs of the Jews* was delayed for forty years, until after Corcos's death.[12] And although Medici never actually preached in Rome (though he did preach in the papal city of Ancona), his story shows how the Roman community, and specifically Corcos, became the voice of protest for Jewish communities throughout Italy.

Corcos's experience with Medici would stand him in good stead when a later preacher also proved offensive, notably in another public letter. The preacher this time was Luigi Pisani, the former rabbi (possibly from Aleppo) who preached vitriolic conversionary sermons in Rome.[13] This

---

10. Corcos, *Memoriale dell'Ebrei contro le prediche di P. Sebastiano Medici Ebreo convertito*, bound in ASVR Atti dellasegreteria del tribunale del cardinale vicario, tom. 5, A14v/29.

11. For discussions of this specific treatise in the context of the blood libel and witchcraft, see Marina Caffiero, *Battesimi forzati: Storie di ebrei, cristiani e convertiti nella Roma dei papi*, 40–42; Caffiero, *Legami pericolosi*, 109–11. For this treatise in other contexts, see Horowitz, "The Eve of the Circumcision." For links between witchcraft and the blood libel generally, see R. Po-Chia Hsia, *The Myth of Ritual Murder: Jews and Magic in Reformation Germany*; Tamar Herzig, *Christ Transformed into a Virgin Woman: Lucia Brocadelli, Heinrich Institoris, and the Defense of the Faith*. On Medici and the literature of Jewish ritual, see Magda Teter, *Blood Libel: On the Trail of an Antisemitic Myth*, 182, 309–10.

12. *Riti e costumi degli ebrei* was published in 1736 and went through seventeen editions in the next sixty-five years.

13. Milano, *Il ghetto di Roma*, 272. For this treatise, see also Caffiero, *Battesimi forzati*, 44, 68.

was a less public case, never published, and conducted in manuscript. As before, Corcos's treatise argues that Pisani has departed from his brief by launching personal insults and concentrating on ritual, not theology. And as before, it plays to Christian interests; Pisani has undermined his own goal of conversion, says Corcos, by discussing ritual and thereby making private ritual matters public: "he is so far from stimulating conversion that he rather serves the opposite purpose."[14] Corcos reminds his readers, again, that the preacher's harsh sermons have led to violence in Bologna.[15] To some extent, the same arguments held good in every case. But it is Corcos's departures from his proven formula in his letter to Pisani that suggest that tensions were rising in the preaching environment.

In the treatise to Pisani, Corcos includes new arguments emphasizing the experience of sermon going and appealing to Catholic sympathies. Corcos argues, first, that Pisani is especially harmful because he explicitly invites the public to attend sermons to Jews—"not just many religious and nobles, but even ordinary people." Because these audiences know little about Judaism and then hear Pisani's excoriations without proper context, they can only conclude the worst about Jews.[16] This, maintains Corcos, makes sermons into even more unpleasant an ordeal than they were before. He reviews Pisani's sermon of the previous Saturday, when the preacher had feigned ignorance of rabbinic tradition in order to jump straight into a diatribe about circumcision and ritual bathing; the presence of Christians for this discussion particularly rankled Corcos.[17]

Second, Corcos compares Pisani to other preachers, sometimes by name, pointing out that the Jews listen civilly to the official predicatore degli ebrei, only to be attacked with insults by the convert Pisani. "After we have listened to the Dominican . . . we are obligated to stay to hear a sermon by a neophyte, who lapsing from Catholic formulas and customs, only exerts himself to invent calumnies against Judaism."[18] Such reasoning would appeal to a Catholic sense of superiority over Judaism and

---

14. "È tanto lontano dallo stimolare alla conversione, che più tosto può servire di contrario motivo." ASVR Atti della segreteria del tribunale del cardinale vicario, tom. 5, 499r. This treatise appears to date from the early eighteenth century.

15. ASVR Atti della segreteria del tribunale del cardinale vicario, tom. 5, 499v.

16. ASVR Atti della segreteria del tribunale del cardinale vicario, tom. 5, 496r.

17. On Corcos's related attempts to reform Jewish circumcision festivities, and Christians commenting on circumsicion, see Horowitz, "The Eve of the Circumcision," 54–56; Yaakov Deutsch, *Judaism in Christian Eyes: Ethnographic Descriptions of Jews and Judaism in Early Modern Europe*, 123–74.

18. ASVR Atti della segreteria del tribunale del cardinale vicario, tom. 5, 496r.

suggest that converts exploited their claims to authenticity. But Corcos's comparisons are also direct and personal:

> [Pisani's] method is totally opposite to that taken by the preacher Mascelli [Girolamo Mascella], who in addition to preaching with the holy text, with inexpressible charity and love admonishes us about morals, but without making use of terms or reproaches that could offend the modesty of the listeners, rather that the listeners are more often obliged to thank him.

Finally, Corcos compares Judaism favorably to Islam. Pisani had apparently preached that Islam is more holy than Judaism, and the Koran more sacred than the law observed by Jews. Corcos responds that "this hurts the ears not only of Jews but [also] . . . whoever else hears it, since one could never suppose that the strict zeal of [the pope] for the Holy Inquisition would tolerate, in the heart of the church, a sect or religion worse than Islam, so despised by Christians."[19] He goes on to list all the ways Judaism is superior to Islam. In addition to genuine anti-Muslim sentiment, these approaches indicate a desperation on Corcos's part, a sense of the risk and precariousness that he felt on behalf of his community. They show, too, what kinds of objections he considered acceptable to the Vicariate.

We have no direct record of the consequences, but we do know, as discussed in chapter 3, that Pisani continued to struggle for security in his new faith. In 1704, he complained about his debts and a legal action against him; by 1707, he was writing IOUs to well-established professors in the world of Hebrew scholarship.[20]

Corcos was named chief rabbi of Rome in 1702, but by the time he attained that title he had, as we have seen, an extensive history of public advocacy on behalf of Jews in Rome, the Papal States, and sometimes across all of Italy. Shortly after his appointment in 1705, he came to the defense of a group of Jewish men at a market fair in Viterbo when they were accused of an attempted blood libel. The treatises Corcos composed in that case drew on the approach and phrasing he had used earlier against Medici and Pisani. He cited church fathers, rabbinic literature, and historical precedent. He even reused his argument about overlooking disagreements between Luther and Calvin. The first version of Corcos's treatise was sent to Placido Eustachio Ghezzi, sometime papal master of

---

19. This and the previous quotation at ASVR Atti della segreteria del tribunale del cardinale vicario, tom. 5, 497v.

20. ASPF, Misc. Gen. XIII, 89r; BAV Borg. lat. 746, 270r.

ceremonies, official at the council that handled conflicts in courts of the Papal States, and brother of the caricaturist who sketched Corcos. The brothers shared a house, and that presumably explains the origins of Corcos's portrait.[21] The second version was printed by the papal print office, its fair use of Hebrew sources approved by Giovanni Pastrizio himself. Its erudition and rhetoric seem to have been admired across religions. Corcos's treatises in this case contributed to the exoneration of the accused Viterbo defendants. Over the long term, they formed the bedrock of future blood libel defense cases for decades.[22] His reputation as a skilled representative and advocate for Jews in troubled interreligious waters was secure. Copies of his petitions were saved by both the università and curial officials for future use.[23]

When the official position of predicatore degli ebrei was given to Lorenzo Virgulti in 1720, Corcos's long experience confronting conversionary preachers and his more recent dealings with blood libel hate speech were called to the test together. Virgulti seems to have come down on the side of believing blood libel accusations. When he preached about them in a sermon to Jews, Corcos took him on. This time, Corcos's objections prompted a detailed written response from the preacher himself. In a lengthy testimonial, preserved in a fair copy manuscript in an elegant hand, Virgulti refuted Corcos's claim that the preacher had overreached in his sermon of the previous Saturday.[24] Virgulti's nonapologetic apology attempts to dismantle Corcos's arguments.

Virgulti's response to Corcos confirms that Catholic preachers, like Jews, could believe that sermons were potentially violent, rhetorically

21. On the Viterbo incident and Placido Eustachio Ghezzi, see Teter, *Blood Libel*, 282. On his brother, see Dorati da Empoli, *Pier Leone Ghezzi*, 73.

22. Tranquillo Vita Corcos, *Summarium. Alla sagra Consulta illus e Reve Monsi Ghezzi ponente per l'università di Roma*; Tranquillo Vita Corcos, *Memoriale Additionale ad altro dato li 26 Settembre 1705*. Both of these are preserved in ACDF St St BB 3 f. They are also held in ASCER 1 Ug 2, Fasciocolo/Faldone 9, Segnatura; ASCER 1 Ug 2, Fasciocolo/Faldone 4, Segnatura. See also Teter, *Blood Libel*, 289–99, 326, 339–43; Caffiero, *Il grande mediatore*, 69–80.

23. For one example, see Teter, *Blood Libel*, 292–93.

24. ASVR Atti della segreteria del tribunale del cardinal vicario, tom. 5, 561r–66r. Republished in Domenico Rocciolo, "Documenti sui catecumeni e neofiti a Roma nel Seicento e Settecento." For Virgulti, see Alberto Zucchi, "Rome domenicana: note storiche: Predicatori domenicani degli ebrei nel sec. XVIII," 122; Parente, "Il confronto ideologico tra l'ebraismo e la Chiesa in Italia," 362–64; Domenico Rocciolo, "Catecumeni e neofiti a Roma tra '500 e '800: provenienza, condizioni sociali e 'padrini' illustri"; Caffiero, *Legami pericolosi*, 32–33 passim; Kenneth R. Stow, *Anna and Tranquillo: Catholic Anxiety and Jewish Protest in the Age of Revolutions*; 175–80. For the Corcos-Virgulti exchanges in the context of the revival of the blood libel, see Caffiero, *Il grande mediatore*, 69–84. Caffiero dates this letter to 1721.

constricted, and public in a hostile way. Virgulti admits that he has "gone over the limits prescribed for conversionary preachers by Gregory XIII because he has not preached with charity and moderation."[25] Virgulti defends himself by saying that preaching with "charity and moderation," as recommended in the original papal legislation on conversionary sermons, actually means pointing out all the many errors, lies, false interpretations of scripture, and depravities of the Jews. He reviews at length nearly the entire list of long-standing smears against Jews, reviving the sorts of slanders Corcos had worked so hard to discredit: the poisoning of wells, the case of Simon of Trent, and other blood libels. Virgulti then insists that Jews are wrong to object when these subjects come up in a public sermon. Why? Because, contends Virgulti, nothing bad will happen to them when he mentions these topics; the sermons are empty:

> Very vain is the specious claim they object to, that with such things the populace is incited against them. . . . What populace can be incited if so few are the Christians who come to the sermons, and all of them are clerics, or [members of] religious [orders], or literate persons, or at least moderate persons, except for a few passersby?[26]

These claims are more complex than Virgulti makes them sound. Read closely, they suggest, first, that his sermon topics might legitimately provoke violence, were it not for the high status and low numbers of the Christian audience. Indeed, violence frequently accompanied conversionary sermons, despite his assertions to the contrary. His words also remind us just how public conversionary sermons remained, even into the eighteenth century. In alleging that few Christians attend sermons, Virgulti actually names five separate categories of recurrent spectators. Finally, his defensive stance shows us the power of Jewish resistance. By objecting to Virgulti's excessive prose, Corcos has forced Virgulti to acknowledge the existence of a limit in the first place. Corcos's objections have put Virgulti on his back foot. He would hit back only later in his 1728 treatise, *The Jewish Catecumen,* with its further insinuations of blood libels and pessimistic take on the successes of Jewish converts.[27]

Corcos also advocated against the *bacchetta,* the baton used to keep discipline, which as we have seen, appeared frequently in contemporary

25. ASVR Atti della segreteria del tribunale del cardinale vicario, tom. 5, fol. 561r.
26. ASVR Atti della segreteria del tribunale del cardinale vicario, tom. 5, fol. 564r.
27. Lorenzo Virgulti, *L'ebreo catecumeno instruito ne' principali misteri della santa fede Cristiana . . . opera utile anche a i Cristiani, che desiderano di sapere i fondamenti della loro Fede.* See also Stow, *Anna and Tranquillo,* 175–80; Caffiero, *Il grande mediatore,* 80–81.

accounts, with detailed descriptions of its use. Corcos's missive, which remains in manuscript in the ASCER archives, lays out his objections to the bacchetta in the strongest possible terms, his arguments again calculated to appeal to Catholic authorities:

> The custom was introduced many years ago that policemen walk through the oratory with sticks in their hands, as if they had to tame irrational animals with little of the decorum of Catholic piety, almost as if they wanted to force the Jews to believe using the stick . . . but now the policemen have been bold enough to move on from threats to hard knocks [*fiere percossi*], especially to beating up women without any cause, or at least without warning. . . . And if people thought that the preacher must get involved in provoking/poking the listeners and making them cry, and not in delighting them, Saint Augustine teaches the opposite, saying that delight bears the most fruit.[28]

Corcos's skill here lies not only in his remarkable familiarity with Christian sources, such as Augustine, but also in his willingness to use them to take an apparently Christian position and wield it against his interlocutors. Citing popes and church fathers, he insists that the bacchetta is a much less persuasive tool of conversion than blandishment would be. Perhaps unsurprisingly for a learned and strategic rabbinic leader, he draws a sharp parallel with the biblical story of Moses, instructed by God to get water from a stone and harshly punished for using force instead of speech. "God wanted to teach Moses that it takes the tongue, not the stick. And because [Moses] wanted to do with blows what should be done with words, God punished him . . . for not understanding the way a superior must treat a subject."[29] Furthermore, Corcos links the use of the bacchetta to the subject of Christians attending conversionary sermons—clearly a perennial course of concern throughout the early modern period. He argues that the presence of Christians at sermons could only worsen the experience for Jewish listeners and praises Innocent XI for having recently restricted it. As proof, he offers the example of a recent special conversionary sermon, held in a different church, with neither a baton nor a Christian audience, pointing out that without these pressures, Jewish behavior was exemplary.[30]

A written, erudite response such as this letter surely held more weight and might bode greater success than would angry objections hastily

28. ASCER 1 Ue 2, inf. 2 fascicolo 8, 1v–2v.
29. ASCER 1 Ue 2, inf. 2 fascicolo 8, 4r–v.
30. ASCER 1 Ue 2, inf. 2 fascicolo 8, 4v–5r.

shouted during a sermon. Did Corcos's treatise land on sympathetic ears? A letter on a scrap of paper in the Vicariate archives suggests not. The treatise found its way to Marcantonio Boldetti, then the deputy in charge of discipline for Jews. It notes that Corcos had turned for help to a bishop within the Holy Office, who had then proposed switching the bacchetta to a fine. But Catholic opinion was not unanimous; Boldetti disagreed with the bishop-inquisitor. In a few brief lines dated 1718, the paper notes that Boldetti gave the matter "mature reflection," but nonetheless reported to his superiors that the baton should be used the next day at the sermon "as usual, despite the fact that Tranquillo has come to give this discourse."[31] Apparently, the beatings really would continue until morale improved, as the line has it.

Corcos's many treatises, and even Virgulti's by contrast, helped to define the norms of anti-Jewish polemic that flourished in sixteenth- and seventeenth-century Italy. Corcos's objections to these three preachers clarified the limits of tolerable conversionary speech by showing where the preachers had departed from the norms of acceptable discourse. Take, for example, the intemperate Melchior Palontrotti, a generation older than Corcos.[32] The titles of his treatises point to an enthusiastic hatred of Judaism: *A Collection of Arguments Drawn from Scripture and the Ancient Rabbinic Traditions That Clearly Prove the Dogmas of the Christian Religion against the Jewish One*; *The Christian's Debate with the Jew That Clearly Proves against the Jew That the Temporal Reduction He Waits for Was Fulfilled in the Liberation of Babylon*; *Lashing against the Obstinacy and Stubbornness of the Ignorant Jews*; *Collection of Many Errors and Chimera Dreamed Up by the Talmudists on the Exegesis of the Bible, and Referring Particularly to R. Salomone (Rashi), Where We See the Great Blindness into Which Judaism Has Fallen for Not Having Accepted the True Light of Jesus Christ Our Lord, True God of Israel*; and others as well.[33]

31. ASVR Atti della segreteria del tribunale del cardinale vicario, tom. 5, fol. 551r. Despite the presentation-ready copy in ASCER, these words suggest that Corcos may have delivered his petition orally.

32. On Palontrotti, see Benjamin Ravid, "'Contra Judaeos' in Seventeenth-Century Italy: Two Responses to the 'Discorso' of Simone Luzzatto by Melchiore Palontrotti and Giulio Morosini"; Giulio Busi, "La Breve raccolta (Venezia, 1649) del polemista antigiudaico Melchiorre Palontrotti."

33. Melchiorre Palontrotti, *Breue raccolta d'argomenti, cauati dalla sac. Scrit. & dall'antiche tradittioni di rabbini, con le quali chiaramente si prouano i dogmi della religion christiana contra l'hebraica perfidia*; Melchiorre Palontrotti, *Disputa del christiano con l'ebreo di Melchior Palontrotti. Ad istanza di Pietro Pauolo Romaldi romano. Doue si proua chiaramente contra l'ebreo, che la riduttione temporale, che aspetta fù adempita nella liberatione di Babilonia*; Melchiorre Palontrotti, *Sferza contro l'ostinatione, et peruicacia*

These sorts of treatises conform on a surface level to standard norms for Jewish polemic. As discussed in earlier chapters, they construct mostly theological arguments and list points of doctrine. Their purpose is to argue either against Judaism as a whole or against rabbinic Judaism in favor of the biblical Israelites. They largely avoid discussion of rituals, money, or blood libel, and do not dwell on Jews as Christ killers. Instead, like most surviving conversionary sermons, they take up cerebral, theological subjects, such as the Trinity, the coming of the Messiah, the status of the Virgin Mary, and similar topics, often with imagined rabbinical refutations. Yet even so, these works are not benign. Palontrotti's content might be orthodox, but his tone is venomously antagonistic throughout. As his titles indicate, his approach might be called persuasion through contempt. His treatises and those of surviving conversionary preachers suggest that the baseline for pulpit rhetoric was already fairly low, not neutral. For Corcos to object that some rhetoric was still unacceptable indicates that spoken sermons could have been far nastier than even the most scornful of published tracts.

Communal Resistance

Written objections such as those of Corcos built on a wide range of techniques for resisting or challenging aspects of conversionary sermons, developed over time by Roman Jews. The results of their efforts demonstrate how Jewish resistance could have both direct and indirect influence on the conversionary campaigns of early modern Rome. These included passive resistance, attempts to change the experience of attending sermons, and new evidence that sermons were routinely, even ritualistically refuted when they were delivered. In every category, we can document small or incremental victories—an aggregation of resentment that ultimately exerted a long-term influence on the nature of conversionary preaching.

Modern histories of Roman Jews describe extensive evidence of passive resistance, referring often to edicts demanding orderly behavior at sermons, obstructionism, continuous yelling, and uproar.[34] Many cite the

---

de gl'ignoranti Ebrei; Melchiorre Palontrotti, *Raccolta di Molti Errori, e Chimere sognate da thalmudisti sopra l'espositioni della Bibia, e riferite particolarmente da R. Salomone dove se vede la gran cecita' nella quale è caduto l'Ebraismo, per non haver accetato la vera luce Giesu Christo Signor nostro, vero Dio d'Israele.*

34. Adriano Prosperi, "L'inquisizione Romana e gli ebrei," 278–79.

common trope that authorities regularly checked for wax plugs in Jewish ears.[35] These depictions probably reflect the most common forms of resistance—what the political scientist James C. Scott has called "everyday resistance" or "weapons of the weak": "the ordinary weapons of relatively powerless groups: foot dragging, dissimulation, desertion, false compliance, pilfering, feigned ignorance."[36] Nuns in Strasbourg, forced to listen to Protestant sermons, tried similar measures, ignoring the preacher, laughing, sleeping, or reading. This is resistance that avoids direct confrontation; it is also the hardest to document directly. Unlike Jews in Rome, nuns at least had space on their side; the preacher came to them, but often found his entrance barred.[37]

Resentment against an unwelcome but mandatory sermon was inevitable, and early modern sources extensively assume, describe, and allow for acts of Jewish resistance. The volume of legislation devoted to keeping order at sermons suggests that Catholic administrators always expected defiance. A typical edict from 1607 ordered "that during the sermon both men and women must stay vigilant, quiet, and not make a racket or immodest gestures of any kind, but should stay attentive, under penalty of one scudo per person."[38] The life of Lorenzo di Brindisi, whose vitae commonly assert that he preached to Jews in Rome, portrays a scene of subterfuge: rabbis of the community, under the guise of keeping order during the sermon, making secret hand gestures to the congregation cryptically refuting a preacher's arguments.[39] Francesco Rovira-Bonet, rector of the House of Catechumens in the 1790s, listed three conversionary preachers personally known to him, all deeply distressed (*travagliati*) by the resistance they encountered from Jews—no surprise, concluded the rector, for anybody familiar with past attempts by Jews to unseat Medici and Andrea De Monte, "whom they absolutely refused to hear."[40] Jews in Rome tailored their acts of resistance to the context, and Jews in other countries

35. Milano, *Il ghetto di Roma*, 278–79; Hermann Vogelstein, *Geschichte der Juden in Rom*, 172–76. For wax as a trope, see Maria Diemling, "Navigating Christian Space: Jews and Christian Images in Early Modern German Lands."

36. James C. Scott, *Weapons of the Weak: Everyday Forms of Peasant Resistance*, xvi.

37. Amy Leonard, *Nails in the Wall: Catholic Nuns in Reformation Germany*, 100–102.

38. AAV Misc. Arm. VII, 347r.

39. Arturo da Carmignano di Brenta, *San Lorenzo da Brindisi, Dottore della chiesa universale (1559–1619)*, 1:291.

40. Francesco Rovira-Bonet, *Armatura de' forti, ovvero, Memorie spettanti agl'infedeli ebrei che siano, o turchi*, 611.

acted similarly when listening to contemporary sermons, blocking out the preacher's words with earplugs or loud chatter, and finding other ways to signal their discontent.[41]

The disorderly scenes of everyday resistance portrayed in modern histories are matched by detailed depictions in guides and descriptions of Rome from the sixteenth and seventeenth centuries. As previously noted, Federico Franzini's description of Rome's pious offerings pulls no punches:

> But because the Jews wouldn't go to hear [the preacher De Monte], and fled him as much as they could, the Jews were forced, a third of them [at a time], to go on Saturdays with women and children from age twelve to hear the word of God ... every Saturday after lunch. And so that they do not sleep and remain humble, there is a policeman with a baton [truncheon] in hand who at the preacher's signal, touches whoever is sleeping, because on entering the church they must give their names to someone next to the door who writes it down. When the preaching is over, the policeman goes to note down the unruly and fines them one *testone* [a half scudo], which is given to the poor Catechumens.[42]

Not only does such a passage confirm the attempt to keep the Jewish audience under tight controls, but it suggests that unruliness at sermons was the norm. Recall the visit of the English diarist John Evelyn to a sermon in the 1640s that paints a similar picture. The listening Jews display "so much malice in their countenances, spitting, humming, coughing & motion, that it is almost impossible they should heare a word."[43]

Carlo Bartolomeo Piazza's *Eusevologio Romano* uses a similar scene as the culmination of his discussion of sermons. He writes admiringly that Gregory XIII set up grave punishments for any Jewish person who might switch places, change names, or send a substitute to a sermon, making no exceptions for rabbis and other officials. He describes the range of punishments for such misbehavior, from the loss of a business permit to corporal punishment and fines. He includes the now-familiar deputy, "who walks around during the time of the sermon, so that [the Jews] will stay awake to hear the word of God." Word has also clearly reached him of the strenuous Jewish resistance to the regular, papal-sanctioned presence

---

41. Diemling, "Navigating Christian Space," 6.

42. Federico Franzini, *Roma Antica e Moderna*, 240.

43. John Evelyn, *Diary: Now First Printed in Full from the Manuscripts Belonging to Mr. John Evelyn, and as Edited by E. S. de Beer*, 291.

of Christians, "which the rabbis and heads of the ghetto have tried many times with artifices, claims, and industriousness to prevent."[44]

Piazza leaves us with a strong picture of conversionary sermons as a contentious environment, where Jewish listeners were heavily policed and fined, and where feigning sleep was the safest and least offensive way to resist conversionary rhetoric, or at least avoid seeming to approve of it. And while our view of likely Jewish behavior at sermons is indirect, descriptions such as these show how thoroughly non-Jews expected that Jews would resist sermons as much as they could. Passages such as Evelyn's point to an eyewitness account tinged both by stereotypes of Jewish stubbornness and a recognition that Jews would necessarily find sermons abhorrent.

Roman Jews became experts in communal advocacy and self-defense, especially regarding conversion. It took collective efforts to bring children or coerced catechumens home from the casa, using procedures honed over centuries.[45] They chose their strategy carefully, bringing complaints increasingly to the Holy Office instead of the Vicariate in the belief that the inquisitional tribunals, though harsh, were more functional and rule abiding.[46] They also actively resisted elements of conversionary preaching, and by those efforts succeeded in changing aspects of the sermon environment. In later years, they advocated to move the minimum age of attendance from twelve to eighteen and keep unmarried women from the sermon.[47] And in its earliest years, as recounted in chapter 3, they succeeded in removing from the pulpit the deeply unpopular convert-preacher De Monte.

Jews also fought together against the constant presence of Christians at sermons. In this case the documentation is plentiful. As Piazza described,

44. Carlo Bartolomeo Piazza, *Eusevologio Romano overo Delle Opere Pie di Roma*, part 2, 153.

45. For examples from various eras, beyond the case given in chapter 1, see Attilio Milano, "L'impari lotta della Comunità di Roma contro la Casa dei catecumeni"; David I. Kertzer, *The Kidnapping of Edgardo Mortara*.

46. For general evidence on Jewish interaction with the Inquisition, see Stephan Wendehorst, Claus Arnold, Antje Bräcker, Hanna Węgrzynek, and John Tedeschi, "The Roman Inquisition, the Index and the Jews: Sources and Perspectives for Research." On choice, see Marina Caffiero, *Forced Baptisms: Histories of Jews, Christians, and Converts in Papal Rome*, 17–18. On inquisitional tribunals in Rome, see Irene Fosi, *Papal Justice: Subjects and Courts in The Papal State, 1500–1700*; John A. Tedeschi, *The Prosecution of Heresy: Collected Studies on the Inquisition in Early Modern Italy*. For a close study of the procedures of an inquisitional tribunal against Jews, see Katharine Aron-Beller, "Disciplining Jews: The Papal Inquisition of Modena, 1598–1630," esp. 727–29.

47. Milano, *Il ghetto di Roma*, 272–73.

Jewish officials resented the idea that conversionary sermons took place in public and sought to make sermons closed to outsiders. They never succeeded in undoing this legislation—sermons remained a public spectacle for as long as they lasted—but such efforts nonetheless made a difference, with ramifications perhaps more profound and widespread than a change in laws might have accomplished. Jewish objections to Christians at sermons caused preachers, and eventually the wider world of Christians interested in Judaism, to confront, examine, and discuss how a conversionary campaign toward Jews should work.

The trail starts with a conversionary sermon that survives in manuscript in the Vatican library. The preacher was Gregorio Boncompagni. As we have seen, despite his orthodoxy and apparent conventionality, Boncompagni departed from the strict rhetorical traditions of conversionary preaching, and instead spoke openly on the more immediate question of Christians who attended and watched conversionary sermons. His useful sermon of July 15, 1673, is devoted entirely to this question: "We ask if it is permitted to preach to the Jews, dispute with a Jew, and preach publicly to the Jews in the presence of Christians. And we resolve the doubts of the Jews."[48] Boncompagni chose an unusual time to give this sermon. This was the second of the series of three Saturdays preceding the 9th of the Hebrew month of Av, the commemoration of the destruction of the Temple in Jerusalem, and the saddest day in the Jewish liturgical calendar. The three weeks before the 9th of Av constitute a special period of mourning, as Boncompagni knew well. He had introduced his sermon the week before July 15 by referring to the start of the three-week mourning period and would make it the focus of his sermon the week after it.[49] Given that the destruction of the Second Temple precipitated the exile that Boncompagni, like all Catholics, considered to be God's eternal punishment of the Jews, the date offered plenty of relevant material for a sermon on conversion. But instead, he abandoned the theme.

The sermon reflects Boncompagni's long experience in the conversionary pulpit and knowledge of Jewish audiences.[50] It offers an extended defense of Christian viewers. By examining it closely, we can begin to see the nature and range of Jewish objections that appear to have prompted it. As we saw in the previous chapter, Boncompagni argued that sermons were preferable to medieval disputations, which he thought put Jewish

48. BAV Borg. lat. 129, 75r.
49. BAV Borg. lat. 129, 69r, 77v.
50. BAV Borg. lat. 129, 75r–77r.

and Catholic doctrine on equal footing. Boncompagni's lengthy argument against disputations also suggests that he was responding directly to specific Jewish protests, the kind Piazza had indicated when he described rabbis who tried to prevent Christians from attending sermons to Jews.

To Boncompagni, seventeenth-century Rome must have seemed an especially difficult place to hold a disputation between Christians and Jews. In theory, he explained in this sermon, disputations should be discouraged because they could encourage interaction and discussions of religion between Jews and Christians. But he knew that Romans could offer a unique objection, which he could imagine: "Why can we not have these disputes in Rome, where Jewish people already interact with Christians, and where learned Christians aren't lacking, and where there are already many frequent discussions of religion between Christians and Jews?"[51] The constant, ongoing interaction between Jews and Christians in Rome was undeniable, as Boncompagni noted. This question merited a specific response and required Boncompagni to find a new reason to reject disputations. He alights on Jewish rowdiness as a new answer:

> Experience teaches that these disputes would be fruitless and would not have good consequences, which is why they happen rarely. Jews . . . don't await the answers to the arguments so as to admit the truth; while one person says something, they think of what they will say to oppose it, and while one mystery is examined, they pass on to another, and at the same time they propose difficulties and never stay on point. Jews, when they dispute, throw out great screeches, because whoever yells the most appears to simple people to have won. They don't dispute in order to find the truth, but to counfound it.[52]

Roman Jews, Boncompagni claims here, were especially unsuited to disputations because they would actively fight their corner.

This sermon, unlike many, had a lasting and traceable impact. As noted in chapter 5, Boncompagni also used the sermon as an opportunity to examine the viability of Christian spectators, and that he later returned to it, repackaging his conclusions into a more flexible format. This sermon appears in a thick manuscript containing 214 other sermons, but on the volume's final sheaves we find his numbered list with the title, "We Ask Whether at the Sermons to Jews, Christians Must Attend the Sermons

51. BAV Borg. lat. 129, 76r.
52. BAV Borg. lat. 129, 76r.

to the Jews, and Respond Yes."[53] Twelve bulleted reasons follow. These summarize the points worked out in Boncompagni's sermon of July 15, 1673. On the following page, a second list reviews the question again, this time condensing the answers into nine reasons: "We ask whether at the sermons to Jews that take place in Rome it is better to exclude Christians as the Jews are currently asking." An answer follows: "We respond that it is better because of the continuous observance over the course of ninety years since Gregory XIII instituted this preaching; it has always been ordered that it be done in public, and that Christians attend" (figure 7.2).[54]

From this phrasing, we can surmise not only that Boncompagni was reluctant to question long-standing practice and papal legislation but also that he had good reason for suddenly adopting this topic during the three weeks of summer mourning. Jews had been pressing to restrict the presence of Christian onlookers, and the question could no longer be avoided. That pressure, in turn, prompted Boncompagni to write a special sermon defending the practice. But Boncompagni's lists reveal even more about the extent of Jewish resistance. One of its bullet points makes this explicit: "Because if the Jews *now* are so insolent during the sermon, what would they do if they were free, without Christians [watching]?"[55] A second reason to allow Christians to watch, in other words, was to tamp down common Jewish unruliness at sermons. This instance suggests, first, that Jews provided some form of active, regular resistance to sermons, and it grated on the preacher, and second, that they advocated so fiercely to remove the Christians from the room that Boncompagni felt compelled to answer them, initially in a sermon, and then in a set of lists summarized for later use.

Boncompagni's extensive justification of the Christian presence at sermons to Jews eventually found a much broader audience. During his reign (1676–89), Innocent XI apparently banned Christians from conversionary sermons; the position had to be defended, and the sermon came in useful. A decade after his sermon of July 15, Boncompagni's close friend and colleague Giulio Bartolocci included a rationale for Christian attendance at sermons. It can be found in the third volume of his magnum opus, the *Bibliotheca Magna Rabbinica*. Bartolocci's arguments draw heavily on Boncompagni's lists, essentially paraphrasing them.[56] In other words,

---

53. BAV Borg. lat. 129, 499r–v. See also the discussion of these lists in chapter 5, and figure 5.1.

54. BAV Borg. lat. 129, 501r.

55. BAV Borg. lat. 129, 499r (emphasis added).

56. Giulio Bartolocci, *Bibliotheca Magna Rabbinica de scriptoribus, & scriptis Hebraicis, ordine alphabetico Hebraicè, & Latinè digestis*, 2:759–60.x

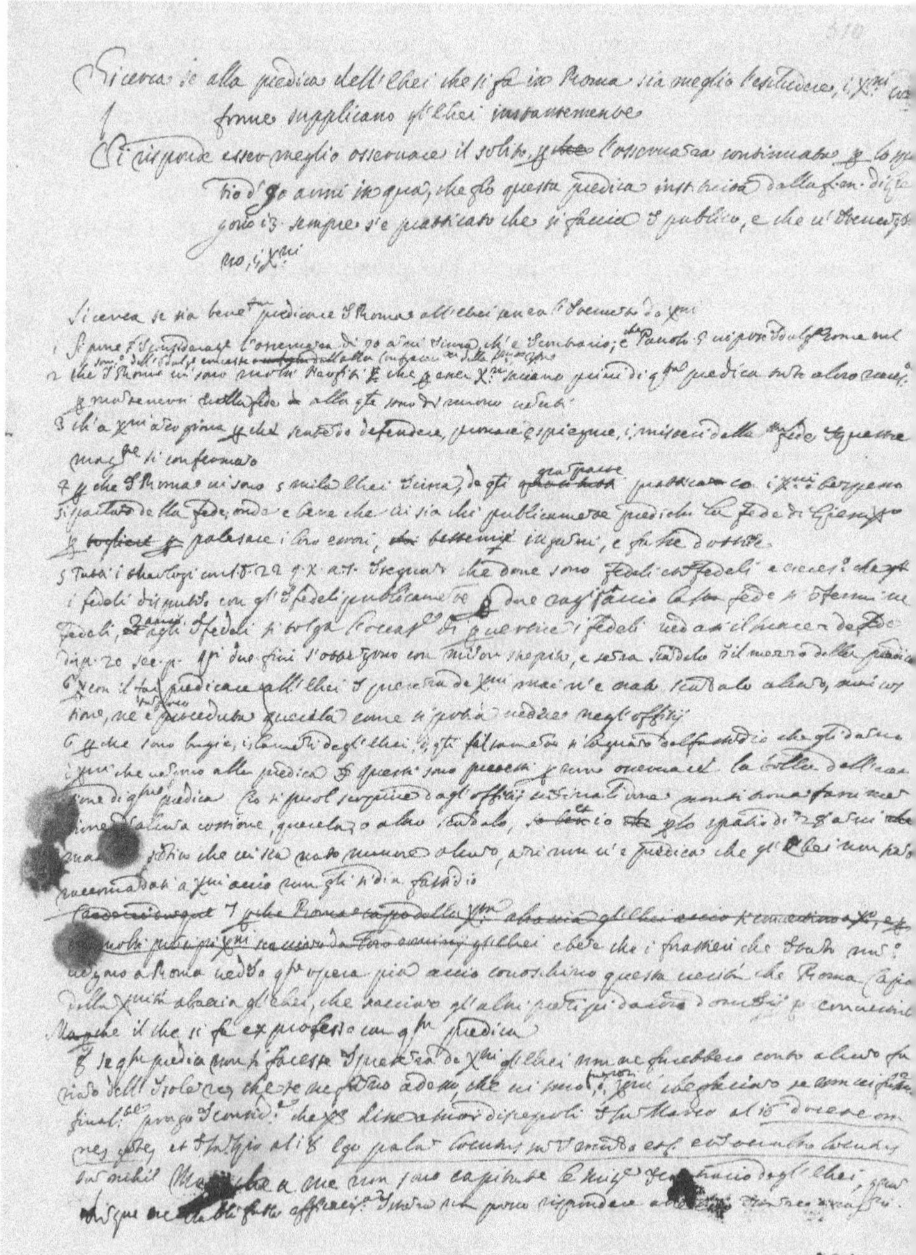

FIGURE 7.2. Reasons why Christians should attend sermons to Jews. Borg. lat. 129, 501r.
© 2021 Biblioteca Apostolica Vaticana.

the discussion in the widely distributed and widely respected *Bibliotheca Magna Rabbinica* had its origin more privately in Boncompagni's sermons. Boncompagni's ideas, first developed in the narrower context of sermons, later reinforced on a much broader scale the Christian interest in watching Jews in early modern Europe.

Christian attendance at forced sermons to Jews was only one issue; Jews in Rome developed a long-standing communal practice of vehemently resisting every aspect of the event, most especially offensive content. This practice probably first began with the removal of the unpopular De Monte and would later bolster Corcos's more formal written objections to the way sermons were held.[57] Evidence of Jewish resistance survives in fragments, but it is plentiful. Gregory Martin's long description of conversionary preaching in the early 1580s mentions rabbis who regularly brought their objections privately to the preacher, who in turn "answereth them presently to satisfie them: and in the next sermon openlie . . . uttereth it . . . to the profite of other lesse obstinate, although he have little hope of the master Rabbine him self that objected it."[58] And when students at the College of Neophytes—future conversionary preachers—were brought back to the oratory to listen to sermons, they were warned not to speak to anybody, particularly Jews, "because the Jews will provoke them into argument."[59]

Notes in Boncompagni's manuscripts indicate that throughout the seventeenth century, resistance to sermons remained a regular and consistent feature of their delivery. One marginal comment at the end of another Boncompagni sermon, noted down more than forty-five years after it was delivered, suggests a lifetime of regular interplay between preachers and Jewish listeners. "This was the first sermon done by me f. Gregorio. It is worth nothing, it was pure practice; the Jews negated it with total ease."[60] Roman Jews seem to have made a habit of policing the border between tolerable and intolerable sermon rhetoric, and letting a preacher know when he had crossed it.

If we return to Boncompagni's many attempts to deliver a sermon on Pope Pius V, just after Pius's beatification in 1672, we see that they are a case in point. Such a sermon, devoted to a near-contemporary saint, departed drastically from the theology and exegesis mandated in the papal legislation. Furthermore, as pope, Pius V had expelled Jews from most of

57. See Barbara Leber, "Jewish Convert in Counter-Reformation Rome," 118–19.

58. Gregory Martin, *Roma Sancta*, 79–80.

59. *Ordini et Constitutioni Fatte per il Collegio di Neofiti*, 14r.

60. BAV Borg. lat. 505, 184r (figure 6.1).

the Papal States and denied Jews the right to own any goods purchased under previous pontificate. A challenge from the audience was foreseeable, and it came. After Boncompagni's first sermon on Pius V, the Jewish audience objected strongly to its unsuitable content. As the opening of the sermon observes in Boncompagni's own hand:

> Having wanted to deliver a sermon on the Blessed Pius V to the Jews, immediately [came] a crowd of rabbis who said to me that this sermon was horrible, incredible, and vain. Horrible, because the adoration of saints is considered idolatry among Jews; incredible, because the sanctity of humans cannot be proven, human testimony being fallible; vain, because if Jews don't believe in Christ, how will they believe in Christians [i.e., saints]?[61]

In the case of this sermon, Jewish protests had tangible results, though perhaps not the ones most hoped for. Boncompagni responded, as he did with the question of Christian spectators at sermons, not by backing down, but by writing a new exculpatory sermon taking on his antagonists. His next sermon on Pius V responded directly to Jewish objections. The sermon summary in the margin parroted the precise language of their complaints: *"The sermon on Pius V to the Jews is not vain but useful, not incredible but credible, not detestable but of great value and religion."*[62] The new sermon eschewed the details of Pius V's biography and concentrated instead on the nature and importance of sanctity along with the public nature of miracles. Indeed, in order to refute Jewish objections, Boncompagni rewrote his discussion of Pius V, transforming it into a general introductory lesson on sainthood to a group of potential future Catholics: "The sermon on Pius V to the Jews is not vain"—began his argument—"because we have no greater sign of the true faithful than demonstrating that saints come from Christians, and saints are those who lived at a heroic level, and through them God worked miracles and grace . . . and who more holy than Pius V?"[63]

This second version of Boncompagni's sermon offered a defense of Catholic doctrine to both Christian and Jewish audiences, and may well have appealed more to both groups, making it arguably more successful than Boncompagni's original idea. In other words, although they were

61. BAV Borg. lat. 129, 487r.
62. BAV Bog. lat. 115, 312r–15r.
63. BAV Bog. lat. 115, 115r.

meant to absorb sermon rhetoric passively, Roman Jews in fact indirectly influenced the content of such preaching through their active protests.

The Jews of Rome employed a wide variety of methods for opposing the sermons forced on them. These ranged from disingenuous acts of passive resistance to objections that could shift the course of conversionary preaching. These methods bore fruit. Jews succeeded in changing the age requirement for attending sermons, removing the first conversionary preacher from the pulpit, and delaying the publication of incendiary works. More notably, they caused various Catholic preachers and officials to review, articulate, and justify their choices, from the use of violence to keep order, to the hostile gaze of Christian onlookers, to the nature of the sermons themselves. These more general contentions—about why sermons were valuable, the nature of sanctity, and others—arose directly in response to Jewish objections. All of these forms of resistance therefore demonstrate the tangible influence of Rome's Jews on both tactics of proselytization and the promotion of early modern Catholic values more broadly.

Some of this influence was, of course, unintended or even the opposite of what Jews hoped for. The attempt to cancel a sermon on Pius V, for example, led instead to an extra sermon. But what kind of resistance and influence were within their grasp? How much success could be expected from Jewish resistance, and how would any success be defined? The possibilities for this community were limited. By the eighteenth century, Italy and especially Rome differed markedly from other countries of Europe in their treatment of Jews. The long process of emancipation had begun; Jewish communities elsewhere had started to obtain the significant civic and political rights that would distinguish modern from medieval and early modern Jewish history.[64] But within the heavily policed confraternal oratory, Rome's Jews could expect far less sweeping success in their protests.

We end up with a picture of varied, even contradictory forms of evidence. As the consummate other, Jews in Rome shaped early modern Catholicism from the outside, but in complex and assorted ways. In the short term, we might suggest that by forcing Catholic authorities to

64. Stow, *Anna and Tranquillo*, 3–4. On the variety of Jewish emancipation experiences across Italy and Europe, see Francesca Bregoli and Federica Francesconi, "Tradition and Transformation in Eighteenth-Century Europe: Jewish Integration in Comparative Perspective." On emancipation as an uneven, contradictory process that nevertheless defines modern Jewish history, see David Sorkin, *Jewish Emancipation*. For varieties within Italy and Rome, see Sorkin, *Jewish Emancipation*, 172–75.

consider, articulate, and defend their positions, Roman Jews contributed to Catholic confessionalization. Over the longer, more uncertain term, in every known case of resistance, we can document incremental effects and small victories, and can consider that this aggregation of defiance helped to make Rome's position on Jews eventually untenable.

Violence Speech and Physical Violence

The antagonism between conversionary preacher and Jewish audience could lead easily to actual bodily harm. Conversionary sermons always took place within a skein of ritualized or semiritualized violence; the weekly encounter of preaching dramatized or heightened tensions that were already menacingly present. Much of the violence between Christians and Jews in early modern Rome was predictable, or ritualized, but it was not static. The tightening anti-Jewish measures of the era not only increased opportunities for staged violence but also allowed for more frequent eruptions of spontaneous incidents.

Anti-Jewish violence punctuated early modern Roman life. Frequent edicts (*bandi*) in Rome sought to limit Christian violence against Jews. Bandi were the primary vehicle for regulating and controlling the population of the city, and these injunctions against Jewish violence are comprehensive:

> This bando orders, prohibits, and commands that no person of whatever status, class, condition, or preeminence, may dare, or presume, directly or indirectly, to bother or impede any Jew in any way: male, female, or child, not to jeer at them [*schernire*], touch them, or offend them in any way, by word or by act, by day or by night, secretly or openly, [lists penalties], and the heads of household are responsible for their servants, fathers for their children, and teachers for their students.

The edict spells out the lashings, with rope or whip, promised for violations, with further punishments "if they had offended a Christian."[65]

Some of these edicts specifically address violence around conversionary sermons. Adriano Prosperi describes the jeering crowds that watched the excursion of hundreds of Jews "from the ghetto to the church of the sermon, between throngs of curious people who commented, laughed,

---

65. ASCER 3 1Tg 2, inf. 7. For the role of edicts in directing urban behavior, see Rose Marie San Juan, *Rome: A City Out of Print*, 22–56.

insulted, and sometimes passed from speech to action." In the early seventeenth century, posters on the door of the oratory and street outside apparently ordered spectators "of whatever status, grade, or condition, under penalty of twenty-five scudi, three lashes of the whip, and other penalties," that they "should not dare or presume to assault or enable the assault of the Jews, whether with deeds or with words, in their going to, coming from, or attending the Saturday sermon."[66]

The edict quoted here is not unique; posters prohibiting Christians from attacking or molesting Jewish people regularly appeared on city walls or ghetto gates in impressive numbers. Surviving examples date from 1591, 1595, 1603, 1606, 1609, 1621, 1623, 1626, 1629, 1633, 1634, 1635, 1636, 1637, 1640, 1641, 1644, 1647, 1655, 1664, 1688, 1699, 1717, 1725, 1727, and 1745.[67] As many as fourteen copies still remain of single editions. Their language is formulaic and varies only slightly. The seventeen editions preserved in the ASCER archive, now restored, show signs of heavy wear, having been posted outdoors. Their publication dates cluster in February and July; perhaps they reflect not only the frenzy of carnival but also the peak of the summer heat. The bandi are usually published by the Apostolic Chamber, which shared oversight of Roman Jews with the Holy Office and Vicariate, demonstrating its ongoing attempt to control the actions of hostile Christians.[68] The quantity of these surviving edicts gives the impression of a lasting face-off, with the implication of assault lurking behind their regular republication.

The threat of violence could erupt all too easily. Although in unscripted daily life Jews and Christians interacted peaceably enough, that peace was fragile; spontaneous actions could easily puncture it. Hostilities could accelerate in both directions. When two millers drove their flour-laden horses through the ghetto in September 1621, knocking into a Jewish resident and triggering the most violent Christian-Jewish riot of the decade, it took the strenuous pursuit of justice by the governor's criminal court to restore equilibrium.[69] Certain seasonal encounters between groups of Christians and Jews seemed likely to unearth more deeply rooted tropes of antagonism that sanctioned and ritualized violence. Some of these took on distinctively Roman forms with connotations beyond Judaism.

66. Prosperi, "L'inquisizione Romana e gli ebrei," 105–6; Attilio Milano, "Un sottile tormento nella vita del Ghetto di Roma: La predica coattiva," 524.

67. ASCER 3 1Tg 2. Inf. 7; AAV Misc. Arm. IV. Similar edicts survive from Bologna and Tuscany.

68. Katherine Aron-Beller, "Ghettoization: The Papal Enclosure and Its Jews," 232.

69. Simona Feci, "The Death of a Miller: A Trial Contra Hebreos in Baroque Rome."

Amnon Linder reads the papal possesso ceremony in Rome as an evolution of Eastertide processions, which typically generated violent rituals around the theologies of the Passion and crucifixion as well as missionary zeal related to the resurrection. The anti-Jewish riots that resulted from the Good Friday Monte di Pietà preaching of 1539 suggest the same.[70] The Roman carnival races featuring elderly Jewish men, running through the streets force-fed and nearly naked, were commonly scheduled between the donkey and other animal races; prostitutes were also conscripted to run. Carnival festivities in Europe and their ancillary violence relied heavily on populations of young, unmarried men, who were disproportionately represented in Rome; ritual violence could escalate easily into hostility and riot.[71] Equally, carnival time falls close to the festival of Purim, when in early modern Rome, Jewish violence and hostility against Christians became more common or even expected.[72]

Most distinctive to Rome, the Vacant See, the unsettled interregnum between popes, was typically characterized by violence and confusion, a result of the mandatory shutdown of the judicial system. The ubiquitous disruption had a solid legal foundation in the fact that there were no consequences for crimes committed during these periods. Normal social conventions slackened. Jews in Rome, whose safety was directly, legally, and historically assured by the figure of the pope, suddenly became fair game on his death in a way that applied only rarely at other times. In his absence, attacks against Jewish people outside the ghetto erupted immediately and almost instinctively. Records paint a scene of a peaceful, busy market in, for example, Piazza Navona suddenly set abuzz with the news of a papal death. Quickly, the Jewish vendors pack up their wares and run for safety as their erstwhile customers start shouting, "Get the Jews—it's the Vacant See!"[73]

70. Amnon Linder, 'The Jews Too Were Not Absent . . . Carrying Moses's Law on Their Shoulders': The Ritual Encounter of Pope and Jews from the Middle Ages to Modern Times," 342–43; Barbara Wisch, "Violent Passions: Plays, Pawnbrokers, and the Jews of Rome, 1539."

71. Julius R. Ruff, *Violence in Early Modern Europe, 1500–1800*, 160–83; Laurie Nussdorfer, "Priestly Rulers, Male Subjects: Swords and Courts in Papal Rome"; Laurie Nussdorfer, "Men at Home in Baroque Rome."

72. Thomas V. Cohen, "The Case of the Mysterious Coil of Rope: Street Life and Jewish Persona in Rome in the Middle of the Sixteenth Century"; Elliott S. Horowitz, *Reckless Rites: Purim and the Legacy of Jewish Violence*, 270–72.

73. John M. Hunt, "Violence and Disorder in the Sede Vacante of Early Modern Rome, 1559–1655," 259–73; Laurie Nussdorfer, "The Vacant See: Ritual and Protest in Early Modern Rome."

In these ways, predictable moments in the calendar or life cycle called for violence, scripted but not necessarily containable, that was otherwise usually controlled. Ritual violence and speech marked all the city's distinguishing ceremonies, from carnival to papal investiture, and accompanied every aspect of its campaign to impose and celebrate religious homogeneity in the early modern period. Scholarship on Italian and European history has often demonstrated how such cases of ongoing and predictable violence between groups could provide useful social functions: they reinforced social order and social discipline, and allowed for, or even established, truce, settlement, and perhaps tolerance between antagonistic religious groups. Conversionary preaching was not aloof from these events. In these and other contexts, violence already included acts of speech, such as insults, subjugation, or reprimand.[74] In addition, as Natalie Zemon Davis has famously shown, religious violence could seek, simultaneously, to reinforce the messages of sermons and cleanse away polluting elements of society. In so doing, perpetrators were "enacting, in symbolic and violent expression, the roles of preachers and priests."[75] For all of these reasons, the purposes and goals of conversionary preaching aligned fully with the patterns of Roman violence toward Jews; both were interdependent and integral parts of Rome's anti-Jewish policy.

The arrival of death inevitably invited comparable turmoil, provoking both scripted and unscripted violence. Just as the death of a pope unleashed assaults on Jewish people across the city during the Vacant See, funerals on a smaller scale brought out attacks and antagonism between Jews and Christians, or fearful measures to prevent them. Jewish cemeteries, unlike Catholic ones, were placed at some distance from the communities of the living—not so far as to prevent frequent visiting, but far enough to differentiate Jewish death rituals from the Catholic cult of the dead and protect Jewish cemeteries from antagonistic passersby. In Rome, the Jewish università had purchased an orchard near the Circo Massimo in 1645 when the older Jewish cemetery near Porta Portese no

74. For three trenchant examples of the vast scholarship on this theme, see David Nirenberg, *Communities of Violence: Persecution of Minorities in the Middle Ages*; Ruff, *Violence in Early Modern Europe, 1500–1800*; Robert C. Davis, *The War of the Fists: Popular Culture and Public Violence in Late Renaissance Venice*. For violence as a "dynamic category" including speech, see Stuart Carroll, *Cultures of Violence: Interpersonal Violence in Historical Perspective*, 8–10.

75. For the interplay between riots, sermons, and pollutions, see Natalie Zemon Davis, "The Rites of Violence: Religious Riot in Sixteenth-Century France," esp. 55–61. For the quotation, Natalie Zemon Davis, "Writing 'The Rites of Violence' and Afterward," 14.

longer sufficed, and had supplemented it with another contiguous plot of land purchased in 1728.[76]

If, as Robert Bonfil argues, "the cemeteries of the Jews . . . convey quite effectively the sense of the Jewish condition in Christian territory . . . the expression of a mentality formed as a mirror image of the Other," then it is no surprise that Jewish cemeteries and funerals became a locus of Christian violence.[77] Bulls from the era of Urban VIII ordered that Jewish graves should be left unmarked, with no tombstones, inscriptions, or other personal indicators.[78] This measure was intended to prevent the desecration and destruction of Jewish cemeteries. Only the tombs of rabbis were allowed a headstone. In the same period, Jewish women were prohibited from accompanying funeral processions into cemeteries and weeping at graves. This regulation sought to prevent women's intense keening from attracting attention and derision from nearby Christians, passing close to the Jewish cemetery.[79] Both of these measures acted on the assumption that Jewish funerals and cemeteries were likely targets.

Tensions surrounding Jewish funerals extended to funeral processions and the spaces they traversed. Urban violence, especially Christian violence against Jews, pooled around liminal sites—doors, windows, and gates—and occasions when Jews left the ghetto in groups or processions.[80] A letter from the vicar of the church of Santa Maria in Cosmedin in the mid-eighteenth century shows how tightly wound and complex tensions, build up over centuries, could erupt into more serious complaints. Santa Maria in Cosmedin sat close to the additional cemetery plot purchased in 1728. The vicar, Carlo Domenico Fuscaglio, sought the help of the cardinal vicar of Rome, with concerns about Jews in the space around his church. He described how the road to the Jewish cemetery crossed in front of Santa Maria in Cosmedin, infusing Jewish funeral processions with danger. Boys in wait attacked those

76. Milano, *Il ghetto di Roma*, 259–61.

77. Robert Bonfil, *Jewish Life in Renaissance Italy*, 281–82.

78. Milano, *Il ghetto di Roma*, 259–67.

79. Milano, *Il ghetto di Roma*, 261–64. Milano reports that the prohibition on tombstones was enforced so thoroughly that when the cemetery was sold, in 1943, to make room for the via del Circo Massimo, no identifying markers remained at all from the older part of the cemetery.

80. Nicholas A. Eckstein, "Prepositional City: Spatial Practice and Micro-Neighborhood in Renaissance Florence." Daniel Jütte, "'They Shall Not Keep Their Doors or Windows Open': Urban Space and the Dynamics of Conflict and Contact in Premodern Jewish–Christian Relations," argues that Christian violence against Jews was especially significant around windows, but must be understood in the broader context of early modern urban violence.

in the procession by throwing jars of urine down from inside the church. Even when the "poor Jews," as Fuscaglio called them, chose other routes, they were so thoroughly harassed that they needed police escort.[81]

This part of Fuscaglio's letter depicts Jews as innocent victims: "Nobody has ever heard that these Jews have ever caused any scandal." In his view, no other churches or streets were safe for Jews; alternative routes would only bring more crowds and more trouble. He remarks, "If for that reason the Jews were prohibited from passing near where there are churches, it would be necessary to prohibit the Jews from leaving the ghetto at all." Fuscaglio sees violence at Jewish funeral processions as an ongoing problem, suggesting a general failure to manipulate or regulate a violent public. He appears here to have significant sympathy for the Jews, who cannot carry out a funeral without encountering unwanted hostility, noting, "This poor community . . . operates under disdain for their religion while they take the greatest care not to cause the slightest scandal, and that therefore it should be ordered that they not be disturbed and upset."[82]

But where the case of Santa Maria in Cosmedin seems a simple issue of aggressors and victims, the stakes are raised when the Jews do not play their scripted role. Fuscaglio's letter later describes a common problem in his church's piazza on Saturdays:

> There is an enormous gathering [of Jews], as many women as men, on the piazza and in front of the church. When the parish priest needs to leave the area, these same people do not move from their places, or withdraw, or give any other sign of reverence. Instead, laughing and joking, they [mock] our sacred services, which is a great scandal and continual occasion for murmuring—not only to those living nearby, but to the foreigners of every nation and condition who rush to this ancient church in great quantity.[83]

These moments take place wholly separately from Jewish funerals; Fuscaglio is at pains to point out that Jews do not perform burials on Saturdays. Presumably the Jewish people crowding around his church were

81. ASVR Atti della segreteria del tribunale del cardinale vicario, tom. 5, 557r–560v. On mandatory police escorts for Jewish funerals during the Vacant See, and at the expense of the Jewish community, see Milano, Il ghetto di Roma, 264–67.

82. ASVR Atti della segreteria del tribunale del cardinale vicario, tom. 5, 557r, 557v, 558r.

83. ASVR Atti della segreteria del tribunale del cardinale vicario, tom. 5, 559v–60r. Santa Maria in Cosmedin has housed the popular "mouth of truth" plaque since the seventeenth century.

those whose number had not been called that week for the sermon. Fuscaglio's greatest concern at this moment in his narrative is public decorum in front of foreigners. None of these groups could be controlled: not the supposedly pious Christians, who violently misbehaved, nor the supposedly victimized Jews, who showed insubordination, nor the touring foreigners, whom Fuscaglio hoped to impress, but whose reactions could not be predicted. The state of Christian-Jewish relations, especially in fraught public spaces and at tense times such as funerals, represent, for Fuscaglio, an integral aspect of the city's international reputation.

Funerals, spectacles, and violence converged in the Roman tradition of *giudiate,* ritual processions explicitly mocking Judaism. Giudiate often involved elaborate staging, with carts, animals, and decoration, offering a parody of well-known Jewish rituals such as circumcision. Rome's fishmongers, living and working next to the ghetto, and familiar by sight with Jewish practice, prepared and staged many giudiate.[84] Giudiate were a particular feature of carnival, but also occurred throughout the year and continued to evolve through the eighteenth century.

The mocking use of animals was a key feature of this ritual. Unsurprisingly, the pig, which encapsulates Jewish otherness, was the most symbolically rich beast in such cases, as it was throughout medieval European history. Christians often defined Jewish difference according to dietary laws and came to associate Jews especially closely with the animal most notoriously forbidden to them. The motif of Jews suckling at a sow was common in medieval Germany, growing increasingly explicit and antisemitic through the seventeenth century.[85] In Rome, cases grave enough to be transferred from the governor's courts to the Holy Office involved masked figures dressed as pigs, or depicted Moses and other rabbis shown as half man, half pig.[86] Pig mockery had precedent in the early modern Papal States. Both Catholic and Jewish sources record an incident in Pesaro, during the Talmud burnings of 1553, when a live, swaddled pig was left overnight in the holy ark of the celebrated synagogue there, to be discovered at morning prayers. In the gleeful Christian retelling, Jewish threats of divine vengeance against the sacrilegious perpetrators were transformed into the

---

84. Milano, *Il ghetto di Roma,* 324–26; Bonfil, *Jewish Life in Renaissance Italy,* 281–82; Caffiero, *Legami Pericolosi,* 362–69.

85. Claudine Fabre-Vassas, *The Singular Beast: Jews, Christians and the Pig.*

86. Caffiero, *Legami Pericolosi,* 363–65.

miraculous spiritual discovery of the "porcine filth of the Talmud," destined for the fire.[87]

Mock funeral processions were the particular specialty of giudiate, complete with animal figures or costumes as well as satiric eulogies. The instigators of a giudiata would walk in a processional through Rome with a casket, performing mocking obsequies, and often carrying a pig in the casket or dressing up as a pig. This tradition only strengthened into the early eighteenth century, when disputes about it ended up in the inquisitional courts. The fattori petitioned to have the license for these processions removed from the fishmongers who held it and sought prohibitions on any disturbance to the funerals of rabbis.[88]

These points, of course, bring us back to the funerary pig who opened this book. The mocking counterprocession of the 1640s, featuring a live pig in its own casket and an erudite but hostile elegy, turned out to leave a legacy. The manuscript that describes Palontrotti's masquerade for the funeral of Corcos also states that this was considered the first giudiata in Rome; this was not true, but it certainly strengthened the funeral giudiata tradition. And as we have now seen, the practice continued afterward for many more decades.[89] As the manuscript portrays the incident, Palontrotti's many incendiary treatises against Judaism propelled him from word into action, from compositions to caskets, and from polemics to pigs. His reliance on long-standing tropes and rituals would not have diminished the drama and affrontery of this innovation, or the level of offense it was intended to cause. Palontrotti employed an event that was already doubly fraught—a funeral and the loss of a revered chief rabbi—to launch his assault at the moment when it would hurt the most.

Palontrotti's giudiata also forces us to reassess the common picture of a relatively harmonious intellectual engagement with Judaism among Rome's scholarly elites. The meticulously prepared manuscript recording the incident is certainly scholarly, with transliterations of the Hebrew words in the song, and translations and annotations carefully keyed to the

87. Girolamo Muzio, *Lettere catholiche del Mutio Iustinopolitano, distinte in quattro libri*, 173–74; Joseph ha-Kohen, *Sefer 'Emeq Ha-Bakha = The Vale of Tears: With the Chronicle of the Anonymous Corrector*, 5:81.

88. ACDF St St Aa2-b, 430r, 515r. See also Caffiero, *Legami Pericolosi*, 364–65. Caffiero links pig mockery to forced baptism and accusations of ritual murder, on the rise again in the eighteenth century.

89. For reviews of the tradition of giudiate before and after this incident, see Martina Mampieri, "When the Rabbi's Soul Entered a Pig: Melchiorre Palontrotti and His Giudiata against the Jews of Rome." Milano, *Il ghetto di Roma*, 323–28, dates them from 1609.

numbered lines of the song.[90] But it also describes Palontrotti's actions in some detail and with a sense of approval for his work against the "foolishness" (*sciochezze*) of the Jews. The whole incident was written up by Giovanni Pastrizio, who appears from his other work to be a more irenic and detached lover of the Hebrew language. This story reminds us that while the drive to convert Jews may have developed separate intellectual and polemical pathways, the two converged easily, without presenting contradictions to contemporaries.

Palontrotti's porcine procession might have left another legacy too. As the reader will have noticed, the much-mourned Rabbi Tranquillo Corcos of the mid-seventeenth-century giudiata bore the same name as the advocate Rabbi Tranquillo Corcos of the late seventeenth and early eighteenth century. Tranquillo Vita Corcos the Younger was born ten years after this funeral. It is plausible that he would have heard stories of the attack and mockery that took place at the funeral of the grandfather for whom he was named, and that the story helped to fuel his fervent, unmatched advocacy against conversionary preachers and on behalf of Roman Jews. His most-repeated argument, in every treatise against a preacher and in his objections to the bacchetta, maintained that gentle speech, contained within communally agreed limits, would always be the most effective tactic. Speech that exceeded those limits was a form of violence.

In an unwitting closing of the circle, the caricaturist Pier Leone Ghezzi later returned to his drawing of Corcos, adding a note describing the rabbi's own funeral procession in 1730: 150 lit torches accompanied his draped coffin throughout the ghetto, and 9 to his burial in the evening.[91] And according to Ghezzi, his subject succeeded in dying in peace, with no whiff of violence. Perhaps Corcos's many acts of advocacy, built on the long practice of Jewish resistance that lay behind them, played a role in giving him a better funeral than his grandfather's.

90. Mampieri, in "Melchiorre Palontrotti and the First Giudiata against the Jews of Rome (1647–48)," showed how the poem is also a valuable example of the *giudeo-romanesco* dialect.

91. BAV Ott. lat. 3114, 19r. See also Elliott S. Horowitz, "Processions, Piety, and Jewish Confraternities," 237.

Epilogue

SERMONS TO JEWS in Rome provided an ideal vehicle for both Catholic self-congratulation and self-definition, and so they endured for an unduly long time. They were abolished in both theory and practice only in 1847. One of the first and most important modern chroniclers of the Catholic Church caught their final years. Gaetano Moroni describes the sermons in the entry on Jews in his vast *Dictionary of Historical-Ecclesiastical Erudition*. Jews still attended sermons, he wrote in 1843, but the number had been reduced to five times a year. The current preacher was Angelo Vincenzo Modena, who usually spoke for about an hour. The sermons now took place at the church of Sant'Angelo in Pescheria, no longer in Trinità dei Pellegrini. Sant'Angelo in Pescheria lies practically inside the ghetto, so there was no longer any sermon procession for Moroni to witness. Moroni insisted that "from all this . . . we clearly come to know how much the Catholic church and its heads, the popes, desire the conversion of the Jews."[1] Nonetheless, the reduction in both frequency and spectacle suggests that expectations for the sermons had lowered over time.

Modena, it turns out, was the last of the permanent predicatori degli ebrei. The upheavals of the French Revolution and Napoleonic era included the opening of the ghetto and a suspension of sermons. When papal power returned after 1814, these and other recent liberties were briefly rescinded. Pope Leo XII reinstated sermons in 1823 in an attempt to reverse the emancipation of Jews in Italy.[2] In the same year, the Swiss

1. Gaetano Moroni, *Dizionario di erudizione storico-ecclesiastica da S. Pietro sino ai nostri giorni*, 27.

2. Alberto Zucchi, "Ragioni della predicazione agli ebrei," 263; Attilio Milano, *Il ghetto di Roma; illustrazioni storiche*, 114–16. Copies of the reinstatement edict are found in ASCER 3 1Tg 2, inf. 7.

FIGURE E.1. Hieronymous Hess, *Die Bekehrung der Juden in Rom* (The Conversion of the Jews in Rome), c. 1821. Courtesy of the Jewish Museum of Switzerland.

artist Hieronymous Hess illustrated the scene (figure E.1). His depiction shows no sympathy with any of the characters. The sneering preacher harangues, Franciscans and Dominicans threaten the congregation, and armed guards watch with boredom. A few Jews listen, but most chatter or roll their eyes; one feigns sleep.

Over the course of the nineteenth century, Jewish life in Rome fell increasingly out of step with the process of Jewish emancipation taking place elsewhere in Europe and the United States. The Roman Catholic Church careened into a crisis of confidence as popes battled against Enlightenment era ideals of rationalism, secularism, and revolution. In their efforts to maintain political power and justify it by divine right, Jewish communities and individual Jewish people often became proxy battle sites.[3] Sermons to Jews were abolished in 1847 by Pio IX, who also put an end to lingering carnival humiliations and opened up the ghetto permanently.

3. For two poignant examples, see Kenneth R. Stow, *Anna and Tranquillo: Catholic Anxiety and Jewish Protest in the Age of Revolutions*, 79–90 passim; David I. Kertzer, *The Kidnapping of Edgardo Mortara*, esp. 85–87.

We can see echoes of this dislocation in the words of the first scholar who wrote in depth about conversionary preachers. Alberto Zucchi, a Dominican writing for the scholarly journal of his order, lamented Pius IX's legislation: "Thus closed forever the sequence of preachers to the Jews . . . after two and a half centuries since its founding. The Dominican Order, with its learned Hebraists, wrote a beautiful page of its history in practicing this salutary ministry in Rome."[4] Zucchi composed his articles in the mid-1930s. His unquestioning appraisal of conversionary sermons as a "beautiful page" in history appeared in 1938, the same year that the Italian fascist regime published the *Manifesto della Razza* in July and decreed antisemitic "racial laws" in the autumn. These laws excluded Jewish people from public office, barred Jewish teachers, professors, and students from places of education, removed and curtailed civil rights and liberties, prohibited "mixed" marriages, and established a census of Jewish Italians and other Jewish residents in Italy that would be used during the war for internment and deportation to concentration and extermination camps. Although the Vatican officially condemned Nazi procedures and called them anti-Christian, many sectors of the Italian church accepted or embraced racist and anti-Jewish policy, and sought to reconcile Catholicism with the fascist regime.[5]

But Zucchi was deluding himself about the success of the "salutary ministry." From the outset, preaching to the Jews could never work, assuming that the benchmark of success was measured in hard conversion numbers. Writing in the same decades, German historian Karl Hoffmann reviewed a history of attempts to justify conversionary preaching, stretching from the moment regular sermons were instituted in the sixteenth century through to the nineteenth. He ended by quoting Pius IX's "most outspoken" cardinal," Carlo Luigi Morichini: "Obligatory preaching in our days was left aside, both for lack of fruit, and because it was deemed easier to lead them to the truth when one has the grace of God. . . . We do as much as we can, but faith and the mutation of the heart happen thanks to God."[6] Morichini admitted that scripted missionizing had its limits, yet like Zucchi, he still insisted on painting a rosy picture of the sermons.

4. Alberto Zucchi, "Rome domenicana: note storiche: Predicatori Domenicani degli Ebrei nel sec. XVIII," 125.

5. Silvana Patriarca and Valeria Deplano, "Nation, 'Race,' and Racisms in Twentieth-Century Italy"; Nina Valbousquet, "Race and Faith: The Catholic Church, Clerical Fascism, and the Shaping of Italian Anti-Semitism and Racism."

6. Carlo Luigi Morichini, *Degli istituti di carità per la sussistenza e l'educazione dei poveri e dei prigionieri in Roma: Libri tre*, 660–61.

However unwillingly the Jews went to the sermons, Morichini wrote, they were nonetheless always moved by the preacher's Christian moderation so that they behaved well and even thanked him at the end of the sermon. We now know how untrue this description could be. But Morichini, from his position in the Curia, had to put the best possible spin on an event that had not managed to fulfill its mandate after 250 years of trying.

Not so Robert Browning (1812–99). His 1855 poem "January 7, Holy-Cross Day" sees conversionary sermons as antiquated and harmful. Browning places the reader among the Roman Jews in the pews. He makes them the narrators of the poem, giving them their own vigorous voice at an event that had relied on and enforced their silence. Browning's Jews are active, even though they are crammed uncomfortably into the pews: "Higgledy piggledy, packed we lie / Rats in a hamper, swine in a stye." They complain. They grumble. They poke fun at the preacher—"I liken his Grace to an acorned hog"—pointing out all of his own sins and throwing back onto him the abuse they have so often borne themselves, not to mention the animal metaphors.[7] They roll their eyes at their compatriots who have taken up Christianity—known entities all: thieves and beggars desperate to improve their circumstances, and one chancer, "four times already converted in." They compare sermons to their other maltreatments in Rome, plan their refutation of the sermon text, and wait resentfully for it to end. Meanwhile, they dream of a better life. They are not heroic, but neither are they imaginary. They are human, and Browning's sympathy lies firmly with them against the preacher.

Browning's take on conversionary sermons was pure conjecture. His poem was inspired by the inscription that still hangs on the facade of the church of San Gregorio della Divina Pietà as a memorial to conversionary sermons. It bears the passage from Isiah 65:2–3, "I have spread out my hands all the day unto a rebellious people, which walketh in a way that was not good, after their own thoughts; / a people that provoketh me to anger continually to my face." Browning had not witnessed the sermons himself during his sojourns in Rome, nor did he see the inscription in person, but he had seen a copy of Hess's picture from the Basle museum.[8] His imagination filled in the rest and turned out to be correct in many ways. Jewish people in Rome really did, we now know, grumble, convert for convenience or multiple times, watch the clock, refute the sermon,

7. Rowena Fowler, "Browning's Jews." See also David Goldstein, "Jews and Robert Browning: Fiction and Fact."

8. Joseph Phelan, "A Source for Robert Browning's 'Holy-Cross Day.'"

and despise the preacher. The inscription itself was erected in 1858 on the orders of Pius IX after he had abolished sermons. Its placement gives the lie to the idea that speech was necessarily a gentle method of persuasion. The church of San Gregorio della Divina Pietà did not host conversionary sermons; it bears the plaque because it sits at an unavoidable entrance to the historical ghetto borders. The inscription was intended as a direct, ongoing rebuke to Jews: convert or be forever despised. The termination of conversionary sermons did not reflect a change in principle or attitude, only of resources and circumstances.

The real value of conversionary sermons—rarely stated, but fully understood—lay outside baptism tallies. Their drama and power depended not on actually converting Jews but rather on capturing the moment of greatest potential for conversion. Jews on the brink of conversion served many useful theological and social functions at once. As despised Jews, they validated the church by their ongoing opposition to it. Unconverted Jews had long played a theological role as living witnesses whose survival validated Christianity.[9] But at the same time, during a sermon, they could be cast as future Christians, actively endorsing the church by choosing to join it. Furthermore, in Rome, local Jews—whether they were recent arrivals or had ancient Roman roots—provided a reassuring spectacle of subjugation, especially for foreign visitors who rarely saw Jewish people in their home regions. But internal distinctions fell away, and different functions merged at a sermon, where the Jews of Rome found themselves deployed into playing the role of "the Jews" in general—those ancient, venerable, and largely imagined antagonists.[10]

Conversionary sermons also prospered in Rome because they gave body to many of the new, big questions facing the post-Tridentine, post-Reformation church. How could Catholics reconcile imagined ideas about "the Jew" with physical communities of Jewish people integrated into the local society? Which was more useful theologically to a revived post-Reformation Catholic church: the imagined Jew as the ancient witness and antagonist to Christianity, or the living Jew who freely chose Catholicism? Which one provided more validation to an embattled Catholic church? What role could the original antagonist play in a church that had since developed powerful new antagonists in the form of Protestants and to some extent Muslims—and was astounded to learn of new populations

9. See especially Jeremy Cohen, *Living Letters of the Law: Ideas of the Jew in Medieval Christianity*.

10. For a more detailed explication of this argument, see Emily Michelson, "Conversionary Preaching and the Jews in Early Modern Rome," 100–104.

overseas that could be evangelized? These questions all essentially contribute to a grander query: the relative value of antiquity versus modernity. The case of conversionary preaching in Rome, a city in the midst of a sweeping spiritual and physical renovation, but boasting the oldest and most continuous Jewish settlement in Europe, uniquely embodies the tension between old and new.

For these reasons, we cannot fully understand the new Catholicism of the early modern period without looking at its reliance on Jews and Judaism, both real and imagined. In the early modern era, Catholics, for the first time, had to promote and defend their religion against viable alternative options for Christian denominations in Europe. At the same time, they embarked on the mission to spread their creed on a broader, more global scale than ever before. These two endeavors were not opposites, but they required many different tools and skills in widely varying contexts. Catholic emissaries were working on many fronts at once and had to retool their arguments for many different audiences.

Jews and Judaism eased that task. The most theologically sound way to confer uniformity and consistency on such a vast endeavor was to take it to a higher plane. The church's oldest, most venerable, but also most despised antagonists made unrivaled straw men for a general defense of Catholicism. Whatever local trouble might be found in strengthening the faith in Poland, Mexico, or Japan, it could be put right on an intellectual level by recourse to the Jewish argument. If Jews were the most stubborn of opponents, then demonstrating to *them* the merits of Catholicism automatically proved the point with regard to newer, lesser-known, less threatening others. This stance made a grand spectacle of Jewish conversion necessary. It might also help to explain why the Congregation of Propaganda Fide engaged so deeply in Hebrew scholarship as part of training and catering to missionaries, even as those missionaries set out for continents that had never encountered a Hebrew alphabet. And it explains the groundswell of support and enthusiasm for conversionary sermons across Rome, and the involvement of its most elite and most vibrant religious institutions.

As a performance, conversionary preaching also insinuated that the church's missionary efforts were benign, relying mostly on persuasion and intellectual argument to achieve conversion. The suggestion of standing above the fray, on the moral high ground, proved useful in an era of bloody, devastating religious wars in Europe, stoked further by fears of a hyperstereotyped violent Islam. This claim to pacifism was not true, of course. Catholic missionary efforts did not eschew violence any more than other religions did. And efforts to convert Jews were not limited to theological debates but employed plenty of vicious strong-arm tactics as well. Jewish life in Rome may have been less deadly than elsewhere in Europe, but sermons and related measures were not benign. They created a hostile environment for Rome's Jews, with consequences that were both violent and demeaning. The close perspective on one weekly event shows us the friction that inhabits the border between speech and violence. Nor were the Jews who attended these sermons passive, pitiable props in any way. Over three centuries of sermon going, their active resistance influenced which arguments preachers would choose in arguing for their church on a global stage. Both individual Jewish people and general ideas of Judaism actively helped to determine the direction of early modern Catholicism as well as the ways it chose to define itself.

These threads of influence and display converged at one highly choreographed, carefully calibrated event, whose repercussions were felt in many places far distant from Rome. Sermons to Jews offered the most reliable and powerful local platform for defining and defending early modern Catholicism as it embarked on its global mission. With these sermons, we see how deeply the early modern Catholic Church commandeered both real and imaginary Jews in order to define and applaud itself—for how long, and at what price. Without them, we can never fully recognize the face that it decided to show to the early modern world.

ACKNOWLEDGMENTS

ACADEMIC COLLEAGUES WILL READ this section first. Count yourselves lucky to encounter here the wise scholars and friends who have improved both this work and the scholarly world, and the libraries and archives that safeguard our histories. Then please read the rest too.

Enormous advantages allowed me to write this book. I enjoy stable, compensated employment, and received extensive support for grant writing, networking, travel, and mentorship. These resources smoothed my access to the benefits that all scholars need, but that not every scholar receives. For this book, I received funding from Villa I Tatti, where I spent a fruitful year as a Robert Lehman fellow, and then from the Carnegie Foundation, Arts and Humanities Research Council (AHRC), and British Academy, which together let me return to Italy for shorter and longer stays. During my AHRC fellowship, I was also warmly welcomed as an honorary fellow at the British School of Rome.

I carried out research and wrote many drafts at many invaluable libraries and archives. My thanks to all the staff at the Archivio Apostolico Vaticano, Archivio della Congregatione per la Dottrina della Fede, Archivio Storico de Propaganda Fide, Archivum Romanum Societatis Iesu, Archivio Storico della Communità Ebraica di Roma, Archivio di Stato di Firenze, Archivio di Stato di Roma, Archivio Storico del Vicariato di Roma, Biblioteca Apostolica Vaticana, Biblioteca Nazionale Centrale di Firenze, Biblioteca Casanatense, Biblioteca Vallicelliana, Biblioteca Nazionale di Roma, library of the British School of Rome, École Française de Rome, John Rylands library in Manchester, and Cecil Roth collection at the Brotherton Library at the University of Leeds. Especial thanks to the experts I met at these institutions: Daniel Ponziani at the ACDF, Domenico Rocciolo at the ASVR, Paolo Vian for his kindness at the BAV, Silvia Haia Antonucci at the ASCER, Valerie Scott at the BSR, and Giovanni Pizzorusso for introducing me to the Propaganda Fide.

In conducting my research, I came close to losing my employment, home, UK residency, and academic foothold when my fellowship at Villa I Tatti put me at odds with the UK Home Office. I would like to acknowledge here the full support of the University of St Andrews during that ordeal. Because of the university's backing then, I can continue to do my work and provide for my family.

Many universities hosted me for conference talks and seminar papers on sermons to Jews, including Trinity College Dublin, Nijmegen, Ben Gurion, St Andrews, Southampton, Leeds, Durham, and Cambridge. I am grateful to the many interlocutors at those events for their productive questions and comments. Various portions of chapters 2, 5, and 7 as well as other scattered passages were published as articles in *Archivio Storico della pietà*, *Religious Orders and Religious Identity Formation c. 1420–1620*, *Past and Present*, and *A Companion to Religious Minorities in Early Modern Rome*. They are reprinted here with permission of the original publishers. Thanks also to Ben Tate, Josh Drake, and Jill Harris at Princeton University Press for their support, Cindy Milstein for astute copyediting, Sheila Hill for help with the index, and the two encouraging and erudite peer reviewers.

This project is more incisive and precise for the wisdom, advice, and generosity of Adam Shear, Anne Coldiron, Barbara Wisch, Bill Shackman, Ed Muir, Marc Michael Epstein, Mary Laven, Piet van Boxel, Simon Ditchfield, Tamar Herzig, and most especially Gillian Steinberg.

Profound thanks, too, to Allison Duncan Kerr, Amy Blakeway, Ana del Campo, Benjamin Ravid, Bernie Cooperman, Bert Roest, Brad Gregory, Camilla Russell, Cáit Power, Caron Gentry, Catherine Fletcher, Catriona Yates, Chris Jones, Daniel Stein Kokin, Davide Baldi, Ed Muir, Ed Wouk, Eva Frojmovic, Euan Cameron, Frances Andrews, Gina Hiatt, Howard Louthan, Ian Campbell, Irene Fosi, Irene Poznanski, JAM, Jennifer De La Guardia, Joseph Ashmore, Kate Ferris, Katherine Aron-Beller, Katrina Olds, Kenneth Stow, Laurie Nussdorfer, Lia Markey, Libby Cohen, Magda Teter, Michael Rocke, Miriam Udel, Moshe Sluhovsky, Nerida Newbingen, Patrick O'Banion, Peter Mazur, Philippa Jackson, Pierre Savy, Piers Baker-Bates, Roberto Rusconi, Roger Mason, Sarah Easterby-Smith, Sarah Frank, Sarah Whyte, Serena di Nepi, Sergio Terracina, Stephanie Shirilan, Thomas-Leo True, Tim Greenwood, Tom Cohen, Ventsday, Erik Ross, OP, and many others. Andrew Drenas, Frank Lacopo, Piet van Boxel, and Jon Hunt shared unpublished work with me, and Frank took emergency photos. The Smart History team taught me new ways to see and convey the experiences of walking to a sermon.

Gregorio Boncompagni Corcos degli Scarinci, OP (d. 1688) and I would have been at loggerheads in person, but he left his lifetime's writing bound in good working order, wrote down some of his own emotions for me to find, and confirmed that we agreed on which topics were most important.

To best convey the extent of my family's support, I need only say that they let me finish the full manuscript in the COVID-19 summer lockdown of 2020 and revisions in the spring lockdown of 2021. I thank them here, but thanking doesn't begin to cover it. More broadly, my parents laid a rock-solid foundation for my intellectual life. My extended families cheered me on. Friends asked encouraging, nonthreatening questions. When I showed my children "just one more" picture, church, or digitized manuscript, I learned from them too. Above all, Bill has believed in me and in this book throughout, even when the path was rocky and the light was dim. As I result, I almost never had to work a full second shift at home, or give up a valuable conference, speaking gig, or research trip. He and our family endured considerable disruption and challenge as they followed me in my long pursuit of this material. I am aware of what they lost as well as what they may have gained by it.

BIBLIOGRAPHY

Manuscript Sources

FLORENCE

Archivio di Stato di Firenze (ASF)

Manoscritti 129

ROME AND VATICAN CITY

Archivio Apostolico Vaticano (AAV)

Arm. LII 18
Fondo Borghese IV
Misc. Arm. IV
Misc. Arm. VII

Archivio della Congregatione per la Dottrina della Fede (ACDF)

Doctrinalia S.O. e voti Doctrinalia 1711–13
QQ 3 L
Res Doctrinales DB I 1618–98St St AA 2 b
St St BB 2 a
St St BB 3 f
St St BB 3 r
St St CC 4 a 7
St St UV 51
St St UV 53
TT 1 b
TT 4 b

Archivio di Stato di Roma (ASR)

Trinità dei Pellegrini, 523

Archivio Storico de Propaganda Fide (ASPF)

Misc. Gen. XII
Misc. Gen. XIII
SC Stamperia I

Archivio Storico del Vicariato di Roma (ASVR)

Atti della segreteria del tribunale del cardinale vicario, tom. 5
Atti della segreteria del tribunale del cardinale vicario, tom. 55
Casa dei Catecumeni 23 N 48
Casa dei Catecumeni 178
Editta Vicarii Urbis, Editti e Bandi 1566–1609
Mandati della Segreteria del tribunale del vicariato, Registrum Mandatorum, 1706–35

Archivio Storico della Comunità Ebraica di Roma (ASCER)

Inventario Fondo università degli ebrei
1 Ue 2
1 Ug 2
3 1Tg 2
Archivum Romanum Societatis Iesu (ARSI)
Opp. NN 313
Opp. NN 336

Biblioteca Apostolica Vaticana (BAV)

Borgiani latini (Borg. lat.) 19
Borg. lat. 47
Borg. lat. 113
Borg. lat. 114
Borg. lat. 115
Borg. lat. 122
Borg. lat. 123
Borg. lat. 124
Borg. lat. 129
Borg. Lat. 192
Borg. lat. 476
Borg. lat. 481
Borg. lat. 499
Borg. lat. 505
Borg. lat. 506
Borg. lat. 555
Borg. lat. 746
Borg. lat. 778
Borg. lat. 790
Neofiti 35
Neofiti 37
Neofiti 38
Ott. lat. 3114
Stamp. Barb. V.IV.68
Urb. lat. 1050

Urb. lat. 1060

Urb. lat. 1072

Vat lat. 14627

Vat. lat. 3561

Vat. lat. 6792

Vat. lat. 6822

Printed Primary Sources

Alfani, Tommaso Maria. *Istoria degli anni santi dal loro principio fino al presente del 1750. Tratta in gran parte da quella del p.l.f. Tommaso Maria Alfani dell'ordine de' predicatori da Domenico Maria Manni accademico fiorentino, con aggiunte notabili del medesimo di memorie, d'inscrizioni, di medaglie.* Florence, 1750.

Allè, Girolamo. *I convinti, e confusi hebrei: opera del M.R.P.M. Girolamo Allè bolognese, dell'ordine di S. Girolamo di fiesole, divisa in alcune prediche da lui predicate nell'antico, & gia patriarcal tempio di san Silvestro di venetia.* Ferrara, Italy, 1619.

——. *Il vecchio giovane, miniera di recondite erudition.* Bologna, 1652.

——. *L' huomo che parla poco, e ragiona molto.* Bologna, 1646.

——. *La contrition trionfante.* Bologna, 1644.

——. *La sconosciuta, e conosciuta sposa di Salomone.* Bologna, 1650.

——. *Le chimere pitagoriche, cabalistiche, chimiche e giudiciarie dissipate dal vento della verità.* Bologna, 1654.

Audeber, Nicolas. *Le Voyage et observations de plusiers choses diverses qui se pevvent remarquer en Italie . . . par le Sieur Audeber conseiller du Roy au Parlement de Bretagne.* 2nd part, 1656. Paris, 1660.

Bellavere, Giovanni Battista. *Doi breui trattati, nell'vno de' quali si raccoglieno diuerse efficaci ragioni contra gli hebrei, et nell'altro dimostrando la grauezza del peccato della lussuria si diffiniscono le sue specie.* Venice, 1609.

Bell'haver, Tommaso. *Dottrina facile et breve per redurre l'Hebreo al conoscimento del vero Messia.* Venice, 1608.

Bartolocci, Giulio. *Bibliotheca Magna Rabbinica de scriptoribus, & scriptis Hebraicis, ordine alphabetico Hebraicè, & Latinè digestis.* 5 vols. Rome, 1675–94.

Biancuzzi, Benedetto. *Indices tres obseruationum miscellaneorum variarumque lectionum.* Rome, 1597.

——. *Institutiones in linguam sanctam Hebraicam.* Rome, 1608.

——. *Lettione fatta alli Hebrei di Roma, nell'Oratorio della Santissima Trinità de' Pellegrini, & Convalescenti, li 8 di ottobre 1605 dal R. D. Benedetto Biancucci . . . Dottore Theologo, et Professore della Lingua Santa nella Sapienza Romana.* Rome, 1606. Autograph copy at BAV Stamp. Barb.V.IV.68.

Borromeo, Federico. *De sacris nostrorum temporum oratoribus libri quinque.* Milan, 1632.

Breve Dichiaratione e descrittione del Teatro Eretto in quest'anno MDxclvi ad honore e culto del santissimo sacramento nella chiesa farnesiana della compagnia di Geisu. Rome, 1666.

Breve Ragguaglio del modo et ordini tenuti in ricevere li pellegrini ambi gli anni santi 1575 e 1600. Rome, 1600.

Buxtorf, Johannes. *Synagoga Iudaica hoc est, Schola Iudaeorum in qua nativitas, institutio, religio, vita, mors, sepulturaq[ue]; ipsorum è libris eorundem a M. Johanne Buxdorfio . . . graphice descripta est.* Hanau, 1614.

Calasanz, José de. *Epistolario di San Giuseppe Calasanzio.* Storia e letteratura (Edizioni di storia e letteratura). Rome: Storia e letteratura, 1950.

Campana, Cesare. *Delle Historie del Mondo descritte dal Sig. Cesare Campana.* Venice, 1597.

Caraffa, Antonio. *Trionfo della santa croce, sermone spirituale, sopra l'annuntiatione della beatissima Vergine. Data in luce per Antonio Caraffa romano, già rabino hebreo fatto christiano.* Pavia and Ferrara, Italy, 1621.

Carretto, Ludovico. *Epistola de Ludovico Carretto ad Hebreos. Sermone di Giulio Innocentio suo figliolo alli Hebrei, et era quando lo fece de età de anni cinque in sei.* Genoa, 1556

Ciantes, Giuseppe. *Della incarnazione del Verbo Divino. Evidentemente difesa dalle opposizioni degli Ebrei colle dottrine medesime de loro maggiori teologi. Discorso di Gioseffo Ciantes.* Rome, 1668.

———. *Della Santissima Trinità, evidentemente provata da i testimoni de gli antichi Ebrei.* Rome, 1668.

———. *Summa diui Thomae Aquinatis ordinis Praedicatorum contra Gentiles. Quam Hebraicè eloquitur Iosephus Ciantes Romanus episcopus Marsicensis ex eodem Ordine assumptus.* Rome, 1657.

Corcos, Tranquillo Vita. *Memoriale Additionale ad altro dato li 26 Settembre 1705.* Rome, 1706.

———. *Memoriale dell'Ebrei contro le prediche di P. Sebastiano Medici Ebreo convertito.* Rome, 1697.

———. *Summarium. Alla sagra Consulta illus e Reve Monsi Ghezzi ponente per l'università di Roma.* Rome, 1706.

Costanzi, Giovanni Antonio. *La verità della cristiana religione contro le vane lusinghe di moderni ebrei.* Rome, 1749.

Costituzioni della venerabile arciconfraternità della santissima trinità de pelegrini & Convalescenti, accresciuti e riformati. Rome, 1821.

Costituzioni della venerabile arciconfraternità della santissima trinità de pelegrini & Convalescenti, novamente riformati e stampati. Rome, 1578.

Cuggiò, Nicolò Antonio. *Della Giurisdittione e prerogative del vicario ei Roma: Opera del canonico Nicolò Antonio Cuggiò segretario del tribunale di Sua Eminenza.* Edited by Domenico Rocciolo. Rome, 2004.

Del Monte, Anna. *Rubare le anime: diario di Anna Del Monte ebrea romana.* Edited by Marina Caffiero. Rome: Viella, 2008.

Della Rosa, Torquato. *Salutario discorso, contra l'hostinatione de gl'Hebrei, nel qual si tratta, e ragiona sopra tre articoli. . . . Composto da me Torquato della Rosa, già rabbino hebreo, & hora per gratia di Dio, fatto christiano.* Modena, Italy, 1639.

Dondori, Giuseppe. *Della pietà di Pistoia.* Pistoia, Italy, 1666.

Duval, Pierre. *Le Voyage et la description d'Italie . . . avec la relation du Voyage fait à Rome par Monsier le Duc e Boüillon en l'année 1644.* Paris, 1660.

Eustachio, Giovanni Paolo. *Salutari discorsi composti da M. Giovan Paolo Eustachio Nolano, già Hebbreo, hor Christiano*. Naples, 1582.

Evelyn, John. *Diary: Now First Printed in Full from the Manuscripts Belonging to Mr. John Evelyn, and as Edited by E. S. de Beer*. Oxford, 1955.

Fanucci, Camillo. *Trattato di tutte l'opere pie dell'alma città di Roma*. Rome, 1602.

Ferretti, Francesco Maria. *Le Verità della Fede Cristiana*. Venice, 1741.

Fioghi, Marco Fabiano. *Dialogo fra il cathecumino et il padre cathechizante, Composto per Fabiano Fioghi dal Monte Santo Savino, Lettore della li guali hebrea nel Collegio de Neophiti, Nel qual si risoluono molti dubij, li quali sogliono far li hebrei, contro la uerità della santa fede christiana, con efficacissime ragioni: & per li santi profeti, & per li rabini*. Rome, 1583.

Franzini, Federico. *Roma Antica e Moderna*. Rome, 1660.

Gaude, Francesco, Luigi Tomassetti, and Charles Cocquelines. *Bullarum, Diplomatum et Privilegiorum Sanctorum Romanorum Pontificum Taurinensis*. Augustae Taurinorum: Seb. Franco, H. Fory et Henrico Dalmazzo editoribus, 1857.

Granada, Luis de. *Il Simbolo della Fede*. Venice, 1585.

Guadagnoli, Filippo. *Apologia pro christiana religione*. Rome, 1631.

Ha-Kohen, Joseph. *Sefer 'Emeq Ha-Bakha = The Vale of Tears: With the Chronicle of the Anonymous Corrector*. Edited by Karin Almbladh. Uppsala, Sweden, 1981.

——. *Vale of Tears (Emek Habacha)*. Translated by Harry S. May. Dordrecht, 1972.

Incisa della Rocchetta, Gianni, and Nello Vian, eds. *Il primo processo per san Filippo Neri del Codice vaticano latino 3798 e in altri esemplari dell'Arichivio dell'Oratorio di Roma*. 4 vols. Vatican City: Biblioteca Apostolica Vaticana, 1957.

Index Librorum Prohibitorum usque ad annum MDCCIV. Regnante Clemente XI. Rome, 1682.

La rappresentatione della conuersione di santa Maria Maddalena. Florence, 1554.

Landrini, Ignazio. *Virginis partus eiusque filii Emmanuel diuinitatis et humanitatis scripturalis dissertatio, atque demonstratio aduersos hebraeos, & haereticos*. Milan, 1639–41.

Lapini, Agostino. *Diario Fiorentino dal 252 al 1596*. Florence, 1900.

Lassels, Richard. *The Voyage of Italy: Or a Compleat Journey through Italy*. Paris, 1670.

Leoni, Giovanni Battista. *La conuersione del peccatore a Dio*. Venice, 1591; 1592.

Marcellino, Evangelista. *Lettioni sopra Daneiele Profeta del RPF Vangelista Marcellino de Min. Osservanti. Fatte in Roma in Araceli*. Venice, 1588.

——. *Lezzioni Diciannove sopra Rut. Del RPF Vangelista Marcellino de' Minori Osservanti*. Florence, 1586.

——. *Predica del venerdi santo fatta nel duomo di Fiorenza, l'anno 1585 dal molto r.p.f. Vangelista Marcellino de' minori osseruanti di San Francesco*. Florence, 1585.

——. *Prediche della Passione e Resurrezione di Giesu Criso nostro Redentore. Fatte l'anno 1592 in Roma dal R.P.F. Vangelista Marcellino*. Florence, 1622.

——. *Sermoni Quindici sopra il salmo centonove fatti a gli Hebrei di Roma*. Florence, 1583.

Martin, Gregory. *Roma Sancta*. Edited by George Bruner Parks. Rome, 1969.

Martin, Raymond. *Pugio fidei Raymundi Martini ordinis Praedicatorum aduersus Mauros, et Iudaeos*. Paris, 1651.

Martinelli, Fioravante. *Roma ricercata nel suo sito*. Rome, 1644.

Medici, Paolo Sebastiano. *Catalogo de neofiti illustri usciti per misericordia di Dio dall'ebraismo e poi rendutisi gloriosi nel cristianesimo per esemplarità di costumi, e profondità di dottrina*. Florence, 1701.

———. *Conversione di Sabbato Nachamù rabbino ebreo in Ancona*. Florence, 1735.

Medici, Vitale. *Omelie fatte alli ebrei di Firenze nella Chiesa di Santa, et Sermoni Fatti in Più compagnie della detta città*. Florence, 1585.

Misson, Maximilien. *A New Voyage to Italy: With Curious Observations on Several Other Countries, as Germany, Switzerland, Savoy, Geneva, Flanders, and Holland. Together with Useful Instructions for Those Who Shall Travel Thither. Done out of French*. 2nd ed. London, 1699.

Misuracchi, Giulio Cesare. *Ragionamento della venuta del Messia contro la durezza & ostinatione hebraica contro la durezza & ostinatione hebraica*. Orvieto, Italy, 1629.

Montaigne, Michel de. *The Complete Works of Montaigne: Essays, Travel Journals, Letters*. Translated by Donald M. Frame. London, 1958.

———. *Montaigne's Travel Journal*. Translated by Donald Murdoch Frame. San Francisco, 1983.

Morichini, Carlo Luigi. *Degli istituti di carità per la sussistenza e l'educazione dei poveri e dei prigionieri in Roma: libri tre*. 1870; repr., Charleston, SC: Nabu Press, 2010.

Moriga, Paolo. *Historia della merauigliosa conuersione, vita essemplare, e beato fine, dell'ill.ma sig.ra Lodouica Torella, contessa di Guastalla*. Milan, 1603.

Morosini, Giulio. *Via della Fede mostrata à gli ebrei . . . Opera non men curiosa che util principalmente per chi conversa o tratta con gli'Ebrei, o predica loro*. Rome, 1683.

Mortoft, Francis. *Francis Mortoft: His Book, Being His Travels through France and Italy, 1658–1659*. Works Issued by the Hakluyt Society. 2nd Ser., No. 57. London: Printed for the Hakluyt Society, 1925.

Munday, Anthony. *The English Roman Life*. Studies in Tudor and Stuart Literature. Oxford: Oxford University Press, 1980.

Musso, Cornelio. *Delle Prediche Quadragesimali*. 2 vols. Venice, 1587.

———. *Prediche sopra il Simbolo de gli Apostoli . . . Predicate in Roma la Quaresima l'Anno MDXLII nella Chiesa di S. Lorenzo in Damaso*.

Muzio, Girolamo. *Lettere catholiche del Mutio Iustinopolitano, distinte in quattro libri*. Venice, 1751.

Nashe, Thomas. *The Unfortunate Traveller*. Edited by J. B. Steane. Hamondsworth, UK: Penguin Classics, 1972.

Natta, Giacomo. *Ragionamento della venuta del messia, contra la durezza, & ostinatione hebraica fatto alla presenza loro, da me Giacomo Natta hebreo fatto christiano, & rabino di Sacra Scrittura*. Parma, 1642.

Negri, Francesco. *Breue, & vtilissimo discorso contra la perfida ostinatione delli Hebrei . . . Fatica di Francesco Negri gia rabino hebreo, & hora per gratia dello Spirito Santo christiano*. Bologna, between 1636 and 1660.

———. *Ragionamento della venuta del messia. Contra la durezza, & ostinatione hebraica. Fatto alla presenza loro da me Francesco Negri ebreo fatto christiano, & rabino di Sacra Scrittura*. Forlì, 1628.

Ordini et Constitutioni Fatte per il Collegio di Neofiti. Rome, 1628.

Orsino, Alessandro. *Ragionamento della venuta del messia, contra la durezza, & ostinatione hebraica. Fatto alla presenza loro da me Alessandro Orsino ebreo fatto christiano & rabino di Sacra Scrittura.* Modona, Forlì, & Rimino, 1629.

Palontrotti, Melchiorre. *Breue raccolta d'argomenti, cauati dalla sac. Scrit. & dall'antiche tradittioni di rabbini, con le quali chiaramente si prouano i dogmi della religion christiana contra l'hebraica perfidia. Opera descritta da Melchior Palontrotti* . . . Venice, 1649.

——. *Disputa del christiano con l'ebreo di Melchior Palontrotti. Ad istanza di Pietro Pauolo Romaldi romano. Doue si proua chiaramente contra l'ebreo, che la riduttione temporale, che aspetta fù adempita nella liberatione di Babilonia.* Rome, 1647.

——. *Raccolta di Molti Errori, e Chimere sognate da thalmudisti sopra l'espositioni della Bibia, e riferite particolarmente da R. Salomone dove se vede la gran cecita' nella quale è caduto l'Ebraismo, per non haver accetato la vera luce Giesu Christo Signor nostro, vero Dio d'Israele.* Venice, 1649.

——. *Sferza contro l'ostinatione, et peruicacia de gl'ignoranti Ebrei. Di Melchior Palontrotti.* Bracciano, 1643.

Panvinio, Onofrio. *Le Sette Chiese Romane del RPF Onofrio Panvinio.* Rome, 1570.

Peri, Iacopo. *Breve Discorso della via del P.F. Vangelista Marcellino da Pistoia* . . . *Raccolto da Fra Iacopo Peri.* In *Prediche della Passione e Resurrezione di Giesu Criso nostro Redentore Fatte l'anno 1592 in Roma dal R.P.F. Vangelista Marcellino da Pistoia, by Evangelista* Marcellino. Florence, 1622.

Piazza, Carlo Bartolomeo. *Eusevologio Romano overo Delle Opere Pie di Roma.* Rome, 1698.

Pichi, Pietro. *De partu Virginis deiparae aduersùs Iudaeos libri tres.* Rome, 1621.

——. *Epistola a gli Ebrei d'Italia nella quale si dimostra la vanità della loro penitenza. Del P. Maestro F. Pietro Pichi da Trievi Dominicano, Predicatore de gli Ebrei in Roma.* Rome, 1622.

——. *Le Stolte Dottrine de gli Ebrei con la loro confutatione. Opera del P. maestro F. Pietro Pichi da Trieui domenicano. 1625; repr.,* Rome, 1640.

——. *Trattato della passione e morte del Messia contra gli ebrei. Del P.F. Pietro Pichi da Trieui dell'ord. de pred. maestro della sacra theol. predicatore degli ebrei in Roma.* Rome, 1618.

Pinamonte, Giovanni Pietro. *La Sinagoga disingannata: overo via facile à mostrare a qualunque ebreo la falsità della sua setta.* Bologna, 1694.

Pulinari, Dionisio. *Cronache dei Frati Minori della Provincia di Toscana.* Arezzo, Italy: Cooperativa Tipografica, 1913.

Porcacchi, Thomaso. *Delle Prediche di Diversi Illustri Theologi, et Catholici predicatori della Parola di Dio.* Venice, 1565.

Raymond, John. *Jo. Raymond, an Itinerary Contayning a Voyage, Made through Italy, in the Yeare 1646 and 1647.* London, 1648.

Razzi, Serafino. *Sermoni Predicabili dalla prima domenica dell'Avvento fino all'ottava Pasqua di Resurrezzione.* Florence, 1590.

Relationi economiche date all'eminentiss. E reverendiss. Sig. Card. Fulvio Astalli nell'ingresso alla protettione della chiesa della Madonna Santissima de' Monti di Roma. Rome, 1690.

Riera, R. [Rafael]. *L'inesauribile tesoro: la cronaca del giubileo del 1575 di R. Riera*. Edited by Salvatore Ussia. Borgomanero (Novara): Fondazione Achille Marazza, 2000.

Rovira-Bonet, Francesco. *Armatura de' Forti, Ovvero, Memorie spettanti agl'Infedeli Ebrei che siano, o turchi*. Rome, 1794.

Savonarola, Girolamo. *Selected Writings of Girolamo Savonarola: Religion and Politics, 1490–1498*. Edited by Donald Beebe and Anne Borelli. New Haven, CT: Yale University Press, 2006.

Skippon, Francis. *An Account of a Journey Made thro' Part of the Low-Countries, Germany, Italy, and France*. London, 1732.

Statuti della ven. Archiconfraternita della Santissima Trinità de' pellegrini, e convalescenti di Roma, accresciuti e riformati. Dalle stampe di Crispino Puccinelli, 1821.

Talenti, Vincenzo. *Vita del beato Giuseppe Calasanzio, della Madre di Dio, fondatore de' Chierici poveri della Madre di Dio delle scuole pie*. Rome, 1753.

Tasso, Faustino. *Venti Ragionamenti familiari sopra la venuta del Messia, Del R.P. Faustino Tasso, Minore Osservante. Fatte in Napoli ad alcuni Hebrei Per comandamento de gl'Ill.mi e R.mi Vicerè, e Arcivescovo*. Venice, 1585.

Teoli, Antonio. *Esercizj di cristiane virtù insegnate dal gran taumaturgo S. Vincenzo Ferreri dell'ordine de' Predicatori da praticarsi in sette Venerdì ad onore di detto santo. Proposti alla pietà de' suoi divoti. Da un religioso dello stess'ordine*. Rome, 1733.

———. *Storia della vita e del culto di S Vincenzo Ferrerio, dell'ordine de' Predicatori. Composta dal P Lettore Fr Antonino Teoli della congregazione di S sabina del medesimo Ordine, e Predicatore agli Ebrei di Roma*. Rome, 1735.

Totti, Pompilio. *Ritratto di Roma Moderna*. Rome, 1638.

Trevisani, Francesco. *Conferenze Pastorali istruttive sopra la verità della fede Cristiana, fatte da Monsig. Francesco Trevisani con Sara figlia di Salvatore Conegliano Ebreo di Ceneda, ora Suor Francesca Maria Trevisana*. Rome, 1728.

Vicenti, Giovanni Maria. *Il Messia Venuto . . . non solamente necessaria a gli Hebrei, ma molto utile à Cristiani e massime à' Predicatori*. Venice, 1659.

Virgulti, Lorenzo. *L'ebreo catecumeno instruito ne' principali misteri della santa fede Cristiana . . . opera utile anche a i Cristiani, che desiderano di sapere i fondamenti della loro Fede*. Rome, 1728.

Secondary Sources

Abulafia, Anna Sapir. "Introduction." In *Religious Violence between Christians and Jews: Medieval Roots, Modern Perspectives*, edited by Anna Sapir Abulafia, xi–xviii. Basingstoke, UK: Palgrave Macmillan, 2001.

Accame Lanzillotta, Maria, and Emy Dell'Oro, eds. *I 'Mirabilia urbis Romae'*. Tivoli (Rome): Tored, 2004.

Adams, Jonathan, and Jussi Hanska. *The Jewish-Christian Encounter in Medieval Preaching*. Routledge Research in Medieval Studies 6. New York: Routledge, 2015.

Adelman, Howard. "Rabbis and Reality: Public Activities of Jewish Women in Italy during the Renaissance and Catholic Restoration." *Jewish History* 5, no. 1 (April 1, 1991): 27–40.

Ago, Renata. *Gusto for Things: A History of Objects in Seventeenth-Century Rome*. Chicago: University of Chicago Press, 2012.

Åkerman, Susanna. *Queen Christina of Sweden and Her Circle: The Transformation of a Seventeenth-Century Philosophical Libertine*. Leiden: Brill, 1991.

Al Kalak, Matteo. "Converting the Jews: Inquisition and Houses of Catechumens, from Rome to Outlying Areas." In *The Roman Inquisition: Centre versus Peripheries*, edited by Katherine Aron-Beller and Christopher Black, 303–21. Leiden: Brill, 2018.

Al Kalak, Matteo, and Ilaria Pavan. *Un'altra fede: le case dei catecumeni nei territori estensi (1583–1938)*. Biblioteca della Rivista di storia e letteratura religiosa. Studi 27. Florence: Olschki, 2013.

Alberts, Tara. *Conflict and Conversion: Catholicism in Southeast Asia 1500–1700*. Oxford: Oxford University Press, 2013.

Alexander, John H. *From Renaissance to Counter-Reformation: The Architectural Patronage of Carlo Borromeo during the Reign of Pius IV*. Rome: Bulzoni, 2008.

Andersen, Jennifer L. "Anti-Puritanism, Anti-Popery, and Gallows Rhetoric in Thomas Nashe's 'The Unfortunate Traveller.'" *Sixteenth Century Journal* 35, no. 1 (2004): 43–63.

Andreatta, Michela. "The Persuasive Path: Giulio Morosini's Derekh Emunah as a Conversion Narrative." In *Bastards and Believers*, edited by Theodor Dunkelgrün and Paweł Maciejko, 156–81. Philadelphia: University of Pennsylvania Press, 2020.

Andretta, Elisa, and Federica Favino. "Scientific and Medical Knowledge in Early Modern Rome." In *A Companion to Early Modern Rome, 1492–1692*, edited by Pamela M. Jones, Barbara Wisch, and Simon Ditchfield, 515–29. Leiden: Brill, 2019.

Angeli, Giovanni, and Antonino Poppi. *Lettere del Sant'Ufficio di Roma all'Inquisizione di Padova, 1567–1660: Con nuovi documenti sulla carcerazione padovana di Tommaso Campanella in appendice (1594)*. Vol. 51. Padua: Centro Studi Antoniani, 2013.

Ansell, Richard. "Reading and Writing Travels: Maximilien Misson, Samuel Waring and the Afterlives of European Voyages, c. 1687–1714." *English Historical Review* 133, no. 565 (December 11, 2018): 1446–77.

Antinori, Aloisio. *La Magnificenza e l'utile: Progetto urbano e monarchia papale nella Roma del seicento*. Vol. 19. Roma, Storia, Cultura, Immagine 19. Rome: Gangemi, 2008.

Arcelli, Federico. *Banking and Charity in Sixteenth-Century Italy: The Holy Monte di Pietà of Rome (1539–84)*. Leicestershire, UK: Upfront, 2003.

———. *Gli statuti del 1581 del Sacro Monte di Pietà di Roma*. Vol. 15. La politica. Soveria Mannelli: Rubbettino, 1999.

———. *Il Sacro Monte di Pietà di Roma nel XVI secolo (1539–1584): dalla costituzione del Monte all'assegnazione del Banco dei Depositi*. Vol. 2. Economia e storia. Naples: Editoriale scientifica, 2001.

Ardissino, Erminia, and Elisabetta Selmi. *Visibile Teologia: Il Libro Sacro Figurato in Italia Tra Cinquecento e Seicento*. Vol. 101. Temi e Testi. Rome: Edizioni di storia e letteratura, 2012.

Armellini, Mariano. *Le chiese di Roma dal secolo IV al XIX*. Rome: Tipografia Vaticana, 1891.

Arnold, John H. *Inquisition and Power: Catharism and the Confessing Subject in Medieval Languedoc*. Philadelphia: University of Pennsylvania Press, 2013.

Aron-Beller, Katherine. "Disciplining Jews: The Papal Inquisition of Modena, 1598–1630." *Sixteenth Century Journal* 41, no. 3 (2010): 713–29.

———. "Ghettoization: The Papal Enclosure and Its Jews." In *A Companion to Early Modern Rome, 1492–1692*, edited by Pamela M. Jones, Barbara Wisch, and Simon Ditchfield, 232–46. Leiden: Brill, 2019.

———. "The Inquisition, Professing Jews, and Christian Images in Seventeenth-Century Modena." *Church History* 81, no. 3 (September t2012): 575–600.

———. "Would All the Quintessential Jews in Christian Art Please Stand Up?" *Ars Judaica* 8 (2012): 151–53.

Aron-Beller, Katherine, and Christopher F. Black. *The Roman Inquisition: Centre versus Peripheries*. Catholic Christendom, 1300–1700. Leiden: Brill, 2018.

Austin, Kenneth. *The Jews and the Reformation*. New Haven, CT: Yale University Press, 2020.

Bacci, Pietro Giacomo. *The Life of Saint Philip Neri: Apostle of Rome and Founder of the Congregation of the Oratory*. Vol. 2. London: Kegan Paul, Trench, Trübner and Co., 1902.

Baer, Marc David. "History and Religious Conversion." In *The Oxford Handbook of Religious Conversion*, edited by Lewis R. Rambo and Charles E. Farhadian, 25–47. Oxford: Oxford University Press, 2014.

Bale, Anthony Paul. *Feeling Persecuted: Christians, Jews and Images of Violence in the Middle Ages*. London: Reaktion, 2010.

Bamji, Alexandra, Geert H. Janssen, and Mary Laven, eds. *The Ashgate Research Companion to the Counter-Reformation*. Farnham, UK: Ashgate, 2013.

Barone, Giulia. "Gli ordini religiosi e la predicazione." In *Roma sancta: la città delle basiliche*, edited by Marcello Fagiolo, Maria Luisa Madonna, and Lucia Armenante, 109–12. Rome: Gangemi, 1985.

Bauer, Stefan. *The Invention of Papal History: Onofrio Panvinio between Renaissance and Catholic Reform*. Oxford-Warburg Studies. Oxford: Oxford University Press, 2019.

Bemporad, Dora Liscia. "Arredi Sacri: Argenti per un Santuario." In *La Basilica della Santissima Annunziata*, edited by Carlo Sisi, Gabriele Alessandrini, Paolo Bertoncini Sabatini, and Antonio Quattrone, 239–64. Florence: Edifir Edizioni Firenze, 2013.

Benedetti, Sandro. *Architettura del cinquecento romano*. Rome: Istituto Poligrafico e Zecca dello Stato, Libreria dello Stato, 2011.

Benedetti, Sandro, and Marcello Vittorini. *Recupero del ghetto di Roma*. Rome: Multigrafica, 1990.

Benocci, Carla. "Il Complesso assistenziale della SS. Trinità dei Pellegrini: ricerche sullo sviluppo architettonico in relazione ad alcuni anni santi." In *Roma sancta: la città delle basiliche*, edited by Marcello Fagiolo and Maria Luisa Madonna, 101–8. Milan: A. Mondadori, 1985.

Berardini, Valentina. "Discovering Performance Indicators in Late Medieval Sermons." *Medieval Sermon Studies* 54 (2010): 75–86.

Berger, David. "Cum Nimis Absurdum and the Conversion of the Jews." *Jewish Quarterly Review*, New Series, 70, no. 1 (July 1, 1979): 41–49.

———. "Mission to the Jews and Jewish-Christian Contacts in the Polemical Literature of the High Middle Ages." *American Historical Review* 91, no. 3 (June 1, 1986): 576–91.

———. *Persecution, Polemic, and Dialogue: Essays in Jewish-Christian Relations*. Judaism and Jewish Life. Boston: Academic Studies Press, 2010.

Bernabei, Roberta. *Chiese di Roma*. Milano: Electa, 2007.

Bernauer, James William, and Robert A. Maryks. *"The Tragic Couple": Encounters between Jews and Jesuits*. Vol. 169. Studies in the History of Christian Traditions. Leiden: Brill, 2014.

Bianco, Alberto. "Cesare Baronio e la conversione dei Corcos nei documenti d'archivio della Congregazione oratoriana di Roma." In *Baronio e le sue fonti: atti del convegno internazionale di studi, Sora, 10–13 ottobre 2007*, edited by Luigi Gulia. Vol. 4. Sora, Italy: Centro di studi sorani "Vincenzo Patriarca," 2009.

Biblioteca Casanatense. *Le cinquecentine ebraiche: catalogo*. Milan: Aisthesis, 2001.

Biller, Peter. "Christians and Heretics." In *The Cambridge History of Christianity: Volume 4: Christianity in Western Europe, c. 1100–c. 1500*, edited by Miri Rubin and Walter Simons, 4:170–86. Cambridge: Cambridge University Press, 2009.

Birch, Debra J. *Pilgrimage to Rome in the Middle Ages: Continuity and Change*. Rochester, NY: Boydell Press, 1998.

Bishaha, Nancy. *Creating East and West: Renaissance Humanists and the Ottoman Turks*. Philadelphia: University of Pennsylvania Press, 2004.

Black, Christopher F. *The Italian Inquisition*. New Haven, CT: Yale University Press, 2009.

Black, Christopher F., and Pamela Gravestock. *Early Modern Confraternities in Europe and the Americas: International and Interdisciplinary Perspectives*. Farnham, UK: Ashgate Publishing, 2006.

Blennow, Anna, and Stefano Fogelberg Rota. *Rome and the Guidebook Tradition from the Middle Ages to the 20th Century*. Berlin: De Gruyter, 2019.

Blum, Gerd. "Vasari on the Jews: Christian Canon, Conversion, and the Moses of Michelangelo." *Art Bulletin* 95, no. 4 (December 2013): 557–77.

Boholm, Åsa. "Christian Construction of the Other: The Role of Jews in the Early Modern Carnival of Rome." *Journal of Mediterranean Studies* 24, no. 1 (2015): 37–52.

Boiteux, Martine. "Les Juifs dans le Carnaval de la Rome moderne, XVIe–XVIIIe siècles." *Mélanges de l'Ecole française de Rome. Moyen-Age, Temps modernes* 88, no. 2 (1976): 745–87.

———. "Parcours rituels romains à l'époque moderne." In *Cérémonial et rituel à Rome (XVIe–XIXe siècle)*, 27–87. Publications de l'École française de Rome 231. Rome: École Française de Rome, 1997.

———. "Preaching to the Jews in Early Modern Rome: Words and Images." In *The Jewish-Christian Encounter in Medieval Preaching*, edited by Jonathan Adams and Jussi Hanska, 296–322. Routledge Research in Medieval Studies 6. New York: Routledge, 2015.

———. "Violences rituelles: Juifs et Chrétiens dans la Rome pontificale." In *Le destin des rituels: faire corps dans l'espace urbain, Italie-France-Allemagne*, edited by Bertrand Gilles and Ilaria Taddei, 191–207. Rome: École française de Rome, 2008.

Bolgia, Claudia. "An Engraved Architectural Drawing at Santa Maria in Aracoeli, Rome." *Journal of the Society of Architectural Historians* 62, no. 4 (December 2003): 436–47.

———. "The Felici Icon Tabernacle (1372) at S. Maria in Aracoeli, Reconstructed: Lay Patronage, Sculpture and Marian Devotion in Trecento Rome." *Journal of the Warburg and Courtauld Institutes* 68 (2005): 27–72.

———. "The So-called Tribunal of Arnolfo di Cambio at S. Maria in Aracoeli, Rome." *Burlington Magazine* 143, no. 1185 (December 2001): 753–55.

Bonacchi, Gabriella M. *Legge e peccato: anime, corpi, giustizia alla corte dei papi.* Vol. 1081. Biblioteca di Cultura Moderna Laterza. Rome: Laterza, 1995.

Bonadonna Russo, M. Teresa [Maria Teresa]. "La visita alle 'Sette Chiese' attraverso i secoli." In *Via delle sette chiese in Roma: un percorso storico, archeologico, paesistico*, edited by Gabriele M. Guarrera, 5–19. Rome: Gangemi, 1997.

Bonadonna Russo, M. Teresa [Maria Teresa], and Niccolò Del Re. *San Filippo Neri nella realtà romana del xvi secolo: atti del convegno di studio in occasione del iv centenario della morte di San Filippo Neri (1595–1995): Roma, 11–13 Maggio 1995.* Vol. 39. Rome: Società romana di storia patria, 2000.

Bonadonna Russo, Maria Teresa. "Gli Oratoriani." In *Roma sancta: la città delle basiliche*, edited by Marcello Fagiolo, Maria Luisa Madonna, and Lucia Armenante, 2:113–17. Rome: Gangemi, 1985.

———. "Il conversionismo devoto di Filippo Neri tra eredità savonaroliane e rigori inquisitoriali." *Ricerche per la storia religiosa di Roma* 10 (1998): 75–90.

Bonfil, Robert. "An Infant's Missionary Sermon Addressed to the Jews of Rome in 1553." In *New Perspectives on Jewish-Christian Relations: In Honor of David Berger*, edited by Elisheva Carlebach and Jacob J. Schacter, 33:141–74. Leiden: Brill, 2012.

———. *Jewish life in Renaissance Italy.* Translated by Anthony Oldcorn. Berkeley: University of California Press, 1994.

Bonfil, Robert [Reuven]. "Chi era Ludovico Carretto, apostata?" In *E andammo dove il vento ci spinse. La cacciata degli ebrei dalla Spagna*, edited by Guido Nathan Zazzu, 51–58. Genoa: Marietti, 1992.

Bono, Salvatore. *Schiavi: una storia mediterranea (XVI-XIX secolo).* Biblioteca storica. Bologna: Società editrice Il mulino, 2016.

Bonola, Gianfranco. "'Con dolcezza e con riguardo': il semitista parmense G. B. De Rossi e la conversione degli ebrei nel Settecento." *Cristianesimo nella Storia* (1983): 367–435.

Bonora, Elena. *Roma 1564: la congiura contro il papa.* Storia e società. Rome: Laterza, 2011.

Borgerding, Todd. "Preachers, 'Pronunciatio,' and Music: Hearing Rhetoric in Renaissance Sacred Polyphony." *Musical Quarterly* 82, no. 3–4 (October 1, 1998): 586–98.

Borzacchini, Marco. "Il Patrimonio della Trinità dei Pellegrini alla fine del cinquecento." *Ricerche per la storia religiosa di Roma Roma* 5 (1984): 237–60.

Bottero, Carlo. *I conventuali riformati italiani, 1557–1670: vicende e insediamenti.* Vol. 14. Fonti e Studi Francescani. Padua: Centro studi antoniani, 2008.

Bowd, Stephen D. "The Conversion of Margarita: A Wedding Oration in Fifteenth-Century Brescia." *Archivio italiano per la storia della pietà* 25 (2012): 139–66.

Bowd, Stephen D., and J. Donald Cullington. *"On Everyone's Lips": Humanists, Jews, and the Tale of Simon of Trent.* Tempe: Arizona Center for Medieval and Renaissance Studies, 2012.

Bradley, Mark, and Kenneth R. Stow. *Rome, Pollution and Propriety: Dirt, Disease and Hygiene in the Eternal City from Antiquity to Modernity.* British School at Rome Studies. Cambridge: Cambridge University Press, 2012.

Bregoli, Francesca, and Federica Francesconi. "Tradition and Transformation in Eighteenth-Century Europe: Jewish Integration in Comparative Perspective." *Jewish History* 24, no. 3–4 (2010): 235–46.

Brevaglieri, Sabina. *Natural desiderio di sapere: Roma barocca fra vecchi e nuovi mondi.* Prima edizione. Corte dei papi 31. Rome: Viella, 2019.

Browe, Peter. *Die Judenmission im Mittelalter und die Päpste.* Rome: S.A.L.E.R., rappresentanza della Casa Editrice Herder: Typis Pontificiae Universitatis Gregorianae, 1942.

Brundin, Abigail, and Matthew Treherne, eds. *Forms of Faith in Sixteenth Century Italy.* Farnham, UK: Ashgate Publishing, 2009.

Bulgarelli, Tullio. *Gli avvisi a stampa in Roma nel cinquecento. Bibliografia, antologia.* Rome: Istituto di studi romani, 1967.

Burke, Jill, ed. *Art and Identity in Early Modern Rome.* Farnham, UK: Ashgate Publishing, 2008.

Burke, Peter. "How to Become a Counter-Reformation Saint." In *The Counter-Reformation: The Essential Readings,* edited by David M. Luebke, 129–42. Oxford: Blackwell Publishers, 1984.

Burnett, Stephen G. "Calvin's Jewish Interlocutor: Christian Hebraism and Anti-Jewish Polemics during the Reformation." *Bibliothèque d'Humanisme et Renaissance* 55, no. 1 (January 1, 1993): 113–23.

———. *Christian Hebraism in the Reformation Era (1500–1660): Authors, Books, and the Transmission of Jewish Learning.* Leiden: Brill, 2012.

———. *From Christian Hebraism to Jewish Studies: Johannes Buxtorf (1564–1629) and Hebrew Learning in the Seventeenth Century.* Leiden: Brill, 1996.

———. *Philosemitism and Christian Hebraism in the Reformation Era (1500–1620).* Leiden: Brill, 2009.

Burroughs, Charles. "Opacity and Transparence: Networks and Enclaves in the Rome of Sixtus V." *RES: Anthropology and Aesthetics,* no. 41 (April 1, 2002): 56–71.

Busi, Giulio. "La Breve raccolta (Venezia, 1649) del polemista antigiudaico Melchiorre Palontrotti." *Annali di Ca' Foscari* 24 (1985): 1–19.

Buzzi, Franco, and Roberta Ferro. *Federico Borromeo fondatore della Biblioteca Ambrosiana: atti delle giornate di studio 25–27 novembre 2004.* Milan: Biblioteca Ambrosiana, 2005.

Cafà, Valeria. "The Via Papalis in Early Cinquecento Rome: A Contested Space between Roman Families and Curials." *Urban History* 37, no. 3 (2010): 434–51.

Caffiero, Marina. *Battesimi forzati: Storie di ebrei, cristiani e convertiti nella Roma dei papi.* Viella, 2004.

———. "Domenicani, Ebrei, Inquisizione. Tra predicazione forzata e censura libraria." In *Praedicatores, inquisitores, III: I domenicani e l'inquisizione romana. Atti del III seminario internazionale su i domenicani e l'inquisizione. 15–18 febbraio 2006,*

Roma, 205–34. Institutum Historicum Fratrum Praedicatorum Romae. Dissertationes Historicae Fasciculus 33. Rome: Istituto Storico Domenicano, 2008.

———. *Forced Baptisms: Histories of Jews, Christians, and Converts in Papal Rome.* Berkeley: University of California Press, 2012.

———. "Gli ebrei sono eretici? L'Inquisizione romana e gli ebrei tra Cinque e Ottocento." In *I tribunali della fede: continuità e discontinuità dal Medioevo all'età moderna*, edited by Susanna Peyronel Rambaldi, 245–64. Turin: Claudiana, 2007.

———. "I processi di canonizzazione come fonte per la storia dei rapporti tra ebrei e cristiani e delle conversioni." In *Hagiologica: Studi per Réginald Grégoire*, edited by Alessandra Bartolomei Romagnoli, Ugo Paoli, and Fabriano Pierantonio Piatti, 1:115–33. Monastero San Silvestro Abate, 2012.

———. *Il grande mediatore: Tranquillo Vita Corcos, un rabbino nella Roma dei papi.* 1st ed. Rome: Carocci editore, 2019.

———. "Il rabbino, il convertito e la superstizione ebraica. La polemica a distanza fra Tranquillo Vita Corcos e Paolo Sebastiano Medici." In *Prescritto e proscritto: religione e società nell'Italia moderna (secc. XVI–XIX)*, edited by Andrea Cicerchia, Guido Dall'Olio, and Matteo Duni, 127–50. Rome: Carocci editore, 2015.

———. "Introduzione." In *Roma moderna e contemporanea. Ebrei, scambi e conflitti tra XV e XX secolo*, 3–9. Rome: CROMA, 2011.

———. "'La caccia agli ebrei': Inquisizione, Casa dei Catecumeni e battesimi forzati nella Roma moderna." In *Le Inquisizioni cristiane e gli ebrei; tavola rotonda nell'ambito della conferenza annuale della ricerca (Roma, 2001)*, 503–37. Rome: Accademia Nazionale dei Lincei, 2003.

———. *Le radici storiche dell'antisemitismo: nuove fonti e ricerche: atti del seminario di studi, Roma, 13–14 dicembre 2007.* Vol. 94. Libri di Viella 94. Rome: Viella, 2009.

———. *Legami pericolosi: Ebrei e cristiani tra eresia, libri proibiti e stregoneria.* Turin: Enaudi, 2012.

———. "Non solo schiavi. La presenza dei musulmani a Roma in età moderna: il lavoro di un gruppo di ricerca." In *Venire a Roma, restare a Roma: Forestieri e stranieri fra quattrocento e settecento*, edited by Sara Cabibbo and Alessandro Serra, 291–314. Rome: Roma Tre Press, 2017.

Caffiero, Marina, and Anna Esposito, eds. *Judei de urbe. Roma e i suoi ebrei: una storia secolare.* Rome: Ministero per i Beni e le Attività Culturali Direzione Benerale per gli Archivi, 2011.

Calimani, Riccardo. *Storia degli ebrei italiani.* Vol. 2: Dal XVI al XVIII secolo. Milan: Mondadori, 2013.

Cameron, Euan. *Enchanted Europe: Superstition, Reason, and Religion, 1250–1750.* Oxford: Oxford University Press, 2010.

Canepari, Eleonora, and Laurie Nussdorfer. "A Civic Identity." In *A Companion to Early Modern Rome, 1492–1692*, edited by Pamela M. Jones, Barbara Wisch, and Simon Ditchfield, 29–43. Leiden: Brill, 2019.

Cantini, Gustavo. "Cornelio Musso dei frati minori conventuali (1511–1574), predicatore, scrittore e teologo al Concilio di Trento." *Miscellanea Francescana* 41 (1941): 145–74, 424–63.

———. *I Francescani d'Italia di fronte alle dottrine luterane e calviniste durante il cinquecento.* Rome: Pontificium Athenaeum Antonianum, 1948.

Caravale, Giorgio. *Forbidden Prayer: Church Censorship and Devotional Literature in Renaissance Italy.* Farnham, UK: Ashgate Publishing, 2011.

———. *Predicazione e Inquisizione nell'Italia del Cinquecento: Ippolito Chizzola tra eresia e controversia antiprotestante.* Bologna: Il Mulino, 2012.

Carlebach, Elisheva. *Divided Souls: Converts from Judaism in Germany, 1500–1750.* New Haven, CT: Yale University Press, 2001.

Carlebach, Elisheva, Jacob J. Schacter, and David Berger. *New Perspectives on Jewish-Christian Relations: In Honor of David Berger.* Vol. 33. Brill Reference Library of Judaism. Leiden: Brill, 2012.

Carmignano di Brenta, Arturo da. *San Lorenzo da Brindisi, dottore della chiesa universale (1559–1619).* 4 vols. Venice: Curia Provinciale dei FFMM Cappuccini, 1960.

Carroll, Stuart, ed. *Cultures of Violence: Interpersonal Violence in Historical Perspective.* Basingstoke, UK: Palgrave Macmillan, 2007.

Cassen, Flora. "Early Modern Jewish History: Ongoing Trends, Global Directions." *Church History and Religious Culture* 97, no. 3–4 (2017): 393–407.

———. *Marking the Jews in Renaissance Italy: Politics, Religion, and the Power of Symbols.* Cambridge: Cambridge University Press, 2017.

Ceen, Allan. *The Quartiere de' Banchi: Urban Planning in Rome in the First Half of the Cinquecento.* Outstanding Dissertations in the Fine Arts. New York: Garland Pub., 1986.

Champ, Judith F. *The English Pilgrimage to Rome: A Dwelling for the Soul.* Leominster, MA: Gracewing, 2000.

Chaney, Edward. *The Evolution of the Grand Tour: Anglo-Italian Cultural Relations since the Renaissance.* London: Routledge, 1998.

Chazan, Robert. *Barcelona and Beyond: The Disputation of 1263 and Its Aftermath.* Berkeley: University of California Press, 1992.

———. "The Barcelona 'Disputation' of 1263: Christian Missionizing and Jewish Response." *Speculum* 52, no. 4 (1977): 824–42.

———. *Church, State, and Jew in the Middle Ages.* New York: Behrman House, 1980.

———. *Fashioning Jewish Identity in Medieval Western Christendom.* Cambridge: Cambridge University Press, 2004.

———. *Medieval Stereotypes and Modern Antisemitism.* Berkeley: University of California Press, 1997.

Chevé, Charles-François. *Dictionnaire des Conversions, ou Essai d'encyclopédie Historique des Conversions au Catholicisme.* Paris: J. P. Migne, 1852.

Cistellini, Antonio. *San Filippo Neri: L'Oratorio e la Congregazione oratoriana: storia e spiritualità.* Brescia, Italy: Morcelliana, 1989.

Clark, Stuart. *Vanities of the Eye: Vision in Early Modern European Culture.* Oxford: Oxford University Press, 2007.

Clines, Robert John. *A Jewish Jesuit in the Eastern Mediterranean: Early Modern Conversion, Mission, and the Construction of Identity.* New York: Cambridge University Press, 2019.

Clossey, Luke. *Salvation and Globalization in the Early Jesuit Missions.* Cambridge: Cambridge University Press, 2008.

Cochrane, Eric. "Caesar Baronius and the Counter-Reformation." *Catholic Historical Review* 66, no. 1 (January 1980): 53–58.

———. "New Light on Post-Tridentine Italy: A Note on Recent Counter-Reformation Scholarship." *Catholic Historical Review* 56, no. 2 (July 1970): 291–319.

Cohen, Elizabeth S. "Honor and Gender in the Streets of Early Modern Rome." *Journal of Interdisciplinary History* 22, no. 4 (April 1, 1992): 597–625.

———. "Seen and Known: Prostitutes in the Cityscape of Late Sixteenth-Century Rome." *Renaissance Studies* 12, no. 3 (1998): 392–409.

Cohen, Elizabeth S., and Thomas V. Cohen. "Open and Shut: The Social Meanings of the Cinquecento Roman House." *Studies in the Decorative Arts* 9, no. 1 (October 1, 2001): 61–84.

Cohen, Gary B., and Franz A. J. Szabo. *Embodiments of Power: Building Baroque Cities in Europe.* Vol. 10. Austrian and Habsburg Studies. New York: Berghahn Books, 2008.

Cohen, Jeremy. *The Friars and the Jews: The Evolution of Medieval Anti-Judaism.* Ithaca, NY: Cornell University Press, 1988.

———. *Living Letters of the Law: Ideas of the Jew in Medieval Christianity.* Berkeley: University of California Press, 1999.

———. "Scholarship and Intolerance in the Medieval Academy: The Study and Evaluation of Judaism in European Christendom." *American Historical Review* 91, no. 3 (June 1, 1986): 592–613.

———. "'Synagoga Conversa': Honorius Augustodunensis, the Song of Songs, and Christianity's 'Eschatological Jew.'" *Speculum* 79, no. 2 (April 1, 2004): 309–40.

Cohen, Thomas M. "Racial and Ethnic Minorities in the Society of Jesus." In *The Cambridge Companion to the Jesuits,* edited by Thomas Worcester, 199–214. Cambridge: Cambridge University Press, 2008.

Cohen, Thomas V. "The Case of the Mysterious Coil of Rope: Street Life and Jewish Persona in Rome in the Middle of the Sixteenth Century." *Sixteenth Century Journal* 19, no. 2 (Summer 1988): 209–21.

Cohn, Samuel. "Introduction: Symbols and Rituals." In *Late Medieval and Early Modern Ritual: Studies in Italian Urban Culture,* edited by Samuel Kline Cohn, Marcello Fantoni, Franco Franceschi, and Fabrizio Ricciardelli, 7:1–14. Europa Sacra. Turnhout, Belgium: Brepols, 2013.

Colombo, Emanuele. "The Watershed of Conversion: Antonio Possevino, New Christians, and Jews." In *"The Tragic Couple": Encounters between Jews and Jesuits,* edited by James William Bernauer and Robert A. Maryks, 169:25–42. Leiden: Brill, 2014.

Colorni, Vittore. *Salomon Romano alias Filippo Herrera convertito del Cinquecento.* 1993.

Coneys Wainwright, Matthew, and Emily Michelson, eds. *A Companion to Religious Minorities in Early Modern Rome.* Leiden: Brill, 2020.

Connors, Joseph. *Alleanze e inimicizie: l'urbanistica di Roma barocca.* Rome: Laterza, 2005.

Cooperman, Bernard Dov, and Barbara Garvin. *The Jews of Italy: Memory and Identity.* Vol. 7. Bethesda: University Press of Maryland, 2000.

Copeland, Clare. "Sanctity." In *The Ashgate Research Companion to the Counter-Reformation,* edited by Alexandra Bamji, Geert H. Janssen, and Mary Laven, 225–43. Farnham, UK: Ashgate Publishing, 2013.

Corkery, James, and Thomas Worcester. *The Papacy since 1500: From Italian Prince to Universal Pastor.* Cambridge: Cambridge University Press, 2010.

Coster, Will, and Andrew Spicer. *Sacred Space in Early Modern Europe.* Cambridge: Cambridge University Press, 2005.

Coudert, Allison P. "Christian Kabbalah." In *Jewish Mysticism and Kabbalah,* edited by Frederick E. Greenspahn, 159–72. New York: NYU Press, 2011.

Coudert, Allison P., and Jeffrey S. Shoulson, eds. *Hebraica Veritas? Christian Hebraists and the Study of Judaism in Early Modern Europe.* Philadelphia: University of Pennsylvania Press, 2004.

Crum, Roger J., and John T. Paoletti. *Renaissance Florence: A Social History.* New York: Cambridge University Press, 2006.

Daileader, Philip. *Saint Vincent Ferrer, His World and Life: Religion and Society in Late Medieval Europe.* Basingstoke, UK: Palgrave Macmillan, 2016.

Dall'Aglio, Stefano. "Faithful to the Spoken Word: Sermons from Orality to Writing in Early Modern Italy." *Italianist* 34, no. 3 (2014): 463–77.

Dalton, Jessica M. *Between Popes, Inquisitors and Princes: How the First Jesuits Negotiated Religious Crisis in Early Modern Italy.* Leiden: Brill, 2020.

Dan, Joseph. *The Christian Kabbalah: Jewish Mystical Books and Their Christian Interpreters: A Symposium.* Cambridge, MA: Harvard College Library, 1997.

Dandelet, Thomas James. *Spanish Rome 1500-1700.* New Haven, CT: Yale Unversity Press, 2001.

Daniel, Norman. *Islam and the West: The Making of an Image.* Edinburgh: University Press, 1960.

Davis, Natalie Zemon. "The Rites of Violence: Religious Riot in Sixteenth-Century France." *Past and Present* 59, no. 1 (May 1, 1973): 51–91.

———. *Trickster Travels: A Sixteenth-Century Muslim between Worlds.* New York: Hill and Wang, 2007.

———. "Writing 'The Rites of Violence' and Afterward." *Past and Present* 214, no. suppl. 7 (January 1, 2012): 8–29.

Davis, Robert C. *The War of the Fists: Popular Culture and Public Violence in Late Renaissance Venice.* New York: Oxford University Press, 1994.

Davis, Robert C., and Benjamin Ravid, eds. *The Jews of Early Modern Venice.* Baltimore: Johns Hopkins University Press, 2001.

De Boer, Wietse, and Christine Göttler, eds. *Religion and the Senses in Early Modern Europe.* Leiden: Brill, 2013.

De Maio, Romeo. "La Biblioteca Apostolica Vaticana sotto Paolo IV e Pio IV." In *Collectanea Vaticana in honorem Anselmi M. Card. Albareda,* 1:274–313. Vatican City: Biblioteca Apostolica Vaticana, 1962.

———. *Riforme e miti nella Chiesa del Cinquecento.* 2nd ed. Vol. 38. Saggi. Naples: Guida, 1992.

Debby, Nirit Ben-Aryeh. "Jews and Judaism in the Rhetoric of Popular Preachers: The Florentine Sermons of Giovanni Dominici (1356–1419) and Bernardino Da Siena (1380–1444)." *Jewish History* 14, no. 2 (January 1, 2000): 175–200.

———. *The Renaissance Pulpit: Art and Preaching in Tuscany, 1400-1550.* Vol. 6. Late Medieval and Early Modern Studies. Turnhout, Belgium: Brepols, 2007.

DeJob, Charles. "Documents sur les Juifs des États pontificaux." *Revue des études juives* 9 (1884): 77–91.

Del Col, Andrea. *L'inquisizione in Italia: dal XII al XXI secolo.* Milan: Oscar Mondadori, 2006.

Delooz, Pierre. "Pour une étude sociologique de la sainteté canonisée dans l'église catholique."*Archives de Sociologie des Religions* 7, no. 13 (1962): 17–43.

Delph, Ronald K. "Polishing the Papal Image in the Counter-Reformation: The Case of Agostino Steuco." *Sixteenth Century Journal* 23, no. 1 (April 1, 1992): 35–47.

Delumeau, Jean. "Movimento di pellegrini e assistenza nel Cinquecento." In *Roma sancta: la città delle basiliche,* edited by Marcello Fagiolo and Maria Luisa Madonna, 2:91–100. Rome: Gangemi, 1985.

———. *Vie économique et sociale de rome dans la seconde moitié du xvie siècle.* 2 vols. Paris: E. De Boccard, 1957.

D'Errico, Gian Luca. *Il Corano e il pontefice: Ludovico Marracci fra cultura islamica e Curia papale.* Rome: Carocci editore, 2015.

Deutsch, Yaakov. *Judaism in Christian Eyes: Ethnographic Descriptions of Jews and Judaism in Early Modern Europe.* Oxford: Oxford University Press, 2012.

———. "A View of the Jewish Religion: Conceptions of Jewish Practice and Ritual in Early Modern Europe." *Archiv fur Reformationsgeschichte* 3 (2001): 273–95.

Devaney, Thomas. *Enemies in the Plaza: Urban Spectacle and the End of Spanish Frontier Culture, 1460–1492.* Philadelphia: University of Pennsylvania Press, 2015.

Di Nepi, Serena. "Saving Souls, Forgiving Bodies: A New Source and a Working Hypothesis on Slavery, Conversion and Religious Minorities in Early Modern Rome (16th–19th Centuries)." In *A Companion to Religious Minorities in Early Modern Rome,* edited by Matthew Coneys Wainwright and Emily Michelson, 272–97. Leiden: Brill, 2020.

———. *Surviving the Ghetto: Toward a Social History of the Jewish Community in 16th-Century Rome.* English ed. Studies in Jewish History and Culture, vol. 65. Leiden: Brill, 2020.

Diemling, Maria. "Navigating Christian Space: Jews and Christian Images in Early Modern German Lands." *Jewish Culture and History* 12, no. 3 (2010): 397–410.

Ditchfield, Simon. "Decentering the Catholic Reformation: Papacy and Peoples in the Early Modern World." *Archiv für Reformationsgeschichte* 101 (2010): 186–208.

———. "How Not to Be a Counter-Reformation Saint: The Attempted Canonization of Pope Gregory X, 1622–45." *Papers of the British School at Rome* 60 (1992): 379–422.

———. "Reading Rome as a Sacred Landscape, c. 1586–1635." In *Sacred Space in Early Modern Europe,* edited by Will Coster and Andrew Spicer, 167–92. Cambridge: Cambridge University Press, 2005.

Dixon, C. Scott, Dagmar Freist, and Mark Greengrass. *Living with Religious Diversity in Early-Modern Europe.* St. Andrews Studies in Reformation History. Farnham, UK: Ashgate Publishing, 2009.

Donnelly, John Patrick. "Antonio Possevino and Jesuits of Jewish Ancestry." *Archivum Historicum Societatis Iesu* 55 (1986): 3–31.

———. "Antonio Possevino: From Secretary to Papal Legate in Sweden." In *The Mercurian Project: Forming Jesuit Culture, 1573–1580,* edited by Thomas M. McCoog, 323–49. Saint Louis, MO: Institute of Jesuit Sources, 2004.

Dorati da Empoli, Maria Cristina. *Pier Leone Ghezzi: un protagonista del Settecento romano.* Rome: Gangemi Editore, 2008.

Drenas, Andrew J. G. "'The Standard-Bearer of the Roman Church': Lorenzo da Brindisi (1559–1619) and Capuchin Missions in the Holy Roman Empire." PhD diss., University of Oxford, 2014.

Duffy, Eamon. *Saints and Sinners: A History of the Popes.* 3rd ed. New Haven, CT: Yale University Press, 2006.

Dunkelgrün, Theodor, and Pawel Maciejko, eds. *Bastards and Believers: Jewish Converts and Conversion from the Bible to the Present.* Philadelphia: University of Pennsylvania Press, 2020.

Earle, Thomas F., and Kate J. P. Lowe. *Black Africans in Renaissance Europe.* Cambridge: Cambridge University Press, 2005.

Ebgi, Raphael. "Vincenzo Cicogna: A Forgotten Christian Kabbalist." *Materia Giudaica* 23 (2018): 391–405.

Eckstein, Nicholas A. "Prepositional City: Spatial Practice and Micro-Neighborhood in Renaissance Florence." *Renaissance Quarterly* 71, no. 4 (December 1, 2018): 1235–71.

Edwards, John. *The Jews in Christian Europe, 1400–1700.* Christianity and Society in the Modern World. London: Routledge, 1988.

———. *The Jews in Western Europe, 1400–1600.* Manchester Medieval Sources Series. Manchester: Manchester University Press, 1994.

Eire, Carlos M. N. *Reformations: The Early Modern World, 1450–1650.* New Haven, CT: Yale University Press, 2016.

Eisenbichler, Konrad. *The Boys of the Archangel Raphael: A Youth Confraternity in Florence, 1411–1785.* Toronto: University of Toronto Press, 1998.

Eliav-Feldon, Miriam. *Renaissance Impostors and Proofs of Identity.* New York: Palgrave Macmillan, 2012.

Eliav-Felton, Miriam, and Tamar Herzig, eds. *Dissimulation and Deceit in Early Modern Europe.* New York: Palgrave Macmillan, 2015.

Elukin, Jonathan M. *Living Together, Living Apart: Rethinking Jewish-Christian Relations in the Middle Ages.* Jews, Christians, and Muslims from the Ancient to the Modern World. Princeton, NJ: Princeton University Press, 2007.

Endelman, Todd M. *Leaving the Jewish Fold: Conversion and Radical Assimilation in Modern Jewish History.* Princeton, NJ: Princeton University Press, 2015.

Esposito, Anna. "Credito, ebrei, monte di pietà a Roma tra quattro e cinquecento." *Roma moderna e contemporanea* x, no. 3 (December 2002): 559–82.

———. "Gli ebrei di Roma prima del ghetto: Nuovi spunti." In *Monaci, ebrei, santi. Studi per Sofia Boesch Gajano,* edited by Antonio Volpato, 377–94. Rome: Università di Roma Tre, 2008.

———. "Gli ebrei a Roma tra quattro e cinquecento." *Quaderni storici* 18 (1983): 815–46.

———. "La città e i suoi abitanti." In *Roma del Rinascimento,* edited by Antonio Pinelli, 3–48. Storia di Roma dall'antichità ad oggi. Rome: Laterza, 2001.

———. "Pellegrini, stranieri, curiali ed ebrei a Roma." In *Roma medievale,* edited by André Vauchez and Giulia Barone, 1:213–40. Rome: Laterza, 2001.

———. "The Sephardic Communities in Rome in the Early Sixteenth Century." *Imago Temporis. Medium Aevum* 1 (2007): 171–79.

———. *Un'altra Roma: minoranze nazionali e comunità ebraiche tra Medioevo e Rinascimento.* Rome: Il Calamo, 1995.

Esposito, Anna, and M. Procaccia. "Ebrei in giudizio: centro e periferia dello Stato pontificio nella documentazione processuale (secc. XV–XVI)." *Roma moderna e contemporanea* 19, no. 1 (2011): 11–28.

Fabre-Vassas, Claudine. *The Singular Beast: Jews, Christians and the Pig.* New York: Columbia University Press, 1997.

Fagiolo, Marcello, Maria Luisa Madonna, and Lucia Armenante. *Roma Sancta: la città delle basiliche.* Vol. 2. Rome: Gangemi, 1985.

Fagiolo, Marcello, Maria Luisa Madonna, and Lucia Armenante. *Roma 1300–1875: L'arte degli anni santi.* Milan: A. Mondadori, 1984.

Fantoni, Marcello. "Symbols and Rituals: Definition of a Field of Study." In *Late Medieval and Early Modern Ritual: Studies in Italian Urban Culture*, edited by Samuel Cohn, Marcello Fantoni, Franco Franceschi, and Fabrizio Ricciardelli, 7:15–40. Turnhout, Belgium: Brepols, 2013.

Feci, Simona. "The Death of a Miller: A Trial Contra Hebreos in Baroque Rome." *Jewish History* 7, no. 2 (October 1, 1993): 9–27.

Fehleison, Jill R. "Appealing to the Senses: The Forty Hours Celebrations in the Duchy of Chablais, 1597–98." *Sixteenth Century Journal* 36, no. 2 (2005): 375–96.

Fehler, Timothy G., Greta Grace Kroeker, Charles H. Parker, and Jonathan Ray, eds. *Religious Diaspora in Early Modern Europe: Strategies of Exile.* London: Pickering and Chatto, 2014.

Feitler, Bruno. *The Imaginary Synagogue: Anti-Jewish Literature in the Portuguese Early Modern World (16th–18th Centuries).* Leiden: Brill, 2015.

Fenlon, Dermot. 'Pole, Carranza, and the Pulpit'. In *Reforming Catholicism in the England of Mary Tudor: The Achievement of Friar Bartolomé Carranza*, edited by John Edwards and Ronald Truman, 81–98. Farnham, UK: Ashgate Publishing, 2005.

Ferrara, Micol. *Dentro e fuori dal ghetto: I luoghi della presenza ebraica a Roma tra XVI e XIX secolo.* Milan: Mondadori Università, 2015.

Ferrara, Pierina. "La struttura edilizia del 'serraglio' degli ebrei romani (secc. xvi–xix)." *Roma moderna e contemporanea. Ebrei, scambi e conflitti tra XV e XX secolo*, 83–102. Rome: CROMA, 2012.

Findlen, Paula. *Possessing Nature: Museums, Collecting, and Scientific Culture in Early Modern Italy.* Berkeley: University of California Press, 1994.

Fiorani, Francesca. "Post-Tridentine 'Geographia Sacra.' The Galleria Delle Carte Geografiche in the Vatican Palace." *Imago Mundi* 48 (January 1996): 124–48.

Fiorani, Luigi. "'Charità e pietate.' Confraternite e gruppi devoti nella città rinascimentale e barocca." In *Roma, la città del papa*, edited by Luigi Fiorani and Adriano Prosperi: 430–76. Storia d'Italia: annali 16. Turin: G. Einaudi, 2000.

———. "Gli anni santi del Cinque-Seicento e la confraternità della ss. Trinità dei Pellegrini." In *Roma sancta: la città delle basiliche*, edited by Marcello Fagiolo, Maria Luisa Madonna, and Lucia Armenante, 2:85–91. Rome: Gangemi, 1985.

———. "Il Carisma dell'ospitalità: La Confraternità della Trinità dei Pellegrini nei Giubilei Cinque-Secenteschi." In *La Storia dei Giubilei*, edited by Gloria Fossi, Jacques Le Goff, and Claudio M. Strinati, 2:308–25. Florence: Giunti, 1997.

———. *Riti, cerimonie, feste e vita di popolo nella Roma dei papi.* Vol. 12. Roma cristiana. Bologna: Cappelli, 1970.

———. "Verso la nuova città. Conversione e conversionismo a Roma nel Cinque-Seicento." *Ricerche per la storia religiosa di Roma* 10 (1998): 91–186.

Fiorani, Luigi, and Adriano Prosperi, eds. *Roma, la città del papa.* Vol. 16. Storia d'Italia: annali. Turin: G. Einaudi, 2000.

Fischer, Lucia Frattarelli. "Cristiani nuovi e nuovi ebrei in Toscana fra cinque e seicento. legittimazioni e percorsi individuali." In *L'identità dissimulata: giudaizzanti iberici nell'Europa cristiana dell'età moderna,* edited by Pier Cesare Ioly Zorattini, 99–150. Florence: Leo S. Olschki, 2000.

Fitzgerald, D. J. "A Seventeenth Century Hebrew Translation of Saint Thomas." In *Millenarianism and Messianism in Early Modern European Culture, Volume II: Catholic Millenarianism: From Savonarola to the Abbé Grégoire,* edited by Karl A. Kottman, 71–78. Dordrecht: Springer Netherlands, 2001.

Fleck, Andrew. "Anatomizing the Body Politic: The Nation and the Renaissance Body in Thomas Nashe's *The Unfortunate Traveller.*" *Modern Philology* 104, no. 3 (2007): 295–328.

Foa, Anna. "Converts and Conversos in Sixteenth-Century Italy: Marranos in Rome." In *The Jews of Italy: Memory and Identity,* edited by Bernard Dov Cooperman and Barbara Garvin, 109–29. Bethesda: University Press of Maryland, 2000.

———. "Il gioco del proselitismo: Politica delle conversioni e controllo della violenza nella Rome del Cinquecento." In *Ebrei e cristiani nell'Italia medievale e moderna: conversioni, scambi, contrasti,* edited by Michele Luzzati, Michele Olivari, and Alessandra Veronese, 155–70. Rome: Carucci, 1988.

———. "'Limpieza' versus Mission: Church, Religious Orders, and Conversion in the Sixteenth Century." In *Friars and Jews in the Middle Ages and Renaissance,* edited by Steven J. McMichael and Susan E. Myers, 299–311. Leiden: Brill, 2004.

Forcella, Vincenzo. *Iscrizioni delle chiese e d'altri edificii di Roma dal secolo XI fino ai giorni nostri. 1.* Vol. 1. Rome: Cecchini, 1869.

———. *Iscrizioni delle chiese e d'altri edificii di Roma dal secolo XI fino ai giorni nostri. 7.* Vol. 7. Rome: Cecchini, 1876.

Fosi, Irene. "Between Conversion and Reconquest: The Venerable English College between the Late Sixteenth and Seventeenth Centuries." In *A Companion to Religious Minorities in Early Modern Rome,* edited by Matthew Coneys Wainwright and Emily Michelson, 115–40. Leiden: Brill, 2020.

———. "'Con cuore sincero e con fede non finta': conversioni a Roma in età moderna fra controllo e accoglienza." In *Les modes de la conversion confessionnelle à l'époque moderne: autobiographie, altérité et construction des identités religieuses,* edited by Maria Cristina Pitassi and Daniela Solfaroli Camillocci, 215–33. Florence: Olschki, 2010.

———. *Convertire lo straniero: forestieri e Inquisizione a Roma in età moderna.* Corte dei papi 21. Rome: Viella, 2011.

———. "Court and City in the Ceremony of the Possesso in the Sixteenth Century." In *Court and Politics in Papal Rome,* edited by Gianvittorio Signorotto and Maria Antonietta Visceglia, 31–52. Cambridge: Cambridge University Press, 2002.

Fosi, Irene. "Fasto e decadenza degli anni santi." In *Roma, la città del papa,* edited by Luigi Fiorani and Adriano Prosperi, 16:789–821. Storia d'Italia: annali. Turin: G. Einaudi, 2000.

———. *Papal Justice: Subjects and Courts in the Papal State, 1500–1700.* Translated by Thomas V. Cohen. Washington, DC: Catholic University of America Press, 2011.

———. "Percorsi di salvezza. Preparare le strade, accogliere, convertire nella Roma barocca." In *La storia dei giubilei,* edited by Gloria Fossi, Jacques Le Goff, and Claudio M. Strinati, 3:42–83. Florence: Giunti, 1997.

———. "'Procurar a tutt'huomo la conversione degli heretici': Roma e le conversioni nell'Impero nella prima metà del seicento." *Quellen und Forschungen aus italienischen Archiven und Bibliotheken* 88 (2008): 335–68.

———. "A proposito di Nationes a Roma in età moderna: provenienza, appartenenza culturale, integrazione sociale." *Quellen und Forschungen aus italienischen Archiven und Bibliotheken* 97 (2017): 383–93.

———. "*Roma patria comune?* Foreigners in Early Modern Rome." In *Art and Identity in Early Modern Rome,* edited by Jill Burke and Michael Bury, 27–44. Farnham, UK: Ashgate Publishing, 2008.

———. "Usare la biblioteca: la Vaticana nella cultura europea." In *La Vaticana nel Seicento (1590–1700). Una biblioteca di biblioteche,* edited by Claudia Montuschi, 761–98. Vatican City: Biblioteca Apostolica Vaticana, 2014.

Fossi, Gloria, Jacques Le Goff, and Claudio M. Strinati. *La storia dei giubilei.* Florence, Giunti, 1997.

Fowler, Rowena. "Browning's Jews." *Victorian Poetry* 35, no. 3 (1997): 245–65.

Fragnito, Gigliola. "'Cardinals' Courts in Sixteenth-Century Rome." *Journal of Modern History* 65, no. 1 (March 1,1993): 26–56.

———, ed. *Church, Censorship and Culture in Early Modern Italy.* Cambridge: Cambridge University Press, 2001.

———. *La Bibbia al rogo: La censura ecclesiastica e i volgarizzamenti della Scrittura (1471–1605).* Bologna: Il Mulino, 1997.

Francesconi, Federica. "'This Passage Can Also Be Read Differently . . .': How Jews and Christians Censored Hebrew Texts in Early Modern Modena." *Jewish History* 26, no. 1–2 (2012): 139–60.

Frediani, Francesco. *Prose e versi.* Vol. 2. Naples: Stamperia del Vaglio, 1854.

Fredriksen, Paula. *Augustine and the Jews: A Christian Defense of Jews and Judaism.* 1st ed. New York: Doubleday, 2008.

Freiberg, Jack. *The Lateran in 1600: Christian Concord in Counter-Reformation Rome.* Cambridge: Cambridge University Press, 1995.

———. "The Lateran Patronage of Gregory XIII and the Holy Year 1575." *Zeitschrift für Kunstgeschichte* 54, no. 1 (January 1, 1991): 66–87.

Friedman, Jerome. "The Reformation and Jewish Antichristian Polemics." *Bibliothèque d'Humanisme et Renaissance* 41, no. 1 (January 1, 1979): 83–97.

———. "Sixteenth-Century Christian-Hebraica: Scripture and the Renaissance Myth of the Past." *Sixteenth Century Journal* 11, no. 4 (December 1, 1980): 67–85.

Fumaroli, Marc. *L'Âge de l'éloquence: Rhétorique et 'res literaria' de la Renaissance au seuil de l'époque classique.* Paris: Librairie Droz S.A., 2008.

Furstenberg-Levi, Shulamit. "The Book of Homilies of the Convert to Catholicism Vitale Medici: Two Models of Identity." *Archivio Italiano per La Storia della Pietà* 25 (2012): 167–84.

———. "The Boundaries between 'Jewish' and 'Catholic' Space in Counter-Reformation Florence as Seen by the Convert Vitale Medici." *Italia* (2008): 65–90.

————. "The Sermons of a Rabbi Converted to Christianity: Between Synagogue and Church." In *The Turn of the Soul: Representations of Religious Conversion in Early Modern Art and Literature*, edited by Harald Hendrix, Todd Richardson, and Lieke Stelling, 281–98. Leiden: Brill, 2011.

Gamrath, Helge. *Roma sancta renovata: Studi sull'urbanistica di Roma nella seconda metà del sec. xvi con particolare riferimento al pontificato di Sisto V (1585–1590)*. Rome: L'Erma di Bretschneider, 1987.

Garofalo, Fausto. *L'ospedale della ss. Trinita' dei Pellegrini e dei Convalescenti*. Collana di studi storici sull'ospedale di santo spirito in saxia e sugli ospedali romani. Rome: A. Urbinati, 1950.

Gentilcore, David. "'Adapt Yourselves to the People's Capabilities': Missionary Strategies, Methods and Impact in the Kingdom of Naples, 1600–1800." *Journal of Ecclesiastical History* 45, no. 2 (1994): 269–96.

————. "Purging Filth: Plague and Responses to It in Rome, 1657." In *Rome, Pollution and Propriety: Dirt, Disease and Hygiene in the Eternal City from Antiquity to Modernity*, edited by Mark Bradley and Kenneth R. Stow, 153–68. British School at Rome Studies. Cambridge: Cambridge University Press, 2012.

Ghilardi, Massimiliano. "'Quasi che mescoliamo le cose profane con le sacre.' La riscoperta delle catacombe ebraiche di Monteverde nella prima età moderna." In *Judei de urbe. Roma e i suoi ebrei: una storia secolare*, edited by Marina Caffiero and Anna Esposito, 23–52. Rome: Ministero per i beni e le attività culturali direzione generale per gli archivi, 2011.

Ghilardi, Massimiliano, Gaetano Sabatini, Matteo Sanfilippo, and Donatella Strangio, eds. *Ad ultimos usque terrarum terminos in fide propaganda: Roma fra promozione e difesa della fede in età moderna*. Studi di storia delle istituzioni ecclesiastiche 5. Viterbo, Italy: Edizioni Sette città, 2014.

Ghirardo, Diane Yvonne. "The Topography of Prostitution in Renaissance Ferrara." *Journal of the Society of Architectural Historians* 60, no. 4 (2001): 402–31.

Ghobrial, John-Paul A. "The Life and Hard Times of Solomon Negri: An Arabic Teacher in Early Modern Europe." In *The Teaching and Learning of Arabic in Early Modern Europe*, edited by Jan Loop, Alastair Hamilton, and Charles Burnett, 310–31. Leiden: Brill, 2017.

Gies, Joseph. *Life in a Medieval City*. Medieval Life Series. London: Barker, 1969.

Girard, Aurélien. "Teaching and Learning Arabic in Early Modern Rome: Shaping a Missionary Language." In *The Teaching and Learning of Arabic in Early Modern Europe*, edited by Jan Loop, Alastair Hamilton, and Charles Burnett, 189–212. Leiden: Brill, 2017.

Glaser, Eliane. *Judaism without Jews: Philosemitism and Christian Polemic in Early Modern England*. Basingstoke, UK: Palgrave Macmillan, 2007.

Gnoli, Umberto. *Topografia e toponomastica di Roma medioevale e moderna*. Nuova accresciuta. Foligno, Italy: Edizioni dell'arquata, 1984.

Goldberg, Edward L. *Jews and Magic in Medici Florence: The Secret World of Benedetto Blanis*. Toronto: University of Toronto Press, 2011.

Goldish, Matt. "Mystical Messianism." In *Jewish Mysticism and Kabbalah*, edited by Frederick E. Greenspahn, 115–38. Insights and Scholarship. New York: NYU Press, 2011.

Goldstein, David. "Jews and Robert Browning: Fiction and Fact." *Jewish Historical Studies* 30 (1987): 125–34.

Gordini, Gian Domenico. *Storie di pellegrini, di briganti e di Anni Santi*. Vol. 3. Chiesa Sotto Inchiesta 3. Turin: Marietti, 1974.

Gotor, Miguel. *I beati del papa: Santità, inquisizione e obbedienza in età moderna*. Florence: Leo S. Olschki, 2002.

———. "Le vite di San Pio V dal 1572 al 1712 tra censura, agiografia e storia." In *Pio V nella società e nella politica del suo tempo*, edited by Maurilio Guasco and Angelo Torre, 207–49. Bologna: Il mulino, 2005.

Graizbord, David L. *Souls in Dispute: Converso Identities in Iberia and the Jewish Diaspora, 1580–1700*. Philadelphia: University of Pennsylvania Press, 2004.

Grayzel, Solomon. *The Church and the Jews in the XIIIth Century*. Vol. 2, 1254–1314. Detroit: Wayne State University Press, 1989.

Graziano, Frank. *Wounds of Love: The Mystical Marriage of Saint Rose of Lima*. Oxford: Oxford University Press, 2004.

Grendler, Paul. *The Roman Inquisition and the Venetian Press, 1540–1605*. Princeton, NJ: Princeton University Press, 1977.

Groppi, Angela. *Gli abitanti del ghetto di Roma: Descriptio hebreorum del 1733*. Rome: Viella, 2014.

Gutwirth, Eleazar. "Conversions to Christianity amongst Fifteenth-Century Spanish Jews: An Alternative Explanation." In *Shlomo Simonsohn Jubilie Volume: Studies on the History of the Jews in the Middle Ages and Renaissance Period*, edited by Daniel Carpi, 97–121. Tel Aviv: Tel Aviv University, 1993.

Hacker, Joseph, and Adam Shear, eds. *The Hebrew Book in Early Modern Italy*. Jewish Culture and Contexts. Philadelphia: University of Pennsylvania Press, 2011.

Hadfield, Andrew. "Thomas Nashe, *The Unfortunate Traveller* (1594)." In *Handbook of English Renaissance Literature*, edited by Ingo Berensmeyer, 395–410. Berlin: De Gruyter, 2019.

Hall, Marcia B., ed. *Rome: Artistic Centers of the Italian Renaissance*. Cambridge: Cambridge University Press, 2005.

Hall, Marcia B., and Tracy E. Cooper, eds. *The Sensuous in the Counter-Reformation Church*. Cambridge: Cambridge University Press, 2013.

Hames, Harvey J. *The Art of Conversion: Christianity and Kabbalah in the Thirteenth Century*. Medieval Mediterranean. Vol. 26. Leiden: Brill, 2000.

Hamilton, Donna B. *Anthony Munday and the Catholics, 1560–1633*. Farnham, UK: Ashgate Publishing, 2005.

Hamilton, Sarah, and Andrew Spicer. *Defining the Holy: Sacred Space in Medieval and Early Modern Europe*. Farnham, UK: Ashgate Publishing, 2005.

Hanska, Jussi. "Mendicant Preachers as Disseminators of Anti-Jewish Literary Topoi: The Case of Luca Da Bitonto." In *From Words to Deeds: The Effectiveness of Preaching in the Late Middle Ages*, edited by Maria Giuseppina Muzzarelli, 117–38. Turnhout, Belgium: Brepols, 2014.

Heal, Bridget. *A Magnificent Faith: Art and Identity in Lutheran Germany*. Oxford: Oxford University Press, 2017.

Henderson, John. *Piety and Charity in Late Medieval Florence*. Oxford: Oxford University Press, 1994.

Henkel, Willi. "Verfügungen der Kongregation in der Judenfrage." In *Sacrae Congregationis de Propaganda Fide Memoria Rerum 1622–1972*, 1–2:367–74. Rome: Herder, 1972.

Herzig, Tamar. *Christ Transformed into a Virgin Woman: Lucia Brocadelli, Heinrich Institoris, and the Defense of the Faith.* Rome: Edizioni di storia e letteratura, 2013.

——. *A Convert's Tale: Art, Crime, and Jewish Apostasy in Renaissance Italy.* Cambridge, MA: Harvard University Press, 2019.

——. "The Future of Studying Jewish Conversion in Renaissance Italy." *I Tatti Studies in the Italian Renaissance* 22, no. 2 (Fall 2019): 311–18.

——. "The Hazards of Conversion: Nuns, Jews, and Demons in Late Renaissance Italy." *Church History* 85, no. 3 (September 2016): 468–501.

Heyberger, Bernard. "L'islam dei missionari cattolici (Medio Oriente, Seicento)." In *L'islam visto da Occidente: cultura e religione del Seicento europeo di fronte all'islam: atti del convegno internazionale, Milano, Università degli studi, 17–18 ottobre 2007,* edited by Bernard Heyberger, Mercedes García-Arenal, Emanuele Colombo, and Paola Vismara, 289–314. Genoa: Marietti 1820, 2009.

——. "L'Orient et l'islam dans l'érudition européenne du xvii e siècle." *Dix-septième siècle* 268, no. 3 (2015): 495–508.

——. "Polemic Dialogues between Christians and Muslims in the Seventeenth Century." *Journal of the Economic and Social History of the Orient* 55, no. 2–3 (2012): 495–516.

Heyberger, Bernard, Mercedes García-Arenal, Emanuele Colombo, and Paola Vismara, eds. *L'islam visto da Occidente: cultura e religione del Seicento europeo di fronte all'islam: atti del convegno internazionale, Milano, Università degli studi, 17–18 ottobre 2007.* 1st ed. Genoa: Marietti 1820, 2009.

Hill, Tracey. *Anthony Munday and Civic Culture: Theatre, History, and Power in Early Modern London: 1580–1633.* Manchester: Manchester University Press, 2004.

Hochmann, Michel, and Accademia di Francia, eds. *Villa Medici: Il Sogno di Un Cardinale: Collezioni e Artisti di Ferdinando de' Medici.* Rome: De Luca, 1999.

Hoffmann, Karl. *Ursprung und Anfangstätigkeit des ersten päpstlichen Missionsinstituts; ein Beitrag zur Geschichte der katholischen Juden- und Mohammedanermission im sechzehnten Jahrhundert.* Vol. 4. Veröffentlichungen des Internationalen Instituts für missionswissenchaftliche Forschungen; Missionswissenschaftliche Abhandlungen und Texte. Münster: Aschendorff, 1923.

Holmberg, Eva Joanna. *Jews in the Early Modern English Imagination: A Scattered Nation.* Farnham, UK: Ashgate Publishing, 2011.

Horowitz, Elliott S. "The Eve of the Circumcision: A Chapter in the History of Jewish Nightlife." *Journal of Social History* 23, no. 1 (October 1, 1989): 45–69.

——. "Processions, Piety, and Jewish Confraternities." In *The Jews of Early Modern Venice,* edited by Robert C. Davis and Benjamin Ravid, 231–47. Baltimore: Johns Hopkins University Press, 2001.

——. *Reckless Rites: Purim and the Legacy of Jewish Violence.* Jews, Christians, and Muslims from the Ancient to the Modern World. Princeton, NJ: Princeton University Press, 2006.

——. "The Use and Abuse of Anti-Judaism." *Journal of Religion* 95, no. 1 (January 2015): 94–106.

Hsia, R. Po-Chia. *A Companion to Early Modern Catholic Global Missions.* Leiden: Brill, 2018.

——. *The Myth of Ritual Murder: Jews and Magic in Reformation Germany.* New Haven, CT: Yale University Press, 1988.

——. *Trent 1475: Stories of a Ritual Murder Trial*. New Haven, CT: Yale University Press, 1992.

Hughes, Diane Owen. "Distinguishing Signs: Ear-Rings, Jews and Franciscan Rhetoric in the Italian Renaissance City." *Past and Present*, no. 112 (1986): 3–59.

Hülsen, Christian. *Le chiese di Roma nel medio evo*. Florence: Leo S. Olschki, 1927.

Hunt, John M. "The Conclave from the 'Outside In': Rumor, Speculation, and Disorder in Rome during Early Modern Papal Elections." *Journal of Early Modern History* 16 (2012): 355–82.

——. *The Vacant See in Early Modern Rome: A Social History of the Papal Interregnum*. Leiden: Brill, 2016.

——. "Violence and Disorder in the Sede Vacante of Early Modern Rome, 1559–1655." PhD diss., Ohio State University, 2009.

Iarocci, Bernice. "The Santissima Annunziata of Florence, Medici Portraits, and the Counter Reformation in Italy." PhD diss., Department of Art, University of Toronto, 2015.

Idel, Moshe. "Major Currents in Italian Kabbalah between 1560 and 1660." In *Essential Papers on Jewish Culture in Renaissance and Baroque Italy*, edited by David B. Ruderman, 345–68. New York: NYU Press, 1992.

Infelise, Mario. *I padroni dei libri: il controllo sulla stampa nella prima età moderna*. Prima edizione. Storia e società. Rome: Laterza, 2014.

——. "Roman Avvisi: Information and Politics in the Seventeenth Century." In *Court and Politics in Papal Rome, 1492–1700*, edited by Gianvittorio Signorotto and Maria Antonietta Visceglia, 212–28. Cambridge: Cambridge University Press, 2002.

Ingersoll, Richard Joseph. "The Ritual Use of Public Space in Renaissance Rome." PhD diss., University of California at Berkeley, 1985.

Ioly Zorattini, Pietro. *I nomi degli altri: conversioni a Venezia e nel Friuli Veneto in età moderna*. Florence: Olschki, 2008.

Jack, Gillian. "Sex, Salvation, and the City : The Monastery of Sant'Elisabetta Delle Convertite as a Civic Institution in Florence, 1329–1627." PhD diss., School of History, University of St Andrews, 2018.

Jedin, Hubert. Der Franziskaner Cornelio Musso, Bischof von Bitonto: sein Lebensgang und seine kirchliche Wirksamkeit." *Römische Quartalschrift für christliche Altertumskunde und für Kirchengeschichte* 41 (1993): 207–75.

Jones, Pamela M. *Altarpieces and Their Viewers in the Churches of Rome from Caravaggio to Guido Reni*. Farnham, UK: Ashgate Publishing, 2008.

——. "The Pope as Saint: Pius V in the Eyes of Sixtus V." In *The Papacy since 1500: From Italian Prince to Universal Pastor*, edited by James Corkery and Thomas Worcester, 47–68. Cambridge: Cambridge University Press, 2010.

Jones, Pamela M., Barbara Wisch, and Simon Ditchfield, eds. *A Companion to Early Modern Rome, 1492–1692*. Leiden: Brill, 2019.

Jütte, Daniel. "Interfaith Encounters between Jews and Christians in the Early Modern Period and beyond: Toward a Framework." *American Historical Review* 118, no. 2 (January 4, 2013): 378–400.

——. "'They Shall Not Keep Their Doors or Windows Open': Urban Space and the Dynamics of Conflict and Contact in Premodern Jewish-Christian Relations." *European History Quarterly* 46, no. 2 (April 1, 2016): 209–37.

Kaplan, Debra. *Beyond Expulsion: Jews, Christians, and Reformation Strasbourg.* Stanford, CA: Stanford University Press, 2011.

Kaplan, Debra, and Magda Teter. "Out of the (Historiographic) Ghetto: European Jews and Reformation Narratives." *Sixteenth Century Journal* 40, no. 2 (July 2009): 365–94.

Karant-Nunn, Susan C. *The Reformation of Feeling: Shaping the Religious Emotions in Early Modern Germany.* New York: Oxford University Press, 2010.

Karmon, David E. *The Ruin of the Eternal City: Antiquity and Preservation in Renaissance Rome.* New York: Oxford University Press, 2011.

Katz, Dana E. "'Clamber Not You up to the Casements': On Ghetto Views and Viewing." *Jewish History* 24, no. 2 (January 1, 2010): 127–53.

———. *The Jew in the Art of the Italian Renaissance.* Philadelphia: University of Pennsylvania Press, 2008.

———. *The Jewish Ghetto and the Visual Imagination of Early Modern Venice.* New York: Cambridge University Press, 2017.

Katznelson, Ira, and Miri Rubin. *Religious Conversion: History, Experience and Meaning.* Farnham, UK: Ashgate Publishing, 2014.

Kertzer, David I. *The Kidnapping of Edgardo Mortara.* 1st ed. New York: Alfred Knopf, 1997.

Kitzes, Adam H. "The Hazards of Professional Authorship: Polemic and Fiction in Anthony Munday's English Roman Life." *Renaissance Studies* 31 no. 2 (May 1, 2016): 444–61.

Klaniczay, Gábor. *Procès de Canonisation Au Moyen Âge: Aspects Juridiques et Religieux* Collection de l'École française de Rome 340. Rome: École française de Rome, 2004.

Kleinhenz, Christopher. *Medieval Italy: An Encyclopedia.* Routledge Encyclopedias of the Middle Ages. New York: Routledge, 2004.

Kubersky-Piredda, Susanne, Alexander Koller, and Tobias Daniels. *Identità e rappresentazione: le chiese nazionali a Roma, 1450–1650.* Rome: Campisano editore, 2015.

Lacopo, Frank. "Crisis and Conversion to Catholicism in Early Modern Rome and beyond, c. 1500–c. 1600." MA thesis, Ball State University, 2018.

Lasker, Daniel J. "Jewish Anti-Christian Polemics in the Early Modern Period: Change or Continuity?" In *Tradition, Heterodoxy, and Religious Culture: Judaism and Christianity in the Early Modern Period,* edited by Chanita Goodblatt and Howard T. Kreisel, 469–88. Goldstein-Goren Library of Jewish Thought. Beersheba, Israel: Ben Gurion University of the Negev, 2006.

Lazar, Lance Gabriel. "Negotiating Conversions: Catechumens and the Family in Early Modern Italy." In *Piety and Family in Early Modern Europe: Essays in Honour of Steven Ozment,* edited by Marc R. Forster and Benjamin J. Kaplan, 152–77. Farnham: UK: Ashgate Publishing, 2005.

———. *Working in the Vineyard of the Lord: Jesuit Confraternities in Early Modern Italy.* Toronto: University of Toronto Press, 2005.

Leber, Barbara. "Jewish Convert in Counter-Reformation Rome: Giovanni Paolo Eustachio." PhD diss., University of Maryland, 2001.

Lee, Egmont. *Habitatores in Urbe: The Population of Renaissance Rome = la popolazione di Roma nel Rinascimento.* Collana studi e proposte 4. Rome: Università La Sapienza, 2006.

Lee, Rosemary. "Theologies of Failure: Islamic Conversion in Early Modern Rome." *Essays in History* 45 (January 2012): 59–74.

Leonard, Amy. *Nails in the Wall: Catholic Nuns in Reformation Germany*. Chicago: University of Chicago Press, 2005.

Leone, Massimo. *Saints and Signs: A Semiotic Reading of Conversion in Early Modern Catholicism*. Berlin: De Gruyter, 2010.

Lerner, L. Scott. "Narrating over the Ghetto of Rome." *Jewish Social Studies*, New Series, 8, no. 2–3 (January 1, 2002): 1–38.

Liebes, Yehuda. *Studies in the Zohar*. Edited by Stephanie Nakache, Arnold Schwartz, and Penina Peli. Albany: SUNY Press, 1993.

Liebreich, Karen. *Fallen Order: Intrigue, Heresy, and Scandal in the Rome of Galileo and Caravaggio*. New York: Grove Press, 2004.

Limor, Ora. "Missionary Merchants: Three Medieval Anti-Jewish Works from Genoa." *Journal of Medieval History* 17, no. 1 (1991): 35–51.

Linder, Amnon. "Appendix B: The Reconstructed Complete Encounter during the Possession-Procession of Clement XIII (1758)." *Jewish Quarterly Review* 99, no. 3 (2009).

———. "'The Jews Too Were Not Absent . . . Carrying Moses's Law on Their Shoulders': The Ritual Encounter of Pope and Jews from the Middle Ages to Modern Times." *Jewish Quarterly Review* 99, no. 3 (2009): 323–95.

Lipton, Sara. *Dark Mirror: The Medieval Origins of Anti-Jewish Iconography*. New York: Metropolitan Books, 2014.

Lirosi, Alessia. "Monacare le ebree. Il monastero romano della Ss. Annunziata ai Pantani. Una ricerca in corso." *Rivista di storia del cristianesimo* 1 (2013): 147–80.

Long, Pamela O. *Engineering the Eternal City: Infrastructure, Topography, and the Culture of Knowledge in Late Sixteenth-Century Rome*. Chicago: University of Chicago Press, 2018.

Lotz-Huemann, Ute. "Confessionalization." In *The Ashgate Research Companion to the Counter-Reformation*, edited by Alexandra Bamji, Geert H. Janssen, and Mary Laven, 33–53. Farnham, UK: Ashgate Publishing, 2013.

Louthan, Howard. *Converting Bohemia: Force and Persuasion in the Catholic Reformation*. Cambridge: Cambridge University Press, 2009.

Luria, Keith P. *Sacred Boundaries: Religious Coexistence and Conflict in Early-Modern France*. Washington, DC: Catholic University of America Press, 2005.

Luzzati, Michele, and Albano Biondi. *L'Inquisizione e gli ebrei in Italia*. Vol. 1. Rome: Laterza, 1994.

Luzzati, Michele, Michele Olivari, and Alessandra Veronese, eds. *Ebrei e cristiani nell'Italia medievale e moderna: conversioni, scambi, contrasti: atti del VI Congresso internazionale dell'AISG, S. Miniato, 4–6 novembre 1986*. Rome: Carucci, 1988.

Maag, Karin, and John D. Witvliet. *Worship in Medieval and Early Modern Europe: Change and Continuity in Religious Practice*. Notre Dame: University of Notre Dame Press, 2004.

Macey, Patrick. "The Lauda and the Cult of Savonarola." *Renaissance Quarterly* 45, no. 3 (1992): 439–83.

Maier, Jessica. *Rome Measured and Imagined: Early Modern Maps of the Eternal City*. Chicago: University of Chicago Press, 2015.

Malcolm, Noel. *Useful Enemies: Islam and the Ottoman Empire in Western Political Thought, 1450–1750*. Oxford: Oxford University Press, 2019.

Mampieri, Martina. "'The Jews and Their Doubts': Anti-Jewish Polemics in the Fascicolo Delle Vanità Giudaiche (1583) by Antonino Stabili." In *Yearbook of the Maimonides Centre for Advanced Studies*, 1:59–75. Berlin: De Gruyter, 2016.

———. *Living under the Evil Pope: The Hebrew Chronicle of Pope Paul IV by Benjamin Neḥemiah Ben Elnathan from Civitanova Marche (16th Cent.)*. Studies in Jewish History and Culture, vol. 58. Leiden: Brill, 2020.

———. "When the Rabbi's Soul Entered a Pig: Melchiorre Palontrotti and His Giudiata against the Jews of Rome." *Jewish History* 33, no. 3–4 (2020): 351–75.

———. "Melchiorre Palontrotti and the First Giudiata against the Jews of Rome (1647–48)." Renaissance Society of America Annual Conference, New Orleans, LA, 2018.

Manuel, Frank Edward. *The Broken Staff: Judaism through Christian Eyes*. Cambridge, MA: Harvard University Press, 1992.

Marconcini, Samuela. "La casa dei catecumeni di Livorno." *Ricerche Storiche* 43, no. 3 (2013): 433–54.

———. *Per amor del cielo: farsi cristiani a Firenze tra seicento e settecento*. Premio Istituto Sangalli per la storia religiosa 2. Florence: Florence University Press, 2016.

Marini, Quinto. "Francesco Fulvio Frugoni oratore tra devozione e potere." In *Predicare nel Seicento*, edited by Maria Luisa Doglio and Carlo Delcorno, 105–42. Bologna: Il Mulino, 2011.

Maroni Lumbroso, Matizia, and Antonio Martini. *Le confraternite romane nelle loro chiese*. Rome: Fondazione Marco Besso, 1963.

Martano, Renata. "La missione inutile: la predicazione obbligatoria agli ebrei nella seconda meta del cinquecento." In *Itinerari ebraico-cristiani: società, cultura, mito*, edited by Anna Morisi Guerra, 93–110. Fasano, Italy: Schena, 1987.

Maryks, Robert Aleksander. *The Jesuit Order as a Synagogue of Jews: Jesuits of Jewish Ancestry and Purity-of-Blood Laws in the Early Society of Jesus*. Leiden: Brill, 2010.

Masetti, PT. *Monumenta et Antiquitates veteris disciplinae ordinis praedicatorum ab anno 1216 ad 1348 praesertim in Romana provincia Praefectorumque qui eandem rexerunt Biographica Chronotaxis*. 2 vols. Rome: Tipografia Rev. Cam. Apostolica, 1864.

Masetti Zannini, Gian Ludovico. "La Biblioteca di Andrea Del Monte (Josef Sarfath) e altre librerie di ebrei nel Cinquecento romano." In *Studi di biblioteconomia e storia del libro in onore di Francesco Barberi*, 391–405. Rome: Associazione Italiana Biblioteche, 1976.

Mayer, Thomas F., ed. *Reforming Reformation*. Farnham, UK: Ashgate Publishing, 2012.

———. *The Roman Inquisition: A Papal Bureaucracy and Its Laws in the Age of Galileo*. Philadelphia: University of Pennsylvania Press, 2013.

———. *The Roman Inquisition on the Stage of Italy, c. 1590–1640*. Philadelphia: University of Pennsylvania Press, 2014.

Mazur, Peter A. *Conversion to Catholicism in Early Modern Italy*. New York: Routledge, 2016.

———. "Searcher of Hearts: Cesare Baronio's History of Conversion." *Journal of the History of Ideas* 75, no. 2 (2014): 213–35.

Mazur, Peter A., and Abigail Shinn. "Introduction: Conversion Narratives in the Early Modern World." *Journal of Early Modern History* 17, no. 5–6 (2013): 427–36.

Mazzuchelli, Gian Maria. *Scrittori d'Italia*. Vol. 2. Brescia: G. Bossini, 1753.

McCullough, Peter E. *Sermons at Court: Politics and Religion in Elizabethan and Jacobean Preaching*. Cambridge: Cambridge University Press, 1998.

McGinness, Frederick. "Preaching Ideals and Practice in Counter-Reformation Rome." *Sixteenth Century Journal* 11 (1980): 109–29.

———. *Right Thinking and Sacred Oratory in Counter-Reformation Rome*. Princeton, NJ: Princeton University Press, 1995.

———. "The Rhetoric of Praise and the New Rome of the Counter Reformation." In *Rome in the Renaissance: The City and the Myth. Papers of the Thirteenth Annual Conference of the Center for Medieval and Early Renaissance Studies*, edited by P. A. Ramsey, 355–70. Binghamton, NY: Medieval and Renaissance Texts and Studies, 1982.

McNamara, Celeste. *The Bishop's Burden: Reforming the Catholic Church in Early Modern Italy*. Washington, DC: Catholic University of America Press, 2020.

Menning, Carol Bresnahan. *Charity and State in Late Renaissance Italy: The Monte di Pietà of Florence*. Ithaca, NY: Cornell University Press, 1993.

Merelli, Fedele. "P. Alfonso Lupo cappuccino e san Carlo Borromeo." *L'Italia Francescana* 64, no. 2–3 (1989): 137–348.

Meserve, Margaret. *Empires of Islam in Renaissance Historical Thought*. Cambridge, MA: Harvard University Press, 2008.

Michelson, Emily. "An Italian Explains the English Reformation (with God's Help)." In *From Icons to Eternity: Studies in Religious and Cultural History in Honor of Carlos M. N. Eire*, edited by Emily Michelson, Scott K. Taylor, and Mary Noll Venables, 33–81. Aldershot, UK: Ashgate, 2012.

———. "Conversionary Preaching and the Jews in Early Modern Rome." *Past and Present* 235, no. 1 (2017): 68–104.

———. "Dramatics in (and out of) the Pulpit in Post-Tridentine Italy." *Italianist* 34, no. 3 (2014): 449–62.

———. "Evangelista Marcellino: One Preacher, Two Audiences." *Archivio Italiano per La Storia della Pietà* 25 (2012): 185–202.

———. "How to Write a Conversionary Sermon: Rhetorical Influences and Religious Identity." In *Religious Orders and Religious Identity Formation in Late Medieval and Early Modern Europe, ca. 1420–1620*, edited by Bert Roest and Johanneke Uphoff, 235–51. Leiden: Brill, 2016.

———. *The Pulpit and the Press in Reformation Italy*. Cambridge, MA: Harvard University Press, 2013.

Milano, Attilio. *Bibliografia degli studi sulla storia degli ebrei in Italia, 1964–1966*. Rome, 1966.

———. *Il ghetto di Roma; illustrazioni storiche*. Rome: Staderini, 1964.

———. "L'impari lotta della Comunità di Roma contro la Casa dei catecumeni." *La Rassegna Mensile di Israel* 16, no. 11 (November 1, 1950): 355–68.

———. *Storia degli ebrei in Italia*. Vol. 318. Saggi. Turin: G. Einaudi, 1963.

———. "Un sottile tormento nella vita del Ghetto di Roma: La predica coattiva." *La Rassegna Mensile di Israel* 18, no. 12 (December 1952): 517–32.

Milano, Attilio, and Giovanni Buttelli. "L''Editto sopra gli ebrei' di Papa Pio VI e le mene ricattatorie di un letterato (cont. e fine)." *La Rassegna Mensile di Israel* 19, no. 3 (1953): 118–26.

Milano, Attilio, and Giacomo Giordani. "L''Editto sopra gli ebrei' di Papa Pio VI e le mene ricattatorie di un letterato." *La Rassegna Mensile di Israel* 19, no. 2 (1953): 65–80.

Milner, Stephen J., ed. *At the Margins: Minority Groups in Premodern Italy.* Medieval Cultures. Vol. 39. Minneapolis: University of Minnesota Press, 2005.

Minnich, Nelson. "The Catholic Church and the Pastoral Care of Black Africans in Renaissance Italy." In *Black Africans in Renaissance Europe*, edited by Thomas F. Earle and Kate J. P. Lowe, 280–301. Cambridge: Cambridge University Press, 2005.

Mitchell, Bonner. *Italian Civic Pageantry in the High Renaissance: A Descriptive Bibliography of Triumphal Entries and Selected Other Festivals for State Occasions.* Vol. 89. Biblioteca di Bibliografia Italiana. Florence: L. S. Olschki, 1979.

Molho, Anthony. "Robert Bonfil: A 'Modern' Historian's Moral Imperative." *Jewish History* 9, no. 2 (October 1, 1995): 113–18.

Molnár, Antal, Giovanni Pizzorusso, and Matteo Sanfilippo. *Chiese e nationes a Roma: dalla Scandinavia ai Balcani: Secoli XV–XVIII.* Rome: Viella, 2017.

Momigliano, Arnaldo. *Pagine ebraiche.* 1st ed. Rome: Edizioni di storia e letteratura, 2016.

Mooney, Denis. "The Development of the Roman Carnival over the Eighteenth and Nineteenth Centuries." PhD diss., University of Glasgow, 1988.

Moretti, Massimo. "'Glauci Coloris': Gli Ebrei nell'iconografia sacra di età moderna." *Roma moderna e contemporanea* 19, no. 1 (2011): 29–64.

Morisi Guerra, Anna. "Cultura Ebraica ed esegesi biblica cristiana tra umanesimo e riforma." In *Ebrei e cristiani nell'Italia medievale e moderna: conversioni, scambi, contrasti*, edited by Michele Luzzati, Michele Olivari, and Alessandra Veronese, 209–23. Rome: Carucci, 1988.

Mormando, Franco. *The Preacher's Demons: Bernardino of Siena and the Social Underworld of Early Renaissance Italy.* Chicago: University of Chicago Press, 1999.

Moroni, Gaetano. *Dizionario di erudizione storico-ecclesiastica da S. Pietro sino ai nostri giorni.* Vol. 21. Venice: Tipografia Emiliana, 1843.

Morrison, Karl F. *Understanding Conversion.* Charlottesville: University Press of Virginia, 1992.

Mouchel, Christian. "San Filippo Neri e i Cappuccini: retorica ed eloquenza dopo il Concilio di Trento." *L'Italia francescana* 64, no. 5 (1989): 493–516.

Mrkonjić, Tomislav. *Il teologo Ivan Paštrić (Giovanni Pastrizio) (1636–1708): Vita-opere-concezione della teologia-cristologia.* Rome: Pontificia Facultas theologica "S. Bonaventurae" Ordinis Fratrum Minorum Conventualium in Urbe, 1989.

Muir, Edward. "The Eye of the Procession: Ritual Ways of Seeing in the Renaissance." In *Ceremonial Culture in Pre-Modern Europe*, edited by Nicholas Howe, 129–54. Notre Dame, IN: Notre Dame University Press, 2007.

———. *Ritual in Early Modern Europe.* 2nd ed. Cambridge: Cambridge University Press, 2005.

Muldoon, James, ed. *Varieties of Religious Conversion in the Middle Ages.* Gainesville: University Press of Florida, 1997.

Murphy, Paul V. "Jesuit Rome and Italy." In *The Cambridge Companion to the Jesuits*, edited by Thomas Worcester, 71–87. Cambridge: Cambridge University Press, 2008.

Musto, Ronald G. *Apocalypse in Rome: Cola di Rienzo and the Politics of the New Age*. Berkeley: University of California Press, 2003.

Muzzarelli, Maria Giuseppina. *Ebrei e città d'Italia in età di transizione: Il caso di Cesena dal XIV al XVI Secolo*. Bologna: CLUEB, 1984.

——. *Pescatori di uomini: predicatori e piazze alla fine del medioevo*. Biblioteca Storica. Bologna: Il mulino, 2005.

——. *Verso l'epilogo di una convivenza: Gli ebrei a Bologna nel XVI secolo*. Florence: Giuntina, 1996.

Nanni, Stefania, and Maria Antonietta Visceglia. *La Città del perdono: pellegrinaggi e Anni Santi a Roma in età moderna, 1550-1750*. Rome: Archivio G. Izzi, 1998.

Natali, Ettore. *Il ghetto di Roma. Volume primo*. Rome: Stabilimento Tipografico della Tribuna, 1887.

Nirenberg, David. *Aesthetic Theology and Its Enemies: Judaism in Christian Painting, Poetry, and Politics*. Mandel Lectures in the Humanities. Waltham, MA: Brandeis University Press, 2015.

——. *Anti-Judaism: The Western Tradition*. New York: W. W. Norton and Co., 2013.

——. *Communities of Violence: Persecution of Minorities in the Middle Ages*. Princeton, NJ: Princeton University Press, 2015.

——. "Mass Conversion and Genealogical Mentalities: Jews and Christians in Fifteenth-Century Spain." *Past and Present*, no. 174 (February 1, 2002): 3–41.

——. *Neighboring Faiths: Christianity, Islam, and Judaism in the Middle Ages and Today*. Chicago: University of Chicago Press, 2014.

Norman, Corrie. *Humanist Taste and Franciscan Values: Cornelio Musso and Catholic Preaching in Sixteenth-Century Italy*. Bern: Peter Lang, 1998.

Novikoff, Alex J. *The Medieval Culture of Disputation: Pedagogy, Practice, and Performance*. Philadelphia: University of Pennsylvania Press, 2013.

Noyes, Ruth S. "On the Fringes of Center: Disputed Hagiographic Imagery and the Crisis over the *Beati moderni* in Rome ca. 1600." *Renaissance Quarterly* 64, no. 3 (Fall 2011): 800–846.

Nussdorfer, Laurie. *Brokers of Public Trust: Notaries in Early Modern Rome*. Baltimore: Johns Hopkins University Press, 2009.

——. *Civic Politics in the Rome of Urban VIII*. Princeton, NJ: Princeton University Press, 1992.

——. "Men at Home in Baroque Rome." *I Tatti Studies in the Italian Renaissance* 17, no. 1 (2014): 103–29.

——. "The Politics of Space in Early Modern Rome." *Memoirs of the American Academy in Rome* 42 (1999): 161–86.

——. "Priestly Rulers, Male Subjects: Swords and Courts in Papal Rome." In *Violent Masculinities: Male Aggression in Early Modern Texts and Culture*, edited by Jennifer Feather and Catherine E. Thomas, 109–28. Basingstoke, UK: Palgrave Macmillan, 2013.

——. "The Vacant See: Ritual and Protest in Early Modern Rome." *Sixteenth Century Journal* 18, no. 2 (1987): 173–89.

Ó hAnnracháin, Tadhg. *Catholic Europe, 1592-1648: Centre and Peripheries*. Oxford: Oxford University Press, 2015.

Oberman, Heiko. "Gli ostinati giudei: Mutamento della strategie nell'Europea tardo-medioevale (1300–1600)." In *Ebrei e cristiani nell'Italia medievale e moderna: conversioni, scambi, contrasti*, edited by Michele Luzzati, Michele Olivari, and Alessandra Veronese, 123–40. Rome: Carucci, 1988.

O'Brien, Grant. "The Use of Simple Geometry and the Local Unit of Measurement in the Design of Italian Stringed Keyboard Instruments: An Aid to Attribution and to Organological Analysis." *Galpin Society Journal* 52 (1999): 108–71.

Olszewski, Edward J. "The New World of Pier Leone Ghezzi." *Art Journal* 43, no. 4 (1983): 325–30.

O'Malley, John. "Form, Content, and Influence of Works about Preaching Before Trent: The Franciscan Contribution." In *I frati minori tra '400–'500*, 27–50. Assisi: Università di Perugia, Centro di Studi Francescani, 1986.

——. *Praise and Blame in Renaissance Rome: Rhetoric, Doctrine, and Reform in the Sacred Orators of the Papal Court, c. 1450–1521*. Durham, NC: Duke University Press, 1979.

O'Regan, Noel. *Institutional Patronage in Post-Tridentine Rome: Music at Santissima Trinità Dei Pellegrini, 1550–1650*. London: Routledge, 1995.

Oryshkevich, Irina T. "Accommodating Jews in the New Jerusalem: The Roman Ghetto in the Renaissance." In *Present and Future Memory: Holocaust Studies at the Italian Academy 2008–2016*, edited by Barbara Faedda, 23–28. New York: Italian Academy, 2016.

Ostrow, Steven F. *Art and Spirituality in Counter-Reformation Rome: The Sistine and Pauline Chapels in S. Maria Maggiore*. Cambridge: Cambridge University Press, 1996.

Pagano, Sergio. "L'ospizio dei convertendi di Roma tra carisma missionario e regolamentazione ecclesiastica (1671–1700)." *Ricerche per la storia religiosa di Roma* 10 (1998): 313–90.

Palumbo, Genoveffa. *Giubileo giubilei: Pellegrini e pellegrine, riti, santi, immagini per una storia dei sacri itinerari*. Primo Piano. Rome: RAI ERI, 1999.

——. "I giubilei del cinquecento tra riforma e controriforma." In *La storia dei Giubilei*, edited by Gloria Fossi, Jacques Le Goff, and Claudio M. Strinati, 2:199–237. Florence: Giunti, 1997.

Panetta, Marina. "Itinerari dell'anima: Letteratura devozionale e giubilei nel primo secolo della stampa." In *La storia dei giubilei*, edited by Gloria Fossi, Jacques Le Goff, and Claudio M. Strinati, 2:295–307. Florence: Giunti, 1997.

Parente, Fausto. "Di uno scritto antiebraico della meta del xviii secolo: la verita della cristiana religione contro le vane lusinghe de' moderni ebrei di Giovanni Antonio Costanzi (1705 ca.–1785)." *Italia* 13–15 (2001): 357–95.

——. "Il confronto ideologico tra l'ebraismo e la Chiesa in Italia." In *Italia Judaica. Atti del I Convegno internazionale, Bari, 18–22 maggio, 1981*, 303–81. Rome, 1983.

——. "La Chiesa e il 'Talmud': L'atteggiamento della Chiesa e del mondo cristiano nei confronti del 'Talmud' e degli altri scritti rabbinici, con particolare riguardo all'Italia tra XV e XVI secolo." In *Gli ebrei in Italia*, edited by Corrado Vivanti, 11:521–643. Storia d'Italia: annali. Turin: G. Einaudi, 1996.

——. "La Quabbale Chrétienne, Flavius Mithridate, Pic de la Miraondola, Galatin et la Réafffirmation de la Téorie des deux Strates dans le Talmud." In *Les juifs et l'église romaine à l'époque moderne (XVe–XVIIIe Siècle)*, 29:284–90. Bibliothèque d'études juives. Paris: Honoré Champion, 2007.

———. *Les juifs et l'église romaine à l'époque moderne (XVe–XVIIIe Siècle)*. Vol. 29. Bibliothèque d'études juives. Paris: Honoré Champion, 2007.

———. "Les raisons et justifications de la conversion des Juifs." In *La conversion et le politique à l'époque moderne*, edited by Daniel Tollet, 15–41. Paris: Presses de l'Université Paris-Sorbonne, 2005.

———. "Notes biographiques sur André de Monte." In *Les juifs et l'église romaine à l'époque moderne (XVe–XVIIIe Siècle)*, 29:177–204. Bibliothèque d'études juives. Paris: Honoré Champion, 2007.

Partner, Peter. *Renaissance Rome, 1500–1559: A Portrait of a Society*. Berkeley: University of California Press, 1976.

Patriarca, Silvana, and Valeria Deplano. "Nation, 'Race,' and Racisms in Twentieth-Century Italy." *Modern Italy* 23, no. 4 (November 2018): 349–53.

Pattenden, Miles. "Antonio de Fuenmayor's Life of Pius V: A Pope in Early Modern Spanish Historiography." *Renaissance Studies* 32, no. 2 (n.d.): 183–200.

Pecchiai, Pio. *Il Gesù di Roma*. Società grafica romana, 1952.

———. "Il Secolo XVI." In *Riti, cerimonie, feste e vita di popolo nella Roma dei papi*, edited by Luigi Fiorani, 12:123–76. Roma cristiana. Bologna: Cappelli, 1970.

Pertile, Lino. "Montaigne, Gregory Martin, and Rome." *Bibliothèque d'Humanisme et Renaissance* 50, no. 3 (January 1, 1988): 637–59.

Perugini. "L'Inquisition Romaine et les Israélites." *Revue des études juives* 3 (1881): 94–108.

Pettegree, Andrew. *Reformation and the Culture of Persuasion*. Cambridge: Cambridge University Press, 2005.

Peyronel Rambaldi, Susanna. *I tribunali della fede: continuità e discontinuità dal Medioevo all'età moderna*. Turin: Claudiana, 2007.

Phelan, Joseph. "A Source for Robert Browning's 'Holy-Cross Day.'" *Notes and Queries* 65, no. 3 (July 13, 2018): 382–86.

Phillips, Amy E. "Censorship of Hebrew Books in Sixteenth Century Italy. A Review of a Decade of English and French Language Scholarship." *La Bibliofilía* 118, no. 3 (2016): 409–26.

Piéjus, Anne. "Il savonarolismo di san Filippo Neri attraverso poesie e canti." In *Filippo Neri: un santo dell'età moderna nel V centenario della nascita (1515–2015): Atti del convegno di studi (Roma, Biblioteca Vallicelliana, 16–17 settembre 2015)*, edited by Paola Paesano, 193–206. Rome: Ministero per i beni e le attività culturali, Biblioteca Vallicelliana, 2018.

Pierre Delooz. "Pour une étude sociologique de la sainteté canonisée dans l'Église catholique." *Archives de sociologie des religions* 7, no. 13 (1962): 17–43.

Pifferi, Stefano. *Viaggiatori, penitenti, pellegrini a Roma: Due giubilei a confronto in testi inediti e/o Rari*. Viterbo: Sette città, 2005.

Piladi, Angelico. *Il P. Evangelista Marcellino insigne predicatore ed ecclesiaste del secolo XVI*. Florence: Studi Francescani, 1944.

Pinelli, Antonio. *Roma del rinascimento*. Storia di Roma dall'antichità ad oggi. Rome: Laterza, 2001.

Pitassi, Maria Cristina, and Daniela Solfaroli Camillocci. *Les modes de la conversion confessionnelle à l'époque moderne: autobiographie, altérité et construction des identités religieuses*. Florence: Olschki, 2010.

Pizzorusso, Giovanni. "Agli antipodi di Babele: Propaganda Fide tra immagine cosmopolita e orizzonti romani (XVII–XIX secolo)." In *Roma, la città del papa*, edited by Luigi Fiorani and Adriano Prosperi. Storia d'Italia: annali 16, 479–517. Turin: G. Einaudi, 2000.

———. "I satelliti di Propaganda Fide: il Collegio Urbano e la tipografia poliglotta. Note di ricerca su due istituzioni culturali romane nel XVII secolo." *Melanges de l'école française de Rome Italie et Mediterranee* 116, no. 2 (2004): 471–98.

———. "La preparazione linguistica e controversistica dei missionari per l'Oriente islamico: scuole, testi, insegnanti a Roma e in Italia." In *L'islam visto da Occidente: cultura e religione del seicento europeo difronte all'islam: atti del convegno internazionale, Milano, Università degli studi, 17–18 ottobre 2007*, edited by Bernard Heyberger, Mercedes García-Arenal, Emanuele Colombo, and Paola Vismara, 289–314. Genoa: Marietti 1820, 2009.

———. "Lo 'Stato temporale' della Congregazione de Propaganda Fide nel seicento." In *Ad ultimos usque terrarum terminos in fide propaganda: Roma fra promozione e difesa della fede in età moderna*, edited by Massimiliano Ghilardi, Gaetano Sabatini, Matteo Sanfilippo, and Donatella Strangio, 51–66. Viterbo: Edizioni Sette città, 2014.

Plaisance, Michel, and Nicole Carew-Reid. *Florence in the Time of the Medici: Public Celebrations, Politics, and Literature in the Fifteenth and Sixteenth Centuries.* Toronto: Centre for Reformation and Renaissance Studies, 2008.

Pocino, Willy. *Le confraternite romane.* Studi e documenti. Rome: Edilazio, 2000.

Ponnelle, Louis, and Louis Bordet. *San Filippo Neri e La società romana del suo tempo (1515–1595).* Florence: Libreria editrice fiorentina, 1986.

Ponnelle, Louis, Louis Bordet, and Ralph Francis Kerr. *St. Philip Neri and the Roman Society of His Times (1515–1595).* London: Sheed and Ward, 1979.

Popper, William. *The Censorship of Hebrew Books.* New York: Ktav Publishing House, 1969.

Procaccia, Micaela. "'Bona Voglia' e 'Modica Coactio': Conversioni di Ebrei a Roma nel Secolo XVI." *Ricerche per la storia religiosa di Roma* 10 (1998): 207–34.

Prosperi, Adriano. "Convertirsi nel Cinquecento." *Ricerche per la storia religiosa di Roma* 10 (1998): 17–30.

———. "Incontri rituali: il papa e gli ebrei." In *Gli ebrei in Italia*, edited by Corrado Vivanti: 497–520. Storia d'Italia: annali 11. Turin: G. Einaudi, 1996.

———. *La vocazione: storie di gesuiti tra Cinquecento e Seicento.* Turin: G. Einaudi, 2016.

———. "L'inquisizione Romana e gli ebrei." In *L'Inquisizione e gli ebrei in Italia*, edited by Michele Luzzati, 67–120. Bari: Laterza, 1994.

———. *Tribunali della Coscienza: Inquisitori, confessori, missionari.* Turin: G. Einaudi, 1996.

Prosperi, Adriano, Vincenzo Lavenia, and John A. Tedeschi. *Dizionario storico dell'Inquisizione.* Pisa: Scuola normale superiore, 2010.

Pullan, Brian. "The Conversion of the Jews: The Style of Italy." *Bulletin of the John Rylands University Library of Manchester* 70 (1988): 53–70.

———. "Jewish Banks and Monti di Pietà. In *The Jews of Early Modern Venice*, edited by Robert C. Davis and Benjamin Ravid, 53–72. Baltimore: Johns Hopkins University Press, 2001.

——. *The Jews of Europe and the Inquisition of Venice, 1550–1670*. I. B. London: Tauris, 1998.

R., G. "Bibliografia degli scritti di Attilio Milano." *La Rassegna Mensile di Israel* 36, no. 7/9 Scritti in memoria di Attilio Milano (September 1970): 35–47.

Rambo, Lewis R. *Understanding Religious Conversion*. New Haven, CT: Yale University Press, 1993.

Rambo, Lewis R., and Charles E. Farhadian, eds. *The Oxford Handbook of Religious Conversion*. Oxford: Oxford University Press, 2014.

Ravid, Benjamin. "Christian Travelers in the Ghetto of Venice : Some Preliminary Observations." In *Studies on the Jews of Venice, 1500–1800*, 111–50. Variorum Collected Studies. Farnham, UK: Ashgate Publishing, 2003.

——. "'Contra Judaeos' in Seventeenth-Century Italy: Two Responses to the 'Discorso' of Simone Luzzatto by Melchiore Palontrotti and Giulio Morosini." *AJS Review* 7–8 (January 1, 1982): 301–51.

——. "From Yellow to Red: On the Distinguishing Head-Covering of the Jews of Venice." *Jewish History* 6, no. 1 (1992): 179–210.

——. "How 'Other' Really Was the Jewish Other? The Evidence from Venice." In *Acculturation and Its Discontents: The Italian Jewish Experience between Exclusion and Inclusion*, edited by David N. Myers, Massimo Ciavolella, Peter H. Reill, and Geoffrey Symcox, 19–55. Toronto: University of Toronto Press, 2008.

——. "*New Light on the Ghetti of Venice.*" In *Shlomo Simonsohn Jubilee Volume: Studies on the History of the Jews in the Middle Ages and Renaissance Period*, 149–76. Tel Aviv: Tel Aviv University, 1993.

——. "Venice, Rome, and the Reversion of New Christians to Judaism: A Study in Ragione di Stato." In *L'identità dissimulata: Giudaizzanti iberici nell'Europa cristiana dell'età moderna*, edited by Pier Cesare Ioly Zorattini, 151–94. Florence: Leo S. Olschki, 2000.

Raz-Krakotzkin, Amnon. *The Censor, the Editor, and the Text: The Catholic Church and the Shaping of the Jewish Canon in the Sixteenth Century*. Philadelphia: University of Pennsylvania Press, 2007.

Rebecchini, Guido. "After the Medici. The New Rome of Pope Paul III Farnese." *I Tatti Studies: Essays in the Renaissance* 11 (January 1, 2007): 147–200.

Renda, Francesco. *La fine del giudaismo siciliano: ebrei marrani e inquisizione spagnola prima durante e dopo la cacciata del 1492*. Vol. 31. Biblioteca Siciliana di Storia e Letteratura. Palmero: Sellerio, 1993.

Rietbergen, P. J. A. N. *Power and Religion in Baroque Rome: Barberini Cultural Policies*. Leiden: Brill, 2006.

Riley-Smith, Jonathan. "Christian Violence and the Crusades." In *Religious Violence between Christians and Jews*, edited by A. S. Abulafia, 3–20. London: Palgrave Macmillan, 2002.

Rinne, Katherine. "Urban Ablutions: Cleansing Counter-Reformation Rome." In *Rome, Pollution and Propriety: Dirt, Disease and Hygiene in the Eternal City from Antiquity to Modernity*, edited by Mark Bradley and Kenneth R. Stow, 182–201. Cambridge: Cambridge University Press, 2012.

Rita, Giovanni. "Il Barocco in Sapienza: Università e cultura a Roma nel secolo XVII." In *Luoghi della cultura nella Roma di Borromini*, edited by Barbara Tellini Santoni and Alberto Manodori, 21–84. Rome: Retablo, 2004.

Robinson, David. "Religious Disputations as Theatre: Staging Religious Difference in France after the Wars of Religion." In *Reframing Reformation: Understanding Religious Difference in Early Modern Europe*, edited by Nicholas Terpstra, 31–49. Toronto: Centre for Reformation and Renaissance Studies, 2020.

Rocciolo, Domenico. "Catecumeni e neofiti a Roma tra '500 e '800: provenienza, condizioni sociali e 'padrini' illustri." In *Popolazione e società a Roma dal medioevo all'età contemporanea*, edited by Eugenio Sonnino, 711–24. Rome: Il Calamo, 1998.

———. "Documenti sui catecumeni e neofiti a Roma nel seicento e settecento." *Ricerche per la storia religiosa di Roma* 10 (1998): 391–454.

———. "Ebrei catecumeni alla Madonna ai Monti nel settecento." *Roma moderna e contemporanea. Ebrei, scambi e conflitti tra XV e XX secolo*, 65–81. Rome: CROMA, 2012.

———. "Fra promozione e difesa della fede: Le vicende dei catecumeni e neofiti romani in età moderna." In *Ad ultimos usque terrarum terminos in fide propaganda: Roma fra promozione e difesa della fede in età moderna*, edited by Massimiliano Ghilardi, Gaetano Sabatini, Matteo Sanfilippo, and Donatella Strangio, 147–56. Viterbo: Sette città, 2014.

———. "L'archivio della pia casa dei catecumeni e nofiti di Roma." *Ricerche per la storia religiosa di Roma* 10 (1998): 545–82.

Rodocanachi, E. [Emmanuel]. *Le Saint-Siège et les Juifs; le ghetto à Rome*. Paris: Firmin-Didot, 1891.

Roest, Bert. *Franciscan Literature of Religious Instruction before the Council of Trent*. Leiden: Brill, 2004.

Romani, Mario. *Pellegrini e viaggiatori nell'economia di Roma dal XIV al XVII secolo*. Milan: Vita e pensiero, 1948.

Rosa, Mario. *La contrastata ragione: riforme e religione nell'Italia del Settecento*. Biblioteca del XVIII secolo 12. Rome: Edizioni di storia e letteratura, 2009.

———. "La Santa Sede e gli ebrei nel settecento." In *Gli ebrei in Italia*, edited by Corrado Vivanti, 2:1067–87. Storia d'Italia: annali 11. Turin: G. Einaudi, 1996.

———. *Settecento religioso: politica della ragione e religione del cuore*. Venice: Marsilio, 1999.

Rosen-Prebor, Gila. "Domenico Yerushalmi: His Life, Writings and Work as a Censor." *Materia giudaica: rivista dell'associazione italiana per lo studio del giudaismo* 15–16 (2010–11): 467–481.

Rostagno, Lucia. "Note su Domenico Gerosolimitano: A proposito del recente saggio di M. Austin PARTE I." *Rivista degli studi orientali* 76, no. 1–4 (2002): 231–62.

Roth, Cecil. "Forced Baptisms in Italy: A Contribution to the History of Jewish Persecution." *Jewish Quarterly Review* 27, no. 2 (1936): 117–36.

Rothman, E. Natalie. *Brokering Empire: Trans-Imperial Subjects between Venice and Istanbul*. Ithaca, NY: Cornell University Press, 2012.

Rowe, Erin Kathleen. *Black Saints in Early Modern Global Catholicism*. Cambridge: Cambridge University Press, 2019.

———. "The Spanish Minerva: Imagining Teresa of Avila as Patron Saint in Seventeenth-Century Spain." *Catholic Historical Review* 92, no. 4 (2006): 574–96.

Rowe, Nina. *The Jew, the Cathedral and the Medieval City: Synagoga and Ecclesia in the Thirteenth Century*. Cambridge: Cambridge University Press, 2011.

Rowland, Ingrid D. *The Culture of the High Renaissance: Ancients and Moderns in Sixteenth-Century Rome*. Cambridge: Cambridge University Press, 1998.

——. *Giordano Bruno: Philosopher/Heretic*. Chicago: University of Chicago Press, 2008.

Rubin, Miri. "Europe Remade: Purity and Danger in Late Medieval Europe." *Transactions of the Royal Historical Society*, sixth series, 11 (January 1, 2001): 101–24.

Ruderman, David B. *Early Modern Jewry: A New Cultural History*. Princeton, NJ: Princeton University Press, 2011.

——. "Hope against Hope: Jewish and Christian Messianic Expectations in the Late Middle Ages." In *Essential Papers on Jewish Culture in Renaissance and Baroque Italy*, edited by David B. Ruderman, 299–323. New York: NYU Press, 1992.

——. "A Jewish Apologetic Treatise from Sixteenth Century Bologna." *Hebrew Union College Annual* (1979): 253–76.

Rudt de Collenberg, Wipertus Hugo. "Le baptême des Juifs à Rome de 1614 a 1798 selon les registres de la 'Casa dei Catecumeni': pt. 1: 1614–1676." *Archivum Historiae Pontificiae* 24 (1986): 91–231.

——. "Le baptême des Juifs à Rome de 1614 a 1798 selon les registres de la 'Casa dei Catecumeni': pt. 2: 1676–1730." *Archivum Historiae Pontificiae* 25 (1987): 105–261.

——. "Le baptême des Juifs à Rome de 1614 a 1798 selon les registres de la 'Casa dei Catecumeni': pt. 3: 1730–1798." *Archivum Historiae Pontificiae* 26 (1988): 119–294.

Ruff, Julius R. *Violence in Early Modern Europe, 1500–1800*. New Approaches to European History 22. Cambridge: Cambridge University Press, 2001.

Rusconi, Roberto. "Anti-Jewish Preaching in the Fifteenth Century and Images of Preachers in Italian Renaissance Art." In *Friars and Jews in the Middle Ages and Renaissance*, edited by Steven McMichael and Suzanne Myers, 225–37. Leiden: Brill, 2004.

——. "Predicatori ed ebrei nell'arte italiana del rinascimento." *Iconographica* 3 (2004): 148–61.

——. *Santo Padre: la santità del papa da San Pietro a Giovanni Paolo II*. Rome: Viella, 2011.

Russell, Camilla. "Imagining the 'Indies': Italian Jesuit Petitions for the Overseas Missions at the Turn of the Seventeenth Century." In *L'Europa divisa e i nuovi mondi. Per Adriano Prosperi*, edited by Massimo Donattini, Giuseppe Marcocci, and Stefania Pastore, 2:179–89. Pisa: Scuola Normale Superiore, 2011.

Sacerdote, Gustavo. *I codici ebraici della pia casa dei neofiti in Roma*. Rome: Accademia dei Lincei, 1893.

Salah, Asher. "Rabbinical Dress in Italy." In *Dress and Ideology: Fashioning Identity from Antiquity to the Present*, edited by Shoshana-Rose Marzel and Guy Stiebel, 55–68. London: Bloomsbury, 2015.

Salter, F. R. "The Jews in Fifteenth-Century Florence and Savonarola's Establishment of a Mons Pietatis." *Cambridge Historical Journal* 5, no. 2 (1936): 193–211.

Salzmann, Ariel. "Migrants in Chains: On the Enslavement of Muslims in Renaissance and Enlightenment Europe." *Religions (Basel, Switzerland)* 4, no. 3 (2013): 391–411.

San Juan, Rose Marie. *Rome: A City Out of Print*. Minneapolis: University of Minnesota Press, 2001.

Santus, Cesare. "Wandering Lives: Eastern Christian Pilgrims, Alms-Collectors, and 'Refugees' in Early Modern Rome." In *A Companion to Religious Minorities in Early Modern Rome*, edited by Matthew Coneys Wainwright and Emily Michelson, 237–71. Boston: Brill, 2020.

Sapir Abulafia, Anna. *Christians and Jews in the Twelfth-Century Renaissance.* London: Routledge, 1995.

Satta, Fiamma. "Predicatori agli ebrei, catecumeni e neofiti a Roma nella prima metà del seicento." In *Itinerari ebraico-cristiani: società, cultura, mito,* edited by Anna Morisi Guerra, 111–27. Fasano, Italy: Schena, 1987.

Saxer, Victor. *Sante-Marie-Majeure: Une Basilique de Rome dans l'Histoire de la ville et de son Église (Ve-XIIIe siècle).* Rome: École Française de Rome, 2001.

Schlauch, Margaret. "The Allegory of Church and Synagogue." *Speculum* 14, no. 4 (1939): 448–64.

Scholem, Gershom. *Kabbalah.* Library of Jewish Knowledge. Jerusalem: Keter, 1974.

———. *Major Trends in Jewish Mysticism.* Jerusalem: Schocken Publishing House, 1941.

———. *Origins of the Kabbalah.* Princeton, NJ: Princeton University Press, 1991.

———. *Sabbatai Şevi: The Mystical Messiah, 1626-1676.* Princeton, NJ: Princeton University Press, 1973.

Schwartz, Yossef. "Kabbalah and Conversion: Caramuel and Ciantes on Kabbalah as a Means for the Conversion of the Jews." In *Un' altra modernità: Juan Caramuel Lobkowitz (1606-1682): enciclopedia e probabilismo,* edited by Paolo C. Pissavino and Daniele Sabaino, 175–84. Pisa: Edizioni ETS, 2012.

Scott, James C. *Weapons of the Weak: Everyday Forms of Peasant Resistance.* New Haven, CT: Yale University Press, 1985.

Scott, Susan C., and Barbara Wisch. *Art and Pageantry in the Renaissance and Baroque.* University Park: Pennsylvania State University Press, 1990.

Scott-Warren, Jason. *"Nashe's Stuff."* In *The Oxford Companion to English Prose, c. 1500-1640,* edited by Andrew Hadfield, 204–18. Oxford: Oxford University Press, 2013.

Secret, François. *I cabbalisti cristiani del Rinascimento.* Translated by Pierliugi Zoccatelli. Rome: Arkeios, 2001.

———. *Les kabbalistes chrétiens de la Renaissance.* Collection Sigma 5. Paris: Dunod, 1964.

Segre, Renata. "Il mondo ebraico nei cardinali della Controriforma." *Italia Judaica* 2 (1986): 119–38.

———. "Il mondo ebraico nel carteggio di Carlo Borromeo." *Michael: On the History of the Jews in the Diaspora* 1 (1972): 163–260.

———. "La Controriforma: espulsioni, conversioni, isolamento." In *Gli Ebrei in Italia,* edited by Corrado Vivanti, 709–78. Storia d'Italia: annali 11. Turin: G. Einaudi, 1996.

Serafinelli, Guendalina. "Guido Reni, Clemente Boncompagni Corcos e lo stendardo doppio di San Francesco: Rinvenimenti d'archivio." *Rivista d'Arte* 5, no. 1 (2011): 175–203.

Sermoneta, Joseph B. "Il mestiere del neofito nella Roma del settecento." In *Shlomo Simonsohn Jubilee Volume: Studies on the History of the Jews in the Middle Ages and Renaissance Period,* 213–44. Tel Aviv: Tel Aviv University, 1993.

———. "Tredici giorni nella casa dei conversi: dal diario di una giovane ebrea del 18° secolo." *Michael: On the History of the Jews in the Diaspora* 1 (1972): 261–315.

Shachar, Isaiah. *The Judensau: A Medieval Anti-Jewish Motif and Its History.* London: Warburg Institute, 1974.

Shagan, Ethan H. *The Birth of Modern Belief: Faith and Judgment from the Middle Ages to the Enlightenment.* Princeton, NJ: Princeton University Press, 2018.

Shapiro, James. *Shakespeare and the Jews.* New York: Columbia University Press, 1996.

Shoulson, Jeffrey S. *Fictions of Conversion: Jews, Christians, and Cultures of Change in Early Modern England.* Philadelphia: University of Pennsylvania Press, 2013.

Siebenhüner, Kim. "Conversion, Mobility and the Roman Inquisition in Italy around 1600." *Past and Present,* no. 200 (August 2008): 5–35.

Siegmund, Stefanie. *The Medici State and the Ghetto of Florence: The Construction of an Early Modern Jewish Community.* Stanford, CA: Stanford University Press, 2006.

Signorotto, Gianvittorio, and Maria Antonietta Visceglia. *Court and Politics in Papal Rome, 1492–1700.* Cambridge Studies in Italian History and Culture. Cambridge: Cambridge University Press, 2002.

Simoncini, Giorgio. *Roma: Le Trasformazioni Urbane Nel Cinquecento.* Florence: Leo S. Olschki Editore, 2008.

Simonsohn, Shlomo. *The Apostolic See and the Jews.* Vol. 7. Toronto: Pontifical Institute of Mediaeval Studies, 1991.

———. "Some Well-Known Jewish Converts during the Renaissance." *Revue des Études Juives* 148, no. 1–2 (1989): 17–52.

Sluhovsky, Moshe. *Becoming a New Self: Practices of Belief in Early Modern Catholicism.* Chicago: University of Chicago Press, 2017.

Smith, Gregory, and Jan Gadeyne. *Perspectives on Public Space in Rome, from Antiquity to the Present Day.* Farnham, UK: Ashgate Publishing, 2013.

Smith, Lesley. "The Rewards of Faith: Nicholas of Lyra on Ruth." In *Nicholas of Lyra: The Senses of Scripture,* edited by Philip D. W. Krey and Lesley Smith, 45–58. Leiden: Brill, 2000.

Smoller, Laura Ackerman. *The Saint and the Chopped-Up Baby: The Cult of Vincent Ferrer in Medieval and Early Modern Europe.* Ithaca, NY: Cornell University Press, 2014.

Snow, David A., and Richard Machalek. "The Sociology of Conversion." *Annual Review of Sociology* 10 (1984): 167–90.

Snow, David A., and Cynthia L. Phillips. "The Lofland-Stark Conversion Model: A Critical Reassessment." *Social Problems* 27, no. 4 (1980): 430–47.

Sorkin, David. *Jewish Emancipation.* Princeton, NJ: Princeton University Press, 2019.

Spear, Richard E. *Painting for Profit: The Economic Lives of Seventeenth-Century Italian Painters.* New Haven, CT: Yale University Press, 2010.

Spence, Craig. *Misson, Francis Maximilian [Formerly François Maximilien] (c. 1650–1722), Traveller and Author.* Oxford: Oxford University Press, 2011.

Stella, Pietro. "Tra Roma barocca e Roma capitale: la pietà romana." In *Roma, la città del papa,* edited by Luigi Fiorani and Adriano Prosperi: 755–85. Storia d'Italia: annali 16. Turin: G. Einaudi, 2000.

Stelling, Lieke, Harald Hendrix, and Todd Richardson, eds. *The Turn of the Soul: Representations of Religious Conversion in Early Modern Art and Literature.* Leiden: Brill, 2012.

Stern, David. "The Rabbinic Bible in Its Sixteenth-Century Context." In *The Hebrew Book in Early Modern Italy,* edited by Joseph Hacker and Adam Shear, 76–108. Philadelphia: University of Pennsylvania Press, 2011.

Stinger, Charles L. *The Renaissance in Rome*. Bloomington: University of Indiana Press, 1998.

Stockton, Will. *Playing Dirty, Sexuality and Waste in Early Modern Comedy*. Minneapolis: University of Minnesota Press, 2011.

Stoichiță, Victor Ieronim. *L'image de l'autre: Noirs, Juifs, musulmans et 'Gitans' dans l'art occidental des temps modernes: 1453–1789*. Chaire du Louvre. Paris: Hazan, Musée du Louvre, 2014.

Stolzenberg, Daniel. "Egyptian Oedipus: Antiquarianism, Oriental Studies and Occult Philosophy in the Work of Athanasius Kircher." PhD diss., Stanford University, 2004.

Stopani, Renato. *Le grandi vie di pellegrinaggio del medioevo: le strade per Roma*. Italy]: Centro studi romei, 1986.

———. *A Roma per il giubileo del 1575: Lungo la Francigena con la confraternità della Santissima Trinità*. Florence: Le lettere, 1999.

Storey, Tessa. *Carnal Commerce in Counter-Reformation Rome*. Cambridge: Cambridge University Press, 2008.

Stow, Kenneth R. *Anna and Tranquillo: Catholic Anxiety and Jewish Protest in the Age of Revolutions*. New Haven, CT: Yale University Press, 2016.

———. "The Burning of the Talmud in 1553, in the Light of Sixteenth-Century Catholic Attitudes toward the Talmud." *Bibliothèque d'Humanisme et Renaissance* 34, no. 3 (January 1, 1972): 435–59.

———. *Catholic Thought and Papal Jewry Policy 1555–1593*. New York: Jewish Theological Seminary of America, 1977.

———. "Church, Conversion, and Tradition: The Problem of Jewish Conversion in Sixteenth-Century Italy." *Dimensioni e Problemi della Ricerca Storica* 2 (1996): 26–35.

———. "The Consciousness of Closure: Roman Jewry and Its *Ghet*." In *Essential Papers on Jewish Culture in Renaissance and Baroque Italy*, edited by David B. Ruderman, 386–400. New York: NYU Press, 1992.

———. "I Papi, gli ebrei e la legge." In *Ebrei e cristiani nell'Italia medievale e moderna: conversioni, scambi, contrasti*, edited by Michele Luzzati, Michele Olivari, and Alessandra Veronese, 141–53. Rome: Carucci, 1988.

———. "Introduction." In *The Jews in Rome*, edited by Kenneth R. Stow and Simonsohn, Shlomo, 9–70. Studia Post-Biblica 48. Leiden: Brill, 1995.

———. "The Jewish Dog and 'Shehitah.'" *Interfaces: A Journal of Medieval European Literatures*, no. 5 (2018): 175–93.

———. *The Jews in Rome*. Studia Post Biblica, vol. 48. Leiden: Brill, 1995.

———. "The New Fashioned from the Old: Parallels in Public and Learned Memory and Practice in Sixteenth-Century Jewish Rome." In *The Jews of Italy: Memory and Identity*, edited by Bernard Dov Cooperman and Barbara Garvin, 130–50. Bethesda: University Press of Maryland, 2000.

———. "The Papacy and the Jews: Catholic Reformation and Beyond." *Jewish History* 6, no. 1–2 (1992): 257–79.

———. *Theater of Acculturation: The Roman Ghetto in the 16th Century*. Seattle: University of Washington Press, 2001.

———. "Was the Ghetto Cleaner . . . ?" In *Rome, Pollution and Propriety: Dirt, Disease and Hygiene in the Eternal City from Antiquity to Modernity*, edited by Mark Bradley and Kenneth R. Stow, 169–81. British School at Rome Studies. Cambridge: Cambridge University Press, 2012.

Strong, Eugénie. *La Chiesa Nuova (Santa Maria in Vallicella): guida storica ed artistica*. Rome: Società Editrice d'Arte Illustrata, 1923.

Sturgis, Matthew. *When in Rome: 2000 Years of Roman Sightseeing*. London: Frances Lincoln Limited, 2011.

Sweet, Rosemary. "The Changing View of Rome in the Long Eighteenth Century." *Journal for Eighteenth-Century Studies* 33, no. 2 (2010): 145–64.

Tamilia, Donato. *Il sacro monte de pietà di Roma: ricerche storiche e documenti inediti: contributo alla storia della beneficenza e alla storia economica di Roma*. Rome: Forzani E. C., Tipografi del Senato, 1900.

Tanner, Marie. *Jerusalem on the Hill: Rome and the Vision of St. Peter's in the Renaissance*. London: Harvey Miller Publishers, 2010.

Tartakoff, Paola. *Between Christian and Jew: Conversion and Inquisition in the Crown of Aragon, 1250–1391*. Philadelphia: University of Pennsylvania Press, 2012.

Taylor, Rabun. *Rome: An Urban History from Antiquity to the Present*. Cambridge: Cambridge University Press, 2016.

Tedeschi, John A. *The Prosecution of Heresy: Collected Studies on the Inquisition in Early Modern Italy*. Binghamton, NY: Medieval and Renaissance Texts and Studies, 1991.

Terpstra, Nicholas, ed. *Global Reformations: Transforming Early Modern Religions, Societies, and Cultures*. Abingdon, UK: Routledge, 2019.

———. *Religious Refugees in the Early Modern World: An Alternative History of the Reformation*. New York: Cambridge University Press, 2015.

Teter, Magda. *Blood Libel: On the Trail of an Antisemitic Myth*. Cambridge, MA: Harvard University Press, 2020.

———. *Jews and Heretics in Catholic Poland: A Beleaguered Church in the Post-Reformation Era*. Cambridge: Cambridge University Press, 2006.

———. *Sinners on Trial: Jews and Sacrilege after the Reformation*. Cambridge, MA: Harvard University Press, 2011.

Toaff, Ariel. "Giovanni Antonio Costanzi, ultimo censore di libri ebraici a roma (1745–1756 ca.)." *La Rassegna Mensile di Israel* 67, no. 1–2 (2001): 203–14.

Tosi, Mario. *Il Sacro Monte di pietà di Roma e le sue amministrazioni: il banco di depositi, la depositeria generale della R. Camera Apostolica, la zecca, la depositeria urbana, 1539–1874*. Rome: Cassa di Risparmio di Roma, 1937.

Trivellato, Francesca. *The Promise and Peril of Credit: What a Forgotten Legend about Jews and Finance Tell Us about the Making of European Commercial Society*. Princeton, NJ: Princeton University Press, 2019.

Udel, Miriam. "The 'Jewish Pope' in the 1940s: On Jewish Cultural and Ethnic Plasticity." In *Eastern Europe Unmapped: Beyond Borders and Peripheries*, edited by Irene Kacandes and Yuliya Komska, 31–52. New York: Berghahn Books, 2020.

Valbousquet, Nina. "Race and Faith: The Catholic Church, Clerical Fascism, and the Shaping of Italian Anti-Semitism and Racism." *Modern Italy* 23, no. 4 (November 2018): 355–71.

Valone, Carolyn. "Elena Orsini, Daniele da Volterra, and the Orsini Chapel." *Artibus et Historiae* 11, no. 22 (January 1, 1990): 79–87.

van Boxel, Piet. "Cardinal Santoro and the Expurgation of Hebrew Literature." In *The Roman Inquisition, the Index and the Jews: Contexts, Sources and Perspectives*, edited by Stephan Wendehorst, 9:19–34. Studies in European Judaism, 1568–5004. Leiden: Brill, 2004.

———. "Dowry and the Conversion of the Jews in Sixteenth-Century Rome: Competition between the Church and the Jewish Community." In *Marriage in Italy 1300–1650*, edited by Trevor Dean and K. J. P. Lowe, 116–27. Cambridge: Cambridge University Press, 1998.

———. "Hebrew Books and Censorship in Sixteenth-Century Italy." In *Jewish Books and Their Readers: Aspects of the Intellectual Life of Christians and Jews in Early Modern Europe*, edited by Scott Mandelbrote and Joanna Weinberg, 73–99. Leiden: Brill, 2016.

———. *Jewish Books in Christian Hands: Theology, Exegesis and Conversion under Gregory XIII (1572–1585)*. Vatican City: Biblioteca Apostolica Vaticana, 2016.

———. "Robert Bellarmine Reads Rashi: Rabbinic Bible Commentaries and the Burning of the Talmud." In *The Hebrew Book in Early Modern Italy*, edited by Joseph R. Hacker and Adam Shear, 121–32. Jewish Culture and Contexts. Philadelphia: University of Pennsylvania Press, 2011.

Vannugli, Antonio. "Giacomo Boncompagni duca di Sora e il suo ritratto dipinto da Scipione Pulzone." *Prospettiva* 61–64 (1991): 54–66.

———. "Per Jacopo Zucchi: un' 'Annunciazione' a Bagnoregio ed altre opere." *Prospettiva* 75–76 (1994): 161–73.

Vasco Rocca, Sandra. *SS. Trinità dei Pellegrini*. Chiese di Roma illustrate. Istituto di studi romani. Rome: Fratelli Palombi, 1979.

Vélez, Karin. *The Miraculous Flying House of Loreto: Spreading Catholicism in the Early Modern World*. Princeton, NJ: Princeton University Press, 2019.

Verhoeven, Gerrit. "Calvinist Pilgrimages and Popish Encounters: Religious Identity and Sacred Space on the Dutch Grand Tour (1598–1685)." *Journal of Social History* 43, no. 3 (2010): 615–34.

Villani, Stefano. "Between Information and Proselytism: Seventeenth-Century Italian Texts on Sabbatai Zevi, Their Various Editions and Their Circulation, in Print and Manuscript." *DAAT: A Journal of Jewish Philosophy and Kabbalah* 82, no. 2016 (n.d.): 87–103.

———. "Conversione e famiglia in due testi letterari italiani del seicento." *Studi Storici* 49, no. 4 (2008): 1039–62.

———. "Defining the Church of England in Italy in the Early Modern Times: British Reconciliations in the Documentation of the Inquisition of Pisa." *Revue de Littérature et de Civilisation (XVIe–XVIIIe Siècles)* 31, 2017. https://doi.org/10.4000/episteme.1775.

Visani, Alessandro. "Il Gesuita di Mussollini. Pietro Tacchi Venturi e le leggi razziali del 1938." *Roma moderna e contemporanea. Ebrei, scambi e conflitti tra XV e XX secolo*, 103–20. Rome: CROMA, 2012.

Visceglia, Maria Antonietta. *La città rituale: Roma e le sue cerimonie in età moderna*. Rome: Viella, 2002.

———. "Papal Sovereignty and Civic Rituals in the Early Modern Age." In *Late Medieval and Early Modern Ritual: Studies in Italian Urban Culture*, edited by Samuel

Kline Cohn, Marcello Fantoni, Franco Franceschi, and Fabrizio Ricciardelli, 7:269–98. Turnhout, Belgium: Brepols, 2013.

Vivanti, Corrado, ed. *Gli ebrei in Italia*. Vol. 11. Storia d'Italia: annali. Turin: G. Einaudi, 1996.

Vogelstein, Hermann. *Geschichte der Juden in Rom*. Berlin: Mayer and Müller, 1895.

von Pastor, Ludwig. *History of the Popes*. Edited by Ralph Francis Kerr. 20 vols. London: Kegan Paul, Trench, Trübner and Co., 1930.

Vose, Robin J. E. *Dominicans, Muslims and Jews in the Medieval Crown of Aragon*. Cambridge: Cambridge University Press, 2009.

Waddy, Patricia. *Seventeenth-Century Roman Palaces: Use and the Art of the Plan*. New York: Architectural History Foundation, 1990.

Waite, Gary K. *Jews and Muslims in Seventeenth-Century Discourse: From Religious Enemies to Allies and Friends*. Milton Park, UK: Routledge, 2019.

Walden, Justine. "Muslim Slaves in Early Modern Rome: The Development and Visibility of a Labouring Class." In *A Companion to Religious Minorities in Early Modern Rome*, edited by Matthew Coneys Wainwright and Emily Michelson, 298–323. Boston: Brill, 2020.

Walton, Michael T., and Phyllis J. Walton. "In Defense of the Church Militant: The Censorship of the Rashi Commentary in the Magna Biblia Rabbinica." *Sixteenth Century Journal* 21, no. 3 (1990): 385–400.

Ward, Allyna E. "An Outlandish Travel Chronicle: Farce, History, and Fiction in Thomas Nashe's *The Unfortunate Traveller*." *Yearbook of English Studies* 41, no. 1 (2011): 84–98.

Warwick, Genevieve. 'Ritual Form and Urban Space in Early Modern Rome'. In *Late Medieval and Early Modern Ritual: Studies in Italian Urban Culture*, edited by Samuel Kline Cohn, Marcello Fantoni, Franco Franceschi, and Fabrizio Ricciardelli, v. 7:297–328. Turnhout, Belgium: Brepols, 2013.

Weil, Mark S. "The Devotion of the Forty Hours and Roman Baroque Illusions." *Journal of the Warburg and Courtauld Institutes* 37 (January 1974): 218–48.

Weinberg, Joanna. "A Sixteenth-Century Hebraic Approach to the New Testament." In *History of Scholarship: A Selection of Papers from the Seminar on the History of Scholarship Held Annually at the Warburg Institute*, edited by C. R. Ligota and Jean-Louis Quantin, 231–50. Oxford-Warburg Studies. Oxford: Oxford University Press, 2006.

Wendehorst, Stephan, ed. *The Roman Inquisition, the Index and the Jews: Contexts, Sources and Perspectives*. Vol. 9. Studies in European Judaism, 1568–5004. Leiden: Brill, 2004.

Wendehorst, Stephan, Claus Arnold, Antje Bräcker, Hanna Węgrzynek, and John Tedeschi. "The Roman Inquisition, the Index and the Jews: Sources and Perspectives for Research." *Jewish History* 17, no. 1 (January 1, 2003): 55–76.

Wickersham, Jane. "Results of the Reformation: Ritual, Doctrine and Religious Conversion." *Seventeenth Century* 18, no. 2 (September 1, 2003): 266–89.

Wilson, A. N. "Everything England Used to Be." *New York Times*, May 30, 1993, sec. 7, 6.

Wilson, Stephen. *Saints and Their Cults: Studies in Religious Sociology, Folklore, and History*. Cambridge: Cambridge University Press, 1985.

Wisch, Barbara. "Celebrating the Holy Year of 1575." In *"All the World's a Stage"—Art and Pageantry in the Renaissance and Baroque*, edited by Susan Scott Munshower and Barbara Wisch, 6:82–118. University Park: Department of Art History, Pennsylvania State University, 1990.

———. *"Embracing Peter and Paul: The Arciconfraternita della SS. Trinità dei Pellegrini e Convalescenti and the Cappella della Separazione in Rome. In Space, Place, and Motion: Locating Confraternities in the Late Medieval and Early Modern City,* edited by Diana Bullen Presciutti, 178–216. Leiden: Brill, 2017.

———. "The Matrix: Le Sette Chiese di Roma of 1575 and the Image of Pilgrimage." *Memoirs of the American Academy in Rome,* 2012.

———. "Promoting Piety, Coercing Conversion: The Roman Archconfraternity of the Santissima Trinità dei Pellegrini e Convalescenti and Its Oratory." *Predella: Journal of Visual Arts* 47 (2020): 255–77.

———. Review of *"Il Gran Cardinale": Alessandro Farnese, Patron of the Arts,* by Clare Robertson, *American Historical Review* 98, no. 5 (December 1993): 1642.

———. "Vested Interest: Redressing Jews on Michelangelo's Sistine Ceiling." *Artibus et Historiae* 24, no. 48 (January 1, 2003): 143–72.

———. "Violent Passions: Plays, Pawnbrokers, and the Jews of Rome, 1539." In *Beholding Violence in Medieval and Early Modern Europe,* edited by Allie Terry-Fritsch and Erin Felicia Labbie, 197–213. Farnham, UK: Ashgate Publishing, 2012.

Wisch, Barbara, and Nerida Newbigin. *Acting on Faith: The Confraternity of the Gonfalone in Renaissance Rome.* Philadelphia: Saint Joseph's University Press, 2013.

Wood, Carolyn H., and Peter Iver Kaufman. "Tacito Predicatore: The Annunciation Chapel at the Madonna Dei Monti in Rome." *Catholic Historical Review* 90, no. 4 (2004): 634–49.

Wood, James. "The Radical Origins of Christianity." *New Yorker,* July 3, 2017. https://www.newyorker.com/magazine/2017/07/10/the-radical-origins-of-christianity.

Worcester, Thomas. *The Cambridge Companion to the Jesuits.* Cambridge Companions to Religion. Cambridge: Cambridge University Press, 2008.

Zawart, Anscar. "The History of Franciscan Preaching and of Franciscan Preachers (1209–1927). A Bio-Bibliographical Study." In *Ninth Annual Meeting of the Franciscan Educational Conference,* 242–587. Athol Springs, NY: Franciscan Educational Conference, 1927.

Zorach, Rebecca. *The Virtual Tourist in Renaissance Rome: Printing and Collecting the Speculum Romanae Magnificentiae.* Chicago: University of Chicago Press, 2008.

Zucchi, Alberto. "I predicatori domenicani degli ebrei in Roma." *Memorie Domenicane* (Memorie Domenicane in Roma) 51, no. 5 (1934): 313–22.

———. "I predicatori domenicani degli ebrei nel secolo XVII." *Memorie Domenicane* (Roma domenicana) 52, no. 1 (1935): 42–47.

———. "Il predicatore degli ebrei in Roma." *Memorie Domenicane* (Memorie Domenicane in Roma) 51, no. 3 (1934): 200–205.

———. "Il primo predicatore domenicano degli ebrei. Ancora sul P. Sirleto—Fr. Alessandro Franceschi." *Memorie Domenicane* (Roma domenicana) 51, no. 6 (1934): 375–81.

———. "Ragioni della predicazione agli ebrei." *Memorie Domenicane* (Memorie Domenicane in Roma) 51, no. 4 (1934): 255–64.

———. "Rome domenicana: note storiche: Predicatori Domenicani degli Ebrei nel sec. XVIII." *Memorie Domenicane* 38 (1938): 118–27.

INDEX

Printed works are given their original (Italian) titles as footnoted, even when I have translated them in the text. Converts are listed by birth name or baptismal name, depending on how they were best known, and cross-listed if necessary. Page numbers in italics indicate illustrations.

A NOTE ON THE TYPE

THIS BOOK has been composed in Miller, a Scotch Roman typeface designed by Matthew Carter and first released by Font Bureau in 1997. It resembles Monticello, the typeface developed for The Papers of Thomas Jefferson in the 1940s by C. H. Griffith and P. J. Conkwright and reinterpreted in digital form by Carter in 2003.

Pleasant Jefferson ("P. J.") Conkwright (1905–1986) was Typographer at Princeton University Press from 1939 to 1970. He was an acclaimed book designer and AIGA Medalist.

The ornament used throughout this book was designed by Pierre Simon Fournier (1712–1768) and was a favorite of Conkwright's, used in his design of the *Princeton University Library Chronicle.*